George T. Bettany

A Popular History of the Reformation and Modern Protestantism

George T. Bettany

A Popular History of the Reformation and Modern Protestantism

ISBN/EAN: 9783337836344

Printed in Europe, USA, Canada, Australia, Japan

Cover: Foto ©Lupo / pixelio.de

More available books at **www.hansebooks.com**

A POPULAR HISTORY

OF THE

REFORMATION

AND

MODERN PROTESTANTISM

BY THE LATE

G. T. BETTANY, M.A, B.Sc.

Author of "The World's Religions," "The World's Inhabitants," etc.

WITH MANY ILLUSTRATIONS

LONDON

WARD, LOCK & BOWDEN, LIMITED

WARWICK HOUSE, SALISBURY SQUARE, E.C.

NEW YORK AND MELBOURNE

1895

PUBLISHERS' NOTE

A S the late Mr. G. T. Bettany was, throughout his literary career, closely associated with the publishers of this volume, it may not perhaps be out of place if, in issuing this—the last piece of work he ever did—they take the opportunity of expressing the sense of personal loss with which they regarded his death.

Mr. Bettany undertook nothing on which he was not prepared to bestow patient and painstaking research; and though the unusually wide range of his reading and learning qualified him for writing on many subjects, he touched on none to which, by the spirit in which he wrote, he did not impart earnestness and dignity.

By his too early death the publishers of this volume lost the valued assistance and advice of a scholar of distinction and of a man of letters of fine taste and unerring judgment.

January, 1895.

CONTENTS

ROME AND THE CASTLE OF ST. ANGELO.

POPULAR HISTORY OF THE REFORMATION AND MODERN PROTESTANTISM.

CHAPTER I.

Causes of the Reformation.

What was the Reformation ?—Causes of the Reformation—The Corrupt State of the Church —Papal Misdeeds—Temporal Power of the Papacy—Investiture—Act of Præmunire— Evil Life of Clergy—"Benefit of Clergy"—Abuses of Monastic Orders—The Mendicant Friars—Belief in Authority—Abelard—The Mystics—Eckhart—The Renaissance— The Inquisition—Personal Religion and Beneficence—Complex Causes of Reformation —Effect on the Roman Church.

THE Reformation has sometimes been spoken of as if it had been due solely to the egotism of certain self-willed monks and priests, and to the pride and greed of a number of princes and kings. It has What was the been denounced as blasphemous, heretical, criminal; it has Reformation? been sneered at as hasty, coarse, crude, ignorant; it has been censured as

1   B

injurious to religion and humanity, destroying more valuable things than it supplied in their place, inimical to church order, tradition, and continuity. It has been lauded as restoring the only truth, as renewing the church of the apostolic days, as the heroic witness of god-like men to the salvation and redemption of the world by Christ, as the efficient cause of modern freedom in church and state. By a considerable number of Protestants it is regarded as "a return to Biblical Christianity, to the simple and pure doctrine of the Gospel, divested of all which Protestants regard as a later addition, as the 'ordinance of men' and as a disfigurement of the primitive apostolic type of religion." (Hagenbach.) By not a few it is viewed as "only the first impulse to a movement which is thrusting aside everything which lays claim to authority, and, consequently, regarding the systems of belief drawn up by the Reformers, as barriers to further progress, the utter destruction of which is reserved for modern times." How far it was each or any of these things, it will be our endeavour to set forth without fear or favour, in the spirit of the words, "Prove all things; hold fast that which is true."

The Reformation, as narrowly understood, was the work of certain great Reformers,—Wyclif, Luther, Melanchthon, Zwingli, Calvin, Knox, Cranmer. But we now realise that great men are as much the product as the stimulus of their age, and that great movements are long in preparing, and are due to the impressions, the feelings, the uprisings of centuries. **Causes of the Reformation.** Many causes contributed to produce that remarkable movement known as the Reformation. We will briefly enumerate the chief of these, before proceeding to consider some of them in detail, without, however, attempting to decide the order of their importance or their influence.

The main influences which led to the Reformation were :—

1. The overshadowing growth of the power and claims of the Papacy, the abuses connected with the papal administration, and the immorality and tyranny of many of the Popes.

2. The interference of this Papal power with national and princely rights and liberties, and the antagonism thus produced between Romanism and champions of national liberty.

3. The immorality and practical irreligiousness of many of the secular clergy.

4. The wealth, degeneracy, and corruption of most of the monastic Orders.

5. A revolt of intelligent men against the enforced acceptance of a system of theology, or a scheme of religious practice, on the mere authority of the existing church, when errors in interpretation or lack of competence to interpret might be proved against living churchmen.

6. The Renaissance of intellectual, classical, and artistic culture,

ULRICH ZWINGLI, HEAD OF THE ZURICH SCHOOL OF REFORMERS (1484–1531).

leading on the one hand to a revival of mere paganism, and in reaction from this to a revival of religion, apart from pagan influences.

7. The tyrannical and cruel proceedings of the Inquisition.

8. The continuous germination of practical and heartfelt religion in the characters of such men as the "Friends of God," the "Brethren of the Common Life," and religious reformers like Savonarola.

A work on the "Corrupt State of the Church" dating from the end of the fourteenth or the beginning of the fifteenth century, if not from the pen of Nicolas de Clemanges, rector of the University of Paris in 1393, proceed-

"The Corrupt State of the Church." ing from a writer equally well informed, gives a picture of the Church from within, which cannot be surpassed, for lurid light, by any representations given by enemies from without.   It describes the evils connected with the Papacy as having their prime source

Papal Misdeeds. in the growth of wealth, pride, and the spirit of domination in the Roman pontiffs.   The dignity of the popes and the complex machinery which they worked, necessitated an expenditure rivalling that of the most opulent monarchs.   Money or its equivalent had consequently to be obtained from every possible source.   The territory under the immediate dominion of the Pope was enlarged whenever war or treaty could increase it; and the inhabitants had to pay the utmost taxes they could bear.   Wherever the sovereigns of Christian States did not effectively hinder it, all vacant benefices were claimed for the papal treasury, and many benefices were for this reason long kept vacant.   The loss on filling up a benefice was to be made good somehow, and money payments for presentation were accepted, often from unworthy candidates, by numerous popes, and still more numerous clerical officials; and in addition to this, the first year's income, often fixed at an exorbitant rate, was demanded from the newly presented cleric.   Instead of the primitive system of popular election, or election by members of the church concerned, or appointment by the civil rulers, the popes gradually engrossed to the holy see all church appointments whatever, and therewith introduced an almost inconceivable system of abuses and malversation of local revenues.   One of the worst of the results was the introduction into sacred offices of ignorant, ill-bred, or vicious men, often mere youths, everywhere raising scandal against things that ought not to have been profaned.   The legates and collectors sent out by the popes often outdid their instructions and their examples. Excommunications and interdicts were by them scattered broadcast, often ruining particular churches or monasteries, despoiling them even of their sacred vessels and ornaments; depriving prelates and clergy of Christian burial when dead, or reducing them to beggary while yet alive.   The papal court itself was beset by a crowd of venal officials and hangers-on, more intent on money gain than on securing that justice should be done, and ready to exert all their influence for a pecuniary consideration on the side of the heaviest purse.   The cardinals, formerly a minor body of only local signification, had become, since they could make and unmake popes, to a large extent so haughty that they looked down upon archbishops and even patriarchs, and affected the state of princes. Outrageous pluralists, loaded with incompatible duties, their transactions in simony and nepotism disgusted sycophants and enemies alike.

But the Papacy had not been always in the hands of unworthy or contemptible tenants. Again and again it had been occupied by men who, judged merely as statesmen, were a match for kings like Temporal power Frederick I. of Germany, Henry II. of England, and Louis IX. of the Papacy. of France. From being a nominee of the Frankish emperor, needing also his confirmation when elected, the Pope had come to be elected, independently of any outside power, by the College of Cardinals, and claimed, and often exercised a practical dictatorship over the haughtiest and most powerful temporal princes. This was made effectual by the judicious use of pecuniary influence, by skilfully playing off prince against prince, by utilising rivalries, jealousies and suspicions, and above all by the terrors of the power of the keys, which—extended from the terrestrial to the supernal sphere—could forbid all church services for the living or for the dead, and, it was fondly believed, exclude from or admit to heaven, or shorten or intensify the sufferings of purgatorial purification. A church that could not err, popes above all judgment, claiming to depose emperors, and to absolve subjects from their allegiance—is it to be wondered at that the triumph of such ideas marked the beginning of their downfall?—that human nature, when completely trodden under foot, should turn, and gathering strength, rend its tyrant?

Without going into the question of investitures, or the right to place ecclesiastics in possession of their temporal possessions, which was so long the battleground between popes and princes, it may be Investiture. remarked that the very point of the question was whether the prince was to be merely the Pope's deputy and servant or not. If national or princely liberty meant anything, the prince could not consent to allow the pope to invest a bishop with the temporalities which were in the prince's domain. The popes employed all their threats, launched all their interdicts and bulls and excommunications, and exhausted their skill in continental combinations against the English kings in this matter; but their victories were transient. Neither English king nor English church for any long period endured the tyrannical claims of Rome. When greater claims failed, popes could always demand and often got money, though parliaments frequently cut down the amounts; when civil wars raged, the pope made terms for himself with one or other party. Long before the time of Henry VIII. the essential protest of the nation had

Act of
Præmunire. been made in the famous Act of Præmunire. In its most striking form it repelled the claim that "the Crown of England, which had been so free at all times, that it hath been in no earthly subjection, but immediately subject to God in all things touching the Regality of the said Crown and to none other, should be submitted to the Pope, and the Laws and Statutes of the Realm by him defeated and avoided at his will, in perpetual Destruction of the Sovereignty of the King our Lord, his Crown, his Regality, and of all his Realm, which God defend."

The laity, though often slow to reform their own morals, are quick to discern the flaws in those of the clergy, whose profession pledges them

Evil Life of
Clergy. to lead a pure life. It is not to be inferred that the Church included all the worst people in the dark ages; but there is abundant testimony that very many of the clergy were immoral, self-indulgent, grasping, deceitful, hypocritical, in the ages of which we are speaking. On the Continent, and to a less degree in England, both clergy and bishops were often non-resident, and did literally none of the work for which they were paid; not a few were even murderers, having gained admission to the Church perhaps to cloak their crimes. Many did not make the least pretence to a decent life; many did not even know the language of the country in which they should have ministered. How

"Benefit of
Clergy." monstrous then was the claim of "benefit of clergy," that offending clerics should only be tried by ecclesiastical courts, when the latter habitually inflicted totally inadequate penalties. Yet this was perhaps the most successfully and persistently enforced of all the claims of the Church.

Again and again new orders of monks were founded, as an antidote to the prevailing corruptions, and in order to restore that purity of religion

Abuses of
Monastic
Orders. which it was fondly hoped might be preserved best under monastic vows. No well-meant system of endeavour after a higher life seems to have more fatally tended to corruption than monasticism. Scarcely has a founder departed from this world, before his order, by virtue of his very merits, perhaps, attracting benefactions or stimulating spiritual pride or haughtiness in his followers, becomes rich, proud, luxurious, and often fatally degenerate. And yet we must acknowledge that there is considerable truth in Montalembert's claim that the monasteries "were for ten centuries the schools, the archives, the libraries, the hostelries, the studios, the penitentiaries, and the hospitals of Christian society." But the evil ultimately predominated over the good. The contraries of the virtues aimed at gained the mastery in a multitude of cases. Instead of poverty, riches; instead of abstinence, luxurious living; instead of chastity, licentiousness; instead of a pure heart, impure thoughts and deeds; instead of charity, arrogance and Pharisaism; such were the very frequent fruits of the life which was to purify at any rate the individual, by his quitting the world at large.

Nor was it much better with regard to the mendicant orders which sprang into such universal repute and fame in the thirteenth century. That they were founded out of a true zeal for Christianity *The Mendicant Friars.* and the Church, cannot be doubted; that they grew at first by reason of the attractive ideas they embodied and the hope of attaining holiness, is equally true. But as the cloister had become an inner world as impure as the outer, so the way of mendicant poverty and spiritual helpfulness was beset by pitfalls and temptations which transformed the Dominicans and Franciscans into the spiritual tyrants, the secular ministers and diplomatists, the dispensers of ecclesiastical indulgences, the intercessors with heaven of half the States of Europe. By their quarrels with bishops, their rivalries, their coarse manners, their ignorance, their rapacity, and also, it must be added, by the worse deeds of pretended Friars, they in the fifteenth and sixteenth centuries almost entirely lost their hold of the populace, and incurred hatred.

To an extent which it is difficult to estimate precisely, the growth of Universities had fostered an uprising against the doctrines enforced by the Church, or at any rate against the accepted interpretations *Belief in authority.* of them. The great Anselm had given to theological students a two-edged sword when he said that "faith precedes intellectual belief." If on the one side he had launched a dogma, which is one of the bulwarks of the implicit reception of the Church of Rome, on the other he had set forward a proposition that continually offends and stirs up the reasoning principle in man. The varied ways in which Abelard, early in *Abelard.* the twelfth century, exemplified the working of this spirit, are as an index to what went on in the minds of very many in succeeding centuries. He steadfastly opposed belief without understanding, and recognised that any idolatry might be accepted on that principle. He argued that St. Thomas and St. Paul were led to faith by being convinced of facts. He first taught that we should separate minor questions from the essence, and concentrate attention upon that. Qualifying it with a "perhaps," he says, "what the Gospel has taught concerning faith, hope and charity, might suffice for salvation." He singularly well anticipated a modern principle of controversy, that in order to defend Divine truth adequately, it is necessary to become acquainted with the opponents' standpoint, and to match them at their own weapons, and in their own knowledge. And he went still farther in reference to the doctrine of the Trinity, saying: "We do not promise, on this point, to teach the truth, a task to which we hold that neither ourselves, nor any other mortal is competent; but we promise to teach at least something *probable*, something which approximates near to human reason, and which stands in no contradiction with our holy faith." His famous "Sic et non" (yes and no), in which he set against one another the contrasted views of the fathers on a large number of subjects of faith and morals, was a powerful suggestion of the impossibility of attaining dogmatic uniformity by general consent. "Judge not that ye be not judged," is his emphatic protest. Well would it have been for the mediæval Church if it had remembered this. How modern, too, is his view of inspiration, wherein he recognises that not every line of the writings of the prophets and apostles was inspired, but that the Spirit of God neither bestows all gifts at once on the same individual, nor all enlightenment, "but reveals sometimes this and sometimes that, and in revealing one thing hides another." Even the discussions of scholasticism, the disputes which filled the Universities, had their part in bringing about the Reformation. On the one hand they sharpened the weapon for discussing, on the other they aroused antagonism in fresh original minds, and they tended to occasion revolt in the unlearned mind.

In a very real sense the Mystics helped to prepare the way for the Reformation. And yet they made no revolt against the Church. Their object was, however, to realise the Divine immediately, and to minimise or destroy "self," to overcome the heart's alienation from God by direct and continual contemplation of the Divine perfection. Their method, depending more upon the individual experience than upon books or external authority, was nevertheless highly calculated, in the hands of those in whom opposition to the Church had once been roused, to strengthen that opposition, to give it an independence, a self-sustaining life. The Abbots of St. Victor, near Paris, Bonaventura, and John Eckhart (1260–1329), in different forms emphasised this

The Mystics.

Eckhart.

aspect of spiritual life, and the latter, in particular, speculated on the nature of God so freely that his teaching verges on pantheism. "The eye with which I see God is the same eye with which God sees me. My eye and God's eye are one eye, one vision, one recognition, one love," he says. But his spiritual influence travelled far, and supplied much religious seed for the strong religious growth of the Reformation. He was followed by such men as Suss of Constance and John Tauler, of Strasbourg, and Nicolas of Basle, of whom we must give some account as a preliminary to our sketch of Luther. Thomas à Kempis, in his *Imitation of Christ*, has exemplified for us the extreme of the principle of absolute submissiveness to the Divine Will, and has described a form of religious life quite independent of what the Church may do or order, dependent only on the direct sense of the Divine presence in the heart. So far as mysticism is a form and mode of spiritual freedom, it was of some significance towards the Reformation.

The Renaissance of Art and Letters in the fifteenth century has sometimes been described as corresponding to the Reformation in religion. But while it gave to theological students new implements of The study, in the revived knowledge of Greek, and the recovery of Renaissance. ancient manuscripts of the Bible, and introduced new conceptions of nature and philosophy and art from classical authors and remains, its direct effect on religion was negative and destructive. The educated men of Italy were almost beside themselves at the discovery of a new manuscript or an ancient work of art ; and as they spent their time over learned discussions, they came to take but a perfunctory interest in the church teaching which had always been familiar to them, in the church rites in which the priest went through mechanical duties, and the dogmas which had been infallibly handed down. When popes evidently cared more for classics than for theology, it is not surprising that religion became more pagan and superstitious. In Italy reverence degenerated into neglect and contempt, in Germany and France it was revived by earnest men who began to study the Bible, and to demand a reform of abuses.

We have next to note how the proceedings of the "Holy Inquisition" contributed to sow the seed of the Reformation. It had long been held to be the function of the bishops to inquire into the prevalence of The erroneous teaching, and to stamp it out, largely by the aid of Inquisition. the "secular power" of obedient princes. The Inquisition, properly so-called, was due to Pope Gregory IX., who in 1232 constituted the Dominicans inquisitors into heresy in Toulouse, with appeal only to the Pope. "The suspicion of heresy was sufficient cause for imprisonment; accomplices and criminals were deemed competent witnesses; confession was often extorted by torture." Here, without discussing the Inquisition, we will only point out that when it did not exterminate; it cowed weak minds, and roused resistance in strong ones. If an opinion was repressed, it was often silently held, and left its hereditary impress on offspring. The known unfairness, cruelty and unscrupulousness of the Inquisition in its actual working must breed reaction, if human nature had any virtue left. Fortunately, in England the Inquisition does not rank as one of the exciting causes of the Reformation, for it was never established. But the martyrdom of the Lollards performed a similar office in rousing the popular conscience.

In opposition to dogma, to church authority, to tyranny and immorality in churchmen, we find all through the Middle Ages a protesting minority who cultivated a heartfelt personal religion, and re- **Personal Religion and Beneficence.** jected many of the additions of popes and schoolmen. While many of the sects held extravagant opinions, they served to show that uniformity in religious belief was not natural to mankind. The simple earnest scriptural preaching of Waldo and his followers, the self-renunciation, and inward intercourse with God, of Nicolas of Basle and the "Friends of God," the powerful spiritual preaching of John Tauler, the glow of inspiration of John Ruysbrock, the practical benevolence and self-suppression of Gerard Groot and the Brethren of the Common Life in the Netherlands and the schools they founded, all aided in rousing in the religious consciousness of men a new sense or new combination of feelings, which was destined to have full play in many of the Reformed churches of which we shall have to speak. We must not omit to mention the *Béguinages*, those societies of women founded to attend to the sick and poor while following their own employments, and which have lasted till the present day in Belgium. In various ways these forms of religious devotion all helped to prepare the way for the Reformation.

Thus it will be seen that no one cause can be assigned for the Reformation. It was a complex product of many causes, acting differently, and **Complex Causes of Reformation.** with varying degrees of force, in different countries. It was most vigorous, not merely where abuses were most abundant, but where the races of men were most consolidated by natural feeling, where the rugged independence of national temper and genius was predominant.

The softer southern races, fierce-tempered though they might be, were more influenced by the sensuous ritual of the Church, more indifferent to the intellectual aspects of its teaching than the northern peoples.

Perhaps as much as any one factor, the invention of printing facilitated and spread the Reformation, but did not originate it. The sentiment for popular freedom can scarcely be credited with a great share in its beginning, though it undoubtedly did much to extend the general movement. We must acknowledge the important work towards church reform which was done by many who remained within the Church, and we must also own that the Reformers had at first no thought of separating from the church, which they regarded as the visible body of Christ. By timely concessions and reforms, they might have been kept within the Roman communion. They were forced into their onward course by the masterfulness and want of discernment of popes and cardinals.

Let us also bear in mind that the church against which Protestants protested is not the Roman Church of our own day. It has been in many ways reformed; it has felt the power of Protestantism working incessantly, and has been improved by the spirit of the age in spite of itself, and of its successive dogmas. Impurities and evils which once were common have shrunk or disappeared; ignorance which once largely prevailed has greatly diminished. Persecution has given way to wiser toleration, pitying though it may be. The proportion of noble men and women in the Romish Church is far greater than in the dark mediæval days. We must bear these facts in mind if we are adequately to estimate what it was against which our fathers rose, what evils they had to combat, how fierce was the battle for religious liberty, how difficult the path. While we cannot approve many of their deeds, while we must reject many of their opinions, we should remember the difficulties they had to contend against, the limited light they possessed, compared with our times, the imperfect knowledge, the imperfect experience.

Effect on the Roman Church.

LINCOLN CATHEDRAL, COMPLETED BY THE REFORMING BISHOP GROSSETÊTE.

CHAPTER II.

Early English Reformers.

Robert Grossetête—His Memorial to Pope Innocent IV.—His Last Protest—Roger Bacon —William of Occam—Richard Fitzralph—Thomas Bradwardine—The "Vision of Piers Plowman."

EVEN in the thirteenth century, church abuses in England roused some sturdy churchmen to protest against them; and among these no man deserves more honour than Robert Grossetête, Bishop of Lincoln from **Robert Grossetête.** 1235 to 1253. An Oxford student, he won from Roger Bacon the praise of being "the only man living who was in possession of all the sciences." About 1231 or 1232 a dangerous illness seems to have stirred his conscience as to whether it was right for him to hold several livings at the same time; and soon afterwards he resigned all he held, except a prebendal stall at Lincoln. His character for practical wisdom led to his election to the bishopric in 1235, an onerous charge, extending as it did from Oxford to the north of Lincolnshire. He immediately began to be diligent in reforming abuses, showing a strong sense of the importance of his office, but expecting nothing of others that he was not willing to exemplify in himself. Monks, cathedral and secular clergy were rigorously criticised, and not unfrequently deprived. Against Henry III. he again and again stood forward as the champion of the Church and of English liberties. At his visitations, he preached regularly to the clergy of each rural deanery, hoping thus to reach their congregations, whom he could not address. The residence and the qualifications of pastors he scrutinised with a lynx eye. He strongly opposed both pluralities and the conferring of secular offices on men who should have enough to do in discharging their sacred functions. He was impartial enough to welcome the newly formed mendicant orders, then in the heyday of their awakened zeal for souls, causing the good bishop to say, "The people who walked in darkness have seen a great light."

In a Memorial to Pope Innocent IV. at Lyons, in 1250, he sets forth in a striking form the evils that he wished to remedy,—"the diminution in the number of good shepherds of souls, the increase of wicked shepherds, and the circumscription of the pastoral authority and power. Bad pastors are everywhere the cause of unbelief, division, heresy and vice. . . . Their pride is ever on the increase, and so are their avarice, luxury and extravagance." He boldly traces the evil to its source in the Papal Curia itself. "Not only because it fails to put a stop to these evils as it can and should, but still more because by its dispensations, provisions and collations, it appoints evil shepherds, thinking therein only of the living which it is able to provide for a man, and for the sake of that *handing over many thousands of souls to eternal death.* . . . *He who so sacrifices the pastoral office is a persecutor of Christ in His members.* . . . The cure of souls consists not only in the dispensation of the sacraments, in the singing of ' homo,' and reading of masses, but in the true teaching of the word of life, in rebuking and correcting vice; and, besides all this, in feeding the hungry, giving drink to the thirsty, clothing the naked, lodging the stranger, visiting the sick and the prisoners—especially among the parish priest's own parishioners. . . . When parish churches are made over to monasteries, these evils

His Memorial to Pope Innocent IV.

are made perpetual. . . . Further, the pastoral office, especially of the bishops, is at the present time circumscribed and restrained, particularly in England . . . by the exemptions of privileges of monasteries, for when the inmates of these addict themselves outside their walls to the worst vices, the bishops can take no action against them—their hands are tied by the privileges of the convent."

What one strong, resolute man could do in reforming the abuses of which he complained, Grossetête did; but he had little help from the Pope **Grossetête's** or his Curia. In the year of the bishop's death (1253), the Pope **Last Protest.** sought to induct one of his own grandsons, a youth, into a canonry of Lincoln, setting aside all rule and reason. Grossetête opposed

ROGER BACON (1214-1291).

this successfully in a paper which set forth the sin, recklessness and deception of the papal brief, the murder of men's souls that it involved. He maintained that "the Holy See could not really command a thing which must have sin for its issue; and that it was the duty of a devoted subject of the See to resist it with all his might." So the venerable prelate, at the age of eighty, protested against the malpractices of Rome, as he had often done against the sins of the clergy. He was revered by the nation. His own university eulogised him thus: "Never from the fear of any man had he forborne to do any good action which belonged to his office and duty." Wyclif again and again refers to him, always in the highest terms. If his views had been carried out, the reform in church discipline would have been antedated by two centuries.

Though his fame is much greater in science than in theology, Roger Bacon claims a place here, not only for his services to free inquiry, and for **Roger Bacon.** the endurance of many years' close confinement inflicted by his Franciscan superiors for his plain speaking, but also for his resolute boldness in denouncing abuses. His Compendium of Theology, written in old age, in 1292, deals vigorously with the evils which marred the study of theology. Men occupied their time with treatises and discus-

sions of technical points, instead of with the word of God. Implicit trust
was placed in the teachings of the schoolmen, and no attention was paid to
Greek, Hebrew, and Arabic, and to works, especially the scriptures, originally written in those languages. He exposed the errors of the Latin Vulgate, and insisted that without study of the letter of the originals, the
spiritual teaching of the Bible was often completely misunderstood. He
declaimed against the intrusion of ignorant boys and youths into the
mendicant orders and into benefices. All the orders, he said, were deeply
corrupted. The secular clergy were ignorant, luxurious, and place-seeking.
It is uncertain how far this outspoken work was known and circulated.

Although he spent much of his life on the Continent, William of Occam
(or Ockham, Surrey) deserves mention as a prominent English opponent of
papal misdoings. One of the foremost of the schoolmen, he   William of
interests us here mainly from his support of the belief that Christ   Occam.
and His apostles had been poor, a fact that put to shame the luxury of the
pope and of many prelates. Pope John XXII., rich, luxurious, and corrupt,
could not stand this, and in 1328 imprisoned Occam and others at Avignon.
Occam having escaped, spent much of his later life in exposing the heresies
of the Pope, and in exalting to an extravagant degree the power of temporal princes. He declares, as clearly as any later Reformer, that it is wholly
erroneous, and dangerous to souls, to claim for the Pope absolute power,
spiritual and temporal. We should then all be the Pope's slaves, and the
law of Christ would bring with it intolerable slavery. He denies that the
Pope has power to make new articles of faith, or that he can fall into no sin,
and is infallible. According to him, the whole order of bishops, including
the papal primacy, is but a human order. The unity of the Church does
not depend on there only being one chief pontiff. He exalts the power of
the whole Church, and of a general council far above the Pope ; over all is
Christ alone. Cast out of the Franciscan order, persecuted by the Pope,
Occam expressed the utmost joy in his Christian faith, and trust in God,
and looked forward to a future time when men zealous for truth, righteousness, and the commonweal would discern many truths to which rulers,
councillors, and teachers were blind in his own day.

Richard Fitzralph, Chancellor of Oxford in 1333, and Archbishop of
Armagh from 1349 to 1360, has a place in this chapter because of his strong
opposition to the mendicant orders, which no longer, as in Grosse-   Richard
tête's time, represented the best type of churchmen. Against the   Fitzralph.
virtue of mendicancy, Fitzralph preached a number of sermons in English

at St. Paul's, maintaining that Christ never practised begging and never taught any one to beg, and showing that no man can prudently or holily determine to follow a life of medicancy. For these sermons he had to defend himself in person before the Pope at Avignon in 1357. He was easily able to point to a multitude of evils caused by the prevailing habits and practices of the mendicant friars. They induced many to join their orders, he says, by promises and lies; but Fitzralph maintained that no lie was allowable for a good end. The friars, he said, were eating the people out of their houses, claiming their places as of right. They were disobeying their own rules, seeking after honours and dignities, and accumulating wealth. We cannot but rank Fitzralph in the roll of protestors against the abuses of the Church.

Thomas Bradwardine, Archbishop of Canterbury in 1348–9, was a learned theologian who at Oxford lectured against the current Pelagian view

Thomas Bradwardine. that man is the master of his own actions and can do good of himself apart from Divine grace. His teaching—how like that of many great reformers—was that human actions can have no merit towards God, that man cannot conquer a single temptation without Divine grace, the free and unmerited gift of God. Thus he felt himself to be the champion of the true cause of God, so much so that he entitled his chief work "On the Cause of God against the Pelagians." However much we may differ about the value of the scholastic methods by which he supported his argument, we cannot fail to acknowledge the depth and fervour of his piety. In his prayer near the close of his book, he thus invokes the Saviour: "Good Master, Thou my only Master, Thou who from my youth up, when I gave myself to this work by Thy impulse, hast taught me up to this day all that I have ever learned of the truth, and all that, as Thy pen, I have ever written of it, send down upon me, also now, of Thy great goodness, Thy light . . . Show me, I pray Thee, Thou most learned of all teachers, show to Thy little child, who knows no outlet from the difficulty, how to solve the knot of Thy word so hardly knit," etc.

A little later, and contemporaneously with Wyclif, the state of the Church and of society is vividly pictured for us in the "Vision of Piers

The "Vision of Piers Plowman." Plowman," by William Langland. Without in any way impeaching the doctrines of the Church, Langland's poem confirms all that we have said of the disorders of the Church, the clergy, and the monks. It is of value far beyond its expression of individual observation and opinion—from its wide acceptation by and circulation

among the people, showing that it was regarded as true in essence, and
that a strong spirit of censure was working in the country. All through
the poem the evils pervading the Church are laid bare, contrasted with
simple, lowly goodness and sincere following of the Gospel. It is well
deserving of careful study by all who would realise the state of England
in the latter part of the fourteenth century, when Wyclif studied, wrote,
and preached. In the time of Henry VIII. the following lines were pointed
out as a prophecy singularly fulfilled. We, with our more sober notions,
can readily realise how likely such a prevision was to come to the ardent
worker for reform :—

> " And yet shall come a King and confess you all,
> And beat you, as the Bible telleth, for breaking of your rule.
> And amend you monks, and monials, and canons,
> And put you to your penance *ad pristinum statum ire* "
>
> > (to return to your former state).

KING HENRY VIII.

C

LUTTERWORTH CHURCH, OF WHICH JOHN WYCLIF WAS RECTOR.

CHAPTER III.

John Wyclif, the First great English Reformer.

Wyclif's Importance—Early History—A Royal Chaplain—The Papal Tribute—Wyclif at Bruges—The Good Parliament—Papal Bulls against him—Development of Wyclif's Ideas—On Divine and Civil Lordship—On the Bible—On Grace and Love—On Christ's Sufferings—On the Church—Laity and Clergy—The Papacy—The Sacraments—Transubstantiation.—Condemnation at Oxford—Translation of Bible—The Peasants' War—Attack upon Wyclif—His Later Years and Death—His Character and Influence.

UNDOUBTEDLY Wyclif must have a foremost place in the history of the Reformation, although he did not succeed in securing the adoption of his views, and although in many points his opinions were un-

Wyclif's Importance. like those of later Reformers. Against the preposterous claims of the papacy, he vigorously represented the strong and resolute sense of the English people. Against the extreme doctrines of the schoolmen, he upheld a much more moderate view of the Eucharist and the rights of the Church. Touching the lordship of the upper classes, his teaching led to something approaching socialism. But his great claim on our national gratitude is in connection with his version of the Bible in the language of the people.

John Wyclif, born early in the fourteenth century near Richmond,

in Yorkshire, a scion of an old family, was educated at Balliol College,

BALLIOL COLLEGE, OXFORD, WHERE JOHN WYCLIF WAS EDUCATED.

Oxford; and was so distinguished, that he was chosen its master some time between 1356 and 1360. His classical acquirements were confined

to Latin, Greek being understood by very few in that age; but in the
Early History. dialectic studies which were prominent in those days of logical subtlety, he was a master. He was not far inferior, for his
time, in mathematics and natural philosophy, from which he often drew
illustrations in his sermons and writings. Having passed through the
comparatively elementary stage, as it was then regarded, of study of the
Bible in the Vulgate version, he had no doubt mastered the "Sentences"
of Peter Lombard, then very largely swaying the theological schools, the
Summa Theologica of Thomas Aquinas, and the writings of Grossetête and
of Fitzralph. In 1363 (or probably later) he took the degree of Doctor
Wyclif a Royal Chaplain. of Divinity; and about the same time was appointed one of the
royal chaplains, having already become known as a supporter of
the national side against the papal claims. Indeed, opinions were already
attributed to him which went far beyond the current practice of ecclesiastics. To assert that "no one in holy orders ought to exercise temporal
authority," and that "no ecclesiastic ought to be a holder of property,"
was subversive, at any rate, of established facts.

Wyclif became an eager combatant when challenged by a monkish
opponent to present an argument against the making of an annual payment
Wyclif on Papal Tribute. of 1,000 marks claimed by Pope Urban V. from Edward III.
in 1365, in continuation of the tribute paid by King John. In
1366, Parliament, including the spiritual peers, unanimously decided
against the lawfulness of the demand. This rejection proved the death-
blow to the papal claim of feudal lordship over England and demand for
tribute; it was never again asserted. Wyclif's tract, though it did not
influence this result, set forth several strong arguments against the right
of the Pope to temporal lordship, and against his having any claim on a
kingdom he did nothing to benefit. Wyclif also maintained that King
John had no right to make the surrender he had made to the Pope.

Wyclif continued to lead an active teaching life at Oxford, and to
support the Crown against the Pope. In April, 1374, he was rewarded
Wyclif at Bruges. by the King with the rectory of Lutterworth, in Leicestershire,
and in July of the same year he was named next after the
Bishop of Bangor as one of the King's emissaries to treat with the Papal
nuncios at Bruges regarding certain matters in dispute. During this
mission, if not earlier, Wyclif came into close relations with John of
Gaunt, whose patronage of him was afterwards so marked, especially in the
abortive proceedings before Convocation in 1377. It is considered probable

that Wyclif's writings had not a little to do with the important present-
ment of the "Good Parliament" of 1376 against Church abuses,
and that he thus naturally incurred the hostility of the rich **The Good Parliament, 1376.**
clerics of Convocation. This parliamentary memorial asserted
that the Pope received from England five times as much as the King's
taxes; that foreigners drew the stipends of English livings without ever
seeing their cures; that the Papal Receiver, living in state in London, was
always looking out for English places, and had claimed the first year's
income of all newly conferred livings for the Pope; and that when a
bishopric became vacant, the Pope translated four or five other bishops
from one see to another, in order to obtain the first year's income from each.
All these and many other grievances the State surely had in its own power
to remedy, were it not for the dread influence which the Church had over
men's minds in its power of the keys, of absolution and Church ministrations. In this, as in many other subtle ways, the Church, which was
intended to make minds and hearts truly free, worked so as to enchain and
enslave them. This vigorous protest testifies to the existence of a strong
uprising of the national feeling.

That Wyclif was really the strongest opponent of the papacy in the
English Church at this time is made clear by the fact that, very soon after
Pope Gregory XI. had returned to Rome from the exile of
Avignon in 1377, he launched five Bulls against Wyclif, in- **Papal Bulls against Wyclif.**
tended by different methods to secure his imprisonment for
heresy, and transmission to Rome for judgment. Among the accusations
brought against him, and which he afterwards justified, were: that if the
Church fails in its duty, temporal princes may deprive it of its possessions; that the act of the Pope cannot enable or disable any man, and that
excommunication has no validity unless the offender be self-excommuni-
cated (by sin); that temporal punishments are not lawful as a consequence
of excommunication; that the Pope or any other cleric can only "bind" or
"loose" so far as he conforms to the law of Christ. Wyclif's previous
citation before Convocation, in February, 1377, came to nothing, through a
personal quarrel between John of Gaunt and Courtenay, Bishop of London.
The death of Edward III. put a stop for a time to proceedings under the
Papal Bulls; and Wyclif was chosen to draw up an opinion for the new
king and council as to the lawfulness of preventing the country's gold from
being drained away to supply the Papal demands. Wyclif was recognised
as a national champion; and when in the next year proceedings were at

last taken against him by the Papal commissaries Archbishop Sudbury and Bishop Courtenay, and Wyclif boldly came forward with his answer, the Princess of Wales, acting as regent, forbade the commissaries to proceed to judgment; while the citizens of London forced their way into the court, and noisily expressed themselves on Wyclif's side.   The commis-

JOHN WYCLIF, THE "MORNING STAR" OF THE REFORMATION.

saries contented themselves with forbidding Wyclif to teach the offending doctrines, and let him go free.

The death of Gregory XI. in 1378, and the resulting Papal schism, in which two Popes divided the suffrages of the faithful, had a marked and evident influence on Wyclif's mind.   We must here review the writings of Wyclif previous to this time, so far as they are known.   In many of them he was largely influenced by the scholastic style and definitions, by the current views of the Papacy and tradition, and by a favourable estimate of the mendicant orders. He certainly attached high *Development of Wyclif's Ideas.* importance to the use of the reason and the light of nature in ascertaining or confirming truth, but he had no notion that they could be contrary to anything taught in Scripture. He regarded the law of Christ as the perfect law, and the source of all that is good in every other law. He gradually came to distinguish clearly between *The Authority of the Bible.* the authority of what is taught in the Bible, and the additions made to it by Tradition. He regarded Christ as the true Author of all Scripture, and therefore held its literal inspiration and infallibility. It contained exactly what was most beneficial for men in every position in life. While it was made the only rule, the Church grew rapidly; when it was mixed with traditions, the Church declined. So absolute was his belief in the universal authority of the Bible that he wrote in his treatise, "On the Truth of Scripture," 1378, "It is impossible that any word or any deed of the Christian should be of equal authority with Scripture "—a principle which had to wait for a century and a half before it was enforced by the great Protestant revolt. Wyclif showed in his writings a marvellous knowledge of the Scriptures to which he bowed; yet he by no means rejected the light thrown by the interpretation of the Fathers, and especially when they agreed. That he conceded to all persons the right to read the Bible in the common tongue is evident by the translations he set on foot, and the efforts he made to circulate them.

We need not go into Wyclif's views on the Godhead, creation, etc., since on these subjects he introduced no new conception. But his doctrine of Divine and Civil Lordship or Dominion, though largely metaphysical, contains matter highly calculated to rouse animosity, and even now causing him to be accused of rank socialism.

We cannot precisely date Wyclif's Three Books "On Divine Dominion," forming the preliminary part of his collective "Summa in Theologia." God's rule he declares to be absolute and direct over every *On Divine and Civil Dominion.* creature. In his later "Civil Dominion" he puts forth the corresponding proposition, that no one in mortal sin has a right to any gift of God, while every man in grace has all God's gifts. Carrying this further, any grant made to a wicked man must be contrary to God's will, and so not a real possession. Mortal sin, being a defrauding of God, causes the sinner to forfeit all right to his possessions. The righteous man, on the contrary, is the true lord of all things, even when afflicted, for all things work together for his good. He follows this up to its logical consequence—that frequent antagonist of common sense—that as there are many righteous, and they are all lords of everything, all things should be held in common. As to the proper form of government he is undecided, and will determine nothing, but " it were better that all things should be had in common." Yet he felt that these views applied to an ideal, not an existing practicable state of things, and he discouraged all forcible attempts to set things right unless there should be a strong likelihood of putting an end to tyranny.

Wyclif was remarkably strong in favour of the freedom of man's will, although he also adopted much of the Augustinian view of predestination. Freewill and As to the origin of evil, he regarded all acts as determined by Necessity. God, and not evil in themselves, but only evil if the intention or feeling of the doer is evil. But it is useless to expect him to have solved a question which the wisest of our time cannot settle. As to the The Person of person of Christ, He is both eternally pre-existent and Divine, Christ. and true Man, the centre of humanity, the only Mediator. And Wyclif does not allow to the Virgin Mary or to saints any true mediatorship. The services in their honour, he says, are only of use so far as men's souls are thereby kindled to love for Christ Himself.

Wyclif brings into special prominence the humility, gentleness and poverty of Christ. "The works of Christ," he says, "are the best Christ's interpreters of His law," and therefore his life should be laid Passions. open and made plain in all schools, sermons, and churches. He lays frequent stress on the sufferings of Christ, and in a Passion sermon represents Christ as saying every day in our hearts, "This I suffered for thee ; what dost thou suffer for Me ? " In Wyclif's view the effect of Christ's suffering reaches forward to the world's end and backward to its beginning; it is sufficient for the redemption of many worlds. Man has gained by it more than Adam lost. Yet he believed with Augustine that salvation only extends to the elect.

Without reaching the standpoint of the later reformers, Wyclif attached high importance to faith as well as to " fruitful repentance " and Repentance forsaking of past sins; but he was so far an adherent of creeds and Love. that he laid it down as absolutely necessary to salvation for every Christian to believe, at least implicitly, every article of the faith. But with all eminent divines he places in the forefront of Christian virtue love to God and love to our neighbour. That love manifests itself not only in compassion, but, when needed, in remonstrance and censure. Our greatest duty is that which is nearest to us; but every man ought to discharge the duties of his calling or position, whatever that may be. No man can be neutral as to virtue and vice. Yet man can neither in any way earn grace before or after salvation, nor do works of supererogation or surplus merit. While on these matters he did not advance so far as the Reformers, his teaching certainly struck at the root of many of the Sacerdotal and Papal pretensions.

In his view of the Church, Wyclif was very broad, including in that term the angels and saints in heaven, the militant on earth, and those who are in purgatory, but who will be saved. This inclusiveness What is the Church? shut out all the unsaved, though they might fill high offices in the Church. Ungodly bishops he styles "members of Satan's synagogue." Just as no man can know whether another is truly elect, and therefore we are warned against hasty judgments, so no Christian can be sure of his own final continuance in grace, but each must continually test himself as to his standing in grace, without mortal sin.

As to Church services, Wyclif repeatedly censures their excessive sensuousness and symbolism. He was especially moved against images and reverence paid to them; for they had a mischievous effect on men's minds, leading them to erroneous ideas and idolatry. Sensuous Worship, Images and Relics. From having been in earlier days a believer in the necessity of the help of the Virgin, he in later days expressed himself against the canonisation of saints, the value of worship offered to them, the immoderate veneration of relics, masses for the dead, etc., though he is cautious and moderate in his expressions.

In regard to the relative place of the laity and the clergy in the Church, Wyclif expressed opinions, which, if not exclusively modern, have been very largely ignored even by English Churchmen. He Laity and Clergy. held that every man should know enough to judge for himself about the doctrines he was required to believe; he believed that it was possible for the laity to hold the truth when priests and theologians erred; and he laid it down that the laity, in order to influence the clergy to do their duty or refrain from vice, might withhold the payment of customary revenues to them. He could even conceive it possible that the true Church might for a time consist of laymen alone—a view quite inconsistent with strict apostolical succession. And his denunciations of "false shepherds," of their worldliness, their devotion to noblemen, to sport and drinking, their fleecing the poor, etc., show that he was by no means blind to the failings of his brethren, though he gave just praise to those who earnestly fulfilled their spiritual mission. He held a very modern view of the full authority of the priesthood, believing that in the apostolic times the only orders were presbyters and deacons, the presbyter being at first identical with the bishop; and this gradually gave him a truer insight into the proper meaning of the primacy of the Pope.

POPE URBAN VI., ELECTED 1378; THE RIVAL OF CLEMENT VII.

For a long time, even up to the year 1378, Wyclif spoke with great respect of the Papacy, although limiting its powers by a clear view of the

The Papacy.

rights of states, and he already denied that the Papacy was absolutely necessary and endowed with full power. On the contrary, he held that popes might sin and err in judgment. When Urban VI., however, immediately after his election, expressed the best intentions of reform and righteous administration, Wyclif joyfully welcomed his promises. Even after the election of a rival Pope, Wyclif held to Urban, although he expressed the opinion that if Urban were to wander from the right way, it would be much better to do without either Pope. Urban, however, proceeded to excommunicate his rival and all the Churches that took that rival's side; whereupon Wyclif gave up Urban, believing that neither Pope had anything in common with the Church of God.

Subsequent events intensified Wyclif's alienation from the Papacy. He began to realise that the Papal position was a usurpation, and not founded in right. In one of his latest writings he describes both Popes as antichrists, and charges the Church with stupidity in not withdrawing from both; and he regards it as even blasphemous for the "Roman presbyter" to say without foundation, "We will it to be so." He even came to think that the Papacy was of the devil, and that the veneration rendered to it was of the nature of idolatry, and all the more detestable because Divine honour was paid to a limb of Lucifer. Rough language; but neither clerical nor secular war is accustomed to measure its words. The rival Popes used such language of each other and of each other's adherents; Wyclif applies the same language to both, and to the Papacy in general.

A similar rapid development of Wyclif's ideas upon the Sacraments took place in his later years. It is remarkable how broadly he was capable of thinking on such a subject. Every sacrament he regarded **The** as the sign of a holy thing; and to the holy everything might **Sacraments.** thus be a sacrament. Consequently the number of seven sacraments was too small, viewed in this large sense; but of the seven, the Eucharist and Baptism were the most expressly based upon Scripture. While the sacraments, when rightly administered, had saving efficacy, they must be received in a believing and devout spirit.

It was in 1381 that Wyclif first came forward to attack the doctrine of Transubstantiation or Change of Substance in the Eucharist; and we cannot more clearly express his new view than by quoting **Transubstan-** some of the theses he put forward at Oxford in that year. **tiation denied.** Among them were these: The consecrated Host which we see on the altar is neither Christ nor any part of Him, but the efficacious sign of Him. No passer-by is able to see Christ in the consecrated Host with the bodily eye, but by faith. Transubstantiation, Identification and Impanation (the glorified body of Christ entering into perfect union with the real bread) cannot be founded on Scripture. The Eucharist is in its own nature bread and wine, though having, by virtue of the sacramental words, both the body and blood of Christ at every point. Thus Wyclif believed in a "Real Presence" of Christ's body in the Eucharist, while denying to the priest the power of "making the Body of Christ" out of the bread.

He powerfully contested all teachings, especially those of the schoolmen, which contradicted his view. He so far emancipated himself from current conceptions that he saw the absurdity of maintaining that bread was changed by a miracle into the body of Christ while yet it retained all the physical and sensible qualities of bread; but he held a materialistic view of the "Real Presence" which was very near akin to Luther's later doctrine of Consubstantiation. While he admitted that Christ's body was corporeally and locally in heaven, and not in the sacrament, he had a conception of some peculiar sacramental presence of Christ's body in the Host, by virtue of the words of consecration. Yet he inveighed strongly against the adoration of the Host, as idolatry, while he conformed to the custom of the Church in kneeling before the Host, but only as expressing his devotion to the glorified body of Christ in heaven. Not the miracle of the Romish Church, but still a miracle, was what Wyclif held, and in this he did not advance so far as the later Reformers. Yet in breaking the consecrated bread, it was not the body of Christ that was broken or touched. In brief, his doctrine was that "as Christ is at once God and man, so the sacrament of the altar is at once Christ's body and bread—bread in a natural manner, and body in a sacramental manner."

However far it may be removed from modern Protestant ideas, Wyclif's doctrine was sufficiently novel and heterodox to be viewed with **Wyclif's Teaching condemned at Oxford.** alarm and horror by conservative minds. The Chancellor of Oxford got together a number of doctors of theology and laws, the majority being monks, and mostly of the mendicant orders. These, without expressly condemning Wyclif, declared his two principal theses, denying transubstantiation, to be contrary to the teaching of the Church, and forbade them to be taught in the University, on pain of suspension, excommunication, and imprisonment. Wyclif received this injunction while lecturing on the subject in the Augustinian monastery at Oxford, and at once asserted that neither the Chancellor nor his colleagues could alter his convictions. And although he ceased to discuss the subject publicly in Oxford, his literary teaching was continuous, and to the same effect, in his later years.

Meanwhile Wyclif had in hand his greatest work, the Translation of **Wyclif's Translation of the Bible.** the Bible into English. Although considerable parts of the Bible had been translated or paraphrased into Anglo-Saxon and into Norman-French, and even into Old English, there was nothing generally adapted to and understood by the mass of the laity when read to them by the learned. We have it on the testimony of Wyclif's enemies that he devised and carried out the idea of translating the whole Bible into the vernacular—a work regarded as most condemnable. Wyclif, on the contrary, at some date conceived the ideas that every man ought to know the gospel for himself, and that every man who is saved is a real priest of God's making. The stages by which he advanced to the realisation of his idea can be but dimly seen.

BEGINNING OF ST. JOHN'S GOSPEL: WYCLIF'S VERSION, 1380.

It was mainly the New Testament that Wyclif himself translated out of the Vulgate; while the Old Testament was translated to a certain extent by Nicholas of Hereford, who in 1382 was consequently summoned before a Synod in London for a sermon preached before the University of Oxford, and on being excommunicated, appealed to Rome. There he was imprisoned for years, but at length gained his release and returned to England. It is very probable that Wyclif himself completed the translation of the Apocrypha, and arranged for the multiplication of copies,—some complete, others consisting of portions only,—of single books, or of the gospels and epistles for Sundays and festivals.

Undoubtedly Wyclif's version has numerous imperfections, as it must have, seeing that it was translated from the imperfect Vulgate into a language which was only beginning to be settled, and, moreover, at a time when the principles of satisfactory translation had scarcely begun to be discussed. A vast undertaking it was, in the midst of dangers, accusations of heresy, political troubles, lack of sympathy; an undertaking requiring calm thought, much time and perseverance, and one in which difficult questions had continually to be met and decided. Hereford's version of the Old Testament is a very stiff and literal performance; but Wyclif's work on the New Testament has high merits, rising beyond his other English writings, and deserving to be ranked among the earliest English classics.

It was not long before the work of revision was begun; but Wyclif did not live to complete it. John Purvey, his friend and assistant, carried **Purvey's Revision.** it out on his master's principles, and with many improvements, making the style more flowing and pleasing. Probably the revised version was issued in 1388. It is a mark of the extent to which copies of the earlier and later translations were multiplied, that at the present day nearly two hundred manuscript copies exist, mostly executed during the forty years succeeding Wyclif's death.

While the translation was proceeding, Wyclif was active in other directions. He had preached, before the University of Oxford, many Latin **Wyclif on Preaching.** sermons, in which his scholastic style had full scope. Instead of giving sermons, like most preachers in his time, which were little better than fabulous or incredible tales, or even stories from Ovid and from Roman history, he applied himself to set forth some weighty truth of doctrine or practice. His view of the importance and responsibility of preaching was such as might have been held by a modern evangelical divine. He found fault also with the practice of preachers who cut up the Bible truths as it were into mincemeat, and so loaded the particles with ornament, that personal pride appeared to have the chief share in the sermon. Nice logical and scholastic subtleties, and too much ornament,— these things hindered the gospel. In Wyclif's eyes, it was God's Word that ought to be preached, and in such form as to lead best and most quickly to edification. "In every proclamation of the Gospel," he says, "the true teacher must address himself to the heart, so as to flash the light into the spirit of the hearer, and to bend his will into obedience to the truth."

So eager was Wyclif to diffuse the truths which he had so laboriously acquired, the thoughts he had so earnestly reasoned out, that in his later years he sent out itinerant preachers who preached not only in churches but in public places; and they were so numerous and active in 1382 that Archbishop Courtenay inveighed against them in a mandate to the Bishop of London. And we must think of Wyclif not only as sending these men forth, but also as training and preparing them for their work, whether at Oxford or at Lutterworth we do not know. One of his followers, William Thorpe, spoke of his master as "the greatest scholar of that day; . . . the most virtuous and godly wise man whom I ever heard of, or whom I ever in my life became acquainted with." At first they were, no doubt, all duly ordained; but as the work went on and the opposition of the Church authorities to Wyclif increased, he appears to have dispensed with ordination. Indeed, in one of his sermons he expressly says that the evidence of Divine acceptance is sufficient authority for preaching without a bishop's ordination; and thus Wyclif distinctly ranged himself on the same side as those who maintain in these days that the proof of a Divine commission to preach rests not in the imposition of hands, but in the evidence of holy living and successful preaching.

Wyclif's Itinerant Preachers.

Wyclif's itinerants appear to have been conspicuous examples of poverty and plainness of garb, walking barefoot with a pilgrim's staff, dressed in coarse russet cloth, travelling from village to village, preaching and teaching wherever they could gain an audience—in the public places, or in churchyards and churches when they could gain admission. Holding up the lofty standard of the New Testament, they denounced the sins of pope, clergy, and laity, and sought to promote godly living and reformation of character. Such preaching naturally provoked opposition, especially from those of the papal party, who represented the preachers as undermining the Church and all religion. Wyclif actively defended his assistants in various tracts, and plied his pen to strengthen and encourage his preachers in their work.

Wyclif's enemies, eager to bring a charge against him, accused him with being the cause of the Peasants' War in 1381,[1] and the general dis-

---

[1] We shall not discuss the Peasants' War of 1381, inasmuch as there is no proof of Wyclif being in any way connected with it, as has been alleged.

turbance of social relations. The new Archbishop, Courtenay, already mentioned as an opponent of Wyclif, lent himself readily to a scheme for condemning Wyclif and punishing him and his followers. In May, 1382, he summoned a council of bishops and doctors of theology and laws, which met in the hall of the Dominican Monastery at Blackfriars. During its session an earthquake occurred which frightened some members, who thereupon wished the Council to be broken up. The Archbishop, however, was able to turn the earthquake to account, by representing it as a good omen, signifying the purification of the kingdom from error.

The Earth-quake Council.

The Council, without attacking Wyclif personally, or summoning him to appear, decided to condemn a list of ten articles as heretical, and fourteen others as erroneous, which had partly been set forth at Oxford and partly spread by itinerant preachers. The ten heretical articles include the assertion that bread and wine remain in the Eucharist after consecration ; the denial of Christ's corporeal presence there ; and the statements that " if a bishop or a priest be in mortal sin, he doth not ordain, consecrate, nor baptise ; " that if a man be contrite, confession to any other is superfluous and invalid ; that if the Pope be an evil man, he has no power over the faithful ; that ecclesiastics should have no temporal possessions, etc. Although these doctrines were not directly quoted from Wyclif, there can be no doubt that they were mainly gathered from his teachings, and that he was principally aimed at. This is further evident when we consider the fourteen erroneous articles. These articles denounce excommunication, unless for real breaking of God's law ; and maintain that any deacon or presbyter may preach without license from Pope or bishop ; also that temporal lords may take away their possessions from delinquent Churches.

Even in issuing his mandates forbidding all these teachings, Courtenay neither mentioned Wyclif nor any of his followers. Stringent measures were, however, taken against Hereford, Pepyngdom, and others at Oxford, not without considerable opposition within the University, which then as ever sought to maintain its independence of all outside authority. But this much is certain, that the public preaching of Wyclif's doctrines was repressed, and that several of Wyclif's followers recanted. But it is inexplicable why no open proceedings were taken against Wyclif, when there was so violent a dislike to him in high ecclesiastical quarters, unless it be true that he was so deeply rooted in the affection of

Wyclif's Followers Recant

the English people that to attack him would have been to risk a revolt. At all events, after being excluded from teaching at Oxford, he continued his work at Lutterworth without intermission, although he suffered from a paralytic stroke about the end of 1382.

POPE CLEMENT VII, ELECTED AT AVIGNON, 1378, AS ANTIPOPE TO URBAN VI.

To the last two years of Wyclif's life belong several of his most vigorous English tracts. To the parliament which met near the end of November, 1382, Wyclif addressed a memorial in which he attacked monastic vows as being only inventions of sinful men, and not obligatory. He therefore asked that the members of monastic orders might be free to quit them when they chose, and adhere to the more perfect rule of Jesus Christ only. He argued with great force that if the rules of the Orders were consistent with Christ's rule, they were superfluous; if inconsistent with it, they were harmful. A second article in the memorial supported the King's right to deal with Church temporali-

Wyclif's Memorial to Parliament.

D

ties; a third maintained that tithes and offerings might be withheld from
the clergy if these were unworthy, and that the clergy were much more
bound to do their duty well and set a good example than parishioners to
pay them tithes. A fourth article advocated that Christ's own teaching
about the Eucharist should be taught, and not the false doctrine of transubstantiation. But no practical result followed this memorial, except that
Wyclif was let alone.

When great efforts were continuously made to gain popular support for
a crusade in behalf of Urban VI. against the rival Pope, Clement VII.,
Wyclif on the Wyclif in 1383 published a Latin tract against what he calls
Papal Crusade. the war of the clergy, condemning the whole thing as contrary
to the mind of Christ, and as being a contention merely for worldly power.
The indulgence offered to all who aid the crusade he terms a lie and an
abomination. Those who promote the crusade are enemies of the Church.
He regards the whole quarrel as a consequence of moral apostacy from
Christ and His walk of poverty and purity; and declared that princes are
to blame for endowing the Church with temporal possessions which are
forbidden to Christ's ministers. And as if to show how far Wyclif's bold
spirit was from being quelled by Courtenay's previous action against him,
he addressed a letter to the Archbishop, expressing practically the same
views. The miserable failure of the crusade was an appropriate comment.

Whether, in fact, Wyclif was summoned to Rome by Urban, and
whether Wyclif, in excusing himself on the ground of ill-health, addressed
to him a clear assertion of his main doctrines, appears doubtful. He
spent his last years at Lutterworth, always active, always ready to encounter opposition, and almost expecting martyrdom. In his "Trialogus"
he says, "We have no need to go among the heathen in order to die a
martyr's death; if we preach persistently the law of Christ to Cæsar's
Wyclif's Death. prelates, instantly we shall have a flourishing martyrdom, if
we endure in faith and patience." But, after all, he escaped
judicial condemnation for heresy, excommunication and interference with
his personal liberty. He was engaged in hearing mass in his own parish
church on Innocents' Day, Dec. 28, 1384, when he was a second time struck
down by paralysis, and never spoke again, dying on the last day of the year.

That Wyclif was felt to be a reformer, and a setter-forth of doctrines
unwelcome to many, may be evidenced by the venom with which Walsingham the chronicler described how "John Wyclif,—that organ of the devil,
that enemy of the Church, that author of confusion to the common people,

that idol of heretics, that image of hypocrites, that restorer of schism, that storehouse of lies, that sink of flattery,—being struck by the horrible judgment of God, was struck with palsy, and continued to live in that condition until St. Sylvester's Day, on which he breathed out his malicious spirit into the abodes of darkness." But the position of Wyclif as the first great English reformer is secure.

Wyclif necessarily exemplified some of the defects of his time. He could not help being a scholastic divine, and writing scholastically, in an age when no other education was attainable. When the English language was unformed, and its literature almost non-existent, we must not expect from him a smooth, compact style, still less modern, classical, historical or scientific knowledge. But even his enemies allowed that he was the first scholar of his time : and his translation of the Bible places him high among the creators of the English language. Piercing through all mediæval accretions down to the root of religion, he saw that to make the people religious they must have religious truth at first hand, in their own tongue ; and his single initiative set on foot the procuring of an English Bible.

Wyclif's Character.

Among submissive scholastic theologians, Wyclif carried to its true result the work which scholastic theology had been doing in teaching subtlety of criticism. He applied it,—not so freely as Abelard, it is true, but with more moral earnestness,—first to the criticism of the actual state of the Church and its ministers, a mark of his practical character ; and later to certain doctrines which were causing much actual mischief, in denying the truth taught by Christ. In nothing is he more akin to modern Protestantism than in his thoroughly open criticism of established things. And he refers to ancient and primitive doctrine and practice, and to the direct teaching of Scripture, in a way which ought to commend him to those in our own day whose reverence for antiquity is so overpowering. A great literary artist he was not; but still a great critic, when we consider the state of intellect in his time. He was not one of the fiery souls who convert a nation, nor was he a tender emotionalist. Such emotion as he was possessed of was commonly kept well under control ; but his moral earnestness was great, his force of will and his perseverance were immense, his energy was both incessant and contagious. There is no shadow upon his moral character. With single eye he sought God's glory and the salvation of men. Without Wyclif, and the influence of his translation of the Bible, and his writings, it would have been much more difficult to bring about the Reformation of the Church in England. The Council at Rome in 1412 condemned his writings, and had them burnt on the steps of St. Peter's. The Church Council of Constance in 1415 condemned his doctrines, and thirty years after his death ordered the disinterment and burning of his body. In 1428, Flemyng, Bishop of Lincoln, was found willing to carry out the decree, and after the burning, the Reformer's ashes were scattered in the river Swift at Lutterworth. The republications of his works during the present century and the celebration of the five hundredth anniversary of his death have in recent years emphasised the great place now freely accorded to him.

[*See* Lechler's "Life of Wyclif," translated by Lessing; "Wyclif and Movements for Reform," R. Lane Poole; Perry, "English Church History," vol i.].

JEROME OF PRAGUE, THE FRIEND AND FELLOW TEACHER OF JOHN HUSS.

THE OLD RATHHAUS AT CONSTANCE, WHERE THE CHURCH COUNCIL MET IN 1415.

CHAPTER IV.

John Huss.

Bohemian Students Copy Wyclif's Writings—Milicz—Matthias of Jarrow—John Huss—
Exposes Pretended Miracles—Defends some Wyclifite Doctrines—Becomes Rector of
Prague University—Is Accused to the Archbishop, and Attacked by a Papal Bull—Asserts the Divine Call to Preach—Is Prepared for Martyrdom—Defends Wyclif on Property—Is Excommunicated—A Compromise Arranged—The Crusade against Naples—
Huss on Indulgences—The Bulls Burnt—Huss again Condemned—Is Excommunicated,
and Withdraws from Prague—Writes "On the Church"—The Right of Private Judgment—His Letters—"The Six Errors"—Huss Summoned to Constance—His Journey—
Is Thrown into Prison—Ill-treated—Denied a Fair Hearing—Condemned—Degraded
and Burned—Jerome of Prague—The Hussite War in Bohemia.

THE next scene of incipient reform is to be found in Bohemia, where the Roman Church had long been powerful. But as Ox-ford nourished Wyclif, so the University of Prague, founded in 1348, became the centre of Reform movements in Bohemia; and it was to Adalbert Ranconis, a great teacher at Prague, that the

Bohemian Students Copy Wyclif's Writings.

introduction of Wyclif's doctrines there was indirectly due. The money he left in 1388 to assist Bohemian students to study at Paris or Oxford brought many to the latter place, and the marriage of Richard II. to Anne of Bohemia no doubt increased the attractiveness of England to Bohemians. The foreigners naturally seized upon what seemed newest and truest to them in the theology of England, and many manuscript copies of Wyclif's writings which they made are still in existence, and in some cases have furnished our only knowledge of them.

The reform of Church abuses and a high standard of morals had already been preached at Prague by such men as Conrad of Waldhausen and Milicz of Kremsin. Milicz, an ascetic though a high dignitary, found himself compelled by conscience to resign his wealth and dignity, to adopt a life of poverty, and to preach to the people in the vernacular. Gradually, by his earnestness and denunciations of vice, he made many converts, and drew great audiences. He would often preach five times a day, in Latin, German and Czech. Many were his successes in the reformation of women of ill-fame; so that the quarter of Prague known as "Little Venice" was converted into an abode of piety. After several years of successful labour, he became morbidly self-depreciative, and desired to withdraw into monastic life; but after a short rest from preaching he was again impelled to come forward, by his reflections on various passages of the Bible, referring apparently to the last ages of the Church. He believed the manifold corruptions in the Church, the negligence of pastors, the prevalence of simony, the evil life of all classes indicated the approaching advent of Christ. He therefore, in 1367, went to Rome to Pope Urban V., to inform him of these presages, and of the mission he felt himself charged with to warn and admonish the Church. He desired the Pope to call a general council, at which plans for reform might be devised, including a preaching crusade by men prepared to die for Christ. His attempt to address the populace in St. Peter's was frustrated, and he was apprehended and imprisoned by a Dominican inquisitor. In his confinement his gentle patience was remarkable, and he was at last permitted to deliver his sermon in St. Peter's. Later, Pope Urban gave him satisfactory assurances, and set him free.

On his return to Prague, Milicz established a training college for preachers, with hundreds of members, bound by no vows, but only by a common serious spirit. His beneficence was boundless, at last leaving him without books or warm clothing. He could keep nothing for himself exclusively. But his enemies found heresy in his teaching, and accused him to Gregory XI. at Avignon. Thither Milicz journeyed to plead his own cause in 1374, but died while his case was still undecided.

We might here enlarge on the life and teaching of Matthias of Jarrow, the pupil of Milicz, who forms the link between Milicz and Huss. He is a conspicuous example of a zeal for truth and for apostolical Matthias of purity which, in spite of its reality and fulness of expression, Jarrow. did not effect what others less far-seeing but more disturbing, more combative, might have accomplished. In his teachings are to be found the germs of many of the conten-

JOHN HUSS, THE BOHEMIAN REFORMER (1373-1115).

tions of the Reformers. He exposed the corruptions of the clergy, the self-exaltation of popes and bishops, the excessive multiplication of ecclesiastical laws and human ordinances in place of the simple rule of Christ. "Every Christian," he said, "is already an anointed man and a priest." Neither the priesthood nor membership of a monastic order could render a man more truly a servant of Christ. Profession made no man a Christian; and while man remains in this life, he must ever progress or go backward. The immense distinction made in his time between clergy and laity he attacked unsparingly, and earnestly advocated the giving of the eucharistic cup as well as the bread to the laity. Image-worship he vigorously denounced. He died in 1394.

John Huss, born at Husinetz, in Bohemia, in 1369, of peasant parents, studied at the University of Prague, and in 1398 began to lecture. It was in the same year that Jerome of Prague had returned from John Huss. Oxford, bringing with him many of Wyclif's writings. In previous years, what he had learnt about Wyclif had repelled and horrified Huss; but afterwards the English Reformer began to exercise an increasing attraction on him, so that he made his writings the subject of his lectures.

In 1401 he was appointed preacher of the "Bethlehem" chapel founded in 1391 for vernacular or Czech preaching; and his glowing sermons soon attracted eager audiences. He became known as a man zealous against abuses, and in 1405 was selected, with two others, by the new Archbishop of Prague, Zbynek, to inquire into alleged miracles, in which the blood of Christ was supposed to have appeared, at Wilsnack.   The inquiry re-

Exposes Pretended Miracles. vealed their falsity, and Huss took occasion to expose the fallacy of believing Christ's body or blood to be in any given place on earth, and the false miracles which had been pretended by greedy ecclesiastics.

The next occasion on which Huss stood forward was in direct connection with Wyclif's teaching.   In 1403, a series of doctrines extracted from

Defends some Wyclifite Doctrines. the Englishman's writings were condemned by the University of Prague, although Huss and others defended some of them, and declared that others were not truly derived from Wyclif. But this did not suffice for the anti-Wyclif party; and in 1405 Pope Innocent VII. was induced to issue a Bull to Archbishop Zbynek, to suppress and punish the growing heresy in Bohemia.   He duly published this in 1406, and in 1408 secured a separate condemnation of Wyclif's doctrines by the Bohemian or Czech members of the University.   But the form of the condemnation was a partial Wyclifite victory.   It was enacted that no one should presume to maintain any of the specified propositions in a heretical, erroneous, or scandalous sense.   Liberty was further re- stricted by the prohibition of lectures on specified books of Wyclif, containing his main doctrines.

In 1407, Huss had been chosen to preach before the clergy of the diocese of Prague, and had taken occasion to put forward his views on the duties of the clergy, exhorting them to follow Christ and to initiate re- forms.   Meanwhile the influence of Huss and Jerome at the court of King Wenceslas was undiminished, and the king delighted the national party by

Becomes Rector of Prague University. reversing the weight of votes in the University, giving three votes to the Bohemian "nation," and only one to the Germans and all other foreigners combined.   The Germans, who were much the more numerous party, consequently left Prague in a body, and established the University of Leipsic.   Huss was now elected Rector of the University, but he had a much diminished body of men to rule over. The decline of the University had its reciprocal effect on the estimation of the Rector, to whom the calamity was ascribed.   The king, supporting the

INTERIOR OF ST. PETER'S, ROME.

coming general council at Pisa, to decide between the rival Popes, was fiercely opposed by the Archbishop and clergy; the royal party tried to humble the clericals, and they in turn defied the king. Huss preached in favour of the council, hoping it would do something in the way of reform.

A number of the clergy of Prague accused him to the Archbishop of stirring up the people against the clergy, of terming Rome the seat of antichrist, and of praising Wyclif. An inquisitor was appointed to inquire into the truth of these charges; and probably, as the result of them, Pope Alexander V., in 1409, commanded the *Is accused to the Archbishop.* abjuration of all Wyclif's heresies, which he had heard were widely spread in Bohemia, and the surrender of all his writings. A clause specially aimed at Huss's chapel, forbade preaching in private churches. When this Bull was published in Prague, in March, 1410, it was received with great indignation by the king and many important persons, and Zbynek was accused of being its real *And attacked by a Papal Bull.* author. Huss appealed, as he said, "from the Pope ill-informed to the Pope better informed"; but Zbynek proceeded to demand the surrender of Wyclif's writings, and condemned two hundred volumes to the flames, regardless of their value as private property. Great disturbances were thereby excited among the populace, who further ridiculed the Archbishop in satirical songs. Huss termed the burning "an evil business." "Such burning," he wrote, "never yet removed a single sin from the hearts of men, but only destroyed many truths, many beautiful and fine thoughts, and multiplied among the people disturbances, enmities, suspicions and murders."

The enemies of Huss acknowledged that the enthusiasm for Wyclif in Bohemia was increased by this proceeding. King, queen, nobles and citizens petitioned the new Pope, the infamous John XXIII., to withdraw the condemnation; Huss publicly defended much of Wyclif's teaching, continued to preach, and personally appealed to the Pope. In his tract on the Trinity, in 1410, Huss asserted his desire to accept any teaching which could correct him, if it were founded on Scripture or rational argument. His rule was, whenever he heard a more correct opinion than his own, to give up his earlier opinion with joy and humility, "being well aware that what we know is vastly less than what we do not know." As to the prohibition of his preaching in his private chapel, he *Asserts the Divine Call to Preach.* asserted that the internal call, derived from the Holy Spirit, was of more authority than any outward call, and it might constrain a man to stand forth in opposition to human authority. Every priest or deacon who confessed the truth and practised righteousness had thereby a testimony from God, so that he needed no other proof of his Divine commission.

From this bold declaration Huss rose to the higher flight of asserting his purpose to defend, even to death, the truth which God had enabled him **Is prepared for Martyrdom.** to know, and especially the truth of Holy Scripture, knowing that truth remains and is eternally mighty, and that with God there is no respect of persons. And if the fear of death should terrify him, he had hope in God and His Holy Spirit, that the Lord Himself would give him constancy, and crown him with martyrdom.

Huss at this time also defended Wyclif's doctrine touching the poverty of the Church and clergy, and the right of the civil power to take **Defends Wyclif on Property.** away Church property from unworthy holders. He upheld Wyclif's assertion that no man can rightfully hold any possession if he is in mortal sin; but he did not assert that the ministration of an evil minister was of no avail for the recipients; for God overruled the actions of the evil for the good of His Church. He wrote a tract, "On the Body of Christ," to defend himself against those who charged him with not believing in the presence of Christ's flesh and blood in the Eucharist. He maintained that the body of Christ abode wholly in heaven, but yet was present and eaten spiritually in the sacrament.

Meanwhile Huss was summoned to Rome to answer for himself; but his friends advised him that his journey through Germany would be un- **Huss Excommunicated.** safe. Consequently, in February, 1411, a sentence of excommunication was pronounced against him for his disobedience. Later in the same year he was publicly declared to be a heresiarch, and the city of Prague was laid under an interdict. But many of the clergy refused to observe the interdict, as it had been obtained without a fair hearing of Huss; and those who sought to obey it had to flee the country. So strong was the feeling in Huss's favour, that Archbishop Zbynek arranged **A Compromise arranged.** a compromise, and Huss presented to the University of Prague a declaration in which he vindicated his orthodoxy, and asserted that he had been falsely accused to the Pope.

But a new event upset all calculations, and brought Huss once more into open conflict with the Papal party. John XXIII., in 1412, issued a **The Crusade against Naples.** Bull against Ladislaus, King of Naples, an adherent of his rival, Gregory XII., proclaiming a crusade against him, and promising full indulgence to all who took part in it, or who contributed in money as much as a month's joining in it would have cost them. Huss was summoned by the Papal legate to say whether he would obey the apostolical mandates. "Yes," replied Huss, "the *apostolical* mandates; and as far as the *papal* mandates agree with these, I will obey them most willingly. But if I see anything contrary to these, I will not obey, even though the fire to burn my body were before my eyes." The king had permitted the Bull to be published, and several of Huss's old friends in the University gave their assent to it. Huss now broke with them, and held a public disputation on indulgences, in which he attacked the entire system of granting indulgences for money.

Huss here anticipated Luther's effectual action, more than a century later. He could not approve anything that would not stand the test of Christ's teaching and life. Neither the shedding of blood among Christians—and the King of Naples and his subjects were, at any rate, nominally Christians—nor the laying waste of countries could proceed from love to Christ. And indulgence—that is, remission of sin—could be granted by God only; and priestly absolution was only conditional on the remorse, repentance, faith, and intended obedience of the sinner. Popes, bishops and clergy had no right to fight for temporal power or wealth; and in calling on all persons to destroy Ladislaus and Gregory, the Pope was acting contrary to the example of Christ. The laity who obeyed were blameworthy. He censured the unchristian expressions in the Bull, such as terming the adherents of Ladislaus blasphemers and heretics. As to the pretension to absolve both from guilt and punishment, in return for money for the expedition, the language in which it was offered amounted to a claim of Divine power. "The foolish man of wealth," he said, "is betrayed into a false hope; the law of God is set at nought; the rude people give themselves up more freely to sin; grievous sins are thought lightly of; and the people are robbed of their property. Far be it from the faithful to have anything to do with such indulgences. No case was to be found in the Scriptures of any holy man saying to any one, 'I have forgiven thee thy sins,' still less to offer to absolve from punishment or guilt for a certain number of days." The case against indulgences could not be more clearly or more moderately put.

Huss on Indulgences.

When Huss had thus delivered his soul, Jerome followed in a style far more glowing and inflammatory. Moderation was forgotten for the time. The students and populace got up a procession which carried the Papal Bulls contemptuously through the city, and

The Bulls Burnt.

finally burnt them publicly. Huss had no part in this. The king and court thought it necessary to treat this riotous behaviour seriously, and forbade all public insult of the Pope, or open resistance to the Papal Bulls, on pain of death. But the spirit evoked by Huss and Jerome could not be thus suppressed. Three young artisans, when a priest was offering indulgences for sale, exclaimed, "Thou liest. Master Huss has taught us better than that." They were condemned to death, notwithstanding Huss's appearance in their behalf, and his declaration that their fault was his, and that he deserved to die rather than they. The victims were hailed as martyrs, and so high did popular feeling rise, that others of Huss's followers who had been imprisoned were released.

But Huss's opponents in the University renewed their attack upon him, and the majority of the theological faculty again condemned the forty-

Huss again Condemned. five formerly drawn from Wyclif, together with six propositions specially aimed at Huss. It was declared to be heresy to differ from the Roman Church about the sacraments and power of the kings ; to suppose that antichrist ruled in the Church ; to say that the Fathers and tradition ought not to be followed because they are not in Scripture; to say that relics ought not to be worshipped; to say that priests may not absolve; and that the Pope may not call for contributions and give indulgences to the faithful who loyally come forward. At their request, put forward as a means of securing peace, the king granted an edict forbidding the preaching of these doctrines on penalty of banishment; but he at the same time administered to the theological faculty a sharp rebuff by telling them that they had much better try to refute the doctrines than attempt to crush them by an edict; and he distinctly refused to prohibit the preaching of this or that individual.

Huss's enemies, however, were again busy at Rome against him, and secured his excommunication ; and if he persisted twenty days in dis-

Is Excommunicated and withdraws from Prague. obedience to the Pope, every place that harboured him was to be placed under an interdict. Huss, though he did not in the least admit the validity of this excommunication, found that in order to prevent violent disturbances between the opposing parties, it would be most prudent for him to withdraw for a time from Prague, appealing, as he declared, from the venality of Rome to the one incorruptible, just and infallible Judge, Jesus Christ. An ineffectual attempt to compose matters was made by a synod at Prague, in February, 1413, and a similar result attended the appointment of a commission by the king.

Withdrawing into various country places. Huss occupied himself in

HOUSE OF JOHN HUSS AT CONSTANCE.

open-air preaching, in writing letters to his friends asserting his principles, and in composing his important work on the Church (*De Ecclesiâ*) and various tracts against his opponents.

Huss's doctrine of the Church was such as might be in part quoted by modern Congregationalists in support of their principles. From Christ's words, "Where two or three are gathered together in My name," etc., he argued that *there* would be a true particular Church; and that all the righteous living in Prague were the true Church of Prague. He went further, and said that it would be the height of arrogance for any man, without a special revelation, to assert that he was a true member of the Church. Many were apparent members who were not real members. The Church was divided into very many parts, which together constituted the entire Church. Christ was the all-sufficient head of the Church, which could be adequately governed by His law, interpreted by holy teachers, such as Augustine, Gregory, and Ambrose. Christ could be more really present in His Church in Bohemia than the Pope, who lived 800 miles away. The Papacy as such was derived from the Donation of Constantine, up to which time the Bishop of Rome had but been one among many bishops. Unconditional obedience to Popes and Prelates was unreasonable. Should the Pope bid any one give alms while he left his son to famish, or pomise a fast on him (Huss) which he could not endure, or command him to build towers or to weave, reason must decide against the command. "Wherefore should I not place my own thought before the Pope's dictum?"

Writes "On the Church."

Here Huss distinctly lays down the most important principle, as we take it, of modern Protestantism—the right of private judgment. And this he unflinchingly maintained till his death. In fact, it was practically in defence of this right that he died. He showed most conclusively to what evils the unlimited authority of the Papacy were likely to lead, and he was able to refer to the evil state of the Church in proof of his case. His prayer was, "Almighty Lord, who art the way, the truth, and the life, Thou knowest how few, in these times, walk in Thee, how few follow after Thee, as the Head, in humility, poverty, chastity, labour and patience; help Thy little flock, that they may never forsake Thee, but follow on through the narrow path, even unto Thyself."

The Right of Private Judgment.

Modern Liberationists might be rejoiced to find how heartily Huss is in agreement with them in regard to the worldly possessions of the Church. The whole cause, he said, of the "devilish schism" which divided the Church into fragments adhering to rival Popes, lay

Evil of Church Endowments.

in her worldly endowments and property. To those who charged him with causing division, he asserted that his object was to restore real unity, under the law of Christ in its purity.

One of the smaller works that Huss wrote at this time was a vigorous treatise on "The Six Errors." These were: 1. That of the priests, in asserting that they made the body of Christ in the Mass, thus claiming to create the Creator. 2. That of believing in the Popes and the saints, whereas they ought to believe in God alone. 3. The priests pretending to remit the guilt and penalty of sin to whomsoever they pleased. 4. Implicit obedience to superiors, no matter what they ordered. 5. Making no distinction between a just and an unjust excommunication. 6. Simony, of which he accused the greater part of the clergy. Here again Huss showed himself a true Reformer.

"The Six Errors."

Some of his letters written about this time are remarkable for their force and firmness. "If I cannot make the truth free in all," he writes to Christan, Rector of Prague University, "I will at least not be an enemy to the truth, and will resist to the death all agreement with falsehood. A good death is better than a bad life. One ought never to sin through fear of death. To end this life, by God's grace, is to pass out of misery. The more knowledge of truth a man gains, the harder he has to work. He who speaks the truth, breaks his own neck. He who fears death, loses the joy of living. Truth triumphs over all; he triumphs who dies for the truth; for no calamity can touch him, if no sin has dominion over him." And to the same effect he wrote on many other occasions.

Letters of Huss.

During the year 1413, it was decided to hold a general Council of the Roman Church at Constance, then under the control of the German Emperor, Sigismund, brother of Wenceslaus of Bohemia. It was anxiously hoped by many that this Council would heal the schism in the Church, and reform the abuses which were sapping its strength. The disputes and troubles in Bohemia centring round Huss were naturally prominent subjects for the Council to deal with, and the redoubtable heretic was summoned to appear and defend himself from the charges brought against him.

Huss summoned to Constance.

Nothing loth, Huss prepared for the journey, fortified with the promise of a "safe-conduct" from the Emperor, giving him protection on his journey, and freedom in going, sojourning and returning. It is alleged on behalf of the Roman Catholic hierachy that they were not bound to respect this promise if Huss should be convicted of any heresy deserving punishment. But it was undoubtedly offered to Huss as an inducement to him to attend the Council, and the Emperor ought to have felt bound to see that it was carried out.

In August, 1414, Huss appeared once more in Prague, and by public notice invited any man to convict him, before the Archbishop or his synod, **He starts from** of any heresy; but no one came forward. The Papal inquisitor **Prague.** of Prague, the Bishop of Nazareth, even gave him a full certificate of orthodoxy; and Conrad, the Archbishop of Prague, concurred in making no charge of heresy against him, only saying that he ought to purge himself from the excommunication formerly pronounced. His farewell letter to his old congregation at the Bethlehem chapel was a very touching one. He foresaw by what enemies he should be beset at the Council, but he prayed God to give him wisdom, a skilful tongue, and a spirit to despise persecutions, imprisonment and death. "If my death," he said, " can glorify Christ's name, then may He hasten it, and give me grace to endure with good courage whatever evil may befal me. But if it is better for my salvation that I should return to you, let us beseech God for this—that I may come back to you from the Council without wrong: that I may keep back nothing of the Gospel of Christ; that we may thenceforth come to a purer knowledge of it, and leave a good example to our brethren." Another letter which Huss left behind him for his young disciple Martin, to be opened only after his death, gives careful advice as to his conduct in regard to worldliness, purity, and simplicity, and reveals how self-reproachful Huss was as to his early fondness for sumptuous clothing and superfluities—natural enough in one who had come out of a peasant's cottage. It also tells us that Huss, before entering the priesthood, had spent much time at chess, and often lost his temper over it, which faults he still deplored.

Setting out from Prague on October 11, 1414, he was everywhere welcomed on the route, many Germans eagerly listening to his teaching **His Journey.** and conversation. We may be sure that Huss did not lose his opportunities, and in many places he converted doubters of his teaching into staunch supporters. A striking measure of the common ignorance of the elements of Christian teaching is furnished by the fact that Huss everywhere left behind him for his hosts a copy of the Ten Commandments, sometimes even writing them out during his meals. He was accompanied by three noble Bohemian knights, the most noted of whom,

John of Chlum, has won the regard of all who have the record of the Bohemian martyr's last months.

Arrived at Constance, on November 3, 1414, Huss was at first left in peace, and had liberty to say Mass and to teach daily. But his former friend, John Paletz, of Prague, and others, when they came, busied themselves in accusing and defaming him in public and private, and drew up a form of accusation against him, partly derived from his writings, and partly invented or misrepresented. The worst consequences, it was declared, would fall on the Church in Bohemia if he should be acquitted. Their enmity could not persuade Huss to humbly recant what they alleged; on the contrary, he prepared several discourses for public delivery, in explanation of what he had taught, and in defence of his orthodoxy, asserting that he preached nothing contrary to the general councils or ancient authority of approved Church teachers,—always supposing their doctrine to contain nothing contrary to Scripture. Huss was so active and resolute, and his enemies were so bitter, that they could not refrain from throwing him into prison on November 28, 1414, when he claimed the right to appear before the whole Council in person. On the 6th of December he was confined in a Dominican cloister, in a foul dungeon.

Arrival at Constance.

Is thrown into Prison.

The Emperor, appealed to on behalf of Huss, protested his indignation, and promised that he would set him free; but so potent were the terrors of the Church in those days, that the representation that the Emperor ought not to interfere in matters concerning the faith and heresies frightened Sigismund. The imputation, propagated everywhere by the priests, that he forcibly hindered the course of justice, was too serious for him to encounter. The right of the Church to crush heresy seemed so evident in mediæval times that it required several hundred years to substitute for it the right of free thought and opinion. The Emperor's safe-conduct was violated by the cardinals and bishops, and Sigismund deprecated, yet did not effectively resist, the indignity thus offered to himself.

The Pope now nominated a committee to examine into the matter, calling Huss a dangerous heretic, and thus prejudging him against all justice and right. Even the aid of an advocate was denied him, while the unhealthiness of his dungeon brought on a dangerous illness which threatened to kill him. Under such conditions he had to draw up his defence against accusations heaped together from intercepted letters, expressions in conversation, and distorted passages of his writings.

Is Denied an Advocate.

E

When visited by Paletz, the latter addressed him most harshly and unkindly; and Huss, writing in January, 1415, said, "God has appointed me for my inflexible enemies those to whom I have shown much kindness, and whom I loved from my very heart." Meanwhile he wrote cheerfully and courageously to many friends, and his dreams encouraged him to believe in the future triumph of truth. Eager to use his last days for good, he wrote numerous small treatises in prison—some at the request of his keepers, some on the main doctrines of the Church; displaying minute learning, though he had no reference books at hand. One of these committed him to a new controversy. During his absence from Prague, his

The Cup for the Laity. friend, James of Misa, had openly attacked the withholding of the cup from the laity in the Eucharist, and had begun to administer the sacramental wine regularly. Huss had previously made no statement on the subject; but he now found himself, after careful thought, compelled to say that it was both permitted and profitable that the laity should communicate in both kinds—another subject for his enemies to seize upon.

Meanwhile, Pope John, openly and truthfully accused of a host of crimes, any one of which was sufficient to disqualify him for his office, fled from the Council which he found he could not control. But this event only made matters worse for Huss, who, placed in the custody of the Bishop of Constance, was chained in a tower, in the castle of Gottleben; even at night forbidden to see friends; and treated with such severity as to bring on painful illnesses. At last, after much difficulty, the Bohemian knights

Huss before the Council. obtained for Huss permission to speak in person before the Council, and he was transferred to a Franciscan convent. The castle of Gottleben at once received a fitting prisoner in the person of Pope John XXIII.

While Huss was in Gottleben Castle, the Council had already, on May 4th, condemned the forty-five propositions drawn from Wyclif's writings, and, in fine, all his works, and had taken the extreme step of ordering that his remains should be exhumed and burnt. Jerome of Prague had now arrived at Constance, at first of his own accord, and a second time in consequence of his disobeying a summons from the Council, purporting to be a safe-conduct, but addressing him as a person suspected of errors, for which he must answer before them. On May 23, 1415, he appeared before the Council loaded with fetters, was treated with indignity, and sent back to the harshest confinement, where he lay a whole year.

The Council then deposed John XXIII., and proceeded to condemn the administration of the cup in the Eucharist.

When Huss was at last brought before the Council, his writings containing the passages complained of were laid before him, and he acknowledged them to be his, at the same time offering to retract anything in which he could be proved to be in error. The first article

HUSS DEFENDING HIMSELF BEFORE THE COUNCIL OF CONSTANCE.

charged against him having been read, Huss began to defend it by passages of Scripture, but was met by an outburst of furious clamour, which was renewed whenever he attempted to speak. Astonished, he looked round the assembly calmly, and remained silent. Some declared that he was thus confessing himself convicted of error. Order could not be restored, and the assembly broke up for the day.

On the 7th of June, Huss appeared a second time before the Council, the Emperor Sigismund being present. He was accused of having denied
The Second Day. transubstantiation, a charge he easily refuted; but the Council insisted on accepting the testimony of Huss's enemies, and rejecting his denials. Accused of defending Wyclif's heresies, Huss denied having defended the errors of Wyclif or of any other man ; but he could not agree to the form and terms in which the Council condemned the English reformer. He went fully into the questions relating to Wyclif, in the midst of hostile remarks and derision. As far as possible, endeavours were made to attack Huss on questions involving politics, to show the Emperor and other princes how dangerous he was ; and the question of the safe-conduct coming up, Sigismund exhorted Huss to defend nothing obstinately, but to submit to the Council, and he should be leniently dealt with ; otherwise, if he did not submit, the Emperor would sooner prepare the faggots for him with his own hands than suffer him to go on with the same obstinacy as before. Huss again protested that he would change his opinions without hesitation if he were taught better ; and he was then taken back to prison, after a day of much suffering, during which he saw the last hope of the Emperor's protection disappearing.

Huss had stood firm against all attacks, but longed for an opportunity of making a full explanation of his position, without interruption. The
The Third Day. next day he was again brought forth, and charges drawn from his book, " On the Church," were read. Some he admitted and explained, others he repudiated as not found in his writings, or distorted or misconstrued. As to the charge of saying that dignity, human choice, etc., made no one a member of the Church, he vigorously defended it ; while as to his having declared that when a king, pope, or bishop lay under mortal sin, he was neither king, pope, nor bishop, he explained that such a person was not so in a worthy manner in the sight of God. It is undoubtedly true that Huss's words might be interpreted to mean that no rightful obedience could be claimed by or given to such persons ; yet Huss could point to the deposition of John XXIII. by this very Council as a case in his support. But all these declarations in favour of purity in high places were unwelcome to many in the Council, for they seemed to detract greatly from the Divine authority of the bishops and cardinals ; and John Gerson attacked Huss very powerfully on those questions.

All through Huss was lectured and rated as a prejudged culprit, and at last was told that he must confess that he had erred in the articles alleged against him, and publicly recant them. Huss forcibly pleaded that he could not abjure what he had never taught or thought. The Emperor strongly advised him to abjure anything and everything. He was ready himself to abjure all possible errors—as ready as to disregard the safe-conduct, we might add. But with Huss, words had real meanings, and were not merely counters to juggle with. He could not say he had erred, in such a way as would be for him the utterance of a falsehood; and he could not abjure what he had never taught. Men of our day, who have had no price to pay for their spiritual freedom, may, as they sometimes do, say that Huss was too stiff and inflexible in his maintenance of his own opinions—that he might have bowed to the Council's decision, and still have held his private opinions. But without such martyrs liberty of conscience had been dead ere now. Moreover, Huss soon found out that even if he had recanted in the most explicit form, his recantation would have been suspected; and that in any case it was practically decided that he should be degraded from the priesthood and imprisoned for life. The Emperor joined the chorus against him, declaring that unless he abjured everything alleged against him, he ought to be burned to death. Huss returned to his prison scarcely able to stand after the exhausting ordeal he had gone through, his trusty friend, John of Chlum, supporting and comforting him.

When the proposed form of retractation was sent to Huss, he firmly refused to sign it, "first, because he was called upon to condemn as impious several propositions which he held to be true; and, secondly, because he should thereby scandalize the people of God, to whom he had taught those truths." He maintained inflexibly his view that the author of a book ought to know better than any one else whether it contained the doctrines imputed to him; and he steadfastly refused to allow, contrary to his conscience, that black was white. During four weeks Huss was besought and importuned by all kinds of influences to recant. In the meanwhile he spent his time in writing touching and tenderly affectionate letters to his friends, and to his former congregation. The friends who had become his bitterest enemies—who had inflicted on him the most poignant stabs—were also the objects of his forgiveness. To Paletz he wished to confess himself, but Paletz shrank from the office, although he visited him and besought him to recant; and Huss's words affected him to **His Resolution** tears. The Emperor, having really betrayed Huss, now sought **and Forgiving Spirit.** to save him; but it was too late. Michael de Causis, the most inveterate of his enemies, once a friend, several times visited him and said to his keepers: "By the grace of God we shall soon burn this heretic." For him Huss prayed from the bottom of his heart. Yet he found it at times difficult to rejoice in all trials. "It is easy to say," he wrote, "but difficult to do it." "O Divine Jesus," he prayed, "draw us nigh unto Thee. Feeble as we are, if Thou draw us not, we cannot follow Thee. Fortify my spirit, that it may become strong and resolute. The flesh is weak; but let Thy grace protect, assist, and save us; for without Thee we can do nothing, and are incapable of facing, for Thy sake, a cruel death. Give me a determined mind, an intrepid heart, a pure faith, and perfect charity, that I may be enabled to lay down my life for Thee, with patience and joy."

On the 6th of July, 1415, Huss was brought for the last time before the Council and the Emperor. All the charges against him were once more read over, but he was not now allowed to say anything in his defence, and was pronounced to be an obstinate heretic. This attack Huss repelled :—"I never was obstinate," he said, "but as I have always demanded up to this hour, so now I ask only to be informed of what is better from Holy Scripture." All his writings were condemned to be publicly burnt, and he himself was sentenced to degradation from his priestly office, and to be delivered over to the secular power for execution. When this sentence had been pronounced, Huss fell on his knees and said: "Lord Jesus, forgive my enemies. Thou knowest that they have accused me falsely, and have used against me false testimony and vile calumnies: forgive them of Thy infinite mercy." And mocking laughter followed from many in that evil-minded assembly.

Huss Condemned and sentenced.

Seven bishops were then selected to clothe Huss in priestly vestments and formally to degrade him. Once more called upon to recant, he said: "I now stand before the eyes of my God, without dishonouring whom, as well as meeting the condemnation of my own conscience, I cannot do this." One by one the vestments were removed. He was addressed as "condemned Judas" when the cup of communion was taken from him. A kind of crown or mitre, painted over with devils, and inscribed "Arch-heretic," was placed upon his head. Huss said: "My Lord Jesus wore on my account a crown of thorns; why should not I be willing for His sake to wear this easier though shameful badge?" This done, the bishops said: "Now we give over thy soul to the devil."

Huss's rejoinder was, looking up to heaven: "But I commend into Thy hands, Christ Jesus, my soul, by Thee redeemed."

Led away to the place of execution, Huss saw his books burning in front of the episcopal palace, and smiled. In a meadow outside the city gardens, where the pile of faggots was heaped, Huss knelt down **Huss Martyred.** and prayed in the words of the fifty-first and other Psalms; and his words moved the people to note how excellently he prayed. A priest

JOHN HUSS SUMMONED TO RECANT AT THE STAKE, JULY 6TH, 1415.

being brought to confess him, would not hear him unless he recanted his errors; but he refused to purchase absolution by perjury. Being bound to a stake, surrounded by wood and straw, he once more protested his innocence of the false charges against him, and his joy in death for the truth. "My sermons, books, and writings," he declared, "have all been composed with the sole view of rescuing souls from the tyranny of sin." The fire having been kindled, he began singing with a loud voice, "Jesus, son of the living God, have mercy on me!" As he was singing it for the third time, his voice was choked with smoke; but for some time his lips continued to move, as in prayer. His ashes were thrown into the Rhine.

Thus died at the age of forty-five one of the purest and most Christ-like men the world has ever known. We have dwelt at some length on his **Why Huss Suffered.** sufferings—though many painful details are omitted—partly as a type of many later martyrdoms, which we shall not describe in detail,—partly because Huss was the greatest martyr condemned by a general council of the Roman Church—not by a special tribunal like the Inquisition. What was then done typified the temper of the Church at that time and long afterwards; and it does not require a moment's thought to judge that that kind of procedure was unworthy of humanity, and deserved to be rendered for ever impossible. That a man who declared his assent to the orthodox doctrines of the Church, and only protested against their excess or abuse—and who was actuated by a burning zeal for the very objects for which the Church existed—should have been handed over to be burnt, can only be explained on the view that he touched the hierarchy in some sensitive places, which roused in them an inveterate opposition. Many others, even among his judges, had denounced abuses in the Church; but Huss, like Wyclif, maintained that the temporal power could rightfully take away Church property from unworthy ecclesiastics—thus striking at the root of the temporal influence of the Church. In the second place he valued his conscience above the decisions of the Council; he regarded conscience as supreme, subject to the plain teaching of Scripture. Thus he asserted clearly the rights of the individual conscience, of private judgment, as against the spiritual authority of the Church. He was, as has been well said, a Protestant without knowing it, a Reformer before the Reformation.[1]

A strange fate befell John Gerson, the famous Chancellor of the University of Paris, one of the ruling spirits of the Council and a strong **John Gerson.** opponent of Huss. In retaliation for his strenuous efforts to get the Council to condemn the murder of the Duke of Orleans by his brother the Duke of Burgundy, he was himself accused of many heresies; and although, owing to his influence in the Council, his defence, utterly denying the crime, was listened to and he was not condemned, he

---

[1] See Neander's "Church History," vol. ix; E. de Bonnechose's "Reformers before the Reformation," and "Letters of John Huss."

dared not return to Paris. He spent the rest of his life teaching children at Lyons and writing hymns and devotional books. The Council whose privileges he had done most to exalt, thus placed him on his defence for heresy.

The news of Huss's imprisonment at Constance caused great excitement in Bohemia: riots and attacks upon the clergy followed. When his martyrdom became known, a multitude flocked to his chapel, Proceedings and honoured him as a martyr and saint. The barons and in Bohemia. nobles met and swore to avenge him. Four hundred and fifty-two of them signed a document exalting the character of Huss, and repelling the charges of heresy levelled at Bohemia in general. The University of Prague, which felt itself condemned along with Huss, now, somewhat too late in the day, did him full justice in a noble utterance. King Wenceslaus wavered, though angry at the execution without his sanction of one of his distinguished subjects. At last he encouraged the courageous John Ziska, who was a devoted admirer of Huss, and whose sister, a nun, had been violated by a monk, to avenge the insults done to Bohemia, if he knew any way. The barons met again, and agreed to allow the word of God to be preached freely in accordance with Scripture, within all their jurisdiction, to punish all priests convicted of teaching error, and to repel, by force, if necessary, all unlawful censures.

We must now return to Constance, where Jerome of Prague was lying in prison and suffered most cruelly. The Council were determined, if possible, to gain a victory over the brilliant disciple who had dis- Jerome of seminated the Wyclifite doctrines through several countries, Prague. and had sown strife in several universities. They were somewhat intimidated by the protest of the Bohemian nobles, and feared new agitations. Consequently they called Jerome again and again before them ; and at last they obtained, from his fears and physical weakness, on September 23rd, 1415, a public recantation, so full as of itself to show that it was extorted, not natural and spontaneous. Yet he was not set at liberty. John Paletz and Michael de Causis, fearful of the results of his liberation, raised suspicions as to his recantation, and his imprisonment continued. After many more private examinations, new charges were drawn up, against which he defended himself for two days, May 23rd and 26th, 1416, with great eloquence and presence of mind. Finally, he recounted in a lofty strain the many instances among the heathen, Jews and Christians, of men having fallen victims to false accusations and priestly hatred, concluding with John

Huss, whom he eulogised with enthusiasm. "Nothing," he said, "weighed on him so grievously as that he had, through fear of death, acquiesced in the sentence on that saintly confessor. All that he had said in September in reference to Wyclif and Huss he withdrew. Assuredly," he declared, "he would not be the last who would fall a victim to the cunning malignity of bad priests."

An eye-witness, Poggio of Florence, wrote in a letter from Constance,

MARTINVS V.
man. creat. die ii.
Sedit an. 13. mens. 3.
Februarij an. 1431.

Otho Columna Ro=
Nouemb. ann. 1417.
dies 12. Obijt die 22.
Vac. Sed. dies 8.

POPE MARTIN V., ELECTED, IN 1417, TO END THE SCHISM OF THE WEST.

that Jerome, notwithstanding his long imprisonment in a dark tower full of offensive effluvia, showed such powers as to be worthy of everlasting remembrance. "He stood up fearlessly," says he, "undaunted, not merely contemning death, but even demanding it, so that one might look upon him as a second Cato." He was condemned on May 30th, and perished at the stake like Huss. Poggio relates that "with cheerful looks he went readily and willingly to his end; he feared neither

His Martyr-dom.

death, nor the fire and its torture. No stoic ever suffered death with so firm a soul."

The news of Jerome's death excited the Bohemians to the last degree. The University of Prague formally adopted communion in both kinds, which he had advocated, and which Huss had approved. A solemn fast-day was ordained in memory of the two martyrs. In February, Civil War in Bohemia.

JOHN ZISKA LEADING THE HUSSITES TO BATTLE.

1418, the new Pope, Martin V., issued bulls and briefs excommunicating all obstinate Hussites, and calling upon clergy and civil authorities to proceed against them. Wenceslaus, unstable as ever, wavered between the Hussites and the Papal party. The Hussites, under Ziska, prepared for armed conflict with their opponents. The Papal legate, who arrived charged with the execution of the Pope's bull, was able to carry the King with him, and to initiate harsh proceedings, which exasperated the followers of Huss. Ziska raised his standard in defence of communion in both kinds, and on a hill named *Tabor*, from the booths erected for shelter, the eucharist was admin-

The Taborites. istered on three hundred altars in the open air, in wooden chalices, on July 22, 1419. Marching on Prague by night, they plundered convents, and killed some magistrates in a fierce fight with the Catholics. Wenceslaus died of fright and rage, and his brother Sigismund succeeded to the Bohemian throne. Again and again Ziska defeated great armies led by the new king; and when he died in 1424, his victorious career was continued by the brothers Procopius. The Taborites rejected purgatory and the mediation of saints, did not believe in penances, images and relics, maintained the rights of the laity to preach, and held that priests in mortal sin could not validly administer the sacrament. Thus they held many doctrines of later protestantism. Many rejected transubstantiation and the real presence.

A more moderate party had, however, defined itself as the Calixtines (from *calix*, the cup) or Utraquists (*sub utraque specie*, in both kinds), and

The Calix- tines. in 1420 had agreed to four demands. I. Free preaching of the word of God throughout Bohemia. II. Communion in both kinds. III. Deprivation of the clergy of their temporal lordship. IV. Prohibition and repression of mortal sins and public scandals.—James of Misa and Baron Czenke were among their leaders. Finally Archbishop Conrad adhered to this programme, and at last, in 1433, a compact was made by the Council of Basle, by which the Calixtines were satisfied, the cup being given to all who desired it, and more or less genuine concessions being granted on the other points. From this time the Calixtines gradually became an insignificant party within the Church in Bohemia. The policy of compact with the Roman Church then, as ever, led to subjugation to that Church. Some Calixtines remained in the next century, and joined the Protestant Reformers.

The Taborites suffered their first disastrous defeat, in which the brothers Procopius perished, in 1434; and before long they had to surrender all their fortresses. From this point we cannot follow the internal struggles of Bohemia, only noting that some of the remaining Taborites, together with Waldensian refugees, formed in the next century the Bohemian brethren, in later times more famous as the Moravians, whose noble missionary work and whose influence on John Wesley have given them world-wide fame.

BASLE, FROM THE RHINE FERRY.

CHAPTER V.

The Waldenses, the "Friends of God," and other Reformers before Luther.

Waldo and his Poor Men of Lyons—The Waldenses Excommunicated—Their Character and Persecutions—Nicholas of Basle and the "Friends of God"—John Tauler—His Teaching—Brethren of the Common Life—Gerard Groot—Florentius Radewin—Thomas à Kempis.

LONG before Luther, there had arisen in France a sect which, if its members had been gifted with more vigorous intellect and with greater perseverance, might have anticipated much of his success. But the mediæval Church was strong in its alliance with princes, in its identification of the maintenance of its privileges with those of civil rulers, in the horror of heresy which it had sedulously cultivated; and the printing-press was not yet at work, the revival of learning had not yet broadened the mind and furnished new material for intellectual development. Nevertheless, the Waldenses deserve honourable mention and respectful recognition in the history of the Reformation.

Moved by we scarcely know what impulse, Waldo, a rich merchant of Lyons, about 1170, sought to gain a fuller knowledge of the Scriptures than

could be derived from hearing the lessons read in church, and became
inspired by the desire to model his life in accordance with that
of Christ and His apostles. Having no knowledge of Latin, he
employed priests to translate and transcribe in Provençal numerous books
of the Bible, and passages from the Fathers and theologians, relating to
Christian doctrine and practice. Following what he believed to be a
Divinely approved example, he sold all his property and distributed it to
the poor, thus preceding St. Francis by many years. He then went through
the streets and villages, preaching the gospel and the special teachings he
had derived therefrom, and inciting others to do the same. Thus he set
on foot, without any ordination, the preaching mission of the
Poor Men of Lyons, not considering questions of Church order
in his zeal for the spread of what he believed to be the truth. The
bishops could not approve of this unauthorised activity, and the Archbishop of Lyons forbade him and his followers to intrude themselves into
the office of preaching, and on their disobedience excommunicated them.
Waldo took his stand on Christ's command to His apostles to preach the
gospel to every creature, and thus he raised the whole question of the commission to preach, and the personal freedom or subjection of
Christians to the papacy and bishops. He appealed to Pope
Alexander III. at the third Lateran Council in 1179, presenting
to him a copy of his Provençal Scriptures, and professing adhesion to the
teachings of Ambrose, Augustine, Gregory and Jerome. But the petition
was rejected as that of ignorant and illiterate men; and in 1184 Lucius
III. anathematized the new brotherhood as "those who mendaciously call
themselves by the false name of the *Humiliati*, or Poor Men of Lyons."

Thrown on their own independent efforts, forced to prove their belief
by their works, or succumb, the Poor Men of Lyons travelled far and wide
through Southern France, Northern Italy and Spain, obtaining protection
from nobles and princes in some parts, and establishing numerous schools
in Lombardy and Provence. Even their enemies were constrained to bear
witness to their knowledge and skill in the use of the vernacular Scriptures. After the labours of the day, working men and women assembled
regularly, to hear the word of God read and expounded. Although the
meetings were secret, for fear of the authorities, it is not alleged that any
new or unorthodox doctrine was taught; so far the Waldenses did not an-
ticipate the Reformers; but in going direct to Scriptural teachings, they
certainly were ahead of most of the priests and laity.

Waldo.

His Poor Men of Lyons.

The Waldenses Excommuni-cated.

A little later they are described by one of their enemies as sedate and modest in manners and dress, working diligently in ordinary labour, content with a little, chaste and temperate, moderate in speech, **Their Character.** abstaining from oaths, lies, scurrility, and slander. This excellent character could not, however, protect them from persecution; for their services were in disregard of the authority of the Church. Many were punished in the same persecution as the Albigenses, and they were again formally condemned by the Lateran Council of 1215. The severity of the search made for them caused them to retire more and **Persecutions.** more into secluded localities, especially the upper valleys of the Alps, in Piedmont, which became afterwards celebrated as the valleys of the Vaudois. They were driven by their isolation into complete reliance on private ministrations, and elected their own ministers, who baptized and administered the communion. They relied comparatively little on ceremonial; their ministers were their guides and advisers, not priests. Thus slightly organised, this mountain Church preserved its existence by holding fast its traditional teaching; and in 1487 the Waldenses were important enough to induce Pope Innocent VIII. to issue a bull for their extermination, which was partly carried out by Albert, Archdeacon of Cremona, until Charles II., Duke of Piedmont, interfered to protect them. They had suffered greatly, but continued in existence till the next century, and were glad to learn about the Lutheran movement and to join the Reform movement in the sixteenth century, as we shall detail later. They had had no great leader; they could hardly have had a learned one in the middle ages, when all learning was in the priesthood of the Church; and in several respects they had come into existence before their time. Persecution sufficed, not to crush them, but to prevent their exercising a powerful and growing influence.

Meanwhile, within the Church in France and Germany many were gaining, from the study of the Scriptures and personal meditation, a persuasion that a Divine light could be received directly by the individual soul; that such an intercommunion could take place between the soul and its Maker as to transcend the teaching of the Church, which evidently was full of corruption and needed purification. The innovators had no idea of rebelling against the doctrines of the Church; but they learnt to derive their souls' life direct from the source of all life, without intermediary. The practical side of this mysticism was remarkably displayed by Nicholas of Basle, a youth of good family, who, about 1330, went through

a religious crisis and dedicated his life to God.   For five years he read the
lives of the saints and imitated their austerities; then he was
taught in a vision to give himself up to God, and received
supernatural illumination.   He next set about studying the
Scriptures, and the result was that he became the leader of the "Friends
of God," a brotherhood largely diffused in Southern Germany, and also in
the Netherlands and in Switzerland.   While receiving the doctrines of
the Church, even concerning the Virgin and Purgatory, the "Friends of

Nicholas of
Basle and the
Friends of God.

Benedictine,   Cistercian,   Carthusian,   Dominican,   Franciscan,   Augustine,   Capuchin.
THE CHURCH OF THE MIDDLE AGES; MONASTIC ORDERS.

God" relied largely on visions and revelations.   Among them were some
Dominicans and Franciscans, nuns, and many laymen of note; but they
never formed a sect or took united action.   In fact, their principles could
not easily lead to such action.   Entire submission to the Divine Will, as
they interpreted it, made them care little for temporal matters; they longed
only for the attainment of union with God by themselves and by others.

Nicholas appears, however, to have had some ideas of Church reform,
and in 1377 he, with one companion, went to Rome to urge
Gregory XI., just returned from Avignon, to heal the Church's
maladies.   They failed to stir the Pope sufficiently for their purpose,

Pope Gregory
XI.

whereupon Nicholas is said to have foretold his death within a year. During the next year Nicholas and his followers earnestly prayed for the dispelling of the clouds which hung over the Church. His party rejected both the rival Popes set up after Gregory. After many visions and prophecies had been vouchsafed to the "Friends of God," Nicholas and his principal adherents went out as preachers of repentance, and soon encountered persecution and death. In 1393, Martin of Mainz was burned in Cologne; others met the same fate at Heidelberg, while Nicholas and two of his companions perished at Vienne in Dauphiny. The chief charge against Nicholas was that "he audaciously affirmed that he was in Christ and Christ in him."

Such was the man who largely influenced John Tauler, who in his turn had considerable influence on Martin Luther. Tauler, born at Strasburg in 1290, became a Dominican at eighteen, and while study- **John Tauler.** ing at Paris, took a hearty dislike to the scholastic teachers, declaring that they cared nothing for the One Book of Life. After studying the writings of the priors of St. Victor and St. Augustine, on his return to Strasburg he became attracted by the teachings of the "Friends of God," and was soon noted, in all the cities of the Rhine, for his preaching. In his fiftieth year he received a visit from Nicholas of Basle, which produced such a new development of his spiritual life that he deemed it his conversion, although he was already recognised as a leader by many of the "Friends of God." Nicholas was able to show that Tauler had still lurking in him depths of self-love and self-seeking he had not suspected, and was still in darkness on many essential points. He counselled him to retire from preaching and from public work for a time, that he might meditate on Christ's sufferings and contemplate his own life in the mirror of the Saviour's. We cannot but regard Tauler's consent to this retirement as a strong testimony to the spiritual insight possessed by Nicholas, and the force with which he was able to impress his conviction on so learned and experienced a Dominican. After two years spent as Nicholas had prescribed, and disregarding the mockery of his former friends, Tauler resumed his preaching, and speedily proved that he possessed new powers of searching into hearts and applying religion to the problems of practical life. He became especially remarkable for his deep realization of Christ's life and of His infinite sorrow over the sins of mankind; and he wrote a book in German on "The Imitation of Christ's Life of Poverty." He devoted himself largely to the reformation of the lives of clergy and monks.

F

STRASBURG CATHEDRAL.

Finding that the people, in consequence of the Long Interdict, were left to die in large numbers without priestly ministration, during the Black Death of 1348-9, Tauler devoted himself to administering the sacraments and visiting the sick and dying,—and two other monks, Thomas, prior of the Augustinians in Strasburg, and Ludolph, prior of a Carthusian convent, did likewise. These three issued an address to the clergy, pointing out the injustice of allowing the common people to die without the consolations of religion, merely because a prince or a guilty lord had incurred the displeasure of the Pope, and putting forward the doctrine that "he who confesses the true faith of Christ, and sins only against the person of the Pope, is no heretic." Whether or not many priests were influenced by this address to perform their offices we do not know; but, at any rate, many of the people were enabled to die in peace, through the labours of Tauler and his friends. Naturally they fell under the displeasure of the Bishop of Strasburg, Berthold, who called them to account, burnt their books, and drove them into the retirement of Ludolph's convent. The new Emperor, Charles IV., the Pope's nominee, visited Strasburg at this time, and sent for the three suspected monks, who did not shrink from declaring their mind to him, so forcibly that he expressed himself convinced; but the bishop persisting in his opposition and condemnation, Tauler appears to have judged it prudent to withdraw from the city. He is next met with exercising his ministry at Cologne, where he preached in the church of St. Gertrude's convent of Dominican nuns, and incisively attacked the disorders and worldliness he found prevailing; he advocated spiritual piety as the only true service of God. He returned to Strasburg in 1361, where he died on the 16th of June in the same year, aged seventy years.[1]

In his noble assertion: "God gave all things that they might be a way to Himself, and He only should be the end," Tauler enunciated a doctrine which will never grow old, and might serve for the text of *Tauler's Teaching.* countless sermons without losing its freshness. It cuts through many of the evil excrescences and harmful claims of Pope and priests, and supplies the defence of that inner spiritual religion which Tauler advocated. Station and cloth give no holiness; self-mortification and penance sanctify not; prayers and vows in themselves profit not. All helps that become hindrances fall away from the Christian—images, saints, exercises, and even prayer—as he advances to perfection; but he is by no means to cast them aside voluntarily. Tauler strives to show, what many in our day have not understood, who have persevered in a formalism which their spiritual life has outgrown—that spiritual exercises of all kinds ought to be suited to the needs and state of development of the soul at the time, not modelled on a cast-iron system. From the level of spiritual life, in which formal prayer and petition for benefits was needed, he wished the soul to advance to that stage of communion and union with the Divine, which so many since his time have realized; wherein not even petitions for their own souls' good seemed necessary, and all they had to ask of God related to the welfare of others. But Tauler also guarded his disciples

---

[1] For an account of Tauler, Nicholas, and others of the "Friends of God," see the "Life and Sermons of John Tauler," translated by Miss Susanna Winkworth. London: Smith Elder & Co., 1857; also Neander's "Church History," Vol. ix.

from excess of emotional religion. Sweet emotions, he said, have often turned out to be a weak foundation. Men cannot always be favoured by pleasurable feelings, which enervate and lull into false security; nor ought our thoughts to be turned too much inward on ourselves; we must hasten to seek God by Himself. Notwithstanding terrible conflicts and strange events in the order of God's providence, we are to trust in God, who knows well what He means by it all. Our unfailing refuge, Tauler declares, is the cross and the passion of our Lord Jesus Christ; there the Christian obtains the victory in all his conflicts.

It is astonishing to see what a modern spirit breathes through many of the sermons of Tauler; and in truth the simplicity of great men is ever fresh. If a man has got near to the eternal verity, he can exhort and teach long-distant centuries. Well might Luther say, "I have found in them (Tauler's German discourses) more of profound and clear theology than any one has discovered in all the school-doctors together." His teaching and that of his followers certainly helped to prepare the ground for Luther, and furnished part of the great reformer's spiritual armour.

Turning now to a different side of reforming work, we find in the "Brethren of the Common Life," founded in the Netherlands in the second

Brethren of the Common Life. half of the fourteenth century by Gerard Groot, a serious attempt to carry into practice that ideal of Christian life which monasticism had failed to maintain. Groot, a native of Deventer, a theological student of Paris, a lecturer at Cologne, came home to devote

Gerard Groot. himself to a higher ideal of ministry than he found exemplified around him. Obtaining permission to preach, he filled the churches twice a day, often for three hours at a time. But the priests were jealous of him, and he could obtain no fixed appointment. Yet the earnest worker is not easily foiled; and Groot gathered round him at Deventer a band of young clergymen who engaged in religious exercises and studies, mingled with mechanical occupations, especially the copying of books, by the sale of which they earned a great part of their living. Exacting no vows, prescribing no extraordinary discipline, he established a brotherhood for the willing service of God, a brotherhood which sought only to promote His glory in the most profitable way. Especially useful and notable were the schools they founded.

Florentius Radewin. On the death of Gerard Groot in 1384, his mantle fell on his chief follower, Florentius Radewin, who died in 1400. The brotherhood spread rapidly over the Netherlands and Northern Germany, and fell under the same suspicions and obloquy as the Lollards. They were especially opposed by the mendicant orders. They established some monasteries and nunneries, and gained the approval of Popes Martin V. and Eugenius IV. Many were alienated from them by the mendicant friars, but a large number remained to add their forces to the Reformation.

While their aim was chiefly one of practical beneficence, the Brethren of the Common Life laid great stress on the spiritual cultivation of the soul; and from their convent at Zwolle proceeded, about the middle of the fifteenth century, the famous *De Imitatione Christi* of Thomas à Kempis (1380–1471). Educated at Deventer under Radewin, *Thomas à Kempis.* and having long toiled as a copyist of others' works, he produced in mature life that masterpiece of inward contemplative Christianity, full of passionate devotion to Christ, heartfelt submission to His teaching, and belief in His direct influence on the individual soul. So far as inward thought can go in one direction, making man nothing and God everything, this book goes; but yet it has reference only to one side of spiritual life, and that not the practical life of man as a member of a society, united to his fellow-members by many bonds, and ready to benefit them if he is to maintain and develope himself.

All these in their several places were as so many movements foreshowing the future upheaval. Lives of beneficence among the poor, inward spiritual light, superiority of the rights of the believer to the dictation of popes and priests—all these were taught long before Luther. The great system of the Papal Church was seen by many to be rotten at the core, to involve claims almost destructive of true religion if accepted in their full extent. In our next chapter we shall see what befel a noble man who, in the midst of worldliness, selfishness and vice, strove to purify the Church in Italy.

THE CITY OF FLORENCE, THE SCENE OF SAVONAROLA'S ACTIVITY, SUFFERINGS AND
MARTYRDOM.

CHAPTER VI.

Savonarola, the Martyr of Florence.

Arnold of Brescia—Savonarola—Early Life—Settles at Florence—Sees Visions—His Writ-
ings—Preaches in the Duomo—His Predictions—Death of Lorenzo de' Medici—Vision
of the Sword—Sermons on Noah's Ark—Fall of the Medici—Savonarola's Supremacy
His Foreboding of Martyrdom—Reform of Morals—Bonfire of Vanities—Attacks of
Enemies—Excommunicated by the Pope—Forbidden to Preach—The Ordeal by Fire—
Savonarola Tortured—Condemned—Hung and Burnt.

HITHERTO we have been looking at leaders and movements in the
regions north of the Alps. But there were not wanting preachers
of reform in Italy itself, although the difficulties of their career were
greatly intensified by their nearness to the centre of Papal power. Unfortunately southern enthusiasm was conquered by southern lethargy;
classicism and ornament crushed or concealed reality; corruption generated

70

corruption; and only tardily in our own day is freedom of thought, with rejection of clerical rule, giving new life to the Italian character.

Already in the twelfth century one great reforming name is found in Italy, and it is connected with that of Abelard, mentioned in the first chapter. Arnold, born at Brescia in Lombardy, about the Arnold of
Brescia. beginning of the twelfth century, imbibed from study under Abelard one aspect of his master's teaching, and, as a monk, preached in Italy against the ambition and luxury of the cardinals, abbots, and bishops, maintaining that the clergy ought to be subject to the civil power, and should be stripped of their wealth. His vehement oratory caused the Brescians to expel their bishop, and brought down upon himself a condemnation by the second Lateran Council, in 1139, under Innocent II. Banished from Italy, and driven from France by the hostility of Bernard of Clairvaux, he resumed his preaching at Zurich and Constance. He returned to Italy in 1143, on the death of Innocent, and put himself at the head of an insurrection in Rome against the new Pope. For many years he maintained his influence in Rome against a succession of popes, although he was unable to restrain the excesses of the populace; till at last Adrian IV., in 1155, laid the Papal city under an interdict. This step made the Romans quail, and they exiled Arnold. The emperor, Frederick I., Barbarossa, coming to Rome to be crowned, the Pope induced him to have Arnold arrested. The turbulent monk was strangled and burnt, and his ashes were thrown into the Tiber in 1155. He was no heretic, but his denunciations of clerical abuses and evil life entitle him to a place in our record; though the excesses with which he was connected deprived his movement of much of its weight.

The victorious Papacy reached its culmination in the person of Innocent III., with the promulgation of the doctrines of transubstantiation and of auricular confession, insisting on the power of the priesthood to work a miracle in the Eucharist, and to open or close the door of forgiveness to sinners. These very extravagances had within them the seed of future disaster. The open adoption of the principle that error in the faith was worse than crime, and that the heretic deserved burning, was certain sooner or later to lead to reaction, though it remained active for centuries. The mendicant orders which Innocent sanctioned proved, as we have seen, among the most potent instruments in turning men's affections and intelligence away from the Church. For centuries popes spent their strength in contests with emperors and kings as to temporal power, which could not fail to bring somewhat into discredit their spiritual claims. In Italy no great man was found to resist the claim of the Papacy to universal supremacy; but the rival Popes themselves aroused doubts among the laity on

this point, by each denying the supremacy of the other. The Council of Basle decreed reforms in the Papal administration and in the conduct of the clergy; Pope Eugenius assembled a council at Ferrara which excommunicated the council at Basle. The Renaissance of Art and Letters came, with its enlightenment and refinement, and threatened to lead to a total enervation of morals; and in the midst of this movement a bold attempt to stem the torrent of worldliness was made by Savonarola.

INNOCENT III., THE MOST POWERFUL OF THE POPES (1198–1216).

Savonarola.
Girolamo Savonarola, born at Ferrara on September 21, 1452, was educated to follow his grandfather's profession, that of medicine; but philosophy and the writings of Aquinas fascinated him, and he early became an ascetic devotee;—this tendency was exaggerated by a love-disappointment. In 1474 a sermon of an Augustinian friar induced him to adopt a monastic life, and he entered the Dominican monastery at Bologna in 1475, in despair, as he said, "at seeing vice exalted and virtue degraded throughout Italy." He spent his time in the monastery in the humblest drudgery and the most severe fasting and penance; but he meditated great projects of reforming the Church and the world. After some preliminary trials of his strength as a preacher, he was in 1481 sent to Florence, where he entered the monastery of St. Mark, of which, ten years later, he became prior.

At that time Lorenzo de' Medici was at the zenith of his splendid

career, and Savonarola found much to delight him in Florence. The learning and culture of the friars of St. Mark, the beautiful paintings **Settles in**
with which Fra Angelico had adorned the monastery, filled him **Florence.**
with hope and cheerfulness. He soon found, however, that the gaiety, the
refinement, and luxury of Florence covered a sink of moral corruption.
Thrown inward upon himself, he began to see visions, and to
prophecy Divine vengeance against the city. About this time **Sees Visions.**
he made the acquaintance of Pico, Count of Mirandola, a prodigy of the
erudition of the time, at a chapter of Dominicans, at which the young friar
astonished all hearers, by his fiery denunciations of the corruptions of the
Church and clergy. He began now to preach as he had opportunity, at

Brescia and else-
where in Lombardy,
declaring that the
Church was to be
scourged and then
regenerated, and
that these things
would shortly come
to pass. At length
his fame spread
throughout Italy.
In the summer of
1489 he was recalled
to Florence through
the influence of Pico
of Mirandola with
the Duke Lorenzo,
and began to ex-
pound the Revela-
tion to large congre-
gations in the con-
vent garden. On
August 1, 1489, in

SAVONAROLA, THE MARTYR OF FLORENCE, 1492-1498.

the church of St. Mark, he fairly carried away his auditors with enthusiasm; he seemed to speak with supernatural power.

He now published some of his writings, in which he showed not only
knowledge of philosophy and of the Fathers, but also originality of tre-

ment. He insisted on reasoning from the known to the unknown, and on

His Writings. human free-will. He claimed that men should think for themselves, and not refuse, as so many did in his time, to speak save as the ancients spoke, and to say anything that had not been said before. In his principal work, "The Triumph of the Cross," expounding Christian doctrines according to natural reason, he writes in the preface : "Whereas in this book we shall only discuss by the light of reason, we will refer to no authorities, but proceed as though no reliance could be placed on any man in the world, however wise, but only on natural reason." Thus we see that Savonarola really represented a revolt for liberty of private judgment, and is properly regarded as a precursor of the Reformation.

The crowds who came to hear him grew so great that Savonarola was called to preach in the Duomo, the Cathedral of Florence, in Lent, 1491 ;

Preaches in the Duomo. and his vivid and startling imagery and announcements of coming chastisement had more attraction than ever. He powerfully denounced the corruption of manners of the clergy, the sale of clerical offices and ministrations, the oppression of the poor. In a sermon preached at the palace before Lorenzo himself, he plainly warned him how the city depended on the conduct of its head; how evil was done by leaving things to bad ministers; and told him that "tyrants were incorrigible because they were proud, because they loved flattery, because they would not restore ill-gotten gains." In July, Savonarola became prior of St. Mark's, and refused to pay homage to Lorenzo, whom he regarded as the foe of freedom and the great hindrance to Christian life among the people. When the duke tried to appease him by rich gifts to the convent, Savonarola declared that a faithful dog did not leave off barking because a bone was thrown to him. In answer to further remonstrances he said, "Bid Lorenzo do penance for his sins, for the Lord is no respecter of persons. . . . Though I am a stranger, and he the first in the city, I

His Predictions. shall stay, while he will depart ; " and immediately afterwards, in the Sacristy of St. Mark, he predicted before many witnesses that great changes were impending over Italy, and that Lorenzo, the Pope, and the King of Naples were all near to death. Lorenzo, in retaliation, instigated Fra Marians, the most skilful and popular preacher before Savonarola's rise, to attack him in sermons; but the prior of St. Mark's delivered such an overwhelming reply, and proceeded to attack prevalent vices so powerfully, that Fra Marians gave up the contest. And although Savonarola's sermons would sound crude and ill-digested to modern ears, they were so far superior to the dry scholastic discourses and the vulgar claptrap, which were the two ruling types, that we cannot wonder at their popularity. They were replete with a burning zeal for truth and purity, hatred of vice and indolence, and a deep love for the souls of the people, and often acted magically upon their feelings. The populace knew when they were stirred, and they felt that the stirring was wholesome, and intended for their souls' eternal welfare.

In April, 1492, Lorenzo lay dying, and could not rest without seeing the stern friar, of whom he said : **Death of Lorenzo de' Medici.** "I know no honest friar but this one." When he came, Lorenzo confessed his remorse for three great crimes, and was told that he must not only have a great and living faith in God's mercy, but must restore all his ill-gotten wealth, and the liberties of the people of Florence. At the last

SAVONAROLA'S CELL, IN THE CONVENT OF ST. MARK.

demand, Lorenzo turned his back angrily, without a word, and the friar left him unabsolved. After the duke's death, his son Piero's violent and incompetent rule disgusted the Florentines, and gave increasing influence to Savonarola, whose second prediction was fulfilled in July, by the death of Innocent VIII.

Still further excited by the corrupt election of Alexander VI., the in-

famous Borgia, to the Papacy, Savonarola again saw visions which he be-
Vision of the Sword. lieved to be revelations from heaven. In the most striking of
these he beheld a hand appear in the midst of the heavens,
bearing a sword, with these words inscribed upon it: "Gladius Domini
super terram cito et velociter" (The sword of the Lord above the earth soon
and swiftly). He heard voices proclaiming mercy and punishment; the
sword was turned towards the earth, swords, arrows, and flames rained

STATUE OF LORENZO DE MEDICI,
BY MICHAEL ANGELO.

down, and the world was given
up to war, famine, and pestilence.
After an enforced absence in Bologna, brought about by Piero de
Medici, Savonarola succeeded in
securing the Pope's consent to
Independence of St. Mark. the independence of
St. Mark's monastery,
of the Lombard branch of the
order, and was thenceforth free
to carry out his reforms. He restored the old rule of poverty,
sold the property of the convent,
cut off all superfluous expenditure, and set his friars to work
for their living, those who were
competent transcribing and illu-
minating books, and teaching
painting, sculpture, and architecture. Preaching tours were
organized, the spiritual work of
the friars was made thorough
and pervasive, and the study of
the Scriptures in the original
tongues, and of theology and

philosophy, was vigorously set on foot. The prior himself took the hardest
tasks, living the most self-denying life. The growing repute of the monastery brought new adherents continually, from among the nobles as well
as the lower classes; and converts throughout Tuscany sought union with
the Florentine congregations.

In sermon after sermon Savonarola expounded the entire scheme of primitive orthodox religion as he understood it, combining faith, works, and love in a well-balanced whole. He contrasted with this pure religion the evils introduced by the bishops and priests, the pomp, show and pride of public services, and private behaviour. " In the primitive Church," he declared, " the chalices were of wood, the prelates of gold; in these days the Church had chalices of gold and prelates of wood." In 1494 he completed a famous series of sermons on Noah's Ark; these have only come down to us very imperfectly. Describing vividly the building of the ark, and the gathering together of the righteous to take refuge in it, he predicted the coming of a new Cyrus, who would march triumphantly through Italy. When he came to depict the Deluge, his words, " Behold I will bring the waters upon the earth," resounded like a thunder-clap; and at the same time news came that the army of Charles VIII. of France was passing into Italy. We must not here detail how Piero de' Medici was driven out of Florence, without bloodshed, by the restrain-ing influence of Savonarola; how the extortionate demands of Charles VIII. were reduced; how Florence, left free, set up a free govern-ment by its citizens; how skilfully the prior of St. Mark's ruled the city from his pulpit for some years, reducing taxes, administering strict justice, relieving the starving, and finding work for the unemployed. Indeed, for a while Florence represented Savonarola's ser-mons in action, and it appeared as if that capital was in a fair way to become a truly Christian and model city.

> *Sermons on Noah's Ark.*

> *Fall of the Medici.*

> *Savonarola's Supremacy.*

But this success could not give Savonarola permanent joy. Sad fore-bodings weighed him down. He foresaw and foretold his own martyrdom. An inward fire consumed him. Exalted into ecstasy, he saw the future unrolled before him in visions. Through long night watches, or in the day-time when in the pulpit, his condition was often one of excitement. When his visions came during his sermons, his fervour moved the people in the highest degree. " Men and women of every age and condition, workmen, poets, and philosophers, would burst into passion-ate tears, while the Church re-echoed with their sobs." His visions, the product of an ascetic life, constant dwelling on the Biblical visions, and natural temperament, were sufficiently marked by political acumen to give them a most powerful influence, especially after some of his predictions had been fulfilled. Wrought up to an almost unendurable pitch of emotion, the Florentines could find no relief but in abjuring all vanities and luxuries, living lives of abstinence and prayer, dressing with the utmost simplicity,

> *His Foreboding of Martyrdom.*

singing hymns, and crowding to adopt the monastic life. Children were
banded into a sort of holy militia, charged with an important

Reform of Morals. work in calling people to purity of life. In 1496, Savonarola
by their aid arranged a remarkable procession at the carnival, when the
citizens gave rich gifts to the poor, and monks, crowned with flowers, sang
and danced wildly to the glory of God. In 1497, at the same

Bonfire of Vanities. festival, a great heap of "vanities" was publicly burnt, in
which much of the apparatus of luxury perished. But the pace was too
rapid to last; the excitement was too great to be permanently beneficial;
the bow was drawn too tightly, and reaction set in.

The bitter hostility which the Pope had conceived for Savonarola,
fanned by the suggestions and accusations of his old rival, Fra Marians

Attacks of Enemies. was most powerful in promoting his downfall. At first an
attempt was made to gain him over by a favourite Borgian
method—bribery. After fruitless attempts to get him to quit Florence,
a cardinal's hat was offered to the prior of St. Mark, on condition that he
should change the tone of his sermons. His reply was given publicly, in a
remarkable sermon in the Duomo, on February 17, 1496. He publicly
declared his orthodoxy, but asserted that whenever it was clearly seen that
the commands of superiors were contrary to God's commandments, no one
was bound to obey them. He himself would obey no command to leave
Florence to the detriment of his people. It was not on this occasion
apparently, but on the 20th of August in the same year, that he made the
well-known declaration: "I desire neither hats nor mitres, be they great
or small; I desire nought save that which Thou hast given to thy saints;
it is death, a crimson hat, a hat of blood that I desire!" In a second
sermon he said, "Thou, Rome, art stricken with a mortal disease. Thou
hast lost thy health, and hast forsaken the Lord; thou art sick with sins
and tribulations. If thou wouldst be healed, forsake feasting; forsake
thy pride, thy ambition, thy lusts, and thy greed. . . . Thus saith the
Lord: 'Inasmuch as Italy is full of sanguinary deeds, full of iniquities,
harlots and miserable panders, I will overwhelm her with the scum of the
earth; I will abase her princes, and trample the pride of Rome. These in-
vaders shall capture her sanctuaries and defile her churches." By these
and other Lenten sermons his fame and influence were, if possible, extended
further. His life was daily plotted against by his enemies and guarded by
his friends. Abusive pamphlets against him abounded. But no man
worthy of carrying on his work appeared; he towers above his surroundings

as the one great man. The Florentines, from unbelief and luxury, had rushed into fanaticism and puritanism; but their character was not deep, their reformation was not permanent. They were more interested in securing their political freedom, than in a radical reconstruction of their character and lives.

An attempt to gain control over Savonarola by bringing his convent under a new Tuscan-Roman congregation, governed from Rome, failed; and at the beginning of 1497 the prior was still in high esteem in Florence. But in May his enemies came into office, after a new election, and on Ascension Day his pulpit in the Duomo was insulted, and sharp nails were fixed in the board on which he was accustomed to strike his hand.

Soon afterwards the Pope excommunicated him, but he resisted the sentence as invalid, the Pope, a notorious criminal, having been elected by simony. Later in the year a conspiracy to restore Piero de' Medici was discovered, and five of the conspirators, including **Excommunicated by the Pope.** the aged Bernardo del Nero, were put to death. Savonarola took part against them; but he is reproached for not having interfered to save them. He was further interdicted from preaching in his own convent, and again summoned to Rome, but refused to go. On Christmas Day he publicly celebrated mass, in defiance of the Papal sentence.

At the beginning of 1498 Savonarola's friends were once more in office; he again preached to enormous congregations; and a second sacrifice of "vanities" took place. When another turn of the political wheel brought his enemies to the helm, he returned to St. Mark's, and continued to preach there. He appealed by letter to all the rulers of Europe to assemble a council to condemn the Pope. The latter succeeded in frightening the Florentines by threatening the city with an interdict; and Savonarola was **Forbidden to Preach.** silenced. His enemies were in full possession of power, when a Franciscan friar challenged Savonarola to prove the truth of his doctrines by the ordeal of fire. He had always treated such summonses with contempt; but one of his prominent disciples, Fra Domenico, now took up the challenge, and on the 7th of April, 1498, a vast assembly met to witness the spectacle. The Franciscans hesitated, suggested **The Ordeal by Fire.** obstacles, and at last withdrew; while Savonarola with Fra Domenico remained. The people, defrauded of their diversion, became enraged, and abused the prior of St. Mark's. Next day, after the populace had sacked the convent, Savonarola surrendered and was imprisoned. The Pope ordered the Florentines to send him to Rome; nevertheless, he

was tried in Florence, and tortured day after day.   Under this cruel
Savonarola   treatment he was made to say anything they liked, but always
Tortured and withdrew all "confessions" so soon as he was released from the
Condemned.
rack.   He was forced to sign a falsified version of his confes-
sions; but even then it was quite insufficient to condemn him.   On May

MARTYRDOM OF SAVONAROLA AT FLORENCE, MAY 23RD, 1498.

22nd, he was sentenced to death, with Fra Domenico and Fra Silvestro, by
one of the most unjust votes ever given, under cover of a condemnation
by Papal commissioners.   The night before his death he predicted that
great disasters would befal Florence during the rule of a Pope named
Clement; a prophecy amply fulfilled in 1529.   When he was stripped of
his priestly robes, the Dominican Bishop of Vasona said, "I separate thee

from the Church militant and the Church triumphant." Savonarola replied firmly: "Not from the Church triumphant; that is beyond thy power." The victims were first hung on a cross, and then burnt, their remains being afterwards thrown into the Arno. Savonarola's followers were crushed; but many of them, in their hiding-places, recorded their experiences and wrote biographies of their master.[1]

Hung and Burnt.

A man of repellent and coarse features, and dark complexion, Savonarola was able to enchant beholders by the benevolence and sweetness of his expression. Nervous to a degree, plain of speech, simple in manners, his language rose at times to a vehemence and an eloquence which carried conviction and roused enthusiasm. His truthfulness, integrity, and political insight were such as to make him a truly original character. Without being a reformer of the positive doctrines of the Church, he sought to be a true reformer of her corruptions. His final failure was due to the great number of evil influences by which he was surrounded and attacked; and, secondarily, to the too great stringency of his demands. His fall showed once more the hopelessness of attempting in the fifteenth century to reform the Roman Church and the Papacy from within.

[1] See "Life and Times of Savonarola," by Professor Villari. English Translation, New Edition, 1889.

INTERIOR OF THE CHURCH, SINZIG.

THE AUGUSTINE MONASTERY, WITTENBERG.

CHAPTER VII.

Martin Luther.

HIS HISTORY UP TO THE DIET OF WORMS.

The Printing Press—Luther's Early Life—Luther at Erfurt—Becomes a Monk—His Spiritual Struggles—Staupitz—Repentance and Faith—Lectureship at Wittenberg—Visits Rome—Takes the Doctor's Degree—His Theses on Free-will and Grace—Tetzel Sells Indulgences—Luther's Theses against them—Tetzel's Counter attack—Luther's Paradoxes—His "Solutions"—Philip Melanchthon—Luther and Cajetan at Augsburg—Rowe and Luther—Luther's Disputation with Dr. Eck—His "Address to the German Nobility"—Treatise on the Babylonian Captivity of the Church—Papal Bull against him—Luther Burns it—The Diet of Worms—Luther Outlawed.

WE have now reviewed the main reforming movements which preceded and preluded the rise of Protestantism. So far they had sought to bring about reforms by acting upon the minds of clergy and people from within the Church; and this method was continued until Luther found that it was useless to hope for success against an interested hierarchy. He was favoured by political circumstances, by the gradual diffusion of the teachings of Wyclif and Huss, and by the growth of intelligence during the revival of learning. But the most potent ally of the new movement which was to shake the Church of Rome and the religious consciousness

URSULA COTTA MEETING LUTHER WHEN SINGING IN THE STREETS.

of mankind to their foundations was the printing press. It is impossible to conceive how the success and permanence of the Reformation could have been achieved without that powerful instrumen- The Printing Press. tality. Yet even that might have been effected—when we remember that Christianity itself was established with no such aid.

ROOM AT EISLEBEN IN WHICH LUTHER WAS BORN.

Martin Luther, in several respects the greatest man in the Reformation history, was Luther's Early Life. born on November 10, 1483, at Eisleben, in the district of Mansfeld, Thuringia, Saxony. His parents were John Luther, a well-to-do peasant and miner, and his wife Margaret. When Martin was six months old, his father removed to Mansfeld, where he set up two smelting furnaces, and became one of the town council. The father was a sturdy man, with some traits foreshadowing his son's character, and brought him up with stern discipline and gloomy morality. Luther himself wrote in later life: "My parents were very hard on me, so that I became broken-spirited, and it was from this cause that I subsequently betook myself to a convent." Young Martin distinguished himself at the Latin school of Mansfeld, and was thence sent to a Franciscan school at Magdeburg, and finally to Eisenach, in 1497. His father destined him to be a lawyer, but had little money to aid the project; Martin had to undergo privations as a scholar, till he attracted the attention of Ursula, wife of Conrad Cotta, burgomaster of Eisenach, who took him into her house, and greatly influenced and refined his

LUTHER'S HOUSE AT EISLEBEN.

character. He became a proficient in music, and especially in flute playing. His attachment to the Church, great from childhood, grew stronger.

In 1501 Luther went to Erfurt University, aided now by his father. Having mastered the scholastic philosophy, he received his bachelor's degree at the end of 1502, and then began to teach, and in time turned to the study of Aristotle, and of the New Testament in the original Greek. He mixed with scholars of the Renaissance without becoming paganized or absorbed into classicism. One of his friends was George Burckhard, or Spalatin, who afterwards became the Elector Frederick's chaplain. A noteworthy incident of this period is his coming across an entire Bible in the university library, which greatly interested him, but did not as yet touch him vitally. Early in 1505 he took the Master's Degree, standing second in the list.

Luther at Erfurt.

LUTHER'S STUDY.

About this time several events combined to make a striking change in his life. Deeply affected by the sudden death of a friend, who was killed by lightning at his side during a storm, he exclaimed: "Help, sweet Saint Anne, and I will become a monk." After a gay musical and social evening with friends, he entered an Augustine convent at Erfurt, in July, 1505, greatly to his father's disappointment, taking with him only two books, his Plautus and his Virgil. A severe novitiate awaited him; he literally served his brethren, and begged for them, at the same time outdoing them in austerities and devotional exercises. His request for a Bible was at first

Becomes a Monk.

AUGUSTINE CONVENT AT ERFURT.

granted, but the Bible was afterwards taken away. It was the chosen book of the heretics, he was told; he had far better read the scholastic theology. But he found another Bible, and diligently read it, meanwhile commending himself to one-and-twenty saints. Once he discovered a volume of Huss's sermons—that notable heretic; but he did not read long, fearing contamination.

MARTIN LUTHER, THE APOSTLE OF THE 16TH CENTURY REFORMATION.

On May 2, 1507, Martin Luther was ordained a priest, his father being present, and making him a gift of money, but afterwards upbraiding him with having failed to honour his parents, when he became a monk without consulting them.

Luther now began more than ever to fret about his soul's salvation, which he sought by diligence in good works, while his inner self was darkened by despair.   Staupitz, vicar of the Augustines in Thuringia,

His Spiritual Struggles. a man of learning, saintly, and of some reforming power, visited the monastery during this period of Luther's life, and soon discerned that an inward fire was consuming the thin, worn, cast-

Staupitz. down, melancholy friar.   After a short conversation, their hearts were opened to one another.   Staupitz heard from Luther of his struggles and despair, comforted him by describing his own former conflicts, and recommended him to trust entirely in the merits of Christ, the righteousness of His life, and the expiation of His death. "There is no true repentance," said Staupitz, " but that which begins with the love of God, and of righteousness. . . . If thou wouldst be converted, endeavour not after all these macerations and all these martyrdoms. Love Him who first loved thee."

This great counsel proved to be both an arrow of conviction and a well of comfort to the distressed monk.   Eagerly referring to the Bible, he

Repentance and Faith. gained new light on old passages, and learnt to rejoice in repentance.   At times, again, he was overwhelmed by the thought of his sinfulness, and was appropriately instructed by Staupitz that "Jesus Christ is the Saviour even of those who are great and real sinners, and who deserve utter condemnation."   But could man first choose God, or did God first choose man?   What about Augustine's doctrine of election?—Here Staupitz wisely checked Luther, and bade him not pry too far into the Divine, but to realize that which is manifested in Christ.   He then showed Luther how to view the design of Providence in driving him through such trials and temptations: and, with a prophet-like prevision, he told him, " It is not in vain that God exercises thee by so many conflicts; thou wilt see that He will make use of thee as His minister in great affairs."   And Staupitz followed this by the gift of a Bible, and the advice to study it diligently, throwing aside scholastic systems.   Luther accordingly studied the original Greek of the New Testament, and found in *Metanoia* (repentance, a change of mind and disposition, so inadequately translated by the Vulgate *pœnitentia*) a word full of enlightenment.   He realized that a change of heart made all things new, smoothed every difficulty, and truly united the believer to God through Christ.   He was permanently at peace, though not without seasons of depression.

Now came the opportunity which brought the new man out into the world to influence it.   Frederick, Elector of Saxony, had founded, in 1502, a new university at Wittenberg.   Staupitz, himself one of the professors,

felt that Luther ought not to remain shut up in a convent, and he recommended him to Frederick, in 1508, for a chair at Wittenberg. The appointment was offered and accepted, and Luther started as lecturer on philosophy, at first discoursing on Aristotle. **Lectureship at Wittenberg.**
Early in 1509, however, he began to lecture on the Bible, having taken the degree of bachelor in theology. First the Psalms, then the Epistle to the Romans, were his subjects; and one day he was peculiarly impressed by the passage, " The just shall live by faith," which continued to speak to him, as with a living voice, throughout his life. His fame grew rapidly, and his lecture-room became crowded, even his fellow-professors attending. Staupitz set him to preach, and, speaking from the heart with conviction, he was so eloquent that great congregations gathered to hear him.

WITTENBERG MARKET PLACE, WITH LUTHER'S MONUMENT.

In 1510 or 1511 he was sent to Rome on monastic business, and thus saw the Roman Church in its full and evil development in Italy, under the warlike Julius II. His sojourns in monasteries scandalized him by their revelations of luxurious living and surroundings, and **Visits Rome.**
laxity of morals. At Rome he went from shrine to shrine of martyrs and saints, and he was climbing the steps of the so-called judgment seat of Pilate on his knees, to obtain an indulgence, when once more the words, " The just shall live by faith," pierced his soul, and recalled him to his new life. The ritualism and pomp, with the real emptiness, scoffing spirit, and unbelief of the Roman priests, disgusted him. He left Rome thoroughly disenchanted; his old veneration for the seal of the pontiffs was irrecoverably gone: he found the seat of authority rotten and corrupt.

Soon after Luther returned to Wittenberg, Staupitz pressed him to graduate as Doctor in Theology; and the poor monk's difficulty as to the fees was got over by the Elector himself paying them. He was formally invested with the degree in October, 1512, taking the oath "to devote his whole life to study, and faithfully to expound and defend the Holy Scriptures." He became more and more engrossed in active religious work; now defending Reuchlin in his censure of the proposed destruction of Hebrew books at Cologne; now preaching on the ten commandments, throwing startling lights upon their meaning; daily expounding the Scriptures to the university students; fiercely attacking the scholastic theologians and Aristotelian philosophy. Staupitz, now become Augustinian Vicar-General for Germany, appointed Luther his vicar for Thuringia; and in this office he showed himself a calm, strong and wise administrator, and a zealous guardian of souls. His labours were enormous; his fare was meagre; his courage was conspicuous in the perilous time of plague. But there grew within him an ever-increasing longing to bring forward into the utmost prominence the doctrines of salvation, which he felt and experienced, and which were so little understood or taught by others. Among the books which he recommended at this time were Tauler's sermons, as containing the soundest theology, and the most in agreement with the gospel of any he had ever seen. He drew up ninety-nine propositions, including novel views of doctrine, or revivals of old ones, asserting the natural depravity and impotence of the human will, God's free gift of grace, His election and predestination of His servants, man's continual state of sin without God's grace, the evil of the "works of the law." He sent these theses to Erfurt for discussion, but without result; and to John Mayer, so well known later as Dr. Eck, at Ingolstadt University in Bavaria. But now a new direction was suddenly given to Luther's activity.

Takes the Doctor's Degree.

His Theses on Freewill and Grace.

The new Pope, Leo X., being in want of money for his grand works, to complete St. Peter's at Rome, had sent out a new and plenary commission for the sale of indulgences, in order to accumulate the necessary funds; and John Tetzel, a Dominican friar of evil life, and already experienced in the business, was chosen as salesman for Saxony. He was an unrivalled cheap-jack, wonderfully skilful in vaunting his wares, declaring that he had saved more souls by his indulgences than St. Peter did by his preaching. There was no sin that could not be pardoned through him; his indulgences could save both the living and the dead. The very instant the money chinked at the bottom of his box the

Tetzel sells Indulgences.

ITHER FASTENS THE NINETY-FIVE THESES TO THE CHURCH DOOR AT WITTENBERG, OCTOBER 31ST, 1517.

living were pardoned, and the deceased soul escaped from purgatory to heaven.

Tetzel's skill and promises brought crowds to buy indulgences, and extracted from them the utmost price they were willing and able to contribute. Written documents were granted absolving from all sins, ecclesiastical and civil crimes and penalties, and purgatorial pains, and purporting to restore baptismal innocence and purity. Tetzel established his mart at Jüterbock, close to Wittenberg, in the autumn of 1517; and

Luther's Theses against Indulgences. the reports from thence filled Luther with indignation and distress. On the eve of All Saints' Day, October 31, 1517, he nailed up on the door of the Castle Church of Wittenberg, full of the relics of saints accumulated by successive electors, ninety-five theses against indulgences. This event was really, though unintentionally, the unfurling of the flag of the Reformation.

In these celebrated theses Luther asserted Christ's demand of a lifelong genuine repentance for sin, and denied the Pope's power to remit any penalty but what he himself had imposed. The specific assertions made by Tetzel about indulgences were denied, and it was stated that every true Christian participates in the benefits of Christ or of the Church, without a letter of indulgence. All the Pope could do was to declare the pardon of God to repentant sinners. In a very ingenious way Luther assumed that the Pope was on his side, and claimed his assent to various doctrines declaring true charity, beneficence and prayer far preferable to the purchase of an indulgence; and he was careful not to speak disrespectfully of the Pope. To hope to be saved by indulgences, however, was an empty and lying hope. Thus at one and the same time a great abuse was attacked, and free salvation was proclaimed.

The people were all on fire. Those who had paid for indulgences were dismayed. Priests and laymen copied the theses, and sent them rapidly through Germany. Luther followed his declaration by sermons expounding his views more fully. Many bishops, princes, and learned men were delighted at his boldness, and tacitly assented to his doctrine. Even the Pope was interested and not indignant, and called Luther a fine genius. Frederick Myconius, a young monk at Annaberg, rejected by Tetzel because he had not a sixpence, found joy in Luther's teaching, and became one of his first adherents in open revolt against the Papacy. But Luther was bidden by his bishop to be silent at least for a time; and no immediate open effect seemed to be produced by his bold pronouncement. As an actual combatant he was alone; and his veneration for the Church still kept him back.

Tetzel, bent on crushing Luther, interpreted the attack on indulgences as an attack on the Pope; and at an elaborate discussion at Frankfort-on-Oder, put forward a series of theses extolling the Pope as being *Tetzel's Counter* above the entire Church and the Councils, and as having the *Attack.* sole right to decide in matters of Christian faith, and on the meaning of Scripture. He further denounced such attacks as Luther's as worthy of damnation. A youth of twenty vigorously assailed Tetzel's theses, and the discussion closed without much gain for Tetzel, who took occasion soon after to burn Luther's propositions and his sermon on them. The Wittenberg students, in return, showed their attachment to Luther by burning Tetzel's second theses; but bishops and other dignitaries of the Church were already longing to burn the innovator as a heretic.

The reformer's courage rose with the opposition he had to encounter. He felt that his enemies had no real knowledge which could shake his position, and he was tempted to despise them; but he knew that witnesses to truth had always to forsake all things, and must look for death. He threw himself ardently into controversy, answering various *Controversy.* Dominicans, and also giving forth short popular treatises, such as his Exposition of the Ten Commandments and of the Lord's Prayer, the latter one of the most clear and vigorous of his writings. Dr. Eck's attack on the theses was the most serious he had to meet; it was plausible and learned, and at the same time loaded him with evil epithets, such as "venomous," "seditious," "heretical," "imbecile," "ignoramus." Luther's answer was more moderate, but clearly showed Eck's objections to be merely scholastic, and not drawn from Scripture or from the Fathers. "The supreme pontiff is a man, and may err. . . . Where find we in the Bible that the treasury of Christ's merits is in the hands of the Pope?" were two points in Luther's reply to Eck.

In April, 1518, Luther attended a general meeting of Augustinians in Heidelberg, and took the opportunity to hold a public disputation, in which he asserted and defended a series of "Paradoxes," stat- *Luther's* ing his central doctrines in most striking fashion. His defence *Paradoxes.* against his opponents won him numerous converts, among them a young Dominican friar, Martin Bucer, and John Breutius, a student of Heidelberg, both of whom became notable Reformers, and soon began to diffuse Luther's doctrines.

Returning to Wittenberg, Luther published a moderate exposition of his theses on indulgences, under the title "Solutions," asserting the necessity

His "Solutions." for a thorough reform of the Church, in which the whole of Christendom ought to engage. He boldly said: "I do not trouble myself about what may please or displease the Pope. . . . I listen to the Pope as Pope; that is to say, when he speaks according to the canons, or when he determines some point with the concurrence of a council, but not when he speaks his own mere notions." If he did otherwise he would have to approve of the horrible massacres of Christians by Julius II. And this young man in his twenty-sixth year ventured to send his "Solutions" to the Pope, with an explanatory letter, in which he sought to persuade Leo X. to be on his side.

LUTHER AND MELANCHTHON TRANSLATING THE BIBLE.

Already, however, a cardinal had written to the Elector Frederick in the Pope's name, cautioning him to beware of giving countenance and protection to Luther. The latter seems to have intended a sermon preached on July 15, 1518, as a reply to this letter, for he showed himself fully armed against excommunication. He clearly held the Hussite doctrine, that only his own sins could shut a man out of communion with God; the Papal power could only exclude from the outward ceremonies of

THE CASTLE OF PLEISSENBURG, LEIPSIC, THE SCENE OF THE DISPUTATION OF LUTHER WITH DR. ECK.

the Church. Luther's influence and reputation in Germany increased daily. The Pope bestirred himself, and sent out a summons to Luther to come to Rome for trial; but the Elector Frederick **Luther Summoned to Rome.** induced him to allow Luther to be examined at Augsburg by the Papal legate, Cardinal James de Vio, of Garta, commonly termed Cajetan. The Papal brief, however, was couched in very severe terms against Luther as a heretic, and against all princes and others who should favour or protect him.

Before he had received this summons, however, Luther had made the acquaintance of a man who was destined to have the greatest influence on him, Philip **Philip Melanchthon.** Schwartzerde or Melanchthon, who had just come to Wittenberg, at the age of twenty-one, as professor of classics. Born on February 14, 1497, at Bretten in the Palatinate, and educated at Heidelberg and Tübingen, Melanchthon became a doctor in philosophy at Heidenheim, and soon gained fame for his learning. Although short, slight, and feeble-looking, his conversation and manners were very attractive, and his teaching spread a genuine knowledge and love of Greek.

MEMORIAL MEDAL OF THE CONFESSION OF AUGSBURG, JUNE 25TH, 1530.

Luther met him, and they soon joined in preparing to translate the Bible into German.

Meanwhile, amid many fears and cautions from influential persons as to the dangers he would incur, Luther went to Augsburg in October, 1518, and was at once plied with advice to retract his errors, and with subtle counsel as to how he might maintain false propositions. **Luther and Cajetan at Augsburg.** Luther would only promise humility and due obedience. When he came into the legate's presence, Luther succeeded in obtaining a definition of the main doctrines he was to retract: (1) that the treasury of indulgences granted by the Pope was not constituted of the merits of Christ;

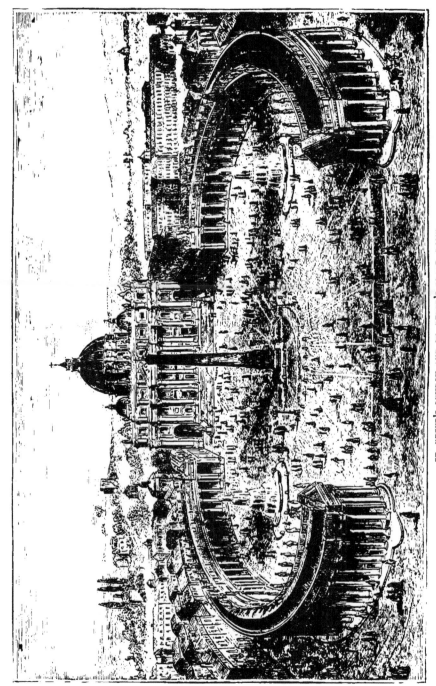

ST. PETER'S CHURCH AND ST. PETER'S PLACE, ROME.

(2) that the recipient of the sacrament must have faith in the grace offered to him. Luther, in controversy with the cardinal, showed such readiness in argument, and advanced such cogent reasons, that the latter at last said, "I will dispute no longer with this beast; it has deep eyes, and marvellous thoughts in its head." At last he enjoined Luther either to retract or to return no more.

Staupitz had come to Augsburg, to comfort Luther, and to arrange matters for him if possible. He absolved him from his vows as an Augustinian, and persuaded him to write a conciliatory letter to Cajetan, in which, however, there was no express retractation. But Staupitz grew timid and quitted Augsburg, leaving the letter to be sent by another. No answer came from Cajetan. Luther, in spite of an imperial safe-conduct which he held, began to fear violence, and withdrew from Augsburg secretly. Cajetan's next proceeding was to write to Frederick, bidding him send Luther to Rome, or banish him. The elector refused. Luther offered to take refuge in France; but after some wavering, the elector bade him remain. The Pope answered Luther in one way by publishing in Germany a bull confirming the doctrine of indulgences as **Rome and** attacked by Luther; and he sent a new legate to Germany, **Luther.** Carl von Miltitz, who met Luther in presence of Spalatin, and made no demands upon him except as to his conduct to the Pope, to whom he requested that Luther should apologise. Luther agreed to do so, and to cease writing or teaching on controverted questions, which the Pope was to have examined by a commission of theologians. This concession Luther afterwards greatly regretted. He had already formally appealed from the Pope to a general council of the Church, and had a protest printed, which was generally diffused contrary to his desire. In this crisis, on January 12, 1519, the Emperor Maximilian died, and it fell to the Elector Frederick to administer the Empire during the interregnum. Luther was safe under his protection. The Pope was anxious to conciliate Frederick in prospect of the new election. Meanwhile, Miltitz was induced to administer such a bitter rebuke to Tetzel that the seller of pardons fell into despair and died shortly after.

In view of political difficulties, it was arranged to put off decision on Luther's affairs till the next Diet, which did not assemble till **Luther's** 1521, at Worms. Luther's students and hearers at Witten- **growing** berg continually increased. A collection of his works was **Influence.** printed at Basle, and widely sold all over Western Europe and in England.

In the midst of his growing popularity, Dr. Eck attacked Luther in thirteen theses, especially asserting the Pope's primacy, and challenged Andrew Bodenstein—better known as Carlstadt, from the place of his birth—a friend and colleague of Luther's, to a public disputation. Luther, finding that the Roman champion was not going to keep silence, put forward a **His Disputation with Dr. Eck.** rival series of theses, the last asserting the forgery of the Isidorian decretals on which Rome relied, and asserting the authority of Scripture and the conclusions of the council of Nicæa. The formal disputation took place at Leipsic in June and July, 1519. Let us here quote the graphic description of a learned spectator, Mosellanus.

"Martin Luther is of the middle size, and has become so lean from the intensity of his studies that you might almost count his bones. He is in the prime of life, and has a clear and sonorous voice. His learning and his knowledge of the Holy Scriptures are incomparable, so that he has almost the whole in his grasp. Besides this, he has a vast fund of arguments and ideas." Candid and affable, accommodating, pleasant and good-humoured, firm and confident in his case, perhaps over-severe and sarcastic in attacking the views of others—such was the champion of reform at this time. Eck, on the contrary, is described as more like a soldier or a butcher than a divine; of good memory, but slow in comprehension; withal of inconceivable impudence. The disputation lasted seventeen days, and in many points Eck confessed himself beaten. "Had I not had a disputation with Doctor Martin on the primacy of the Pope," said Eck, "I might almost have been of one mind with him." Luther maintained that the Greek Church was part of the Church of Christ, and that the Bishop of Rome was only head of the Latin Church by human election. He denied that there could be no Church apart from the Pope. The Church was the communion of the faithful, and could never lack the guidance of the Holy Spirit, who was not always in Popes and councils. Eck at last refused to debate with an opponent who would not abide by the decisions of (so-called) œcumenical councils. The debate ended with much popular excitement. Mosellanus declares that Luther and Carlstadt remained victors in the judgment of all who had learning, mind, and modesty; but Eck, defeated, was more insulting than before.

It was soon felt throughout Germany that there must be open battle between Luther and the Pope. Eck's own secretary, Poliander, joined the Reformers. Melanchthon dated his entire adhesion to Luther from the

Leipsic debate. Luther himself felt redoubled strength, seeing that the Papal system had no better support than Eck's arguments, which he had crushed. He put forth a series of powerful works, such as his sermons on the sacraments, on excommunication, on the priesthood, on good works, his "Address to the Christian Nobility of Germany" on the Reform of Christendom, and his treatise on the Babylonian Captivity of the Church. In the sermons on the sacraments he advocated administration of both the bread and the wine to all communicants. He attacked the doctrine of the efficacy of the sacrament independently of the recipient's state of heart. In his sermons on good works, he showed that they could not take the place of faith, which must always precede them.

Luther on the Sacraments.

The "Address to the Christian Nobility of Germany" attacked the whole sacerdotal system of Rome, as constituting a separate caste of priests. All Christians, he said, constitute the spiritual estate, and the only difference among them belongs to the functions they discharge. Consecration by a bishop might make a hypocrite, but never could make a spiritual man. All true Christians were priests by their baptism in Christ. Thus he powerfully expounded a doctrine on which genuine Protestants will always insist. Caste distinctions among Christians are not part of the spirit of genuine Protestantism. Luther next reviewed the abuses of the Church, and the horrible degeneracy exhibited by Papal magnificence and domination. The methods of attracting money to Rome, of selling offices, he unsparingly denounced. The evil life of many priests was laid bare; and in this connection the bold reformer attacked the celibacy of the clergy, and recommended their marriage. The evils of monasticism were fully exposed; the disastrous work of the Papal legates was denounced; the dissipation attending Church festivals, Church dedications, was censured. One notable passage dealt with the burning of heretics, especially the case of Huss. Luther had already, on carefully reading Huss's works, discovered that he himself held and taught all the views of Huss. He now denounced all burning of heretics. They ought to be refuted by Scripture, not by fire. He called upon the German empire at any rate to put an end to these abuses within its limits.

Address to the German Nobility.

This address, bold and incisive in its tone, had an unprecedented sale, and made Luther many friends. The Germans were roused by a sort of national feeling. An equally vigorous book followed, "On the Babylonian Captivity of the Church" (October, 1520), showing how the Church had been carried captive by the Papacy, and

On the Babylonian Captivity of the Church.

how the sacraments had been perverted by its priestcraft. "I declare," wrote Luther, "that neither Pope, bishop, nor any man has power to impose the smallest matter on a Christian unless with his own consent." Here was set forth the true charter of Christian liberty. Meanwhile, the Emperor Maximilian had died in 1519, and, after considerable delay, his son, Charles V., was elected Emperor. To him, not yet twenty-one, Luther, early in 1520, addressed a respectful appeal for fair treatment.

Eck had been at Rome busily engaged in bringing about Luther's condemnation. At last he obtained a bull condemning forty-one proposi-
Papal Bull against Luther. tions asserted to be Luther's, some of them clearly Augustinian and orthodox, others denying the primacy and infallibility of the Popes. One of the condemned heresies is this: "To burn heretics is against the will of the Holy Ghost." From the moment of receiving this bull, bishops were to seek out Luther's erroneous writings and burn them publicly. As for Luther himself, he might be received again into the Church on retracting within sixty days; if not, he and his adherents were condemned as obstinate heretics. This bull, published at Rome on July 15, 1520, was brought by Eck to Leipsic, and published there in October. But he got little but ridicule where he had formerly had so much applause; and he took refuge in Coburg. At Erfurt, whither he carried the bull after a time, the students tore the copies to pieces. He dared not visit Wittenberg.

Luther, in reply, called the Pope Antichrist, and his bull impious and false. He laughed it to scorn, and proceeded to burn it. He wrote thus
Luther burns the Bull. to Spalatin: "In the year 1520, on the 10th of December, at the ninth hour, were burnt, at Wittenberg, at the east gate, near the sacred cross, all the books of the Pope; the Decree, the Decretals, the Extravagance of Clement VI., and the latest Bull of Leo X." Another professor lighted the bonfire; Luther threw the bull on the flames.

This declaration of war was the signal for great popular excitement in Germany. The people rejoiced at the bold stand thus taken for freedom
His Protest. from Papal shackles. On December 17, 1520, Luther drew up a solemn protest appealing from the Pope to a general council of the Church. The Pope commanded the Emperor to bestir himself to crush heresy in Germany. Whereupon he summoned Luther before him at the Diet of Worms, opened in January, 1521. The Papal nuncio desired that Luther should be condemned unheard, as being already convicted by the Pope. The German princes agreed that he should be simply

called upon to retract, and the Emperor gave Luther a safe-conduct, under which he came to Worms on April 16.   Before he left Witten- **The Diet of** berg he planned with his friend, Lucas Cranach, the artist, a **Worms.** book of woodcuts representing the contrast between Christianity and popery, with brief descriptions, such as Christ washing the disciples' feet, contrasted with the Pope holding out his toe to be kissed ; Christ bearing

LUTHER BURNING THE POPE'S BULL AT WITTENBERG, DEC. 10TH, 1520.

the cross, the Pope carried on men's shoulders through Rome; Christ driving out the money-changers, the Pope selling indulgences with heaps of money before him.   On the 28th of March Luther had been publicly excommunicated at Rome by the Pope.

We must pass by the notable incidents of Luther's journey and arrival.   When called before the Emperor and the Diet, he spent an hour

in fervent prayer, and then faced the assembly boldly. Being called upon
Luther's Firmness. to answer whether he retracted the contents of his books, he
asked for time for careful consideration. On the next day,
April 18, he replied that his writings were of three kinds: (1) those which
his opponents did not find fault with—these he could not retract; (2) those
condemning the Papacy and its acts, which had ruined Christendom—these
it would be mean and wicked to retract; (3) those in which he had made
attacks on private persons with more vehemence perhaps than was right—
these he did not retract, lest he should sanction their impieties. He would
retract anything on being convinced of its error from the writings of the
prophets and apostles. Being again challenged to retract, Luther said:
" I cannot submit my faith either to the Pope or to councils, inasmuch as

THE EMPEROR CHARLES V.

they have often fallen into error, and
even into gross contradictions with
themselves. If then I be not convinced by Scripture or by evident
reasons, . . . I neither can nor
will retract anything." After a further defence of his argument that
councils had erred, Luther said, when
the Emperor had given a sign to end
the discussion, "Here stand I: I
cannot do otherwise: God help me.
Amen."

Spalatin and many others highly
approved Luther's attitude. Some
Italian and Spanish dukes wished the safe-conduct revoked and Luther
Luther Outlawed. burnt. The Emperor declared that he would respect the safe-
conduct, and let Luther return whence he came unhurt; but his
doctrines must be condemned. After three days had been given to Luther for
further consideration, during which many theologians and others sought to
shake him, he was allowed to leave Worms on April 26. On May 8 Charles
V. proclaimed the severest condemnation of Luther as a madman, a fiend, an
inciter to bloodshed and sedition, and a damnable heretic. Every one was
forbidden to shelter or succour him, and was ordered after a certain date to
seize and detain him. Such was the ban of the empire proclaimed against
Luther. By the Elector Frederick's orders he was seized near Eisenach,
and concealed in the fortified castle of the Wartburg.

LUTHER'S STUDY IN THE WARTBURG, HIS PLACE OF REFUGE AFTER THE DIET OF WORMS.

FRIEDRICHSHAFEN, ON THE LAKE OF CONSTANCE.

CHAPTER VIII.

Zwingli and the Early Swiss Reformers.

Religion in Switzerland — Ulrich Zwingli—Pastor of Glarus—Opposes Indulgences— Appointed Preacher at Zurich—Zwingli's Persuasive Preaching—He Visits Basle—Plot Against His Life—Martyrdom of Galster—Zwingli and Mercenary Service—Abstinence from Meat—Progress of Gospel Preaching—Zwingli and His Enemies—His Marriage— Assembly at Einsiedeln—Zwingli's Sixty-seven Theses—Conference at Zurich—Papal Offers to Zwingli—Images—Hottinger Martyred—Disputation at Zurich—Zwingli on Congregations as Churches—Images Given Up—The Diet against Zurich—Martyrdom of the Wirths—The Lord's Supper Restored at Zurich.

SWITZERLAND, unlike Germany, had long overthrown the tyranny of princes; and the democracy, imperfectly educated in many places, was slowly feeling its way along the path of liberty. Considerable independence of Rome in religious matters had already been *Religion in* established, and Zurich had specially distinguished itself in *Switzerland.* this particular. The Genevans opposed an obstinate resistance to the pretentions of their bishop. But in the mountainous districts much superstition remained; miracles and ecclesiastical fables still obtained credit; and the priests made profit of the people's ignorance, and often set morality at defiance.

Although Luther's early writings might have been expected to arouse a reforming spirit in Switzerland, the first movements in that country were of home growth, and not inspired by the great German innovator.

Ulrich Zwingli. Ulrich Zwingli, born seven weeks after Luther, on New Year's Day, 1484, at Wildhaus, in the Toggenburg valley above Zurich, was the first of the great Swiss reformers. He was the son of a mountain herdsman and baillie, who sent him to school at Basle. In 1497 he was transferred to the academy of Lupulus at Berne. To avoid the allurements of the Dominicans, his father afterwards transferred him to Vienna University. At 18 he returned to Basle to teach in a school, and at the same time to attend the university, where he studied scholastic theology and philosophy till he was tired of them. In November, 1505, Thomas Wittembach arrived at Basle from Tübingen, and taught theology on a more liberal system than usual, prognosticating the downfall of scholastic theology, and declaring that the death of Christ was the sole ransom for the sins of humanity. Zwingli and a young friend, Leo Judah, afterwards his faithful colleague, were among Wittembach's most zealous hearers, and we must credit Wittembach with accomplishing an important work in promoting Zwingli's religious developement.

In 1506, the people of Glarus, not far from Wildhaus, chose young Zwingli for their pastor, rejecting a nominee of the Pope. After his Pastor of Glarus. ordination, Zwingli devoted himself to parish work and to classical study; but he had a brief interval of service in Italy with the Swiss mercenaries engaged to fight for the Pope against the French. His knowledge of the evils caused by Swiss mercenary service led him to denounce the practice vigorously. In 1513 he devoted himself energetically to the study of classical and Scriptural Greek, and determined to seek the interpretation of the Bible mainly from itself, by comparing passages which illustrated one another. The great Erasmus visited Basle in 1514, and that liberal-minded scholar soon recognised the ability of Zwingli. Among other friends whom the pastor of Glarus made at this time were Oswald Myconius, rector of a school at Basle, and John Hausschein or Œcolampadius, a native of Franconia, born in 1482, educated at Heidelberg, and appointed pastor of Basle in 1515. In that year Zwingli again visited Italy as chaplain of a body of Swiss troops, and was present at the battle of Marignano, when Francis I. defeated the Papal army. The experience gained in this campaign intensified Zwingli's conviction of the necessity of reform in the Church; and on his return he devoted himself more than ever to Scriptural preaching.

In 1516 Zwingli was appointed as priest and preacher to the Abbey

Church of Einsiedeln, a famous place of pilgrimage. Here he was dismayed at the abject superstition of the pilgrims, and their ignorance in religious matters; and he declared to them that *Preaches at Einsiedeln.* Christ alone can forgive sins, and can save everywhere, independent of pilgrimages or visits to holy places. As a consequence, the receipts of the shrine rapidly fell off.

Zwingli was equally outspoken on the evils of the Papacy to Cardinal Shinner, to the legate Pucci and to Capito, the friend of Œcolampadius. The legate sought to attach him by the offer of a Papal chaplaincy, but this did not silence the reformer. In August, 1518, a Carmelite friar named Samson visited Schwytz, selling indulgences, and this *Opposes Indulgences.* aroused in Zwingli an opposition similar to that of Luther to Tetzel. His fame went abroad in Switzerland, and in many cities were to be found personal friends or attached converts of the mountain pastor. Oswald Myconius, who had, in 1516, become master of the cathedral school at Zurich, in 1518 recommended Zwingli as preacher in the principal church of Zurich. Zwingli was elected after a sharp contest, and removed to Zurich in December, leaving his friend Leo *Appointed Preacher at Zurich.* Judah as his successor at Einsiedeln. He found that he was expected to pay more attention to increasing the revenues of the Church than to serious preaching. But he plainly told the canons who appointed him, and whose neglected work he was elected to do, that he was going to spend his main strength on preaching. "The life of Jesus," he said, "has been too long concealed from the people. . . . It is to the glory of God, to the praise of His only Son, to the real salvation of souls, and to their instruction in the true faith, that I shall consecrate my ministry. . . . I will speak with modesty, and give no man cause of offence."

Thus on New Year's Day, 1519, after Germany had for more than a year been stirred by Luther's denunciation of Tetzel's practices, the Swiss Reformation may be said to have actually begun, when Zwingli delivered his first sermon as preacher at Zurich. His lucid and *Zwingli's Persuasive Preaching.* attractive exposition of the gospel, his proclamation of salvation through Christ alone, his energetic exhortation to repentance, his unsparing denunciation of vice, luxury, intemperance and oppression, drew round him all that was best in Zurich, though the conventional and conservative among the congregations stood aloof. With admirable discretion Zwingli kept a prudent course. He avoided such determined, exciting opposition as Luther had aroused, and showed an affability and geniality towards the peasantry which won their hearts, and led many of the principal burgesses to become his adherents. He took great delight in music, and was himself a skilful performer on the flute and the harp. At the same time he studied zealously, especially devoting himself to Hebrew.

Early in 1519, Samson, the seller of indulgences, approached Zurich. He had already met with much success, but had likewise encountered considerable opposition. He had had a sharp contest at Bremgarten with Dean Bullinger, father of the celebrated reformer Henry Bullinger, and the dean hastened to Zurich before Samson, to complain of him to the Swiss Diet. The Bishop of Constance sided with the dean, and had refused

MAYENCE MARKET PLACE AND CATHEDRAL.

to license Samson. Zwingli had preached energetically against indulgences. The Diet therefore forbad Samson to enter Zurich, and he was soon after recalled to Italy. Warned perhaps by the strife already aroused in Germany, the Pope withdrew early from the contest concerning indulgences in Switzerland.

Zwingli's strenuous labours affected his health; and while he was regaining his strength at the baths at Pfeffers, the plague visited Zurich. He returned at once, weak as he was, and devoted himself to the sick and the dying. Presently he was himself struck down, and for a long time was in a dangerous condition. During this period of enforced suspension of his activity, Switzerland realized his worth more than ever, and his own character matured. Rising from his sick bed, filled with new fire and energy, Zwingli had to mourn the removal of his friend Myconius to Lucerne.

Early in 1520 he visited his old friends at Basle. His preaching there

ZWINGLI PREACHING IN ZURICH CATHEDRAL.

was more powerful than ever. Capito (1478-1541), a former lecturer at Freiburg University, who had studied Luther's writings, and Zwingli Visits Basle. was now preacher at Basle Cathedral, was delighted at hearing Zwingli, whose doctrine, already biblical, became more truly reforming. In the same year he was appointed chaplain to Albert, Archbishop of Mainz. He was succeeded by his pupil and friend Hedio, who not only publicly expounded the gospel of St. Matthew, but held private meetings for evangelical instruction. The adherents of the Papacy became alarmed at the progress of the novel teachings of Zwingli and his friends, and Myconius and Hedio apprehended active opposition. Zwingli, always inclined to the ways of quietness, went on preaching without faltering, and the great cathedral at Zurich was crowded. Switzers from all the cantons thronged to hear him, and carried home the gospel teaching. The magistrates of Zurich, anxious to put a stop to the unscriptural and foolish preaching of the monks, ordered, in 1520, that nothing should be introduced into a sermon but what was founded on the Bible. Thus began that interference of the civil power with Church services which has proved so great a subject of contention ever since. The adherents of the monks plotted against the life of their chief opponent, Zwingli; and on January 1, 1521, the first blood shed for the Reformation Martyrdom of Galster at Schaffhausen. was poured forth at Schaffhausen, when an old man named Galster, who had denounced priests, with relic-worship and other superstitions, was beheaded by the authorities.

During this time Zwingli was gaining many friends, who afterwards became prominent reformers. Such were Berthold Haller, the gentle and eloquent preacher of Berne; Henry Bullinger, newly arrived from his studies in Germany; and Gerold Meyer, whose widowed mother, Anna Reinhard, was afterwards to be Zwingli's wife. In 1521, Zwingli and Mercenary Service. Zwingli strongly opposed the sending of a detachment from Zurich to fight for the Pope against other Swiss mercenaries engaged by France; but he was overruled. He made a satirical reference to this event, in the next year, when, attacking the practice of abstinence from meat at special seasons, he said that certain defenders of Abstinence from Meat. such abstinence were, nevertheless, quite willing to sell human flesh to foreigners, and drag it to death. But he did not himself break through the established customs of abstinence, or omit saying mass, although some of the more violent of his adherents, such as Roubli, openly ate meat on fast-days. Faber, vicar of the Bishop of Constance, and a strong partisan of the Papacy, now returned from Rome, and, hearing of these proceedings, sent a deputation to Zurich from the bishop, complaining that doctrines new, startling, and seditious were being taught there. Zwingli seized an opportunity of answering these complaints before the council of two hundred, and vigorously preached a simple gospel. As to abstinence, it was agreed to invite the Pope and Cardinals to explain its principle and necessity, and meanwhile abstinence from meat during Lent was enjoined. In April, 1522, he published his work "On the Free Use of Meats."

THE CITY AND CATHEDRAL OF CONSTANCE.

While some parts of Switzerland became more devoted to the Papacy than ever, and the Swiss Diet had forbidden the preaching of new doctrines which caused dissension, the Reformation was making

Progress of Gospel Preaching. progress at many points. John Wanner was preaching Christ in the cathedral of Constance; Francis Lambert, a French Franciscan, who had been compelled to leave Avignon for reading Luther's writings, declaimed at Geneva, Lausanne, Berne and Zurich, against the errors of the Church, the "sacrifice" of the mass, and the superstitions of the religious orders; Conrad Schmid, at Lucerne, preached the gospel in German; at Berne, a mystery play held up the Pope and the clergy to ridicule under the title, "Devourers of the Dead"; and, somewhat tardily, the Bernese found out a trick that had been played upon them by monks, who foisted off an ordinary skull as the sacred head of St. Anne, mother of the Virgin. In Appenzell, in the Grisons, and elsewhere, enlightened men preached the gospel and made converts.

Zwingli's enemies did not pause in their opposition. The Bishop of Constance sought to influence the canons of Zurich against him. In reply, Zwingli wrote his "Architetes," defending himself, and prognosticating the fall of the Romish ceremonies. The Zurich Council were induced to prohibit preaching against the monks. Zwingli refused to preach at all, unless he was left unhampered, as bishop and pastor of Zurich; thus assuming the old significance of the word *episcopus*. He was open to reprehension by any one, he said, if he asserted anything contrary to the gospel. *Zwingli and his Enemies.*

Meanwhile, numerous scandals in connection with the priests turned the attention of the Swiss reformers to the marriage question, and they realized that the time had come for a new departure. They saw that the celibacy of the clergy was a comparatively modern innovation, and noted that St. Paul wrote about true bishops as husbands and fathers. Xylotect, of Lucerne, was already married. Zwingli married Anna Reinhard about 1522, though he kept the marriage secret till 1524, thinking the knowledge of it might injure his usefulness. *Zwingli's Marriage.*

About the end of June, 1522, Zwingli called an assembly of evangelical clergy at Einsiedeln, which adopted addresses to the Swiss Diet and the Bishop of Constance in favour of full freedom to preach the gospel, and of the abolition of compulsory celibacy of the clergy. This was the first united act of the reforming party in Switzerland. The presentation of the petition to the Diet was the signal for much active opposition to the reform movement, and one of its first effects was the dismissal and banishment of Oswald Myconius from Lucerne, a city which has, to this day, remained almost exclusively Roman Catholic. Zwingli comforted Myconius, and was able to obtain for him the chaplaincy of Einsiedeln, in succession to Leo Judah, who was appointed to St. Peter's Church, Zurich; thus bringing him close to Zwingli. *Assembly at Einsiedeln.*

Towards the end of 1522, an Augustinian monk, preaching in St.

Peter's, proclaimed that man of himself could satisfy God's justice. Pope Leo X., who was present, at once contested the doctrine, and this act led to the summoning of a conference at Zurich, at which Zwingli was called upon to give an account of his doctrine. As a preliminary step, he *Zwingli's Sixty-* published sixty-seven propositions or theses, comprising the *seven Theses.* principal doctrines he sought to maintain. These theses asserted that Christ is the only way to salvation; that the gospel contains all truth; that the mass is no sacrifice, but a commemoration of the one sacrifice of the cross; that the power of the Pope and of the bishops has no foundation in Scripture; that all Christians are brethren; that the prohibition of the lawful marriage of priests is a great scandal; that Scripture knows nothing of purgatory. The theses contained other anti-Roman doctrines.

On January 29, 1523, the conference was opened, attended by the bishop's deputies, including Faber, by townsmen, clergy, and people of dis-*Conference at* tinction from a distance. When Zwingli asserted that he had *Zurich.* preached salvation in Christ alone, and that for this he was called a heretic and rebel, and declared himself ready to be convinced, Faber refused to argue, saying he had been only sent to listen. Three summonses were despatched to all Zwingli's opponents, citing them to come forward, but no one appeared. The Council of Zurich met in the afternoon, and resolved that Zwingli, not having been reprehended by any one, should continue to preach, and that the other priests of the canton should teach nothing which they could not establish by Scripture. Faber now angrily contended that Zwingli's theses were contrary to the doctrine of Christ; but he refused to prove his statement except at Paris, Cologne, or Freiburg. But scarcely was the conference concluded, when a Papal *Papal Offers* legate arrived, prepared to offer the bold Swiss reformer any-*to Zwingli.* thing short of the popedom itself. The Pope had treated Luther as an enemy; he tried to propitiate Zwingli. But his efforts were useless: Zwingli was far less attached to the historic system of the Papacy than Luther, who had been deeply imbued with the monastic spirit.

A book published by a young priest named Louis Helzer, entitled "God's Judgment against Images," about this time, produced a great sen-*Images.* sation in Zurich; and a citizen named Claud Hottinger was moved to pull down a richly carved crucifix which was held in great reverence at Stadelhofen, just outside Zurich. The sacrilege was so startling that the Zurich council caused Hottinger and his assistants to be apprehended, and a little later Hottinger and his friend Hochrutiner were banished from the canton for two years. Having talked freely against images in various places, Hottinger was apprehended in a Baden village in February, 1524, and remitted to the Diet sitting at Lucerne, which without delay condemned him to death and had him beheaded. **Hottinger Martyred.**

Meanwhile there had been further destruction of images at Zurich, and the magistrates resolved to hold a disputation on the question, so that the Roman advocates might have full opportunity to state their case according to Scripture. In October, 1523, there assembled a great meeting of the grand Council of Zurich, with 350 priests; but though the other cantons were invited, only Schaffhausen and St. Gall sent deputies, and the bishops refused to be present or to be represented. Zwingli spoke first, and demanded a return to the Christian liberty of primitive times, asserting that the universal Church was to be found wherever there were believers, while particular Churches were found in separate places. Popes, cardinals, and councils, he said, were neither the universal Church nor one particular Church. The assembly here gathered together was the Church of Zurich, and had the right to ordain whatever appeared good to it, and conformable to Scripture. Thus was the doctrine of congregationalism and independency for the first time powerfully asserted. **Disputation at Zurich, Oct., 1523.** **Zwingli on Congregations as Churches.**

A feeble opponent declared he would wait for a council, and would obey his bishop, even if that prelate were a rogue. Zwingli ridiculed the idea of waiting for a council, and carried the meeting with him in his practical revolt from obedience to the Bishop of Constance. The image question now came up, and after several priests had defended the worship of images without adducing Scriptural arguments, Zwingli and others easily refuted them by Biblical quotations; and many priests who had hitherto defended image worship gave up the case. On a second day the doctrine of the mass was attacked by Zwingli, and his views were agreed to by many. By common consent, the men of Zurich "let Christ return into their territory and resume His ancient empire!" Zwingli and many others were astonished and deeply moved at the triumph of their views. From that time the Bishop of Constance had no power in Zurich; the pastors in town and country went forward boldly in gospel teaching; Zwingli maintained a moderate position, not desiring hastily to abolish the mass, inclined rather to build up than to **Images given up.**

cast down.   Oswald Myconius, invited to Zurich to take charge of a school, expounded the New Testament daily in a church.

The Swiss Diet, almost unanimous against the Reformation, after beheading Hottinger, sought to coerce the city of Zurich.   This assembly

The Diet against Zurich. directed the Zurichers to dismiss Zwingli and his followers, and to join with the Diet in remedying the injuries inflicted on the Papacy.   Zurich replied by abolishing the annual Whit-Monday procession to Einsiedeln, by burying a quantity of relics, and by ordering that the images should be removed from the churches throughout the canton, and that the ornaments should be sold for the benefit of the poor.   A new baptismal service, purified of non-Scriptural matter, was also drawn up.

Moved by a Papal brief, the Swiss Diet in July, 1524, sent a deputation to Zurich, Schaffhausen and Appenzell, to inform them of the Diet's resolution to put down the new doctrines, and to punish the adherents of those doctrines with severity ; thus the so-called free confederation assumed collectively a tyrannical power in religious matters.   The Zurichers, firmly grounded in a truer principle of liberty, declared, in answer, that in matters of faith they would obey the Word of God alone. A number of states, including Lucerne, Schwytz, Uri and Zug, all zealous adherents of Rome, thereupon announced that they would no longer sit in Diet with Zurich.

The illegal arrest of Œxlin, pastor of Burg, a friend of Zwingli, in July, 1524, led to an attempt at rescue by Wirth, the vice-baillie of Stammheim, and his two sons, young priests of reforming tendencies. Failing in the attempt, their followers seized a Carthusian monastery at Ittingen, and after perpetrating some excesses, burnt it to the ground. The deputies of the Catholic cantons were indignant, and denounced Zwingli as the promoter of these movements.   The Zurichers apprehended

Martyrdom of the Wirths. Wirth and his sons, with Rutiman, baillie of Mossbaum, and claimed the right to deal with them at their pleasure.   The Diet also claimed them, and succeeded in gaining the custody of them, notwithstanding Zwingli's opposition, on condition of dealing with them only as regarded the late incidents,—not concerning any matter of creed. The elder Wirth was accused of having destroyed an image of St. Anne ; against Adrian Wirth it was alleged that he was married, and was a follower of Zwingli and Luther.   To show the extent of religious bigotry in those days, it suffices to mention that one influential man declared he would have done anything to gain a pardon for the elder Wirth, if he had been guilty of robbery or murder, but that as he had burnt St. Anne, die he must. On September 28, 1524, Wirth himself, his son John, and Rutiman were condemned to death by deputies from nine cantons; and they were beheaded the same day.

This execution produced a profound sensation, and appears to have given some impulse to the reforming movement at Zurich. Things were now ripe for the abolition of the mass. On April 11, 1525, **The Lord's Supper restored at Zurich.** Zwingli, Leo Judah, and Oswald Myconius, asked the grand Council of Zurich to permit the Lord's Supper to be restored to its primitive simplicity. Objection being made that Christ's words in its institution were, "This is My body," Zwingli said that the Greek word in the original meant not only "is" but "signifies," and quoted many examples of its use in a figurative sense. This argument convinced the few objectors; and it was determined that the mass should no longer be celebrated in Zurich, and that on the next day, April 12 (the Thursday before Easter), the practice of apostolical times should be restored.

On that day there was witnessed in Zurich the first solemn observance, in modern times, of the simple celebration of the Lord's Supper, at tables whereon bread and wine were set forth. The deacons read the appropriate passages of Scripture, the pastors exhorted their people, each of the recipients, kneeling, broke off a piece of the bread on the platter, and drank from the wooden goblets handed round. All felt that they had attained to something more hearty, something savouring more of true communion, than the mass afforded them. Rejoicing in their renewed feeling of brotherhood, old enemies embraced each other; and Zwingli gave thanks, in one of those outpourings of jubilation which have often burst from prophets and reformers at the acme of their career, to be frequently followed by disappointment, when the people forgot their first love. "Peace," he said, "makes her abode in our town; dissimulation, dissension, envy and quarrelling have disappeared from amongst us. Whence can such concord have arisen, if not from the Lord, and from the tendency of the doctrine we preach to produce order and peace?"

Coming events were destined to pronounce a strange comment on this declaration.

WRESTLING IN PRAYER IN THE CONVENT CELL AT ERFURT.

CHAPTER IX.

𝔏𝔲𝔱𝔥𝔢𝔯 𝔞𝔫𝔡 𝔏𝔲𝔱𝔥𝔢𝔯𝔞𝔫𝔦𝔰𝔪; 𝔱𝔬 𝔱𝔥𝔢 𝔇𝔦𝔢𝔱 𝔬𝔣 𝔖𝔭𝔦𝔯𝔢𝔰, 1526.

Luther as an Organizer—His Activity at the Wartburg—His Forcible Language—Dangerous Teaching on Sin—Clerical Celibacy—Confession—Translation of the Bible—Retirement of Augustinian Monks—Carlstadt at Wittenberg—The Mass Abolished—The Zwickau Prophets—Extremes at Wittenberg—Luther Reappears—Preaches in Favour of Charity and Tolerance—Interview with the Prophets—Luther Discourages Violence—Melanchthon's " Common Places "—Luther and Henry VIII.—Adrian VI. and the Diet at Nuremberg—The Hundred Grievances—The Pope and the Elector Frederick of Saxony—Persecutions of Lutherans—Campeggio and the Diet—Convention of Ratisbon—Luther's Publications—The Knights' War—Luther on Church Organization—His Marriage—Carlstadt's Proceedings—Münzer and the Peasants' War—Death of the Elector Frederick—Progress of Reform—The Diet of Spires, 1526.

HAVING raised the standard of revolt against the Papacy, and proved his steadfastness when brow-beaten by emperor and cardinals and princes, Luther had now to guide the independent development of his movement; and it must be owned that while he was a tower of strength *Luther as an* in many ways, he was not so well qualified as a later reformer, *Organizer.* John Calvin, to devise a new plan of Church order and government, or to inaugurate a complete course of theological doctrine. Deeply imbued with ecclesiastical notions and routine, but more impressed by the Divine authority of monarchs than of popes, he was not prepared for sturdy and persistent opposition to the Emperor, nor for a root-and-branch extermination of Roman practices and doctrines. He yielded episcopal rights

112

to civil authorities, and thereby hampered the developement of the Reformed Church, splitting it up into as many Churches as there were Protestant states in Germany, and not reserving for the Churches that freedom of action which is essential to its most healthy growth and wellbeing. In consequence of his too great devotion to the authority of princes, he failed to take the popular side in the Peasants' War, at a time when his moderating influence might have been most beneficial. But he conferred on Germany

LUTHER, THE AUGUSTINE MONK, AT THE CONVENT AT ERFURT.

the inestimable benefits of his German Bible and his stirring and comforting hymns.

Nominally a prisoner in the Wartburg, but in reality protected and kept from danger—dressed as a knight, and growing a beard—Luther, at first, did not chafe against restraint, but sought to turn to good account the enforced leisure of what he called his Patmos. His Activity at the Wartburg. There is no more remarkable picture of mental activity than the record of

I

these months of seclusion; but at times, as we learn from his letters, Luther was beset by temptations, physical and spiritual, which were as acute as those that had assailed him in the Augustinian convent at Erfurt. His safety and his place of refuge became known to his friends at Wittenberg, and he was enabled to communicate with them. He wrote frequently to Melanchthon and to Spalatin, and to the latter he entrusted for publication his short treatises on the Mass, on Vows of Celibacy, and against the New Idol at Halle (the sale of indulgences newly authorized by the Archbishop of Mayence); but Spalatin, from prudential motives, kept them unpublished, greatly to Luther's vexation. In a letter to the archbishop on November 15th, 1521, Luther's energy finds characteristic expression in his words. "Did you think that Luther was dead?" he asks. "No, no, Luther is not dead; he lives, and, fortified by the protection of that God who has already humiliated the Pope, is ready to begin with the Archbishop of Mayence a game that nobody, perhaps, expected. You are now warned; if your grace will not abandon those idolatrous practices, I shall take the matter actively in hand, I, a man of faith and of eternity; I will treat you as I have treated the Pope, and will show the world what difference there is between a wolf and a bishop."

It is an impressive indication of Luther's importance, even when under the ban of the empire, occupying no official station, standing at the *His Forcible* head of no organized body, that the archbishop replied humbly *Language.* to this fierce epistle, and promised amendment; but the moderating hand of Capito, who was now in attendance on him, may perhaps have suggested his conciliatory answer; and we know that Capito at the same time rebuked Luther for his intemperate language to the archbishop. But the great Reformer was surcharged with force. His expressions were often coarse, and therefore all the better fitted to seize and hold the masses of the people, who must be the ultimate upholders of a movement universal in its scope. Any one wishing to make a study of forcible language will do well to read Luther's letters and treatises. In this respect Luther is a homely Carlyle; and this is one of the reasons why many people of taste and refinement shrink from Luther. But it is possible to regret, and to refrain from imitating the foibles and infirmities of a great man, and at the same time fully to recognise how these very failings constitute important factors in creating that essential element in the leader of a revolutionary movement, a commanding personality, not pliable, but uncompromisingly resolute; not vacillating, but decided or even

tyrannical. Without a resolute militant head, in act and word, no great
revolt is possible. We have seen that before Luther's time strong men had
attacked the Papacy. It required all his exceptional strength to succeed, in
the face of the disunion of the German states, the prestige of the Emperor
and the terrors of the unseen, as represented by the priests.

LUTHER GIVING RELIGIOUS INSTRUCTION TO CHILDREN.

But Luther's letters undoubtedly lay him open to some charges difficult
to refute. For instance, in a letter to Melanchthon, he says:
"If you are a preacher of grace, preach not a fictitious grace,   **Dangerous
teaching on
sin.**
but a true grace. If it is a true grace, let it conquer true, not
fictitious sin. God does not save fictitious sinners. Be a sinner and sin

bravely (or sturdily); but still more bravely believe and rejoice in Christ, who is the conqueror of sin, of death, and of the world. Sin is a necessity, so long as we are in our present state. It is enough that we have known, through the riches of glory, the Lamb of God, that taketh away the sins of the world. From Him sin will not separate us, although a thousand thousand times in one day we commit fornication or murder. . . . Pray bravely, for you are the bravest of sinners."

It is one of the misfortunes connected with vehement natures, that when powerfully moved they go to extremes, totally regardless of the bearing of their language or acts in some direction quite apart from the one they have in view. Thus they prepare for their followers stumbling-blocks, and provide points of attack for adverse critics. At the same time they are delivered from the snare of being worshipped; for the clay in their composition is evident. No doubt Luther had been greatly exasperated by having forced upon his notice those namby-pamby sinners and dilettante saints, whose temptations are less than a pin's prick to a robust warrior, and whose saintliness is as the faint gloss on a thin sheet of paper compared with the hammered-on mail of a brave man-of-war. Strenuous himself, full of powerful impulses, he could respect the robust sinner whose sins were human yieldings to natural impulses, and whose repentance was an equally sincere homage to God, and an intense heartfelt cry for pardon, through the merits of Christ,—while he despised the feeble, vacillating, rosewater sinner, doing wrong from very feebleness of nature, and holding to the right with an equally feeble grasp. "Be in earnest in whatever you do," he says. "If you have been a great sinner, God has provided a greater redemption." It has been suggested that this letter, or part of it, is a forgery, and also that it is simply a hyperbolical way of expressing the heinousness of sin and the magnificence of redemption. But it appears simpler to admit this letter as genuine, and with considerable sorrow at its violence of language, to explain it as an instance of those extremes into which Luther was not unfrequently carried by that very vehemence of nature of which we have spoken.

Clerical celibacy, monastic vows, and auricular confession, were among the important subjects on which Luther now came to a definite conclusion. His own experience provided him with sufficient arguments

Clerical celibacy. against celibacy as an enforced discipline. The language of St. Paul in 1 Tim. iv., identifying those who forbid marriage as "seducing spirits" and "teachers of devils' doctrines," was borne out by his own knowledge of the vices encouraged by clerical celibacy. Luther rightly discerned the type of Christian pastor described by St. Paul, as a minister working among men whose temptations and experiences were like his own, not a priest of a separate caste. On monastic vows he was also becoming clear. He decisively pronounced against the validity of all vows taken under compulsion, and those taken by persons under the age of mature choice or under adult years. Again, monastic vows taken as a means of securing salvation, under the belief in their efficacy, he declared void from their certain lack of efficacy in that direction. He now acknowledged to his father that he had been wrong in his own hasty assumption of monastic vows. He was quite ready to give up all obligations of the kind that were inconsistent with free Christian life. Especially did he clearly discern the true value of the so-called chastity of the monastic state, and he transferred that term to the pure natural married life. The ideal of Scripture is purity in the unmarried, and the true faithful union of the married.

Concerning auricular confession, Luther himself acknowledged the frequent benefit he had received from it. He thought it was often an advantage to a man to confess, to declare his repentance, to the minister of God's word; yet he considered the practice open to <small>Luther on Confession.</small> many abuses, and especially when celibate priests received the confessions of maidens and wives, and questioned them in detail. But confession was to be made, according to St. James, " one to another; " "whence it should follow that the confessors should confess likewise to <small>Luther's Works, vol. 17.</small> their penitents," a very different ideal to that of the Roman Church.

In 1521 the Mass, too, became repugnant to him. He resolved never again to celebrate a private mass. But the most important work which Luther accomplished in the Wartburg was certainly his translation of the Bible, beginning with the New Testament, <small>Translation of the Bible.</small> from the original Greek, according to Erasmus's fourth edition. He had already translated detached portions, which were eagerly welcomed. He possessed various special qualifications for the work. A man sprung from the people, a man socially inclined, he was familiar with the people's language, he knew the power of idiomatic phrases, the adhesive power of simple, vigorous words. He also was steeped in Bible thought, in the atmosphere and aroma of Scripture. He was, above all things, in earnest, as the prophets were in earnest. He knew the Bible tongues as few men of his time knew them. His native Saxon or Franconian, used by the emperor and princes, and most widely spread of all the German dialects, was the vehicle of his translation; and he wielded it with such skill that his Bible became the standard of German, as the English translation became the backbone of English. The New Testament in German was published on September 21st, 1522. When he came to work upon the Old Testament, late in 1522, a sort of syndicate of translators, including Melanchthon, met once a week in Luther's house, and Luther describes them as labouring hard at the difficult task of bringing out the prophets in the Teuton language, making the Hebrew writers speak German.

Another movement was progressing, without Luther's aid, in the Augustinian monastery at Wittenberg. The Reformation

HOUSE AT FRANKFORT INHABITED BY LUTHER.

Retirement of Augustinian Monks.

had been earnestly preached there by Gabriel Zwilling, who demanded the abolition of private masses and administration of the eucharist in both kinds. The prior held out against the unanimous opinion of the monks; but their vehement declaration led the theological faculty of Wittenberg to declare in their favour. Melanchthon's fifty-five propositions, expounding the non-sacrificial character of the mass, were powerful weapons in the contest; and the mass itself was only saved for the time by the authority of the Elector Frederick. Zwilling then proceeded to attack the entire monastic system. "No one in a convent," he asserted, "keeps God's commandments. Vows of chastity, poverty and obedience, are contrary to the Gospel." The result was, that a body of thirteen monks left the monastery. A chapter of Augustinians in Thuringia held at Wittenberg, in December, agreed that monastic vows, though not sinful, were not obligatory, and that any monk who desired to do so was free to leave his cell. They also resolved to abolish the practice of begging extensively carried on by the monks, and the saying of masses for money. Of those who remained in the monasteries, it was decided that the more learned should become religious teachers, while the rest were to maintain themselves by their own labour.

In this place it may be well to note some facts concerning the man who was most prominent in Wittenberg during Luther's enforced retirement, Andrew Bodestein of Carlstadt, mostly known by the name of his native place. Carlstadt after studying at Rome and Witten- Carlstadt at Wittenberg. berg, at which latter place he was made professor of theology and archdeacon in 1513, had at first opposed Luther for his denunciation of scholastic theology; but afterwards ranged himself on the reformer's side; he, indeed, went to an extreme of mysticism. Although, according to Melanchthon, Carlstadt had neither sound learning nor deep piety, he was a sufficiently prominent personage to find himself attacked by Dr. Eck, and to conduct the earlier part of the famous Leipsic disputation, though he was not a match for Eck. In 1520 Carlstadt manifested a spirit of rivalry with Luther, in a work on the Scriptures, in which he attacked Luther, though he agreed with him as to the supreme authority of the Bible; but he stood firmly by Luther when the pope's bull against the great reformer was issued. In 1521, he took the lead at Wittenberg in attacking the Romish ceremonies and practices, publishing a treatise on celibacy and monasticism, and arguing constantly against the maintenance of the mass. He was one of those too eager men who precipitate changes without being strong or wise enough to pilot a ship safely through perilous waters. In The Mass Abolished. October, 1521, he celebrated the Lord's supper according to the reformed simple rite secretly, with twelve friends, and on the following

Christmas Day he celebrated it in the same way publicly in the parish church, pronouncing the words of consecration in German, and distributing the bread and wine to all comers. No open opposition arose, and the practice, as introduced by Carlstadt, continued and extended. Carlstadt married in January, 1522, and in the same month the university gave its sanction to a reformed scheme of services for the parish church.

A new element, afterwards productive of much danger and strife, was

THE WARTBURG, THE "PATMOS" OF LUTHER IN 1521.

now added to the Reformation. At Zwickau on the Bohemian frontier,

The Zwickau Prophets. numerous eager advocates of the reformed doctrines had gone far beyond Luther. Their faith had degenerated into fanaticism; they had become known as the Zwickau prophets. Chief among them was Nicholas Storck, a weaver, who professed to have received direct instruction concerning holy things from the angel Gabriel in a vision. This man chose twelve apostles and seventy-two disciples, and attempted to

revive apostolic methods of practice. He evidently anticipated his eleva-
tion to supreme authority. He and his adherents became separated from
the rest of the reformers by their hostility to infant baptism, and by their
uncompromising declaration that only adult baptism was of value. Later,
under Thomas Münzer, the Carlstadt division acquired a more thorough
organisation and became known as Anabaptists (re-baptizers). The Zwickau
pastor, a follower of Luther, rejected their pretensions, and after disturbing
the church services, they proceeded to Wittenberg. Here they asserted
their claim to immediate intercourse with God, and declared that they had
the power of prophesying things to come, and had received apostolic
authority.

Melanchthon was confounded at their assurance. But while he feared to
do anything against what might be a true work of God's Spirit, was at the
same time impressed by the plausibility of their doctrine of baptism. He
felt that the matter must be referred to Luther. The latter, when appealed
to, by no means approved of the Zwickau men; still he warned the Elector
of the danger of imprisoning them. Religious liberty had found in him a
true friend. Carlstadt, though he did not accept anabaptism, or several of
the extreme doctrines of the prophets, appeared to become more impetuous
from the day of their arrival, and was for precipitately abolishing all customs and practices which he held to be evil. In particular he was strong
in his attack on images, and his stirring language led to several   Extremes at
disturbances, in which churches were invaded and the images   Wittenberg.
and pictures they contained were battered and destroyed. A puritanic
mania seized on many spirits; many asserted that all places of amusement
ought to be closed. Carlstadt began even to despise academic study, and to
advise his pupils to return to their homes; in this matter the master of the
Wittenberg boys' school followed his example. Fanaticism and the anti-
liberal spirit were fast gaining ground.

Luther had already taken hurried counsel with his friends at Wittenberg
in a sudden and secret visit to that town in November, 1521; in March, 1522,
he felt called upon to risk everything, and reappear openly, dar-   Luther
ing all consequences. The condemnation of his doctrines by   reappears.
the Sorbonne, so ably answered by Melanchthon, had not been sufficient
to draw him from his place of refuge; but the disorder and degeneracy at
Wittenberg constrained him to come forward. The Elector besought him to
remain quietly at the Wartburg, especially because Duke George of
Saxony had moved the imperial government to more active measures

against such priests as departed from Roman forms and ceremonies. But Luther was not to be moved by fear. "I would have entered Worms," he wrote, "even though there had been as many devils in that city as there were tiles on the roofs." Duke George was far less to be dreaded than a single devil. Had the same things happened at Leipsic as at Wittenberg, Luther would have gone thither, "though it should rain Duke Georges for nine days, each nine times more furious than he." Luther asked for no special protection; any one who desired to seize or kill him might do so. His resolve was to rest on the protection of God alone.

Thus did Luther come forth from his Patmos to moderate the storm. He was received with enthusiasm. On Sunday the 9th of March, 1522, and on *Preaches in favour of charity and tolerance.* seven following days, he preached in the parish church, declaring vigorously his disapproval of the violent acts of which he had heard, and calling for the exercise of charity and tolerance. He reminded his hearers that he himself had been content to let the Word of God work its own results; he had never sought to do anything by violence, and he had refrained at Worms from every action that might bring about insurrection. "I will not use force or compulsion with any one. In this life every one must not do what he has a right to do, but must forego his rights, and consider what is useful to his brother. Do not make a 'must be' out of a 'may be,' as you have now been doing, that you may not have to answer for those whom you have misled by your uncharitable liberty." As he successively reviewed the chief doctrines and practices that required reforming, the congregations grew more and more interested. The fanatic passions which had been roused were allayed. Many acknowledged their error; even Carlstadt resumed his lectures.

When the principal "prophets," Storck and Stübner, returned to Wittenberg from a preaching journey, they sought an interview with Luther, *Interview with the prophets.* to whom they expounded their views. "Nothing you have said is based on Holy Scripture," he replied. "It is all mere fable." Cellarius, one of their ardent adherents, raved and stormed at this "shameful" speech. Luther calmly called on the prophets to prove their apostleship by miracles, as St. Paul had done. Stübner asserted that he could tell what was passing in Luther's mind, that he was beginning to believe in Stübner's doctrine. "The Lord rebuke thee, Satan!" exclaimed Luther. Still rougher language followed, Cellarius becoming more violent than ever. But the same day the prophets quitted Wittenberg, and peace was re-established.

Luther continued to live in the Augustinian monastery and to wear his monkish garb. The movement of the Reformation progressed, on the basis that nothing was to be rejected unless it was found to be opposed to a clear declaration of Scripture,—thus the German was separated from the Swiss movement, which latter rejected everything that was not distinctly authorised by Scripture. All violence was consistently discouraged by Luther. His "Address to all Christians to avoid uproar and insurrection," written before he had left the Wartburg, gives the keynote of his position on this matter. He considered that

Luther
discourages
violence.

LUTHER AND HIS WIFE, CATHARINA VON BORA.

only the civil magistrate had the right to use force; only by influencing the civil power were Christians permitted to seek change. Such was the teaching of Luther. But this method would leave Christian liberty at the mercy of tyrants.

Luther's influence induced Zwilling to resume his preaching, and Capito to leave the archbishop, and preach the gospel at Strasburg. The reformed doctrines, as set forth by Melanchthon in his "*Loci Communes*" or "Theological Common-places," were becoming widely spread. This compendium of theology based on Scrip-

Melanchthon's
"Common-
places."

ture, stated in simple clear language all that seemed most essential ; and Luther declared that it could not be refuted. In this early form it went almost to an extreme of fatalism, asserting that "all things happen necessarily ; " it represented God's grace as irresistible, working by His immutable will, thus denying man's freedom of will in everything. This view Melanchthon afterwards modified considerably. The scholarship and refine-

PHILIP MELANCHTHON, THE FRIEND OF LUTHER, BORN 1497, DIED 1560.

ment which this work displayed were of great service in securing adherents for the reformed doctrines.

The influence of the Wittenberg Reformers was spreading to England; but at first the interest felt in them appeared in strange guise. Henry **Luther and** VIII., so soon as he heard of the decree of the Diet of Worms **Henry VIII.** caused Luther's works to be burnt at St. Paul's. The king's vanity led him to attack Luther in terms of unbridled license, in his

" Defence of the Seven Sacraments." It was by this work he won from Leo
X. the title "Defender of the Faith." Luther had little difficulty in refuting the royal arguments; but his anger led him to retort upon the king
in equally strong language. " If a king of England," " spits his impudent
lies in my face, I have a right, in my turn, to throw them back down his
very throat. . . . He thought to himself, doubtless, 'Luther is so
hunted about, he will have no opportunity of replying to me.' . . .
Ah, ha, my worthy Henry! you have reckoned without your host in this
matter; you have had your say, and I will have mine; you shall hear truths
that will not amuse you at all; I'll make you smart for your tricks."
Bishop Fisher and Sir Thomas More both replied to Luther, and Henry
wrote to the Elector Frederick and the Duke of Saxony, charging them
promptly to extinguish Luther's sect, and to that end to shed blood fearlessly, if necessary.

About the same time Luther, in a treatise "on the Secular Power,"
showed his keen contempt for the wickedness and folly which characterised
the actions of most princes, and ridiculed their pretensions as " Defenders
of the Faith." Yet he had had some reason for satisfaction at
the attitude of the German Diet in 1522, at Nuremberg, which **Adrian VI and the Diet at Nuremberg.**
replied to the demand of the new pope, Adrian VI., for the
execution of the Edict of Worms, by rehearsing the grievances of Germany.
The new pope was prepared to receive a demand for gradual reform, but
found his intentions thwarted by a crowd of officials who profited by abuses.
The German Diet demanded the holding of a free œcumenical council of the
church within a year to correct abuses, and was content to leave matters
of doctrine open until then. When the papal legate desired to apprehend
the preachers who were proclaiming the reformed doctrines in Nuremberg,
the magistrates declared they would in such a case release them by force.
The Diet drew up a list of a hundred grievances of Germany **The Hundred Grievances.**
against Rome, mainly drawn from Luther's address to the
German nobility. Until these matters were decided upon, nothing was to be
taught except "the true, pure, sincere and holy Gospel and approved writings,"—what these approved writings were, was not clearly defined.

The papal legate could make no favourable answer; but Pope Adrian
soon after addressed the Elector Frederick in a brief which sought to win
him over, by calling Luther a sacrilegious man, who trampled **The Pope and Frederick.**
with his filthy feet on the images of the saints, and hounded on
the laity to imbrue their hands in the blood of the priests, and to overthrow

the churches; who stole away virgins consecrated to Christ, and gave them to the devil. Such false charges were little likely to make Frederick turn from Luther. On the contrary, he contemplated the probable necessity of taking up arms for the Reformation; Luther and Melanchthon deprecated this idea. Many princes, however, were influenced by the papal brief. Duke George of Saxony imprisoned monks and priests who followed Luther, ordered all copies of the German New Testament to be given up to the magistrates, and recalled Saxon students from Wittenberg and other **Persecutions** reforming universities. Austria, Wurtemberg, and Brunswick **of Lutherans.** adopted the same course; and in the Netherlands, which stood the immediate power of the Emperor Charles V., persecution began. The Augustinian monks at Antwerp, who had resolutely preached the Lutheran doctrines, were imprisoned and condemned to death. Some escaped; but on July 1, 1523, three of them—Henry Voes, John Esch, and Lambert Thorn, were burnt to death. The Prior Probst, who had at first retracted, afterwards returned to the Reformer's party, and finally escaped, to take refuge with Luther at Wittenberg. Many other persecutions of Lutherans took place within German states.

Pope Adrian died on the 14th of September, 1523. His successor, Clement VII., a member of the Medici family, was solely bent upon main- **Campeggio and** taining and increasing the papal authority. He sent one of **the Diet.** the ablest cardinals, Campeggio, to the next imperial diet, which met at Nuremberg, in January, 1524, with directions strenuously to demand the execution of the Edict of Worms. The Diet replied by asking what had become of the Hundred Grievances that were to have been discussed. The legate affected to have received no official information on the subject. The Diet promised to observe the Edict of Worms " as far as possible," which, in most German states, meant not all. The assembly urged with much insistence the demand for an œcumenical council, but also resolved that a Diet should be convoked for November, by which religious questions should be settled. That the controverted points might be satisfactorily dealt with, the several states were requested to obtain statements on the subject from their divines.

The adherents of the papal party were highly exasperated at the idea that a secular council should presume to decide on Church matters. The pope wrote to the emperor, and actively sought new supporters in Germany; he at last gained over the Dukes of Bavaria by giving up to them a fifth of the Bavarian church revenues. He felt sure of the support of the

Archduke of Austria, Charles V.'s brother, and other important princes. Towards the close of 1524, the anti-reforming princes met at Ratisbon, and bound themselves to carry out the Edicts of Worms and Nuremberg, to permit no changes in public worship, and to put down heresy by every means in their power. At the same time they admitted the need for some reforms, especially in the conduct of the priests. Cardinal Campeggio promised to put an end to certain papal abuses connected with appointments and indulgences. Thus the definite division of Germany into two camps was effected. *Convention of Ratisbon.*

On the other hand, Brandenburg, Franconia, and various states besides, agreed in condemning the mass and its abuses, the adoration of saints, and the pope's supremacy.

Meanwhile Luther's activity had been uninterrupted. Among a number of other publications, in 1523 he issued the "Order of the Worship of God," in which he provided a simplified arrangement for the services of the Church in German, with a moderate amount of deviation from the old Latin form of prayer. He next issued an "Order for the Mass" in Latin, which was soon afterwards translated into German, inserting numerous simple hymns. In 1524 his first German hymn-book appeared. A Baptismal Service followed, and then a prayer-book. A summary of Christian truth for the common people, and a short catechism for the instruction of children were among his next publications. His separate publications in 1522 amounted to a hundred and thirty; in 1523, to a hundred and eighty. While at first he had stood almost alone as an anti-Roman author, in 1523 there were no fewer than two hundred and fifteen publications in Germany on his side; while only twenty Romanist works were put forth to oppose him. *Luther's publications.*

In the midst of his extraordinary literary activity, Luther visited many parts of Germany, preaching as opportunity offered. Thus at Zwickau, within the territories of Duke George, he preached to twenty-five thousand hearers in the public square. In many other places his followers boldly set forth his doctrines. Wittenberg had become the centre of a great national movement.

We must here briefly refer to a movement which, professing to be on Luther's side, did great harm to the Reformation,—the War of the Knights, under Franz von Sickingen, who acted under the influence of the accomplished and eccentric Ulrich von Hutten. Fascinated by the idea of uniting all Germany under the Emperor by the *The Knights' War.*

dethronement of the princes, Sickingen, in 1522, attacked the Elector Archbishop of Treves. His party adopted extreme reforming opinions from Switzerland, and called on Luther to support them. But he refused, maintaining his policy of holding entirely aloof from political complications.

FRANZ VON SICKINGEN.
From a Portrait by Albert Dürer.

After some months of warfare, Sickingen's enterprise failed, and he himself, besieged in his castle of Landshut by the Landgrave Philip of Hesse and the Palsgrave Louis, was mortally wounded, and died in May, 1523. Luther's cause was somewhat damaged by his abortive attempt.

At first Luther was for reconstructing everything in Church organisation on apostolic lines. He was against irrevocable vows, and considered the priest should be elected by the suffrages of the people, and afterwards confirmed by the bishop. All Christians, he wrote, were priests;— all might teach the word of God, administer baptism, and consecrate

Luther on Church Organisms.

the bread and wine. If the minister ceased to be faithful to his trust, he ought to be deposed. But he was far from desiring to subject all churches to one unvarying rule; nor did he think there should be a Council of

Reformers to establish uniformity of ceremonies. He certainly was not a perfect organiser; he was rather a giant warrior.

In October, 1524, though still continuing to live in the convent, Luther finally put aside the monastic garb, and adopted a gown such as the Lutheran clergy still wear in Germany. Many nuns who had left convents sought his aid towards their restoration to society; and he actu-

THE PEASANT WAR: THE INSURGENTS AND THEIR LEADERS.

ally maintained many of them for considerable periods. He gave wise advice as to the distribution of monastic funds when the monks quitted their cells. One of a company of nine liberated nuns was Catherine von Bora, a woman of a noble Saxon family. She obtained a position of usefulness in Wittenberg, where Luther often met her. At first he regarded her as proud. He was, moreover, frightened at the idea of a monk marrying, and often expressed his unwillingness to marry. Luther had in-

K

terested himself to get Catherine comfortably married.   The lady had, in refusing a proposed match, declared herself to be willing to marry Luther or his friend Amsdorf, but she would not accept the man who offered his hand.   This caused Luther to reconsider the question of his
His marriage. marrying, and by May, 1525, he had arranged, much to his father's satisfaction, to marry Catherine.   In June, 1525, he took her to wife himself.   She proved a most valuable helpmeet, resolute and clever.   She bore him numerous children, towards whom his affection was most attractively displayed.   This marriage of Luther, as a public action, was more important than the corresponding step taken by Zwingli. The latter married simply as a priest.   He was not under monastic vows, Luther and his wife had both taken monastic vows of celibacy, and their breaking through these signified that they abandoned the belief in the binding nature of such engagements, and in the holiness of monastic life. Luther became a strong advocate of marriage for priest, prince, and peasant alike.

Carlstadt had retired, some time before this, from the Wittenberg arena, worsted in conflict with Luther, who could not endure his unstable,
Carlstadt's proceedings. frequently extravagant, teaching.   Carlstadt laid more stress upon the opposition to Roman ceremonies and doctrines than upon the foundation of Christian life in the Gospel, and wanted his own views to prevail.   He came especially into conflict with Luther on the subject of the Eucharist, which Luther interpreted in a sense partly Romish, especially asserting both the real presence of Christ and the continuance of bread and wine in the consecrated elements.   Carlstadt went so far as to deny even the spiritual presence of Christ in the sacrament, and this, in Luther's eyes, profaned the Eucharist.   The two men could not continue to teach in harmony in the same town.   Accordingly, in 1523, Carlstadt left Wittenberg, and took the pastorate of Orlamunde, where he preached his doctrines in a form calculated to excite the peasantry to violence against the Church.   Thence he went to Jena, and set up a printing press to distribute his works.   On being recalled to Wittenberg, whence he still continued to draw his salary, and being visited at Jena and argued with by Luther, Carlstadt represented himself as suffering persecution from his fellow reformer.   Banished, thereupon, from Saxony by Frederick the Elector, he betook himself to Strasburg, and then to Basle, where he published several treatises.

Luther was next brought into relation with the Peasants' War—a tremendous outbreak, of which Thomas Münzer, one of the Zwickau prophets, had taken advantage to promulgate and spread his lawless and fanatical religious opinions. He had been expelled from Saxony, and proceeded to the Upper Rhine district on the Swiss frontier, where **Münzer and the** his anabaptist doctrine found much support. He demanded **Peasants' War.** the organisation of an army of saints who should be ready for any Divine work. This idea exactly suited the discontented peasantry of that time, smarting under many grievances. Luther felt compelled, in a letter to the Saxon princes, vehemently to attack the "false prophets"; exposing the fallacies of their doctrines, and showing the wisdom of his own method. Münzer had reviled Luther for his sociability and his anti-ascetic doctrine. Luther defended himself, and attacked Münzer's asceticism. He also strongly deprecated Münzer's appeal to force. The peasants' movement grew into a revolt. The more moderate among them appealed to Luther for aid, and stated their case in twelve articles. Besides demanding the redress of political grievances and relief from oppression, they claimed for the congregations the right of choosing and of dismissing their ministers, the abolition of compulsory feudal service, and an appeal to the Scriptures on doubtful points of religion. Luther, in an address to the lords, adequately acknowledged the grievances of the peasants, and urged reform; but he strongly discouraged the peasants' appeal to force.

The outbreak became more violent, and various outrages were committed on the nobles and princes. Whereupon, in the heat of his indignation, Luther issued a violent pamphlet "Against the Robbing, Murdering hordes of Peasants," which contains advice to massacre the peasants like mad dogs. The princes roused themselves, and the revolt was put down with ruthless cruelty and slaughter in 1525.

Many moderate persons suffered because they were friendly to the Reformation. Luther had gone too far, and had damaged his own cause. He learnt that war is a great evil, and, when once set on foot, often does more harm than good even to a just cause. His enemies took advantage of a warlike condition of things to persecute his adherents, and even his own congregations in friendly states were demoralised. In May, 1525, died Luther's patron, the Elector Frederick VII. of Saxony, sur- **Death of the** named the Wise. He had been a true friend of reform, and his **Elector Frederick.** last words to his people are worthy of record. "Dear children," he wrote, "if I have ever offended any of you, I pray you to forgive me for the love of God; we princes do many things to the poor people that we ought not to do." He seemed to have a presentiment of the modern reign of democracy, for he wrote to his brother and successor, John, "If God wills to have it so, things will turn out in a way to bring about government by the common man." In the same month Münzer was defeated, taken prisoner, and executed.

ELECTOR JOHN FREDERICK OF SAXONY.

Matters looked dark for the reforming movement. No new princes were gained over, and some who had previously favoured the reformers now sought to temporise with the papal party. Nothing was decided with regard to religious matters at the Augsburg Diet of 1525. But the princes who really cared for reform drew more closely together. In February, 1526, the Landgrave Philip of Hesse, the most energetic leader among them, and the Elector John of Saxony, ratified a formal alliance at Torgau. The latter had already decided to abolish, in his own territory, all rites that were contrary to Scripture. Albert, Margrave of Brandenburg, afterwards Duke of Prussia, Grand Master of the Teutonic Knights, by Luther's advice absolved all the knights from their vows, and the monasteries in his states

Progress of Reform.

were converted into hospitals. In 1525 many steps were taken toward establishing the new church order. An especially important measure was the ordination of ministers by the reformers at Wittenberg. This followed naturally from Luther's principles. He denied the Divine right of bishops as a distinct spiritual order. All clergymen were the servants, the ministers of the congregation.

Many of the reforming princes met at Magdeburg, early in June, 1526, and solemnly pledged "their estates, lives, states, and subjects, for the maintenance of the holy Word of God." Luther and Melanchthon were for peaceful measures, but the Romish party made no secret of their resolve to crush the new heresy. The emperor deputed his brother the Archduke Ferdinand to preside at the Diet of Spires, in June, instructing him to carry out his wishes. The Diet, being bidden to consult as to ways and means of establishing good Christian faith and order, pending the meeting of a free council of the Church, attempted to arrive at a solution of difficulties by appointing committees to consider means for reforming abuses in the Church. The committee of princes, including several prince bishops, agreed to permit the marriage of clerics, and administration of the Sacrament in both kinds, the abolition of private masses, and the use of German with Latin in the Church services. It was also agreed that the Word of God should be preached according to sound understanding, Scripture being always interpreted by Scripture.

The Diet of Spires, 1526.

At a final general committee, strongly reforming resolutions were about to be passed, when an admonition from the emperor was issued, requiring that nothing should be done contrary to the established doctrine or practice of the Church, and that the Edict of Worms should be carried out. This injunction produced a great effect, as it was evident that the emperor if openly opposed, intended an appeal to force. But before the Diet had time to send its message representing the impossibility of executing the edict, the emperor had modified his line of action, so far as to consent to the suspension of the edict, and to acquiesce in the demand for a Church council. A compromise was thus effected, whereby, in September, 1526, the Diet agreed that until the meeting of a general council each state should so act and bear itself, in all matters concerning the Edict of Worms, "as it hoped and trusted to answer for it to God and the emperor," a temporising, whose effect was to give time to the reform movement to consolidate and organise itself. The temporary peace in Germany enabled Charles V. to undertake active measures against the pope, with whom he had quarrelled; and the Reformers, in 1827, beheld this great supporter of the papacy seize Italy and sack Rome. When the "two swords" of the Church, the spiritual and the temporal, were thus turned one against the other, there appeared to be great hope for the progress of free religious reform.

BERNE, ONE OF THE CHIEF SEATS OF THE REFORMATION.

CHAPTER X.

𝕮𝖍𝖊 𝕽𝖊𝖋𝖔𝖗𝖒𝖆𝖙𝖎𝖔𝖓 𝖎𝖓 𝕹𝖔𝖗𝖙𝖍-𝖂𝖊𝖘𝖙 𝕾𝖜𝖎𝖙𝖟𝖊𝖗𝖑𝖆𝖓𝖉, 𝖋𝖗𝖔𝖒 1525 𝖙𝖔 1531.

Zwingli compared with Luther—Church order at Zurich—Berne—Erasmus at Basle—Œcolampadius—Disputes with Eck at Baden—The Anabaptists—The Berne Disputation—Reform in Basle—Discussion at Marburg—League of Catholic Cantons—Battle of Kappel—Death of Zwingli—His Character—His Doctrines—Predestination—The Sacraments—Universal Sinfulness of Man—Salvation of Children.

IT has already been noted that Zwingli broke more completely with Rome and Romish practices than Luther. Zwingli was what we should now term a more radical reformer than the Wittenberg doctor. He was less in sympathy with the historical growths which had arisen within the Christian community, but entirely gave himself up to whatever could be founded upon, and proved from, Scripture. Purification of the Church from positive error and abuse was the leading idea of the German reformer, restoration of the Church to

Zwingli compared with Luther.

apostolic standards and practices was that of his Swiss contemporary. Zwingli had been born and educated in a free state exempt from the rule of princes; Luther had never been outside their predominating influence. Both reformers were opposed to excesses; but the systems they established were singularly influenced by the civil conditions of their respective states.

In the year 1525, Zwingli succeeded in introducing a complete Christian order into Zurich. The affairs of religion were controlled by a synod, consisting of all the clergy, and several members of the great council of Zurich; and this synod exercised episcopal functions. Men were elected by each congregation, to co-operate with the pastor, to maintain a proper observance of the sabbath and the due keeping of the marriage vows, and to admonish those who led an unchristian life. The final disciplinary step was to exclude an offender from the Eucharist, and if he infringed civil laws, to denounce him to the authorities. Zwingli was able to report concerning his new church system: " The apostolic, true, holy church of God has the real pure doctrine, of prayer, breaking of bread, holy baptism, confession, repentance, amendments, and forgiveness of sins. This the church at Zurich has also. The customs the early church considered necessary, the church at Zurich also maintains. Marriage, she confirms in good order, and with prayer to God. The saints are remembered with honour, whose love and faith are to be imitated. The dead are buried decently, but without observing ceremonies which are not authorised in the word of God. Fasting and almsgiving, which were highly valued by the early Christians, have also in Zurich their honourable Christian order. The beloved young ones are diligently instructed in the fundamental doctrines of the true Christian religion. That it has no external ornaments of gold and silver, pictures, carved and engraved images, is owing to the fact that the early church did not have these things, and even rejected them, therefore the church at Zurich laid aside the ceremonies and returned to ancient simplicity." This was a truly noble and high-minded scheme of life and church government. If we have now a fuller life, religious and civil, a more expansive ideal, it is still folly to look down upon and disparage the steps by which the present stage of developement was rendered possible. And after the abuses of indulgences, relic and image worship, private masses and other Roman appliances had been put down, it was essential that one or more Puritan periods of reaction should follow.

Church order at Zurich.

It is not necessary to particularise all the stages of the reforming movement in other cantons. In Berne the De Wattevilles and Berthold

Berne. Haller worked energetically for reform; and the council, while discountenancing Luther's writings, enjoined free preaching, on the basis of the Old and New Testaments only. On the other hand, it banished two controversialists: Sebastian Meyer, an anti-monachist, and Heim, a champion of the Romish mass and of the doctrine of good works. Many nuns, nevertheless, left the convents and married.

At Basle, Erasmus, of whose life we shall have to speak further, had in 1524 published those "Colloquies" in which monkish practices, fasts and

Erasmus at Basle. indulgences, and many other Romish abuses are so effectively ridiculed. The Colloquies were followed in 1525 by his book on Free-will, a work written to refute Luther's doctrine of attributing everything to the grace of God; and this was succeeded by other anti-Lutheran writings. But by his Greek New Testament, Erasmus more than counterbalanced the harm done to the cause of the Reformation by anything he wrote.

DESIDERIUS ERASMUS, BORN AT ROTTERDAM, 1467; DIED AT BASLE, 1536.

Meanwhile Œcolampadius, who had a chequered career, first as pastor of Basle, from **Œcolampadius.** 1515 to 1518, next as pastor of Augsburg, then as a monk, and afterwards as chaplain to Franz von Sickingen, returned to Basle at the end of 1522, and was advised by Zwingli at the Zurich disputation, to make a firm stand for the reformed doctrines. When he attempted to introduce these at Basle he found that the learned scholars of the university were altogether disinclined to make changes; and it was not till after Œcolampadius had spent a year in successful preaching and public disputations, that the council were induced

Dispute with Eck at Baden. to make some reforms in the convents, and to sanction the discontinuance of some superstitious practices. In 1526 he was selected in Zwingli's place, to dispute with the redoubtable Eck at Baden, and eighteen days were spent in discussing the principal tenets of Zwingli, Eck exhibiting throughout the conference his old violence of manner and expression. A versifier of the time has thus satirised this fervid controversialist's peculiarities of manner.

> " Eck stamps, and thumps, and storms and swears,—
> And, as his creed, he still declares
> Whate'er the pope and cardinals
> Pronounce as doctrine to their thralls."

Œcolampadius, with his calm placidity, courage and ability, which made his opponents wish he was on their side, was a perfect contrast to the violent Eck. Berthold Haller followed, and then Œcolampadius resumed the argument. On some points Eck could only appeal to the usage of the church. Every day Zwingli received reports of what had passed, and sent advice to his champions. At the close, Eck's thesis was signed by the great majority of those present. There was great scoffing at Zwingli's non-appearance, which was due to fear for his personal safety among such inveterate enemies; and the Diet declared that Zwingli, who had stayed away, and his followers who had "refused to allow themselves to be convinced," were excluded from the universal church.

But the reports received from Baden impressed the religious community of Basle and Berne in favour of Œcolampadius and Haller. At St. Gall images were removed from the parish churches, and the people sold their jewels and golden ornaments to found charitable institutions with the proceeds. In many other places, the reform movement progressed rapidly after the Baden disputation.

The anabaptists, expelled from Germany, had meanwhile taken refuge in Switzerland, and had gained over to their side several Swiss converts of importance, including Conrad Gaebel, Felix Manz, Roubli, formerly pastor of Basle, and Lewis Herzer. They endeavoured to form a community of their own, and made such progress that the Zurich Council held a public disputation concerning their doctrines, in November, 1525. The anabaptists were unconvinced, and contradiction rendered them more fanatical. Some of them, who belonged to Zurich, were imprisoned, and the strangers were banished. An eloquent friar surnamed Blaurock, joined them; and Gaebel gained great influence in St. Gall. A treatise on baptism, written by Zwingli, roused them to fury; and they exhibited wild excitement, mingled with the most childish behaviour, in the streets and public places; alleging as a reason, that Christ had enjoined His

The Anabaptists.

disciples to become as little children.   A fanatical murder perpetrated at an anabaptist feast on Shrove Tuesday, 1526, near St Gall, roused sensible men to put down their excesses.   But the fanatics went further than ever in their follies.   Thereupon their opponents drowned Manz on Jan. 5th, 1527, and scourged Blaurock with cords.   That unhappy man proved

EXCESS OF THE REFORMATION, CAPTURED CITIZENS TRIED BY AN ANABAPTIST LEADER.

equally unacceptable to Catholics and Reformers; and he was at last burnt to death in 1529, by the Roman Catholics, in the Tyrol.   Thus it became fully manifest, that the Reform movement had not yet produced true religious liberty.   There was, unfortunately, too great a confusion between civil and religious authority.   The idea of entire freedom in forming religious opinions was not grasped.   The doctrine of infallibility reigned

in both camps, only in each it was based on a different principle. It
had yet to dawn on Reformers that the most diverse interpretations and
systems could be drawn from, or built upon, their infallible Scriptures. It
is satisfactory to find that Zwingli took no part in these extreme measures
adopted against the anabaptists.

In 1527, matters came to a crisis in Berne. The friends of reform
gained a majority in the councils, and discussions in every parish
strengthened and developed public opinion against the mass *The Berne Dis-*
and the papal system. A number of the city companies declared *putation.*
for reform, and discontinued their Romish practices. When public opinion
had ripened, the Council of Berne resolved to call an assembly, open to all
Swiss, priests and laymen, to discuss disputed points, on the basis of the
Bible alone. The Swiss bishops refused to attend; but the number of
ecclesiastics present amounted to three hundred and fifty. The first
meeting was on the 7th of January, 1528. The reformers were led by
Zwingli, Haller, Œcolampadius, Bucer and Capito: while Treger of Freiburg
was the only disputant of note on the Catholic side. The first thesis of
the Reformers affirmed that the Christian church, of which Christ is the
sole head, is born of the Word of God, abides therein, and does not listen
to the voice of a stranger. The next point of discussion declared that
Christ was the only salvation,—that church laws were rightly derived
only from the Word of God. Then followed a thesis denying that there
was any proof in Scripture that the body and blood of Christ are
corporeally present in the bread and wine of the Eucharist,—and another
thesis contained an equally explicit denial of the sacrificial character of
the mass. Zwingli set forth this thesis of denial so powerfully in church
on the 19th of January, that a priest, then about to celebrate mass in one
of the chapels, became violently agitated, and publicly stripped off his
sacerdotal vestments, declaring, "If the mass does not rest on a more
solid foundation, I can celebrate it no longer."

This conversion of a priest at the very altar struck the Romanists dumb.
Three days afterwards, on the festival of St. Vincent, the patron saint of
the city of Berne, no priest appeared at church to say mass. An organist
at vespers, being left alone, played a morning hymn. Thereupon some
violent partisans made an attack upon the organ and destroyed it, thus
commencing that savage antagonism to musical instruments, which continued among Scotch Presbyterians till quite recent years.

Various other articles were denounced as contrary to scripture, as prayers

to saints, the doctrine of purgatory, the adoration of images and pictures,
Victory of the Reformers. and the celibacy of the clergy. The papal opposition was feeble; and finally the Bernese councils decided that the mass should be abolished, and that all ornaments might be removed from churches by those who had placed them there. As might have been expected, this decision was followed by some lamentable scenes of destruction. Zwingli preached with great power in the cathedral on the 28th of January, commenting forcibly on the images which lay before him, "conquered, mute, and shattered," and urging the people to maintain the liberty they had acquired. On the 7th of February, 1528, the councils definitely threw off the yoke of the Romish bishops. The rural parishes almost unanimously accepted the Reformation. In Berne, an active Puritanism soon made itself manifest; excesses of all kinds were repressed, and a consistory was appointed to watch over public morals. The monasteries were transformed into charitable institutions, and their monks and nuns, the former occupants, were pensioned off. At Easter the Eucharist was received by vast congregations according to the reformed practice of Zwingli. Berne joined Zurich and Constance in a union in defence of the Reformation. To this union before long were added St. Gall, Schaffhausen, Basle and Mühlhausen.

In Basle a long struggle went on, much influenced by the action of Berne. Œcolampadius gained more and more influence. He married a **Reform in Basle.** widow, and Erasmus sneered at "the comedy," as he called it. But Œcolampadius was in the ascendant, and the Reform tendency became so marked that Erasmus resolved to leave the city. In the place of the Romanising professors, Oswald Myconius, Sebastian Münster, and other Reformers were invited to Basle. The religious change was not effected without a democratic uprising, which not only achieved its primary object, the reform of religion, but also secured for the householders a share in the election of the councils. Bonfires were lighted in the cathedral close, to burn the fragments of the altars and ornaments of the church.

The Diet of Spires, early in 1529, had produced the celebrated Protest of the German Reforming princes. Charles V. and the papal party prepared to crush the reformers. Many of these, noting the divergences between the doctrines of Luther and Zwingli, saw how much stronger the Reformation would become if its adherents were all agreed on the most important points; and sought to bring about an alliance between the

Swiss and the German Protestant States. Philip of Hesse, in particular, desired to secure this end. But Luther's violent maintenance of his own opinions on the Eucharist stood in the way. He had more than once acrimoniously attacked the Zwinglian teaching, and scorned Zwingli's calm and charitable appeals for peace and concord.

Philip of Hesse took the initiative in inviting Zwingli and other Swiss theologians to meet and discuss matters at Marburg. Melanchthon

VIEW OF MARBURG, THE SEAT OF THE CONFERENCE OF 1529.

regarded the project with favour, for he did not attach much importance to the differences of opinion between Zwingli and Luther. The latter was with difficulty persuaded to be present. Zwingli's attendance was not favoured by the Zurich council, owing to the dangers apprehended from the papists. He set out secretly by night for Marburg. Œcolampadius was the other principal Swiss disputant. The Reformers were agreed as to fourteen articles and were divided on the fifteenth; Luther affirming and Zwingli denying the corporeal presence of the Body and Blood of Christ in the Eucharist. It is to be lamented that Luther showed considerable intolerance of any view differing from his own, and at one interview sternly refused Zwingli's proffered hand. But an amicable conclusion was finally arrived at, and thus an important gain resulted from the conference. Yet Zwingli was by no means satisfied when he quitted Marburg. "Lutheranism," he wrote to Philip of Hesse, "will be as heavy as popery." Both Luther and Zwingli claimed the victory; but Zwingli certainly gained more supporters for his doctrines through the Marburg conference than he lost.

Earlier in the same year, war had been imminent between Reformers and Catholics in Switzerland. The five Catholic Cantons of Lucerne, Zug, Uri, Schwyz, and Unterwalden, had concluded a league,

League of Catholic Cantons. with Ferdinand of Austria; and when it came to their turn, alternately with Zurich, to control Thurgau and the other districts on the Upper Rhine, they oppressed the reformers, treated them with great cruelty, and put several to death. Zurich stood up for freedom in religious matters, and prepared for war. Zwingli wrote to his friends in Berne: "The existing peace, which many continue to favour, in reality is war; the war that I desire is peace. There is no security for the truth, nor any safety for its confessors, unless the pillars of tyrannical government are overthrown. Undoubtedly we are called upon to trust in God alone; but we are also called upon to defend our righteous cause, and like Gideon and Joshua, pour out our blood for God and fatherland." Such were the principles on which Zwingli advocated a resort to arms; and it is very difficult to gainsay them, except on the basis of passive obedience and complete non-resistance.

Thus Zwingli took up arms with his fellow townsmen; but Berne hung back, leaving Zurich to bear the brunt of the combat. Zurich was in the field before the allied Catholics were ready; they accordingly sought a truce. Some honourable incidents brightened the life of the camps, such as the dismissal, on one occasion, of hungry Catholic captives, fed and refreshed, by the Zurichers, and the supplying of distressed Catholic soldiers with bread on another. On the 26th of June, 1529, a treaty of

Peace of Kappel. peace was signed at Kappel. Its principal article declared that neither party should attack the other on account of any article of religion, and that the districts alternately governed by both might decide, by a vote, whether they would adopt the Reformation." At the same time the forest cantons agreed to give up their alliance with Austria.

But Zwingli felt that this was but a hollow peace. The Romanists continued to persecute the reformers. Zwingli fully perceived that the true solution of the difficulty lay in the formation of an equitable representative government, and in the cessation of the control of outlying districts by the forest cantons. Therefore, he wished to get rid of the undue preponderance they then enjoyed in the Diet. He urged Zurich and Berne to keep up an agitation until they should secure this object; but Berne hung back, desiring in the first instance to achieve religious freedom alone. It advocated the closing of frontier lines of the forest states, in order to cut off their Blockade of supplies, and stop all intercourse with them. Zurich was unwill- forest Cantons. ing to go to this length, and Zwingli strongly opposed the measure. But Berne insisted, and the step was taken. The result was as injurious to the trade of Zurich as to the welfare of the Catholic cantons. Zwingli's opponents in Zurich grew stronger, and openly derided him; consequently, on the 26th of July, 1531, he appeared before the Grand Council, and resigned his pastorship. It was at once felt that this resignation, if carried out, would be a ruinous blow to Zurich, and he was strongly importuned to withdraw it. After a hesitation of three days, caused by unsatisfactory principles actuating many of the chief men of Zurich, Zwingli resumed his pastorate and his incessant labours for the gospel. He urged the abandoning of the frontier blockade, which was exasperating the forest cantons, and intensifying their opposition to religious reform. Thereupon, the forest states secretly armed; and it was announced at Zurich, too late for any practical good, that Kappel was threatened by a large Battle of force. Zwingli marched out, according to Swiss custom, with Kappel. the Zurich troops; but they were hopelessly inferior to their opponents in numbers, and a great body of ardent reformers perished on the disastrous ▮▮▮ on the 11th of October, 1531, including twenty-five ▮▮▮ them was Zwingli himself, who when attacked made no ▮▮▮ His death was considered the greatest loss of all. When mortally wounded, he said; "What matters it? They can kill Zwingli killed. the body, but not the soul." These words form the inscription on a great boulder, that marks the spot where Zwingli died. The rage and hatred that animated the Catholic army may be judged by the fact that the great Reformer's body was hacked to pieces, and burnt, and his ashes were scattered to the winds. Grief at this terrible disaster killed Œcolampadius, who died on the 24th of November. All Catholic Germany and Switzerland exulted; the Reformed party mourned. But Leo Judah,

Zwingli's faithful assistant, took courage, and said: "He yet lives, and will for ever live. The noble hero has left a memorial of renown that no flame of fire can consume."

Ulrich Zwingli was a truly independent and original father of the Reformation. Bred in an atmosphere of very considerable liberty, he was **His character.** never enslaved by Rome, and he gradually developed a conception of a purified church, which, considering his time, and the visible example he had to guide him, was extraordinary for its boldness, its foundation upon the general popular voice and support, and the extent to which it satisfied religious needs. And, to a considerable extent, he saw his ideal realised in Zurich and elsewhere. Nor was his statemanship less enlightened than his views of church government. In private life and in social intercourse he was uniformly genial and urbane. On festive occasions, he often contributed to the general enjoyment by playing a musical instrument, and by singing hymns, of which he had composed both the music and the verses. It was natural that his chief subjects of conversation were the Bible, so long a sealed book to the masses, and the matters that bore upon the reform of church and state. He was remarkable for simplicity of life, and his general cheerfulness was conspicuous; but his indignation could at times be fiery and scathing. He had what many Reformers lacked, considerable capacity for toleration.

His labours were great, but his habits of orderly despatch enabled him to work rapidly. He wrote much, but his literary works were eclipsed **His Doctrines.** by those of Luther and Calvin. His main doctrines are contained in the theses of 1523 at Zurich, those of 1528 at Bern, in his confession of faith sent to Charles V. at the Diet of Augsburg, 1530, and another similar declaration addressed to Francis in July 1531. In the latter document he says: "We do and the sacraments, we only guard them against as the perpetual Virgin and Mother of God;[1] but we do not in the proper sense of the term, which we know she herself tolerate. The sacraments we honour as signs or symbols but not as the holy things themselves."

Basing his teaching on the supreme authority of Scripture, Zwingli viewed the salvation of sinners as due to unconditional election or predestination, faith being only the organ of appropriation. Herein he differed

[1] Using the term as restricted to the human nature united with the Divine Word or Logos.

from Luther, who placed faith in the background. The fall of man, Zwingli regarded as foreknown and foreordained; but though God fore-ordained sin, His action is free from sin, for He is not bound **Predestination.** by law. Those who hear the gospel and reject it in unbelief, are foreordained to eternal punishment. But he allowed that there might be many heathen destined to salvation. This doctrine of predestination in the main accords with that of St. Augustine.

THE CASTLE OF HEIDELBERG, IN THE PALATINATE.

The sacraments of baptism and the Lord's Supper Zwingli taught no absolute and necessary connection between the sign and the signified. Communion with Christ, he declared, does **The** not depend on the act of the priest, but on the faith of the reci- **Sacraments.** pient. Yet he considered the sacraments, as divinely instituted, necessary and efficacious, not empty signs. "They are also," he said, "means of grace, and public testimonies of faith." The Lord's Supper is a commemoration, not a repetition of Christ's atoning sacrifice; the bread and wine only signify, but are not really, the body and blood of the Saviour. His body is

L

in heaven, and cannot be everywhere or in many places at the same time. Zwingli therefore rejected every form of the doctrine of the corporeal presence of Christ in the Eucharist, and supported his figurative interpretation of Christ's word, of institution, by a multitude of Scripture passages. Nevertheless he asserted his belief that Christ is really present in the Lord's Supper, basing it on Matthew xviii. 20; but the literal presence and the eating of His body by the recipients of the Sacrament he considered to be far from the truth, and contrary to the nature of faith. He believed, however, " that the true body of Christ is eaten in the Communion, in a sacramental and spiritual manner, by the religious, believing, and pious heart." This has been felt by many to be the simplest, clearest, and most intelligible theory of the Holy Communion. It involves no physical difficulties, and requires no miracle. It is accepted by Armenians generally, and by a very large number of Protestants of all denominations.

On the question of man's universal sinfulness and need of regeneration, Zwingli was in full agreement with Luther; but he went beyond St.

Universal Sinfulness of Man. Augustine, in regarding it as foreknown and even foreordained by God, before the fall of man, together with the plan of redemption. This is called the supralapsarian view, contrasted with the infralapsarian, which looks upon the sin of man as a consequence of the disobedience of Adam, and not a necessary el—

creation. "Original sin" Zwingli regarded

fection rather than as punishable guilt.

certainly more in accordance with wide view

the other; but it has always shocked those wh

God should allow sin, or appear to foreorda

looks upon it as means or a step towards m

that it is man's own fault if he does not accept

As to the salvation of children, Zwingli

many of Calvin's followers, and various Cath

Salvation of repeatedly, that all elect children

Children. or not, by Christ's atonement; and

that all children dying in infancy belong to th

lieve in the salvation of the children of heathe

great step in advance of Romanism and high A

ing St. Augustine, regard unbaptized children a

opinions may differ, there can be no doubt as t

integrity, his earnest desire to present truth fully and

AN EVENT OF THE REFORMATION; PRINTING LUTHER'S BIBLE.

CHAPTER XI.

William Farel and the Swiss Reformation till 1536.

Western Switzerland and France—William Farel—Faber or Lefèvre—The Bible in French—Farel in South-East France—At Montbéliard—In Switzerland—At Aigle—His Iconoclasm at Neufchatel—Defeat of the Romanists—Farel Wounded—Visits Orbe—Peter Viret—Farel and the Waldenses—The Geneva Struggle—The Huguenots—Reformed Teaching at Geneva—Olivétan—Farel enters Geneva—Cited before the Council—His Life in Danger—Leaves Geneva—Sends Froment—The Priest Weruli Killed—Arrest and Release of Reformers—Froment and Furbity—Farel Returns to Geneva—A Plot Frustrated—Maisonneuve condemned at Lyons—Released by Francis I.—New Adherents of Reform—Departure of Catholic Officials—Reaction in Switzerland—Geneva in Arms—Reformers Burnt and Poisoned—Olivétan's French Bible—Images Destroyed—Mass Discontinued—Geneva Blockaded—Battle of Ginguis—Aid from Berne—Geneva saved—Pacific Reconstruction—Calvin at Geneva—First Confession of Basle, 1534—First Helvetic Confession, 1536.

A S Northern and North-Eastern Switzerland are naturally associated with Germany, so Western Switzerland is connected to France. Hence the affinity between them in the history of the Reformation. It must be admitted that German Switzerland had her own universities, while the studious youth of the French cantons were accustomed to choose Paris for their university course. But there was always

Western Switzerland and France.

147

much resort to German universities from the north-eastern states, and the Rhine was a natural connecting link between the two countries. France and French Switzerland were yet more closely brought together in the Reformation in the persons of two representative reformers, William Farel and John Calvin.

Farel was born in 1489, of a noble family, in a manor house in the French Upper Alps, three leagues from Gap, in Dauphiny. He was brought up in entire devotion to Romish practices. An ardent student, **William Farel.** he proceeded to Paris in 1510, and soon came under the influence of a doctor of theology, Lefèvre or Faber, a native of Picardy. Lefèvre was a man of low birth and diminutive stature, but a person of great learning, and a zealous student of the Bible, although he still fully conformed to the practices of the Church. Farel took up the **Faber or Lefèvre.** study of the Bible, after an extreme but unsatisfying veneration of saints and relics, and an eager devotion to philosophy and scholastic theology; and he soon perceived the antagonism of its teaching to many of the practices of the church. Studying St. Paul's epistles, Lefèvre found in them all the same doctrine of justification by faith which attracted the attention of Luther about the same time. "It is God alone," he said, "wholly His grace, through faith, justifies us unto everlasting life." In addition, he demonstrated how the teaching of St. James, concerning works, could be reconciled with that of St. Paul. Farel at once embraced the new doctrine (apparently in 1512); with a further teaching, which acknowledged the Divine election, not man's choice, as the sole source of salvation. Lefèvre also emphatically denounced the corrupt practices of bishops and clergy, and Farel eagerly followed in his wake, finally giving up what he had till then retained, the invocation of saints.

With this last stronghold, the whole papal position was overturned in his mind; he began to detest it as diabolical. Applying himself diligently to Greek and Hebrew, he gained strength in his reformed principles. Lefèvre's teaching was welcomed by William Briçonnet, the Bishop of Meaux, who expounded it to Margaret of Valois, sister of Francis I.; and soon the princess became a convert. But the hopes of the reformers were damped by the concordat, established with the pope after the battle of Marignano. In March, 1518, the university opposed this arrangement, but was soon brought to acquiesce in it. A persecutor of the reformers soon appeared in the violent and unscrupulous Noel Bedier or Beda; and though Francis I. refused to take steps against the new teachers, Beda contrived to render their lives a burden to them.

In 1520, copies of Luther's disputation with Dr. Eck at Leipsic were examined by the Sorbonne, and in the end condemned to be burnt as heretical. Lefèvre sought refuge at Meaux with the friendly bishop, who was occupying himself in repressing church scandals, and founding a theological school, in which he invited Lefèvre, Farel, Mazurier, Gerard and Arnold Roussel to teach. From this school proceeded, in 1522, a French translation of the New Testament, chiefly the work of Lefèvre, and in 1525 a French version of the Psalms. Many adherents were gained for the new teaching, and a number of investigators resorted to Meaux for instruction, and returned home to spread the light they had gained. In 1526, Lefèvre's translation of the Pentateuch appeared, and in 1530 he completed his translation of the whole Bible, which has been the basis for most of the subsequent French translations. He died at Nérac in 1536, where Margaret of Valois, sister of Francis I. and afterwards Queen of Navarre, had given him her protection during the persecutions which had broken out.

These persecutions caused a general flight of the reformers, although some, like Mazurier, recanted; and it was to this exodus that French Switzerland owed the great successes of Farel as a preacher of the Reformation. After converting his brothers to his views, and suffering persecution at Gap, Farel travelled through the country of the Durance and the Isère, preaching in houses and in the fields. Amongst other converts, he gained over Anémond de Coet, a member of a noble Dauphiny family, who visited Luther at Wittenberg, urged him to come to France, and induced him to write to Duke Charles of Savoy a declaration of his faith, and an appeal for the duke's aid in propagating the reformed doctrines. At Basle, early in 1524, Anémond was joined by Farel, whose zeal and learning attracted Œcolampadius, while he refused to visit Erasmus, who was now exhibiting marked hostility to the new movement. Erasmus bitterly attacked Farel and the other French refugees in Basle. Farel offered to appear publicly, and defend the reformed doctrines. Thereupon the university forbad its members to attend any such discussion; while the council of Basle supported Farel and Œcolampadius, the latter of whom expounded his own and his co-religionist's position, but found no opponent.

In May, 1524, Farel visited Schaffhausen, Zurich, and Constance. At Zurich he enjoyed pleasant intercourse with Zwingli and Oswald Myconnis. On returning to Basle, he found himself, through Erasmus's influence,

THE FANATICS OF THE REFORMATION—DESTRUCTION OF IMAGES AND ORNAMENTS
IN CHURCHES.

forbidden to remain in that city. He took refuge at Strasburg, where he

became intimate with Capito, Bucer, and Hedio.   Returning secretly to
Basle, he was privately ordained by Œcolampadius to preach in
Montbéliard, where Duke Ulrich of Wurtemberg permitted **At Montbéliard.**
him to resume his activity, and where his energy procured him success.
During this time he was incessantly writing and translating into French
little didactic books and pamphlets, which Anémond printed at Basle, and
diffused by means of colporteurs, who also distributed Lefèvre's New
Testament.   Metz was evangelised by his friend the Chevalier d'Esch.

Farel was now guilty of a grave indiscretion.   At Montbéliard, on St.
Anthony's day, near the end of February, 1525, he imprudently seized from
a priest an image of the saint which was being carried in procession, and
threw it into the river.   The popular indignation aroused by this act
obliged him to fly the city.   He escaped to Basle, where not long after
he received the news that Anémond de Coct was dead.   A little later Farel
went to Strasburg; and there, in the autumn, he was joined by Lefèvre, who
had newly escaped from France, where Briçonnet, overcome by persecution,
had condemned Luther's teaching and recanted the reformed doctrines; at
Nancy, in August, Pastor Schach was burnt to death; James Pavanno
suffered at Paris, where also a hermit of Livry was burnt at a slow fire
in front of Notre Dame.   But among the terrified spectators who witnessed these atrocities in Paris was a timid student of sixteen, who was
destined to issue from the capital as one of the mightiest forces of the
Reformation.

When Lefèvre and others of the French refugees returned to France
on the release of Francis I. from captivity by Charles V., after the treaty
of Madrid, Farel betook himself to Switzerland; and with a moderation not
usual with him, concealed his name and his influence, as a schoolmaster,
under the assumed name of Ursinus, at Aigle, one of the most
southern towns in Switzerland, then under the jurisdiction of **At Aigle.**
Berne.   Here he devoted himself to further study, and in consequence
adopted Zwingli's form of doctrine in preference to Luther's.   After
having temperately argued against purgatory and the invocation of saints,
he one day, in March or April, 1527, threw off his incognito, and ascended
the pulpit as William Farel, with a licence from the council of Berne to
expound the Scriptures.   A turbulent polemic campaign followed; at one
time Farel gained ground, at another his opponents were in the ascendant.
Then followed the disputation at Berne, in January, 1528, of which mention
has been made (p. 139).   One of the consequences of this conference was

the granting of an enlarged commission to Farel to preach in French Switzerland.

Farel now showed himself more impetuous, eager, impulsive and even violent than ever, in his anti-Romish crusade. The little man with red beard, sparkling eyes, and expressive mouth, attacked popery with an intrepid air and with a voice of thunder. At times he carried all before him, but his victories were often followed by a reaction. At Neufchatel, in 1530, in order to provoke the dissolute and vicious canons to attack him, he had posted up large placards exhibiting the following uncompromising declaration: "All who say mass are robbers, murderers, and seducers of the people." **His Iconoclasm at Neufchatel.** This audacious challenge brought an armed crowd down from the cathedral, who demolished the placards, while the canons cited Farel before the city authorities as a slanderer. Farel boldly endeavoured to justify himself by quotations from the gospels; and the council, anxious to avoid taking a perilous step, referred the cause to a higher tribunal; and it was finally relegated to the decision of the emperor and a general council. The populace insisted that Farel should have a church to preach in, and by main force installed him in the pulpit of a hospital chapel. So soon as he was established there, he ordered the painted and carved figures which decorated the pulpit to be destroyed. Iconoclasm was a form of war which presented itself as a necessity to Farel's fiery energy; and wherever he attained ascendancy, destruction of venerated objects followed. The Genevese and Scotch principle of destroying root and branch "Popery and idols," may be traced in its origin to the most restless of iconoclasts.

It was in a village near Neufchatel, on the festival of the Assumption, that Farel one day entered the pulpit while the priest was beginning to celebrate mass. Farel's friend Anthony Bryve snatched the Host from the priest's hands, declaring: "This is not the God you should worship." In the terrified silence which followed, Farel began to preach; but was interrupted by the arrival of a crowd, summoned by the ringing of alarm bells from the belfry. The exasperated throng would have summarily drowned both Farel and Bryve, had not some Neufchatel people interfered. The turbulent reformers were, however, thrown into a dungeon in the castle of Valanzin, and were not released until the citizens of Neufchatel claimed them.

Farel returned to Neufchatel, and soon was carried in triumph into the cathedral, which was forcibly seized by the reforming party.

Roused by his powerful eloquence, the townsmen seized mattocks, axes, and hammers, and destroyed statues, paintings, crucifixes, altars, everything in fact that, according to their view, was at variance with the second commandment. The iconoclasts seized the patens and threw them into the Seyon; the consecrated bread they distributed among themselves, and proceeded to eat it, as a proof that it remained mere bread. An inscription engraved on a pillar in the church, recorded that "on the 23rd October, 1530, the idolatry of this place was overthrown by the burgesses." But in this violence the reformers exhibited an amount of intolerance as great as had been ever shown by Rome.

The official who governed Neufchatel, under the Duchess of Longueville, to whom the city had been restored in 1529, proposed to decide the question of the Reformation by a popular vote; and this proposal was carried into effect in the presence of three Bernese commissioners. The vote, taken early in November, was in favour of the reformers; **Defeat of the** and it was decided that mass should no longer be celebrated in **Romanists.** the cathedral; the Romish party took refuge in the chapel of the castle. Farel, strangely enough, does not appear in these proceedings; probably, for once, he had learnt the art of conquering by avoiding the appearance of undue activity. Some of the canons became reformers; others emigrated to the Val de Travers. Two marble tables were substituted for the high altar of the cathedral, and the pulpit was stripped of all ornament. Farel, assisted by Jean de Bély, preached throughout the territory of Neufchatel, gaining many converts by his untiring activity. His life was frequently in danger from the adherents of Rome. In March, 1531, the Duchess of Longueville's son proclaimed freedom of conscience throughout the state of Neufchatel, at the same time seizing the property of the canons.

Near the end of 1530, during an evangelistic tour on the banks of the Lake of Neufchatel, Farel was wounded by the populace at St. Blaise, who had been stirred up to this violence by the priests. He **Farel wounded.** was rescued by his friends, and taken to Morat, where he was compelled to remain quiet for some time. Here he received the adhesion of a young convert from Dauphiné, Christopher Faber, who had been a medical student at Montpelier, and who appeared so suitable for the work that Farel speedily sent him to preach at Neufchatel.

Scarcely had Farel recovered from his wounds when he heard that a seller of indulgences had established his traffic in the neighbouring city of Orbe, at the foot of the Jura. Appearing in the market place where the

monk was offering his indulgences for sale, Farel suddenly accosted him;
"Have you indulgences for a person who has killed his father
and mother?" and without waiting for an answer, stepped
on to the edge of the basin of the public fountain, and in resounding tones
called upon the people to ask pardon of the Saviour, instead of buying
indulgences, which could not wipe away sins. A few converts were
made; and though Farel himself could not safely remain at Orbe, his
work was carried on with a turbulence and excitement which make the
story of the movement, as told by D'Aubigné, highly dramatic and
interesting. After many striking incidents, in which the violence of the
papists was curbed by the control exercised by Berne over the city, Farel
returned; and orders from Berne compelled the people to give him a hearing. His success, however, at that time was not great.

Visits Orbe.

But a more sober and discreet reformer arose in Orbe itself, in the
person of Peter Viret (born 1511), who after studying in Paris at the same
time as Calvin, returned home, and, incited by Farel, began to
preach in 1531, at the early age of twenty. Some notable
conversions followed; and on Whitsunday, Farel administered the Holy
Communion according to the reformed rite, to their converts, at six in the
morning. At this time Christopher Holbard distinguished himself as an
iconoclast; he pulled down all the altars in the city's seven churches.
This outrage, and similar excesses, caused the papal party to regain power;
and it was not till 1554 that the reformed worship was established at
Orbe.

Peter Viret.

In July, 1532, after a brief mission at Grandson and Morat, Farel
received an invitation from the Waldenses of Piedmont, to attend their
synod at Angrogne, to explain the points in which the reformers went beyond the Waldensian traditional practices and
principles. Farel and his friend Saunier accordingly journeyed to Angrogne, and on the 12th of September and the following days expounded
the reformed doctrines. He recommended, moreover, that the Waldensians
should cease their occasional attendance at mass, and no longer allow the
Romish priests to baptize their children. In demanding a complete rejection of Romish ceremonial, he was supported by many Waldenses, who
declared that his teaching agreed with the doctrine bequeathed to them
by their fathers. He gained the advantage over those pastors of the
Waldenses who wished still to temporise with Rome, and by a majority
the reformed teaching was adopted. A short confession of seventeen articles,

Farel and the Waldenses.

the original of which is now to be seen in the Cambridge University Library, was thereupon drawn up for the guidance of the community.

On their return from Angrogne, Farel and Saunier determined to visit Geneva, where the ground had already been to some extent prepared for them. The quarrels and rivalries of the Dukes of Savoy, the **The Genevan** Genevese counts and the prince bishops of Geneva, had resulted **Struggle.** in producing a revolution in the city of Lake Leman, and the citizens had entered into an alliance with Fribourg and Berne. Here it may be noted

RELIGIOUS PERSECUTION, WALDENSIAN COMMUNITIES DRIVEN FROM THEIR HOMES INTO EXILE.

that the term "Huguenots" originated in this struggle at Geneva. It was really a French rendering of the word "Eidgenossen" (confederates) applied to the Swiss cantons, and was used as a term of reproach by the Duke of Savoy's party. It was at first pronounced variously, Eid- **The Huguenots.** guenots, Eignots, Huguenots, and the last of these forms, being connected with the name of Besançon Hugues, one of the Geneva leaders, became at length the established one. It was originally simply a political name, and not until many years later did the Roman Catholics of France apply it to their Protestant countrymen, by way of contumely, denouncing them as foreigners and republicans.

In the year 1523, "some people called evangelists came from France" to Geneva, and various Genevans "talked with them and bought their books," including the French New Testament of Lefèvre. Some of the citizens, who sought the help of Berne in 1525, became acquainted with the reformed doctrines there, and brought them back on their return in 1526. Thomas de Hofen, a friend of Zwingli, a Bernese deputy to Geneva, in 1527, instructed the principal families concerning the Bible and its authority, and salvation by Christ alone. The prince-bishop, unable to control the citizens, left Geneva in August, 1527. The citizens of Geneva were excommunicated by the pope, and laid under an interdict. They refused to have the excommunication published or executed.

Reformed teaching at Geneva.

The Reformation in Geneva arose in the first instance rather from a determination to abolish the abuses of papal and clerical power, than from questions concerning doctrine. Charles V., under whom Geneva was nominally an imperial city, endeavoured to check the current by ordering the people of Geneva to arrest and punish all Lutheran preachers. They answered simply, "Sire, we intend to live, as in past times, according to God and the law of Jesus Christ." The papists raised an outcry against the Huguenots who had begun to eat meat in Lent; the Huguenots retaliated by calling for punishment in cases of debauchery among priests. In the autumn of 1530, when a Swiss army arrived to defend Geneva from the Duke of Savoy and the prince-bishop, Bernese soldiers, of the reformed religion, took their chaplain into the cathedral, and held a service in German according to their own form of worship. Another minister distributed many copies of the Scriptures and of various writings of the Reformers in French. The pope endeavoured to gain back the people of Geneva by proclaiming special indulgences for certain acts of devotion. The indulgences aroused the anger of the people, and made them turn defiantly towards the reformed teaching. The defeat of Zwingli at Kappel, and the death of Zwingli, however, revived the hopes and energies of the Romanist party.

At this time there had taken refuge in Geneva, Peter Olivétan, a cousin of Calvin's, who had been instrumental in converting Calvin himself, and was now teaching the children of Chautemps, a councillor. Olivétan's conversation impressed upon Chautemps and others the Scriptural doctrines, and the zealous preacher even sought to convert

Olivétan in Geneva.

priests. When the pope, in June, 1532, proclaimed new indulgences, the Huguenots published as an antidote, "the great general pardon of Jesus Christ." Their manifesto was couched in these terms, "God, our Heavenly Father, promises a general pardon of all his sins to every one who feels sincere repentance and possesses a lively faith in the death and promises of Jesus Christ." This placard greatly offended the Romanists, and caused a tumult. The Catholic citizens of Fribourg hotly supported their co-religionists, and caused Olivétan's preaching to be forbidden. The priests began to demand from private persons the surrender of all copies of the New Testament in their possession; but this proceeding strengthened the reforming party, and the council ordered that in every church the gospel should be preached according to the truth, without any mixture of fables or other human inventions.

On October 2nd, 1532, Farel and Saunier entered Geneva, met Olivétan, and delivered letters from Berne to some of the chief Huguenots. On the next day, in his inn, Farel expounded to a select body of citizen patriots the evils arising from the action of priests and *Farel enters Geneva.* popes, and exhorted them to turn to a religion based entirely on scripture. Many declared for "the Lord Jesus Christ alone." At a second meeting he spoke particularly of salvation by grace, and against reliance on works.

Farel and Saunier were cited before the council, and Farel was charged with stirring up tumult and rebellion everywhere. He replied: "I simply proclaim the truth. I am ready to prove out of God's Word *Cited before* that my doctrine is true; and not only to sacrifice my ease, *the council.* but to shed the last drop of my blood for it." He produced letters written in his favour from Berne, and so impressed the council, that the two Reformers were dismissed with the simple admonition not to disturb the public tranquility by new doctrines.

An episcopal council, however, treated them in a very different manner. Farel was overwhelmed with reproaches for daring to preach without episcopal authority, and was vehemently abused as "a wicked devil." He replied with noble moderation, claiming his right, as an ambassador of Jesus Christ, to teach all who would hear him. But when he accused the priests of troubling the world by their traditions, human inventions, and dissolute lives, they "fixed their burning eyes on Farel," and one man accused him of blasphemy in the words of Matthew xxvi. 65, 66. *His life in* A general cry arose "To the Rhone; kill him, kill the Lutheran *danger.* hound." They beat the reformers, spat upon them, and would have carried out the intention of slaying them, but for the interference of the magistrates, who had guaranteed the safety of the accused persons. The council of ecclesiastics then let them go, on condition that they quitted

Leaves Geneva. the city within six hours; but a party of inferior priests endeavoured to stab Farel, who with Saunier had great difficulty in escaping from their violence. Olivétan soon followed them, and the three met at Yverdon, south of the Lake of Neufchatel. Farel persuaded Olivétan to undertake a French translation of the Bible, and with some others, a mission to the Waldenses, who contributed 500 gold crowns to the cost of its publication. A disciple of his, Fabri, introduced the gospel throughout the territory of Neufchatel.

Unable as yet to return to Geneva, Farel sent thither his youthful convert from Dauphiné, Anthony Froment, who first attracted notice, like

Sends Anthony Froment. Farel at Aigle, by opening a school, whence he gradually diffused the reformed doctrines. Madam Levet, the wife of a prominent citizen, was a notable convert, and became an active teacher. The vicar of La Madeleine, who undertook a disputation against the reformers, failed to substantiate his positions with any scripture proofs. On New Year's morning, 1533, Froment was compelled to preach in the Molard, a large square, so great a crowd had assembled to hear him. After a noble

Froment preaches in the Molard extempore prayer, he took for his text the words: "Beware of false prophets," and powerfully exposed Romish malpractices and false doctrines. The priests urged the council to apprehend him, and he was obliged to go into hiding; and at length, after some further disorder, he was compelled to leave Geneva for Yverdon.

The Geneva reformers, deprived of the services of Froment, chose Guérin, one of their number, as their pastor; and he administered the

Guérin and Olivétan. Lord's Supper to them about the middle of March. The papal party raised such a disturbance after this, that Guérin too retired to Yverdon. A Dominican inquisitor, early in Lent, attacked the reformers in a sermon, which moved Olivétan, who had been zealously working at his translation of the Bible, to answer him on the spot. The priests thereupon secured his banishment without hearing or appeal.

Baudichon de la Maisonneuve and Salomon now obtained a letter from the Bernese council, protesting indignantly against the in-

An armed attack threatened. justice inflicted upon Farel, and the molestation of the reformers generally. A body of catholics thereupon proceeded to the Genevese council, and formed a plot to destroy the reformers. They assembled in arms, and were about to proceed to extremities, when the intervention of some Fribourg merchants produced a truce. The great council decreed that no novelty should be introduced in religious proceedings; but that as to the mass, every one was to be left at liberty to act according to his own conscience; that no one should preach without a licence, and that every preacher should prove his assertions by scriptural authority. This idea, however, was not thoroughly carried out at the time.

Early in May, under the excitement of the bellicose conversation and preaching of a priest named Wernli, a riot occurred. It was mainly due to a mistaken idea that the heretics were assembling to plunder the churches. Wernli himself, who led the attack for the catholics, perished in the fight. His death was represented as a martyrdom. At this juncture Pope Clement commanded the prince-bishop to return to Geneva. Meanwhile deputies from Berne, in May, were recommending the Genevese to permit every man to follow his own conscience; advising that the mass and images should remain for those who approved of them, while one church should be set apart for the reformed worship. *The priest Wernli killed.*

The prince-bishop, returning to Geneva early in July, 1833, endeavoured to carry matters with a high hand. Vandel, Perret, Levet, Madame Chautemps and others of the reformed party were arrested by his orders; Chautemps, Maisonneuve and others escaped. The catholics were eager to avenge Wernli's death at any cost. Accordingly Maisonneuve, at the head of fifty reformers, surprised the bishop at night, and compelled him to surrender his prisoners to the Genevese syndics. This incident so intimidated him, that on the 14th of July, 1533, he fled from the city, never to return. The prisoners were released; but one man, who was convincingly proved to have taken part in Wernli's death, was beheaded. *Arrest of and release of Reformers.*

Soon afterwards Froment returned to Geneva, with Alexander Dumoulin; and their persuasive oratory gained many adherents for the gospel. The bishop issued a prohibition of all preaching, except such as he should license, and a Dominican named Furbitz, a Doctor of the Sorbonne, was introduced to attack the reformers. He outdid his predecessors in violence, denouncing as blasphemers, thieves and murderers, all those who read the scriptures in the vulgar tongue; all who would not obey the pope and the clergy, he declared, belonged to the devil's flock. Froment answered his assertions and denunciations boldly and openly in the church, and Furbitz had nothing to say in rejoinder. The *Froment and Furbitz.*

bold reformer was with difficulty rescued from the vengeance of the Catholics, and with Dumoulin and Maisonneuve set out for Berne to appeal for aid.   Farel was sent back with Maisonneuve, in December, 1533, with a letter from the Bernese council, complaining of the treatment the reformers had received at Geneva, and demanding that a church should be assigned to Farel wherein he might preach.   In January, 1534, a public disputation was held between Farel and Furbitz.

Farel returns to Geneva.

Meanwhile a plot was concocted for a " coup d'état " in Geneva.   The bishop, in concert with the Duke of Saxony, planned to appoint a lieutenant in temporal matters, with full power to punish criminals ; his authority was to supersede the constitutional government of Geneva.   But one of his agents wantonly murdered a Huguenot, and this led to the discovery of the whole scheme and the punishment of the murderer.   A short time after, the council recommended the reformers to take any church they could gain possession of ; and soon Farel was set to preach in the great court of the convent at Rive.   Numerous converts were gained, and baptism according to the primitive form was introduced.

Plot for a coup d'état frustrated.

Maisonneuve, who had frequently visited Lyons as a merchant, and had become known as a reformer, was seized, brought before an inquisitorial court at Lyons, and condemned to death as a heretic ; but after some months' imprisonment, he was set at liberty by order of Francis I., at the instance of the Bernese envoys, Diesbach and Schoener.

Maisonneuve condemned at Lyons.

Released by Francis I.

On the Sunday after Easter, 1534, Farel performed the service according to the reformed order.   When Farel, on Whitsunday, was about to administer the Lord's Supper, Louis Bernard, one of the cathedral dignitaries, came up to the table, put off his sacerdotal vestments, and said : " I will live and die with you, for Jesus Christ's sake."   It was considered a triumph for reform, when an ex-Knight of Rhodes and Malta, Pierre Gaudet, came to Geneva and professed the new faith.   Around the bivouac fires of citizen-soldiers, who kept under arms to guard Geneva from sudden attacks, Farel, Vinet, and Froment in familiar converse inculcated their doctrines ; and it was said that at these assemblies more people were won to the gospel, than were converted by public preaching.   Louis Bernard married, and became a member of the council.   Another plot to seize Geneva for the bishop and the Duke of Saxony was balked ; and the principal adherents of the catholics fled.   To render the defence of the city more practicable, a great

New adherents of Reform.

Departure of Catholic Officials.

part of the suburbs beyond the walls were destroyed, and the inhabitants received within the circuit of the city. The bishop cut off food supplies from Geneva, as far as possible; and from his several castles around the town kept armed watch upon all who left or entered it. Then, much to the relief of the reformers, he transferred his episcopal officers, council, court, etc., to Gex. He formally excommunicated the council and citizens of Geneva, threatening with the same penalty all who should listen to the heretical preachers, and even all who entered the city.

The Genevese still pursued a non-revolutionary policy, and on the 7th October, 1534, they appealed to the pope, complaining that the Bishop had deprived them of their franchises and jurisdiction. To their memorial no answer was returned. The Duke of Savoy demanded that the reformed preachers should be dismissed. The council of Geneva replied that they would sooner set fire to their city, renounce their wives and children, and lose their lives, than obey this order. Reaction in Strangely enough, at this juncture the Swiss Diet, and even Switzerland. the Bernese, overcome just then by a catholic reaction, admonished Geneva to reinstate the bishop and the duke in authority. Geneva was left to fight the battle alone.

Abandoned by their former allies, the citizens of Geneva repaired their fortifications, melted down bells to recast them into cannon, prepared and furbished up their arms, and prayed to God for success in Geneva in their course. They elected a majority of Huguenot magistrates arms. and councillors, and the reformers gained ground daily. A Franciscan monk preached gospel sermons, and was attacked by catholic brawlers, who were punished for their violence. Gaudet, the ex-Knight of Malta, was decoyed into the bishop's castle of Perney; he was tortured, and burnt to death. An attempt was made to poison Farel, Froment and Viret; in the case of the last-named it had nearly succeeded. Reformers burnt and poisoned. The poisoner, a woman suborned by priests and monks, was apprehended, convicted, and beheaded. Soon afterwards, Jacques Bernard, brother of Louis, and superior of the Franciscan convent, was converted by Farel, and preached the Gospel in the convent church.

In April of that year (1535), Farel persuaded Jacques Bernard to offer to defend the reformed doctrines in a public disputation. The meeting thus promoted took place at Whitsuntide, and the reformers Olivétan's had a distinct victory. Early in June appeared Olivétan's French Bible. French Bible, printed at Neufchâtel; it was soon widely circulated.

M

While the magistrates of Geneva temporised, Farel, at the call of his followers, preached in the principal churches, and at last in the cathedral itself, without permission. The citizen reformers, Maisonneuve, Vaudel, and Perrin, on Aug. 9th, 1535, headed a somewhat tumultuous throng, which

Images destroyed. destroyed images, pictures, and objects of Romish ceremonial in several churches, and in the process discovered many mechanical contrivances for pretended miracles. The civic council of two hundred met next day, and, on Farel's urgent motion, ordered that mass

Mass discontinued. should no longer be celebrated; at the same time forbidding further destruction of images. The valuables of the churches were removed into safe custody. The greater number of the priests, monks and nuns left the city. The 10th of August, 1535, is celebrated as the first day of the Reformation at Geneva.

A hospital was established in the convent of St. Claire, under Salomon, and a school under Saunier. The episcopal palace was converted into a prison—a change which the reformers declared to be more in name than in fact, considering how many prisoners the building had formerly held, and how it had been used to subvert liberty.

On the 30th of August the Duke of Savoy proclaimed Geneva as infected with plague, and forbade all his subjects, on pain of death, to

Geneva blockaded. have intercourse with its inhabitants; and he prepared to subdue the city by force. The Emperor Charles V. called on the Swiss Diet to help him. Berne held back from aiding Geneva. At last a force from Neufchâtel marched towards Geneva, and won the

Battle of Ginguis. battle of Ginguis, on the 11th and 12th of October, against the Savoyards. But the fruits of this victory were lost through the diplomacy of the enemy. Several attacks by the Savoyard forces were beaten back by Geneva; and, moved by the urgent entreaties of Maisonneuve, the Bernese resolved to aid their old ally. Berthold

Aid from Berne. Haller, rising from his death-bed, encouraged the army of six thousand men that marched from Berne on the 22nd of January, 1536, under Francis Nägeli. Meanwhile Geneva had been closely blockaded, and was suffering from famine. After compelling all their opponents to

Geneva saved. retire, the Bernese entered Geneva as liberators on the 30th of January. The council of the city recorded on their books the sentence: "The power of God has confounded the presumption and the foolish audacity of our enemies."

The bishop's castle and the robber strongholds in the neighbourhood were seized and destroyed, the word being given: "Spare the tyrants, but destroy their dens!" On the 6th of February, 1536, one of the magistrates declared that all animosities engendered in the struggle should be laid aside, all quarrels forgotten, all hateful names dropped. In the choice of new syndics and councillors a spirit of fairness was displayed towards the Romanists. The people of Geneva were saved from further alarms at that time, by the invasion of Savoy by Francis I. The castle of Chillon was taken by the citizens of Geneva and Berne, and Bonnivard, the prior of St. Victor, who had done so much for the liberties of Geneva, was set free.

Pacific reconstruction.

CASTLE OF CHILLON, ON THE LAKE OF GENEVA, THE PLACE OF BONNIVARD'S IMPRISONMENT.

On the 21st of May, at a grand assembly in the cathedral, the people of Geneva passed the following resolution: "We will with one accord desire, with God's help, to live under that holy, evangelical law, and according to God's Word as it is preached to us. We desire to renounce all masses, images, idols, and other papal ceremonies and abuses, and to live in union with one another in consonance with justice." A Latin inscription, composed by Farel, was fixed up over one of the city gates, and later over the entrance to the Hotel de Ville, stating that "The tyranny of the Roman Antichrist having been overthrown, and his superstitions abolished, in the year 1535 . . . the senate and people of

Geneva had set up this monument to proclaim to future ages their gratitude to God."

Farel was over-burdened with work, for Froment had gone to Aigle, and Viret to Neufchâtel. Finding few suitable helpers, he looked for some powerful new force. It was then that his eye lit upon John Calvin, who had been driven from France, and was travelling in search of work and opportunities for study. Calvin had already published his celebrated "Institutes of the Christian Religion." One evening in July, 1536, he

VIEW OF THE CITY AND LAKE OF GENEVA, WITH ROUSSEAU'S ISLAND.

Calvin at Geneva. arrived at Geneva, intending to pass through rapidly. Farel had read the "Institutes," and felt that the author of this work was the man above all others for Geneva. By a sort of Divine constraint **Compelled to stay at Farel.** he compelled Calvin to stay and become the leader in perhaps the most remarkable effort of the Reformation.

The influence of Œcolampadius at Basle lasted after his death. He had prepared a brief confession of faith, which was revised by his successor, Oswald Myconius, who had removed from Zurich after Zwingli's death, and promulgated by the magistrates in January, 1534. It was afterwards adopted by the allied city of Mühlhausen, and hence is sometimes known as the Mühlhausen Confession. It puts forth the principal Zwinglian doctrines in moderate terms, and condemns the views of the anabaptists. This confession is still upheld by the church of Basle. First Confession of Basle, 1534.

Henry Bullinger was Zwingli's successor at Zurich, where he exercised great influence, maintaining the freedom of the pulpit, and defending the Zwinglian doctrines on the sacraments. He was largely concerned in drawing up the first Helvetic Confession in 1536, the earliest which represented the whole of the reformed cantons. First Helvetic Confession, Basle, 1536. It is also known as the Second Confession of Basle, from the place where it was drawn up. Bucer and Capito, the Strasburg reformers, had been zealously promoting a union between the German and Swiss reformed churches; and it was thought that a general agreement among the Swiss would render this project easier to attain. A number of divines, including Bullinger, Myconius, and Leo Judah, selected by the magistrates of Zurich, Berne, Basle, Schaffhausen, St. Gall, Mühlhausen, and Biel, met Bucer and Capito at Basle in January and February, 1536. The confession they drew up consists of twenty-seven articles, and is fuller than the first Confession of Basle. It allows a certain authority to the Fathers, provided they do not depart from the rule of interpreting scripture by scripture, but gives no weight to other "traditions of men." Man is declared to have been originally created perfect, and endowed with an immortal soul; but by his own fault he brought ruin on the whole race. There is no salvation for man but through Christ. Human free will is exercised naturally only in choosing evil, for without divine grace we are unable to choose the good. Christ is the only Mediator, Intercessor, Victim, Priest, Lord and King Faith is a sure and steadfast apprehension of the things hoped for from God's benevolence, and it puts no trust in works. The church is built of living stones (or members) as the spouse of Christ ; and membership in the visible church is essential, except as a singular privilege granted by God. The right to minister in the church is given by the free gift of God, confirmed in general by the suffrage of the church and the Christian magistrates. The ministers are pastors only, not priests ; but their power and rights are freely given. Regarding the sacraments, something beyond the Zwinglian doctrine is allowed. The signs are stated to be signs of real things, in the Lord's Supper, signs of the communion of the body of the Lord ; but the whole value of the sacraments is in the things signified.

There is a real spiritual, not material, presence of Christ, who gives His body and blood to believers. To godly magistrates is allotted the right to suppress and punish blasphemy, the care of seeing that the pure Word of God is truly and sincerely preached, and the duty of educating youth in a godly fashion; of properly providing persons for the ministry, and ministering to the wants of the poor, besides other general public duties. Thus a definite standard of belief was set up for all the reformed cantons.

FACSIMILE OF LUTHER'S MS.—THE FIRST LINES OF HIS HYMN, "EIN FESTE BURG IST UNSER GOTT" (A MIGHTY FORTRESS IS OUR GOD).

SATIRE OF THE REFORMATION PERIOD.

CHRIST AND ANTICHRIST, BY LUCAS KRANACH, PAINTER TO CHARLES V.

1. *Christ washing His apostle's feet.*   2. *The Pope's foot kissed by many monarchs.*

CHAPTER XII.

John Calvin's Life and Work, to the year 1538.

Calvin's Early Life—Study in Paris—Calvin and Olivétan—Calvin's Conversion—Louis Berquin—His Martyrdom—Calvin and Wolmar at Orleans—At Bourges—At Paris again—Writings of Margaret of Valois—Nicholas Cop's Address—Calvin's Escape—Calvin at Saintonge and Nérac—Events in Paris—Burning of Alexander Camus—Calvin's Evangelistic Labours—Calvin and Servetus, 1534—Psycho-Pannychia—The Placards—Calvin at Basle—Writes his "Institutes"—Address to Francis I.—Calvin visits Ferrara—Arrested and Rescued—Revisits France—Farel and Calvin at Geneva—Calvin Reader in Theology—Disputation at Lausanne—Calvin's Scheme of Church Order—Spirituals Expelled—Caroli and Calvin—Bucer and Capito at Berne—Agreement on the Sacrament—Severe Discipline at Geneva—Dissensions at Berne—Bernese Usage enforced at Geneva—Calvin and Farel refuse the Communion—The Pastors Banished from Geneva.

NOWHERE was a reformation of the Church more needed than in France. Nowhere was this necessity more frankly admitted by those who had the interests of religion at heart. But most of those who wished well to reform had too little strength themselves to undertake a task which was rendered most difficult by the autocracy of the sovereign.

Even the strongest man of the Reformation failed to carry France with him; failed, that is, to overcome the inveterate superstition of the majority of the French people.

John Calvin was born on July 10th, 1509, at Noyon, in Picardy. He was the son of a notary and secretary to the diocese of Noyon; a pious

Calvin's early life. man, devoted to the church, Calvin was educated with the De Mommors, a noble Picard family, and at the college of the Capettes in Noyon. At an early age he showed much talent. As a boy

he was gentle and submissive. Long afterwards friends remembered his habitual compliance with his father's stern injunctions. Timid and retiring, he grew up with a strong attachment to church rites and ceremonies. His father had sufficient influence to secure for him the benefice of Gesine, before he was twelve years old. He was accordingly destined for the church, and received the tonsure. In 1523, at the age

JOHN CALVIN, BORN AT NOYON, DIED AT GENEVA, 1561.

of fourteen, he entered the College of La Marche, in Paris, under Mathurin

Study in Paris. Cordier, who afterwards took refuge with him in Switzerland. In 1526 he was transferred to the Montaign College to prepare for the priesthood. Here he made great progress in classics and philosophy. His character was, however, already very definitely formed, and had taken an ascetic turn. He openly and severely censured the faults of his fellow-students. Beda, the principal, was delighted with this young man, who never missed a fast or a mass. Absorbed in his learning, the zealous student often forgot his meals, or sat up nearly all night over his books. Naturally he outstripped his contemporaries. In 1527, his father, who appears to have been sufficiently eager for his advancement, obtained for him a second living, before he had even been ordained a priest.

By this time the Reformation was beginning to make a stir in Paris; and Lefèvre, Farel, Briçonnet and others were advancing in the path of scriptural study. Young Olivétan, Calvin's cousin, a native of Noyon, became an adherent of the new views, and was eager to influence his relative, who obstinately resisted his arguments. But Calvin grew alarmed concerning his own salvation; and like Luther in the convent, endeavoured to ensure his soul's health by zealous compliance with priestly directions, by prayer to saints, and similar means. He found that the scriptures exposed his sins, and bitterly reproached him for them. With much groaning and weeping, he utterly condemned his past manner of life, and threw himself upon the mercy of God in Christ; but he was still restrained by reverence for the Church, from whose majesty he thought nothing must be allowed to detract. His friends urged that the pope was not constituted head of the church either by the voice of God, or by a lawful call of the church; and by searching the scriptures Calvin became convinced that the true order of the church had been lost, and Christian liberty overthrown. Still he clung to the Catholic Church so long as he might do so and yet hold to what he believed to be the truth. At what precise date his conversion—which he described as sudden,—took place, we do not know; but it probably occurred in Paris in 1527.

Calvin and Olivétan.

Calvin's conversion.

Meanwhile Louis Berquin, a gentleman of Artois, had been attracting notice as a reformer, and had been with difficulty rescued by Margaret of Valois from persecution and perhaps death, in 1523 and 1524. In November, 1526, he was once more set free by Francis I. on his return from Spain. He proceeded to attack Beda the arch-papist, for his impious writings, and, having succeeded in prevailing on the king to interdict Beda's polemical writings, he proceeded to attack the Sorbonne as a whole. The Papists redoubled their violence; and they burnt to death De la Tour, a nobleman who had visited Scotland in the train of John Duke of Albany, and "sowed many Lutheran errors there." The Chancellor, Cardinal Duprat, Archbishop of Sens, organised provincial councils, which denounced the Lutherans. The mutilation of images of the Virgin and the infant

Louis Berquin.

Jesus at a Paris street-corner, at Whitsuntide, 1528, by unknown hands, caused a great sensation, which the papists utilised to commence a hot persecution. Francis I. was led to view this act as a defiance of his authority. Many persons were burnt or otherwise punished for alleged heresy. Berquin, refusing to fly, was arrested in March, 1529, convicted of belonging to the sect of Luther, and of having written wicked books against the majesty of God and His glorious mother. Despite the exer-

His martyr- dom. tions of Budæus, a Sorbonne doctor, on his behalf, Berquin, who refused to retract, was strangled and then burnt on the Grève at Paris, on the 22nd of April, 1529. Berquin's character was such as to make even men who were not his friends, declare that so good a Christian had not died for over a hundred years; and his death caused widespread sorrow throughout France.

While these evil things were being done, Calvin had been withdrawn by his father from Paris to Orleans, where he was to study law. Among

Calvin and Wolmar at Orleans. the friends he made was a German, Melchior Wolmar, professor of Greek, who inspired Calvin with his love of Greek literature, especially the Greek Testament, and also imparted to him some knowledge of the course the Reformation in Germany was taking. Wolmar explained to Calvin Luther's teaching concerning free grace and justification by faith. Calvin, for his part, found himself torn by continued internal conflicts. Many accused him of separating from the church, and some declared he ought to be expelled. His intellect impressed even his adversaries, as being in the highest degree keen and subtle; indeed he was frequently selected as substitute for the professors. After his day's study of law, which was destined powerfully to influence his systematisation of Christian belief, he would spend a large portion of the night in studying the scriptures. Many sought religious instruction from him in private, and his ingenuity was often taxed to obtain solitude and leisure for his own studies. Those families who secured his instruction found that he taught with admirable depth and solidity. When in the

At Bourges. autumn of 1528 he transferred himself to the University of Bourges, Wolmar, who accompanied him thither, pressed him to devote his life to evangelistic labours; and his successes in the city and neighbourhood encouraged him to this course, although his modesty rendered him very unwilling to put himself forward.

In 1529 his father died, about the time of Berquin's martyrdom. Still seeking to effect reform from within, Calvin accepted from the

De Mommor who was abbot of St. Eloy, the living of Pont l' Evêque in Normandy, in place of St. Martin's. He preached at Noyon with varying results, and then betook himself to Paris, where, Calvin at Paris again. says Beza, he soon "gave himself entirely up to God," and studied theology with enthusiasm. He taught others as opportunities arose; but meanwhile Beda was attacking the Hebrew and Greek professors, Danès, Vatable and others whose teachings seemed dangerous to the church. The Sorbonne condemned their declaration that Greek and Hebrew were essential to the understanding of the scriptures; but the French parliament dismissed the charges brought against the professors. Margaret of Valois, who had now become Queen of Navarre, caused a prayer-book to be translated into French by her confessor Petit, Bishop of Senlis, wherein the prayers to the Virgin and the saints were omitted.

Meanwhile Calvin, who had a great admiration for the noble sentiments of Seneca, had published a commentary on that philosopher's treatise on Clemency. He resisted the temptation to enter the service of Margaret of Navarre; but she persuaded her chaplain Gerard Roussel to preach evangelical sermons at the Louvre, throughout the Lent of 1533. She next obtained permission for two evangelical Augustinians, Conrault and Berthaud, to preach in Paris. The Sorbonnists were roused, and denounced Roussel, and Beda vigorously fanned the flame of discord. The king for a time silenced both parties. Then Beda, Le Picard and Mathurin, the fiercest of the papists, were banished from Paris to a distance of thirty leagues, while Roussel was once more allowed to preach.

Meanwhile a marriage was arranged between Henry of Orleans, second son of Francis I., and Catherine de Medici, niece of Pope Clement. This marriage had very disastrous results to the French Reformation. The Sorbonnists were emboldened to denounce the Queen of Navarre's "Mirror of the Sinful Soul," of which a new edition Writings of Margaret of Valois. was published in 1533, as containing heresy, because it attributed pardon for sin solely to God's grace through Christ. Her "Tales," at first only privately circulated, included unsparing exposures of the evil life of the monks as regarded morality. The doctors did not succeed in exciting Francis to enmity against his sister. But during the marriage preparations, the pope published a bull against heretics.

During this time Calvin was quietly sowing the seed of the Reformation in Paris. His friend Nicholas Cop, son of the king's physician, had become Rector of the Sorbonne; and in November, 1533, had to deliver an

inaugural address on All Saints' Day. He persuaded Calvin to write an
Nicholas Cop's address. address for him, containing an exposition of the reformed principles. Its delivery produced such a commotion, that Cop was

THE SCHLOSSKIRCHE AT WITTENBERG, ON THE DOOR AT WHICH MARTIN LUTHER NAILED
THE THESES IN 1517.

summoned before the Parliament to defend himself. Matters looked so
threatening that, on his receiving a timely warning of his certain condemna-

tion, Cop escaped from Paris, and ultimately got safe to Basle. Margaret had an interview with Calvin, and promised to do everything in her power to allay the storm. But an attempt was made to seize him, and he only escaped through a stratagem of his friends, who twisted Calvin's escape. his bed-clothes into a rope and let him down from his window while the officers were knocking at the door of his room. His papers and letters were seized, and were afterwards used against their writers. A suburban vine-dresser favourable to the reformed doctrines changed clothes with him; and he started on his wanderings with a hoe on one shoulder and a wallet on the other. Many other reformers left Paris at the same time.

After making some stay with the Sieur de Happeville beyond Versailles, Calvin reached Saintonge, where he tarried awhile with Louis de Tillet, canon of Angoulême; afterwards he proceeded to Nérac, the residence of the Queen of Navarre, where he met Lefèvre. Calvin at Saintonge and Nérac. Beda and Picard obtained leave to return to Paris, and soon set a persecution on foot. Early in 1534, the Parliament of Paris ordered that every person convicted of Lutheranism on the testimony of two witnesses should be burnt. In Paris alone three hundred persons were Events in Paris. arrested. Beda sought to have Roussel burnt; but the king required that he should first be refuted, and this Beda failed to do. Soon, by Margaret's influence, Roussel, Conrault, and Berthaud were set free; while Beda, Le Picard and Le Clerq were in their turn imprisoned, for having slandered the king in a protest against their former banishment.

Alexander Camus, formerly the Dominican friar Laurent de la Croix, having left Paris and monastic life, and received instruction from Farel and Froment in Geneva, had been condemned by the Genevan magistrates under priestly influence, but released, from fear of Burning of Alexander Camus. Francis. Returning to Lyons, he preached and taught incessantly; until at Easter, 1534, he was arrested and condemned to death; on appeal, he was transferred to Paris. He was cruelly tortured, condemned, degraded, and burnt alive. Yet Francis, who at this time aided Duke Ulric to regain Würtemberg for Protestantism, in the autumn of 1534, fortified by moderate declarations from Melanchthon, Bucer, and Capito, proposed to the Sorbonne a reformation stated in still more moderate terms.

Calvin, in the province of Anjou, had been teaching and exhorting with vigour and success, and had sketched out the first ideas of his famous

"Institutes." He had already told Roussel and Lefèvre that no change would be sufficient, short of the destruction of catholicism, and the setting up of a new church. Lefèvre predicted his future power, but bade him be on his guard against being hurried away by the extreme ardour of his character; recommending him to take Melanchthon as his pattern, and always to temper his zeal with charity. Calvin, on the other hand, was distressed at the unmistakable leniency towards catholicism which these elder reformers occasionally displayed. His motto was: "Above all things we must confess our Lord fully, without shrinking from anything soever." He went to Poitiers, where he made many converts and held meetings in certain caves in the neighbourhood. One day he celebrated the Lord's Supper in one of those caves, since known as Calvin's grotto.

Calvin proposes to found a new church.

His evangelistic labours extended through the castles, abbeys, and villages around Poitiers. One of his converts, Ponthus, abbot of Valence, gave up his abbacy and entered the married state. Calvin sent out several of the converted monks to preach in various districts, and their eloquence on the one hand gained adherents, while, on the other, it aroused violent opposition. Reaching Noyon early in May, Calvin announced his resignation of his benefices, refusing the priesthood, which he should have received at the age of twenty-five.

His Evangelistic labours.

Returning to Paris in the early summer of 1534, Calvin found many circumstances apparently favourable. But his host La Forge, in the Rue St. Martin, besought him not to trust too much to the king's good-will; and to beware of teaching in public, for it would be risking his life. He consequently limited his instructions to private meetings, which were chiefly attended by the humble classes. He had controversies with Quintin and other fanatics, who declared that they were inspired by the Holy Spirit, and that all things they did were lawful, and in fact acts of God. Their specious doctrines made many converts.

Calvin was now to hear of Michael Servetus, a brilliant young Spanish physician and man of learning, who anticipated some of Harvey's discoveries concerning the circulation of the blood. Strongly biassed in an anti-papal direction, he went to visit Œcolampadius at Basle, and Bucer and Capito at Strasburg, and endeavoured to influence them by arguments contained in his essay, "The Errors concerning the Trinity," 1531, to which Melanchthon paid much attention, though he considered that the work showed many marks of a fanatical spirit. Serve-

Calvin and Servetus, 1534.

tus called believers in the Trinity tritheists, and declared that Christ was God, not by nature, but by likeness, not through nature, but through grace. He challenged Calvin to a conference, but when the appointed day came did not appear. In this year Calvin published his "Psycho-pannychia," or "Sleep of the Soul," combating the ideas that the soul had lost its immortality by the Fall, and that the spirit sleeps after death till the judgment day. He held that the soul retains its intelligent consciousness after its separation from the body; and was severe on those who believed otherwise.

To obtain more leisure, Calvin left Paris with his friend Du Tillet, and proceeded to Strasburg. He had scarcely got safely there when a storm arose through the simultaneous issue in Paris and all over France, of certain placards and tracts drawn up by Farel at the request of some advanced reformers. The placards inveighed in considerable detail against "the horrible, great, and unbearable abuses of the popish mass"; denouncing it as idolatry, and setting forth the Zwinglian teaching. After a short stay at Strasburg, Calvin went on to Basle, where he found congenial friends, and applied himself diligently to the study of Hebrew. On the way to Basle he had visited Erasmus at Freiburg, but found the old scholar still more alarmed at his proposed innovations than at Luther.

At Basle Calvin heard of the martyrdom of many of his old friends in Paris and France, and of the representations of Francis I. to the German Protestant princes, by which he assured them that he was only repressing the errors of the anabaptists, and the opponents of the civil authority. These things moved Calvin to write his great work, the "Institutes of the Christian Religion," a confession of the reformed faith as he held it. The work originally consisted of but six chapters dealing with Law, Faith, Prayer, the Sacrament, Christian Liberty, and Church and State, but was afterwards repeatedly revised and greatly enlarged. The French address to Francis I. is dated the 1st of August, 1536, and the book probably appeared originally in a French form.

Calvin's address to Francis I. was a bold avowal of the reformed doctrines and a summons to the king to hear the truth and do justice to the reformers. "A reign," wrote the undaunted censor, "which has not God's glory for its aim, is not a real rule but a mere brigandage." He exalted his doctrine as invincible, far above all the

Marginal notes:
Psycho-pannychia.

The Placards.

Calvin at Basle.

Writes His "Institutes."

Address to Francis I.

power and glory of the world; and inveighed against his opponents, who, he said, "made the kitchen their religion." The reformers were not

FREIBURG, THE ABODE OF ERASMUS, WITH THE CATHEDRAL.

despisers of the ancients, the Fathers; for indeed they drew the greater part of their doctrines from them; but it was Christ alone who was to be obeyed wholly and without exception. Moreover, it was a Father of the church, Pope Gelasius, who asserted that the substance of bread and wine remains in the Eucharist. Again, it was a Father, St. Augustine, who pronounced it rash, in an obscure question, to decide either way without clear and evident authority from Scripture. It was a Father, Paphnutius, who desired that the clergy should be forbidden to marry, and who pronounced married life to be a state of chastity. By many other priests Calvin showed that it was not the reformers, but the Romanists who rejected the Fathers.

Calvin refused to be judged by custom and tradition; and claimed that the church might exist without any visible form or splendour; its only essentials being the pure preaching of the Word of God, and the due administration of the sacraments. The tone of the entire address is statesmanlike and dignified.

Having seen his great work through the press, Calvin went to Ferrara on a visit to the Duchess of Este, a daughter of Louis XII. of France, of whose piety he had heard much, whom he influenced in favour of the reformed doctrines, and who continued his lifelong friend. *Calvin visits Ferrara.* Many Italians of distinction heard him preach, including Titian the painter, and several were converted. At Ferrara, Calvin heard of the appointment of his friend Gerard Roussel to a bishopric, at the request of Margaret of Valois, and was filled with regret at the prospective perversion by Romish seductions, of so excellent a man.

The Inquisition, alarmed at Calvin's growing influence, persuaded the Duke d'Este to banish the Frenchmen who surrounded his wife; and suddenly arrested Calvin, designing to carry him to Bologna, *Arrested and rescued.* in the States of the Church, for trial. When they were halfway to their destination, his captors were stopped by armed men, sent no doubt by the duchess, and compelled to release him. Calvin escaped, and was next heard of at Aosta. He passed through Switzerland, reached Basle, and thence proceeded to Strasburg; then, early in 1536, he boldly resolved to visit Noyon once more, relying on a relaxation of severity in *Revisits France.* France. At Noyon, he found that his brother Charles had died confessing the gospel, and without receiving priestly ministrations. Returning, he took the route through Geneva, which happened to be the safest one. He still had no conception of the great *At Geneva.* part he was to play in the Reformation. "I will try to earn my living in a private station," he said. But Farel found him out in Geneva, and exhorted him to take a leading position there. Calvin objected that he was

N

not fitted for such a part; that he had other work to do; that he needed to learn rather than teach; that he was timid and pusillanimous.

Farel and Calvin.

All was in vain against the powerful insistence of Farel. The impetuous reformer, in passionate emotion, raised his hand towards heaven, and exclaimed: "You are thinking only of your own tranquillity; you care for nothing but your studies! Be it so. In the name of Almighty God, I declare that if you do not answer His summons, He will not bless your plans." He even invoked a curse on Calvin's studies, if that reformer refused to help Geneva in her necessity. Calvin trembled; he felt as if the hand of God was laid on him, so that he could not leave the place.

LAUSANNE, THE SCENE OF THE "DISPUTATION."

"And he did more, and that more promptly," says Farel, "than any one else could have done."

In the latter part of August, 1536, Calvin began to preach to large congregations in the cathedral at Geneva; and under the date of the 5th of September the registry of the council shows the following record: "Master William Farel explains that the lecture which that Frenchman had begun at St. Pierre's was necessary; wherefore he prayed that they would consider about retaining

Calvin Reader in Theology.

him and providing for his support. Upon which it was re-solved to provide for his maintenance." But Calvin at first refused a regular appointment as preacher, preferring the office of "Reader in Theology," or Professor of Sacred Literature in the Geneva church. His main subject was, "the exposition, defence, and application of the great facts of Christianity." He was not especially concerned for dis-cipline, and the magistrates and council of Geneva had undertaken to watch over morals, and compel people to hear sermons before he had appeared.

At the end of September Farel and Calvin went to Lausanne, to attend a great public disputation on the reformed doctrines, to be held in the cathedral. Viret had already sowed the seed of Reformation **Disputation** in Lausanne, which had recently come under the rule of Berne. **at Lausanne.** In the disputation, the reformers were very successful; and Calvin distinguished himself by quoting from the Fathers in favour of his views, and by vigorously attacking the high pretensions of Pope Hildebrand concerning the papal power. A Franciscan monk, Jean Tandy, converted by his arguments, there and then threw off his monastic dress, and joined the reformers. The defenders of Rome were almost silenced. On the 10th of October, the council of Lausanne resolved to close all the houses of ill-fame in the town. On the 19th, the chief magistrate and council of Berne ordered the destruction of "images, idols, and altars" throughout the Vaudois country. Caroli was appointed chief pastor of Lausanne, with Viret as his assistant. In other parts of the Vaud country Farel was able to settle various French emigrants as pastors. At the end of 1536, the council of Berne proclaimed a complete reformation of religion in its new territories, and published numerous regulations for promoting good morals and decent behaviour.

About the end of 1536 Calvin was regularly appointed pastor of the church in Geneva. He soon began to be active in his pastoral functions, and, as a first step, drew up a catechism to which he added a Confession of Faith. Early in 1537, in conjunction with Farel, **Calvin's scheme of church order.** he laid before the council his first rules for church procedure, recommending celebration of the Lord's Supper once a month, although he preferred a weekly celebration, but the council thought that four celebrations a year would be more solemn, and more beneficial. To effect the exclusion of persons of evil life, Calvin proposed to use excommunication, and to have laymen chosen to report on individual conduct, in order that persons who would not amend their lives, might be excluded from communion. The celebration of marriage and the education of children were further provided for; and the council decreed "that no shop should be open on Sundays during the time of divine service: that all persons who had images and idols in their houses should destroy them or bring them to be burnt: that no one should sing foolish songs, or play at games of chance; and that the Syndic Porral and Jean Goulay should be commissioned to see that good morals were maintained in the city, and that people led lives conformable to the will of God." This decree may be taken as the definite establishment of sabbatarianism and Puritanism. Unfortunately Calvin, Farel, and Conrault insisted on pressing for the public acceptance the reformed articles of faith by the people individually; and thus began that enforcement of religious profession by the State, which has perhaps caused more people to turn away from religious observances than have been estranged through natural corruption. Many at this time refused to conform.

Two of the "Spirituals," followers of Quintin, named Herman and Benoit, now came to Geneva and asserted their direct inspiration by God,

Spirituals expelled. and the identity of God with their souls. Farel and Calvin exposed the fallacy of their views in a public disputation, in March, 1537. Herman and Benoit were unable to prove their doctrine from Scripture, and the council of Geneva banished them, and every member of their sect, "for ever," on pain of death. It was a mistaken notion of the age that stability was to be attained by banishing or crushing every opponent of the prevalent beliefs. But Calvin soon afterwards resisted the introduction in the Church of a tyranny which would brand every man as a heretic who refused to express himself in terms dictated by another.

By an unfortunate error of judgment, the vainglorious and vicious, but clever Caroli, who had the prestige attached to the title of a Doctor of the

Caroli and Calvin. Sorbonne, had been made pastor of Lausanne. His aim was to set up a kind of reformation of his own, with doctrines peculiar to himself. When Viret pointed out the evil of a reformer preaching his own private views without consultation with his colleagues, Caroli was indignant; but when Calvin was summoned from Geneva, to attend a consistory to inquire into Caroli's teaching, and this assembly had condemned him to retract his teaching concerning prayers for the dead, he obeyed the command even in an abject fashion. Jealous of Calvin, Farel and Viret, he resolved to turn the tables upon them, and accused them and many other reformers of Arianism. The disproof of this charge was sufficiently easy, and Calvin, with characteristic energy exposed Caroli's malice. He defended himself from a charge of not using the terms "Trinity," "substance," or "persons," as given in the Athanasian creed, by saying that he had thought it advisable in works of a popular and practical character, such as the "Confession," to avoid using terms that were not to be found in Scripture; but that these terms were to be found in his "Institutes." Caroli precipitately withdrew his charges. Shortly afterwards, the Genevese pastors were called upon to state what they knew of Caroli's moral character, before a synod at Berne. Caroli thereupon confessed to much vice, and to having delivered over to death two young men whose conduct in hanging up some images he had himself approved. He was suspended and deprived of his living and banished. He fled to the cardinal of Tournon, and made his peace with the Roman church; but he obtained no new benefice.

Meanwhile Bucer and Capito were zealously working to bring about a union between the German and the Swiss reformers. The question of the

MARTIN BUCER, COADJUTOR OF CRANMER IN THE REFORMATION.

Communion was the great point of difference. Kolb and Haller of Berne had died in 1535 and 1536; and Kunz and Sebastian Mayer, pupils of Luther and Bucer, had succeeded them at Berne. Megander, however, an inflexible Zwinglian, still possessed the chief influence in that city. A synod was convoked there in September, 1537, to which Calvin, Farel and Viret were invited; and at this meeting

Bucer and Capito at Berne.

Bucer endeavoured to show that Zwingli's views were not irreconcilable with those of Luther. When Megander, in strong language, had roused opposition, and agreement seemed impossible, Calvin addressed the synod in a conciliatory and judicious speech, describing the spiritual life be-

Agreement on the sacrament. stowed by Christ as consisting not only in making His followers alive by His Spirit, but also in His rendering them partakers by His Spirit of His life-giving flesh. "The Spirit nourished them with the flesh and blood of the Lord, under the symbols of bread and wine. Christ's local presence was withdrawn; but His spiritual presence remained." Bucer was delighted, and he and Capito signed a form representing their united views; and for the time all was peace.

Returning to Geneva, the reformers proceeded with a success which was too complete to last. The Geneva council too readily followed their

Severe discipline at Geneva. suggestions. At Calvin's request, it was ordained that all children should attend the "Christian" school, and that the Confession should be exacted from those who had not yet taken it. There were many in Geneva who had been warmly in favour of the Reformation so long as it meant merely deliverance from papal oppression, but who were by no means strongly imbued with the strict views on faith and morals inculcated by the French immigrants. On November 12th, 1537, many still refused the confession, including all the inhabitants of a street appropriated to the German Swiss, and also some of the most important citizens. The council resolved that all the recusants should be banished.

At the beginning of 1538, Calvin, finding that disorder and immorality were growing, gave notice that none who led evil lives should be admitted to the Communion on the following Sunday; and the reforming pastors requested the council to maintain them in carrying out that exclusion. The council recoiled from the step, and ordered the pastors not to refuse the sacrament to any one. It was accordingly administered indiscriminately, and disorder grew apace.

After some weeks of disturbance, new syndics were elected,—men entirely opposed to the rigid reform policy. Yet so strong was the tendency to regulate conduct in Geneva, that when Calvin and Farel complained of the disorders which were multiplying, the syndics ordered that no one should sing indecent songs introducing the names of inhabitants of Geneva, and that no one should stir up discord or strife, on pain of imprisonment. The council proceeded to adopt other more doubtful political measures which Calvin censured; whereupon the preachers were warned not to meddle with the magistrates' business, but to confine themselves to preaching the gospel.

About the same time dissensions were growing in Berne. Bucer's catechism had been printed by the council of Berne without consulting Megander; and when the latter vigorously censured certain *Dissensions at* Lutheran expressions in it, he was dismissed from his pastor- *Berne.* ship. This event caused a great excitement from Zurich to Geneva. Numerous other proceedings at Berne tended to produce divisions. Calvin wished the government of the Church to be independent of the State, while the magistrates of Berne were for assuming episcopal functions. At Berne wafers and unleavened bread were still used at the Lord's Supper, and several Romish festivals were celebrated; while at Geneva ordinary bread was given, and Sunday was the only festival observed. In order, if possible, to attain outward unity, a synod was convoked at Lausanne in March, 1538; but from the composition of this assembly it was a foregone conclusion that the Berne usages should be accepted. Calvin and Farel desired that such matters should be settled by church assemblies, not by government delegates; and they asked that the matter should be referred to an assembly representing the whole Reformed Church of Switzerland. But this request was not granted.

From the synod of Lausanne a letter was despatched to the Geneva council, praying that its decisions might be accepted. This was promptly agreed to, and Calvin and Farel were summoned to declare *Bernese Usage* whether they would conform. This was on Good Friday, and the *enforced at* celebration of the Communion was to follow on Easter Day. *Geneva.* Calvin offered to accept whatever the general assembly he wished for should decree, and undertook to make no changes in the interim. But the council ordered that the Supper should nevertheless be celebrated according to the usages of Berne. Thus the State once more claimed to rule the Church. This blow to the authority of Calvin and Farel was followed by much disorder, of which one form was the frequent discharge of musketry in front of the pastors' houses. Their lives even appeared to be in danger. The aged Conrault, who had been forbidden to preach, on Saturday morning delivered an angry and intemperate sermon, rebuking the prevalent vices, and was imprisoned in consequence. A number of influential citizens, with Calvin and Farel, protested against this "wicked and unjust" incarceration; but fruitlessly, for they would not modify their own action to gain Conrault's release. The council resolved to forbid Calvin and Farel to preach, unless

Calvin and Farel refuse the Communion. they undertook to celebrate Communion in the fashion of Berne. The two reformers decided, for the time being, not to administer the rite at all, "in the midst of these divisions, gangs, and blasphemies, and with profligacies multiplying around them."

A disturbance appeared imminent; but Calvin never thought of abandoning his position. "I considered myself," he says, "as placed by the hand of God at a post from which I could not withdraw. Nevertheless, if I were to tell the least part of the cares, or rather the miseries, which we were forced to endure throughout a whole year, I am sure you would think it incredible. I can assure you that not a day has passed in which I did not ten times wish for death." On the 21st of April, 1538, both Calvin and Farel preached, explaining their position, in the midst of hostile manifestations. Fortunately, although swords were drawn, the day passed without bloodshed. The council of Two Hundred assembled next day; and in view of the fact that Calvin, Farel and Conrault had preached when forbidden to do so, the three pastors were forbidden to occupy the pulpit any more

The Pastors Banished from Geneva. within the territory of Geneva, and were ordered to quit the city so soon as their successors should be appointed. Calvin claimed to be allowed to give an account of his conduct to the general council of the people. This request was refused, and the general council by a majority ordered them to leave the city within three days.

When this decision was announced to Calvin, he said: "If we had served men, we might certainly consider ourselves badly repaid; but, happily for us, we serve a greater Master, who pays His servants even what He does not owe them." Farel simply remarked: "It is well; it is from God." But Calvin afterwards avowed: "I cannot express what trouble and distress filled my heart night and day; and every time I think of it, I still inwardly tremble." It was probably on the 26th of April that Calvin, Farel, and Conrault left Geneva, which they had laboured so conscientiously to serve.

A remarkably mixed issue was thus opened. Was the State to rule the Church, and had the ministers no rights? Was not the minister to have power to turn back evil livers from the Communion? Were usages adopted at Berne to be thrust on Geneva? Was public authority to overcome the individual conscience? The citizens of Geneva, intolerant of prince-bishops, popes and dukes, could by no means submit to the dictation of French pastors. Would the Reformation win, or the papacy?

LUTHER'S ROOM IN THE WARTBURG.

CHAPTER XIII.

Luther and Lutheranism: from the Diet of Spires, 1526, to the Confession of Augsburg, 1530.

Lambert's Church Organization in Hesse—Luther's Erastianism—Melanchthon's "Instructions"—Visitation of Saxon Churches—Luther's Catechisms—The Pope and the Emperor—Sack of Rome—Disquiet in Germany—Diet of Spires, 1529—The *Status quo* Maintained, with Restrictions on Reformers—Protest of Reforming Princes—Principle of Protestantism—Conference of Marburg, 1529—Luther Rejects Zwingli's Hand—Articles of Agreement—Article on the Eucharist—Dangers Threatening the Reformers—Diet of Augsburg—The Emperor's Attitude—Confession of Augsburg—Melanchthon's Concessions—Tetrapolitan Confession—The Refutation—Melanchthon's Weakness—Edict of Augsburg—The Confession and the Apology.

THE Diet of Spires had given breathing time to the Genevan Reformers, and an opportunity of building up their new organization. The existence of many small states led to the adoption of varied methods of church government. Among them all, that adopted by Philip of Hesse was the most democratic. It was devised by Francis Lambert, a monk from Avignon, who had thrown off the cowl. Lambert asserted that it belonged to the Church, the congregation of faithful servants of God, to judge on matters of faith—disregarding the ignorance of the many, and the necessity of drawing some line. No bishops of Rome, nor any others, were recognised as rulers, or as representatives of Christ; all Christians were declared to be participators in Christ's priesthood. Thus the State and the hierarchy were alike ignored as controlling the Christian Church. Churches were to elect their own pastors, who were identified with the original bishops or overseers. They were servants of the Church, and ought not to be lords, princes, or gover-

LUCAS KRANACH, FRIEND OF LUTHER, AND ENGRAVER
OF HIS PORTRAIT.

nors. Each minister was to be consecrated by the imposition of hands of three ministers. They might be deposed by the Church for any scandalous conduct. A meeting of the men of each Church was to be held every Sunday, to regulate Church business; and a general synod of the whole Church of the country was to assemble every year. Three visitors were to be chosen annually (afterwards six superintendents, appointed for life). They were to examine the ministers, confirm those who gave satisfaction, and arrange for the execution of the decrees of the synod. Thus, while the power of bishops was denied, the very church which rejected them appointed men to discharge episcopal functions.

Luther was at first in favour of a purely democratic organization. He had advised the Bohemians to choose their pastors in the Church assemblies, and to ordain them by imposition of hands by the chief men. But as time went on, he found that the average members of the Church were too ignorant to have this function entrusted to them; he therefore turned to the princes as representing the people, although he by no means intended their influence to be permanently chief. He was not Erastian in principle, but only from motives of expediency.

Luther's Erastianism.

On the 22nd of October, 1526, he urged the Elector of Saxony to compel the inhabitants who desired neither pastors nor schools, to receive these means of grace; to appoint four visitors, two to deal with tithes and

ERFURT CATHEDRAL.

church property, and the other two with doctrines, schools, churches and pastors. And he followed up his letter by a personal appeal to the Elector, which was successful. Melanchthon was appointed to draw up instructions to the visitors, and Luther published his *German Mass*, or **Melanchthon's Instructions.** order of church ceremonies. Melanchthon went very far in conservatism. " Retain as much of the old ceremonies," he wrote, " as can be retained. Do not innovate much, for every innovation is harmful to the populace." The Latin liturgy was retained with only a few German hymns; communion in one kind was permitted to those who had scruples about receiving it in both kinds; confession to the priest was allowed, without being compulsory; and numerous saints' days, and the wearing of priestly vestments, were kept up. Many of the Papal party hailed this moderation as a withdrawal from the Reformers' position, others jeered at the internal dissensions among the Reformers. Luther, however, approved **Visitation of Saxon Churches.** of Melanchthon's instructions, with trifling alterations. The visitation began in October and November, 1528, Luther, Melanchthon, Spalatin, and Thuring being the principal visitors. They dismissed priests of notoriously immoral life, suppressed convents, provided for public worship, and the religious instruction of children, and maintained the abolition of celibacy among priests. Luther's catechisms, published in 1529, after his visitation had revealed much ignorance about the elements of religion, were powerful instruments in the spread and adoption of evangelical doctrines.

As a specimen of Luther's teaching in its simplest form we extract some of the explanations of the Shorter Catechism. The doctrine of re- **Luther's Catechisms.** demption is thus set forth : " I believe that Jesus Christ, true God, begotten of the Father from eternity, and also true man, born of the Virgin Mary, is my Lord ; who has redeemed me, a lost and condemned man, secured and delivered me from *all sins*, from death, and from the power of the devil, not with gold or silver, but with His holy, precious blood, and with His innocent sufferings and death; in order that I might be His own, live under Him in His kingdom, and serve Him in everlasting righteousness, innocence, and blessedness, even as He is risen from the dead, and lives and reigns for ever. This is most certainly true." As to the efficacy of baptism, he says : " It is not water, indeed, that does it, but the Word of God which is with and in the water, and faith, which trusts in the Word of God in the water. For without the Word of God the water is nothing but water, and no baptism ; but with the Word of God it is a baptism—that is, a gracious water of life and a washing of regeneration in the Holy Ghost, as St. Paul says (Tit. iii. 5–7)."

Schaff describes the Smaller Catechism as " truly a great little book, with as many thoughts as words, and every word telling and sticking to the heart as well as the memory. . . . Luther himself wrote no better book." This is but a moderate testimony compared with many in which the work is extravagantly lauded. Yet it omits many subjects of great importance, and follows the Roman Church in omitting the second commandment, and breaking up the tenth into two, to make up the proper number. It is asserted that in German and in translations it has had a wider circulation than any other book except the Bible.

Meanwhile in Franconia, in Silesia, in Friesland, in Holstein and Sleswig the Lutheran Reformation had been adopted, and important additions to the Reformers' ranks were made in Bohemia and Hungary.

Having got all he could from the Diet of Spires in 1526, Charles V. turned his arms

COPY OF PICTURE FROM AN OLD BIBLIA PAUPERUM (BIBLE FOR THE POOR).

against Pope Clement, whose alliance of neutrality with Francis I. had made him obnoxious to the Emperor, and whose absolution of *The Pope and* Francis from his promises to Charles in the Treaty of *the Emperor.* Madrid, increased this hostility. On the 6th of May, 1527, Rome was sacked by the imperial army. Luther said: "Rome has been

miserably laid waste, Christ ordaining that the Emperor, who, in behalf of
Sack of Rome. the Pope, was to have struck down Luther, should, in behalf
of Luther, strike down the Pope." The Pope, imprisoned
by Charles, made terms with him to secure his release, but yet tried to trim
between Charles and Francis. He finally decided for Charles, and granted
absolution to all who had been concerned in the sack of Rome, while in
June, 1528, Charles agreed to take active steps against the Lutherans.

The Catholic German princes had been active in persecuting the Reformers, imprisoning, torturing, and burning many; and rumours that they
Disquiet in Germany. were about to coerce the Protestant princes were confirmed by
a skilful forgery of an agreement to that effect by Otho Pack,
Vice-chancellor of Saxony. Philip of Hesse was for taking the offensive, in
order not to be surprised by numbers, but Luther and Melanchthon by
earnest entreaties dissuaded him. Yet, although the anti-Protestant alliance was a fiction, it was a fiction that had much truth in it; and at
another Diet of Spires, in March, 1529, Charles designed to reclaim all
Germany for the Papacy.

When the Diet met, strife soon arose between the retainers of the
opposing princes, who, on their part, scarcely had any intercourse with one
Diet of Spires, 1529. another. The majority was Catholic, and forbade the Elector
of Saxony and the Landgrave of Hesse from having evangelical
service in their residences. On March 15th the Emperor's commissaries
announced that the resolution of toleration passed by the late Diet of
Spires, having given rise to serious disorder, the Emperor had annulled it
by his imperial authority.

A commission was appointed to report upon this announcement.
Its members were evidently disinclined to accept absolutely whatever
Charles proposed; but it included a majority of Catholics, among whom
The *status quo* maintained with restrictions on the Reformers. were Eck, Faber, and the archbishop of Salzburg. They came
to a resolution to maintain the existing state of things; declar-
ing that all future innovations should be forbidden in places
where the Edict of Worms had been already carried out; that
no new reform should be introduced in states where it was impracticable
to conform to the Edict of Worms; that no Catholic should be permitted
to embrace Lutheranism, and that the Episcopal jurisdiction should be
accepted. Finally, "those who denied the sacrament of the true body and
blood of Christ should in no wise be tolerated, any more than the anabaptists."

THE SACKING OF ROME BY THE LANZNECHTE.

This resolution, adopted by the Diet on April 7th, though apparently tolerant, was more stringent in setting bounds to the spread of the

THE LANDSKNECHTE SACKING A NOBLEMAN'S HOUSE, AT ROME.

Reformation, and in its enforcement of the Roman hierarchy. At a consultation between the Elector of Saxony, the Landgrave of Hesse, the Margrave of Brandenburg, the Prince of Ainhalt, the Chancellor of Lune-

Protest of Reforming Princes. burg, and the representatives of the free cities, it was resolved to draw up a Protest reviewing the situation and declining to accept the resolution of the Diet. After enumerating the events which led to their decision, they asserted their acceptance of the Word of God, the Bible, as the only rule of doctrine. Adhesion to the resolution would be acting against their conscience, renouncing a doctrine they believed to be Christian. They besought the Diet to weigh carefully their grievances and their motives. "If you do not yield to our request,"

STATUE OF PHILIP OF HESSE.

they went on, "WE PROTEST by these presents, . . . that we for us, and our people, neither consent nor adhere in any manner whatsoever to the proposed decree, in anything that is contrary to God, to His holy Word, to our right conscience, to the salvation of our souls, and to the last decree of Spires."

From this celebrated protest of the 19th of April, 1529, the terms Protestant **Principle of Protestantism.** and Protestantism have been derived. It certainly embodied a far more rational principle than that which subjects men's consciences to the authority of a fallible Pope or Church. Provided we can ascertain with certainty what the Word of God is, subjection to it as a rule of conduct and doctrine is the only rational course. The Reformers, however, little versed in criticism or historical inquiry, for which indeed the methods and apparatus were not yet in existence, assumed too readily that the Bible, as they knew it, was from beginning to end the Word of God, and free from error, and having set up a method of "interpreting Scripture by Scripture," they thought they had secured themselves from all risk of error. But the divergences of opinion which presently became manifest among the more learned of the Reformers on such important questions as the Sacraments might have sufficed to show that there was no real medium between the acceptance of an infallible interpreter of Scripture, and the allowance of wide differences of opinion. Had they but recognized this, they might also have learnt the wisdom of limiting greatly the number of articles of belief required of their adherents.

The formal statement of the Protest concluded with an appeal " from all past, present or future vexatious measures, to his Imperial Majesty, and to a free and universal assembly of holy Christendom." The Diet broke up, after having formally passed the resolution against which the Protestants had objected. Many expected war. Luther thought that the Diet had come to an end almost without results, so little did he comprehend the future significance of the Protest. Philip of Hesse was eager to form an agreement, and to act in union with the Zwinglians; Luther opposed this. He had stated his doctrine of consubstantiation and attacked Zwingli's views on the Sacrament in pamphlet after pamphlet of impetuous strength; and Zwingli had replied with coolness and irony. Philip of Hesse thought a meeting and a personal discussion might produce concord. Luther and Melanchthon at last could not resist his pressing invitation, which Zwingli and Œcolampadius accepted with joy. Bucer and Hedro were also among the landgrave's visitors, who began their discussions on the 1st of October, 1529, at Marburg.

After preliminary private discussions between Melanchthon and Zwingli, and between Luther and Œcolampadius, the public conference began on the 2nd of October, in the Knights' Hall of the Castle of Marburg. Luther commenced by writing in chalk on the cloth covering the conference table, "*Hoc est corpus meum*," his watchword; and in his first speech he said he should always differ from his opponents on this question. "Christ has said, This is My Body. Let them show me that a body is not a body. I reject reason, common sense, carnal arguments, and mathematical proofs. God is above mathematics"—a truly unreasonable speech, acceptable only to those who think that because a thing is unreasonable, therefore it must be true. Œcolampadius urged that many figures are used in Scripture, as for instance, "I am the vine." D'Aubigné points out acutely that even Romanists see a figure of speech in "This is My body," interpreting it to include "My blood" and "My Divinity." Luther refused to recognise any figure in this important sentence, and insisted that the eating of His body was a command of Christ which must be obeyed. Zwingli interpreted the saying of Jesus (John vi. 63) as meaning that to eat His flesh corporeally profited nothing,

Conference of Marburg, 1529.

o

and said that the soul is fed with the Spirit, and not with the flesh. He quoted many passages of Scripture in which the sign is described by the thing signified. Lambert, the reformer of Hesse, was converted to Zwingli's view. Luther continued inflexible, and the two leaders grew rather hot in their retorts. After further disputing, Luther said, "I believe that Christ's body is in heaven, but I also believe that it is in the Sacrament. It concerns me little whether it is against nature, provided it is not against faith. Christ is substantially in the Sacrament, even as He was born of the Virgin." Zwingli replied: "He ascended into heaven. If Christ is in heaven as regards His body, how can He be in the bread? The word of God teaches us that He was like His brethren in all things. He therefore cannot be in several places at once." Luther rejoined:

ŒCOLAMPADIUS, ONE OF THE SWISS REFORMERS, BORN, 1482; DIED, 1531.

"Since my Lord Jesus Christ says, *Hoc est corpus meum,* I believe His body is really there." Zwingli rising and striking the table, made answer: You maintain then, doctor, that Christ's body is really *there, there. There* is an adverb of place. Christ's body is then of such a nature as to exist in a place. If it is in a place, it is in heaven, whence it follows that it is not in the bread." Luther's reply was: "I have nothing to do with mathematical proofs. As soon as the words of consecration are pronounced over the bread, the body is there, however wicked be the priest who pronounces them." Zwingli was constrained to retort with some justice: "You are thus re-establishing Popery." He prolonged the argument by appeals to metaphysics, and to some of the Fathers. But Luther was immovable. He even seized the cloth on which he had written his watchword and held it up before his opponents as his ultimatum. "Let our adversaries behave as we do," he said, too much after the manner of a pope. "We cannot," answered the Swiss. "I leave you to God's judgment, and pray

Him to enlighten you," said Luther. "We do the same," concluded

MARBURG CASTLE, THE SCENE OF THE CONFERENCE BETWEEN THE SWISS AND WITTENBERG REFORMERS, 1529.

Œcolampadius, while Zwingli, trembling with emotion, sat silent, and then burst into tears.

Earnestly and repeatedly the landgrave endeavoured to bring about a union, but to no purpose. At last, at a final meeting, Zwingli suggested that they should signify their union in things they agreed in. "There is no one on earth with whom I more desire to be united than with you," said he and his comrades, approaching the Wittenbergers. "Acknowledge them as brothers," said the landgrave. Zwingli with tears in his eyes held out his hand to Luther; but the Saxon was possessed by his unbending spirit, and with the words, several times repeated, "You have a different spirit from ours," he rejected the hand of Zwingli and the brotherly feeling with which it was offered, to his lasting discredit.

Luther rejects Zwingli's hand.

JUSTUS JONAS, ONE OF THE GERMAN REFORMERS EXPELLED FROM HALLE, 1546; DIED, 1555.

Further fierce debates arose; Luther was indisposed to recognise as brothers those who differed from him on so important a subject. He could not understand how they could wish for such recognition. But the gentler spirit and longsuffering of the Swiss at last prevailed. Luther offered them the hand of peace and charity, which they grasped fervently. The landgrave eagerly urged that they should let the Christian world know that they were agreed on all questions except the Eucharist. Luther was deputed to draw up the articles, and set about the work with real moderation, believing, however, that the Swiss would never agree to what he wrote. Finally, he produced fifteen articles, and as he read them one by one, it was found that all the assembly were in agreement concerning God, the Trinity, the Divinity and Humanity of Christ, His death and resurrection, original sin, justification by faith, the work of the Holy Spirit, the Word of God, baptism, good works, confession, civil order, and tradition. The fifteenth article, on the Eucharist, was also found to be framed in such terms that

Articles of agreement.

all could sign it, and this was done with joy on October 4th, 1529. We quote this important article :—

LUTHER'S STUDY AT THE UNIVERSITY OF WITTENBERG.

‘ "We all believe, with regard to the Lord's Supper, that it ought to be celebrated in both kinds, according to the primitive institution; that the

Mass is not a work by which a Christian obtains pardon for another man, Article on the whether dead or alive ; that the sacrament of the altar is the Eucharist. sacrament of the very body and very blood of Jesus Christ; and that the spiritual eating of this body and blood is specially necessary to every true Christian. In like manner, as to the use of the Sacrament, we are agreed that, like the Word, it was ordained of Almighty God, in order that weak consciences might be excited by the Holy Ghost to faith and charity, and although at present we are not agreed on the question whether the real body and blood of Christ are corporeally present in the bread and wine, yet both the interested parties shall cherish more and more a truly Christian charity for one another, so far as conscience permits, and we will all earnestly implore the Lord to condescend by His Spirit to confirm us in the sound doctrine."

Thus Luther made some amends for his previous inflexibility and harshness. The Zwinglian and the Lutheran views are two intermediate opinions between the extremes of transubstantiation and of merely commemoration in the Lord's Supper. This is not a matter as to which it can be said that all the doctrines are true, or contain some portion of the truth ; but it may be allowed that the important thing is that the benefit of communion sought should be attained, that the Christian spirit should be manifested. Christians nowadays cannot be defined by their receiving the sacrament with a certain dogmatic belief, but, as Christ said, "by their fruits shall ye know them." In asserting that the faith of the recipient was essential to his deriving the benefit given by the grace of God, and that it did not depend on the act of a priest to confer it, the article definitely rejected the high sacramentarian doctrine held by the Church of Rome, and by many Ritualists in the Anglican Church. "Now that we are agreed," said Zwingli, "the Papists will no longer hope that Luther will ever be one of them." Papists, Anabaptists, Spirituals or Mystics, were dismayed and vexed at the unity that resulted from the Council at Marburg.

We cannot here detail the most interesting personal history of Luther during this period, but must pass on to the Diet of Augsburg, in 1530. Luther, after leaving Marburg, had revised his articles in a manner which laid greater stress on his own views, and sought to impose this on the south German cities, with whom a league for mutual defence was projected by the Elector of Saxony and the Margrave of Brandenburg. The deputies of Ulm and Strasburg rejected the revised articles at Schwabach. Charles

V. had refused to receive the Protest of Spires, and had arrested the convoys who brought it. It appeared that he meant war against the Protestants. The elector and landgrave were alarmed, and thought they must needs fight. But Luther, influenced by his too great submissiveness to imperial authority, said: "We would rather die ten times than see our Gospel cause one drop of blood to be shed. . . We shall do more by our prayers than all our enemies by their boastings If the emperor requires us to be given up to his tribunals, we are ready to appear." Luther's advice ultimately prevailed; and although it has been much censured, we may say with Ranke, "Never was a course of action more purely conscientious." **Dangers threatening the Reformers.**

The immediate result appeared to be favourable. Charles V., although he was still determined to bring back the erring States to the Catholic faith by fire and sword, if necessary, after the peace of Bologna summoned a Diet at Augsburg in January, 1530, expressing his desire to allay divisions, to give a charitable hearing to all sides, to weigh all opinions carefully, and to bring men to Christian truth. **Diet of Augsburg summoned.** The papal party in Germany, however, drew up statements of their grievances, and expressed a strong desire that the innovations in religion should be rooted out and abolished. The Elector of Saxony, after consulting Luther, requested Melanchthon to draw up articles on which his party were agreed. When the elector set out for Augsburg, Luther composed and sang the fine hymn, *Ein' feste Burg*, "A strong tower is our God," to encourage the hearts of many who feared the result of the Diet. It was sung during the Diet in Augsburg, and in all the Saxon churches, and has on myriad occasions since inspirited the dejected and troubled, and given them new life. But Luther himself, while on the journey, was bidden to stay behind at Coburg, for fear that his unbending nature and strong voice should irritate their opponents, and make mischief. As soon as the Diet met, in June, after Charles had been crowned by the Pope at Bologna, he demanded that the Protestant princes should discontinue the evangelical preachings they had established in Augsburg. The Margrave of Brandenburg said: "Sire, rather than renounce God's Word, I will kneel down on this spot to have my head cut off." Nor was the Emperor's desire that they should take part in the Corpus Christi procession more favourably received. But at length, by the advice of Luther and Melanchthon, they yielded with regard to the preaching, on the Emperor promising to silence the other party also. This step, **The Confessor's attitude.**

however, took away much of Luther's respect for Charles V. Endeavours were made to stifle the Reformation by various intrigues. The Archbishop of Salerno was allowed to preach against the Reformers. Melanchthon's timidity was played upon; but the Elector John of Saxony, who was bolder than he, vowed to give up nothing of the faith. He had already read Melanchthon's Protestant confession, prepared at Coburg, which was polished and repolished, and approved of by Luther, who, however, would have written more strongly himself. Melanchthon, to preserve unity with the Catholic Church, would even have limited his essential demands to three points, communion in two kinds, marriage of the clergy, and abolition of private masses, having persuaded himself that justification by faith was really a doctrine of the Roman Church.

It was at last granted that the Confession of the Protestant princes should be read in open diet, by the Chancellor of Saxony, Brück; and for *Confession of Augsburg.* two hours his sonorous voice resounded in the chapel of the Palatine Palace, where the reading took place. After a historical introduction, with profession of readiness to expound and compare views, and to defend them in a general, free, and Christian Council, the confession is divided into two parts, the first enumerating the chief articles of faith, stated in a manner according as nearly with the Roman views as Melanchthon found possible; the second, detailing the abuses of the Roman Church which the Reformers had corrected. It asserts the ancient doctrines of the Church as laid down in the œcumenical creeds, repudiating Unitarianism, Arianism, and all the heresies condemned by the early Councils. Its definition of original sin is " that, after Adam's fall, all men begotten after the common course of nature are born with sin; that is, without the fear of God, without trust in Him, and with fleshly appetite "; and that this brought eternal death upon all who are not born again by baptism and the Holy Spirit. Men are "justified freely for Christ's sake, through faith, when they believe that they are received into favour, and their sins forgiven for Christ's sake, who by His death hath satisfied for our sins."

The Church is defined as the congregation of saints, or assembly of all believers, in which the gospel is purely preached and the sacraments administered according to the gospel. It is sufficient for the true unity of the Church, to agree concerning the doctrine of the gospel and the administration of the sacraments, nor is it necessary that human traditions, rites, and ceremonies, should be everywhere alike.   Baptism is necessary

THE CATHEDRAL OF SPIRES.

to salvation, and children are to be baptised.   As to the Lord's Supper, the presence of the true body and blood under the form of bread and wine is asserted. But the Communion is only of benefit to those that receive it with faith. Man's free will has no power to work righteousness, which power is the gift of the Spirit of God. Good works are necessary, though they are not the means of salvation. Saints are not to be invoked or prayed to, for Christ is the only Mediator. Among the Romish errors repudiated in the second part, are celibacy of the clergy, the celebration of masses for money, private masses, the sacrificial character of the mass, the enumeration of sins at confession, special mortifications and peculiarities of abstinence, rigidity and special merits of monastic vows, and jurisdiction of bishops beyond what is plainly taught by the gospel.

This confession, which was at first modestly termed an Apology, was signed by the Elector of Saxony, the Margrave of Brandenburg, the two Dukes of Luneburg, the Landgrave of Hesse, John Frederick Duke of Saxony, the Prince of Anhalt and the representatives of two free cities. It is throughout expressed in clear, gentle, dignified language, and contains nothing harsh or abusive. It pleads only for toleration and peace, and might have been made the basis of an accommodation with Rome. But Catholic princes and divines would hear of no compromise; and a commission of divines (including enemies of reform such as Eck, Faber, and a number of vicars of bishops), was appointed to draw up a refutation of the Confession.

Meanwhile things looked black for the Reformers; and Melanchthon quailed at the prospect. Influenced by the favourable expressions of some Melanchthon's Concessions. of the papal party, he was willing to bow to the Pope's authority, if the Pontiff would tolerate "certain little things that it is no longer possible for us to change." If this submissiveness failed to effect its object, it is at least clear that nothing was left undone, short of absolute retractation and submission, by the Reformers, to put themselves in accord with Rome. But Luther, at the same period, wrote: "Sooner than yield, I would suffer the most terrible evils. Concede so much the less, the more your adversaries require. God will not aid us until we are abandoned by all." Fortunately for the Reform movement, when Melanchthon saw Cardinal Compeggio, the papal legate, that prelate, while professing goodwill refused to make any concessions; and he was soon supported by definite instructions from the Pope, urging Charles to crush the Reformation by force.

The first attempted Refutation of the Confession, two hundred and eighty pages in length, hastily drawn up, was full of violence and abuse, and was sent back to be revised and shortened. The indig- **Tetrapolitan** nation of the Emperor had been further excited by the presen- **Confession.** tation of the " Tetrapolitan Confession " drawn up by Bucer and Capito on Zwinglian lines for the four cities of Strasburg, Constance, Memmingen, and Lindau; and by the arrival of Zwingli's " Confession," addressed to the Emperor personally, and repudiating many Romish ceremonies and beliefs that the Lutherans were willing to retain. The differences between these Confessions showed that the Reformers were not united: there was hope that such a divided party might be easily defeated.

LUTHER'S MONUMENT AT WITTENBERG.

The revised Refutation presented **The** on Au-
"Refutation." gust 3rd, 1530, approved of some articles of the Confession, and gave way as to the necessity of faith in the recipient of the Eucharist; but maintained that men are born with the fear of God, that good works are meritorious, and that, when united with faith, they justify the believer. It likewise upheld the seven sacraments, the mass, transubstantiation, the withdrawal of the cup, celibacy of the clergy, and the invocation of saints. It also upheld the divine origin of the Papacy

and bishops, and the necessity of submission to it. It was declared on behalf of the Emperor that he found the articles of this Refutation orthodox and catholic; and he required the Protestants to abandon their Confession, and adhere to all the articles which had been read.

For a time the Protestants were dismayed; but Luther, in correspondence with them, was always bold and courageous. "God," he wrote, "will choose the manner, the time, and the place suitable for deliverance, and He will not linger. . . . It is no matter if Luther perishes: if Christ conquers, Luther conquers also." The Protestant princes asked Melanchthon to prepare an answer to the Refutation, and this he did in the form of an Apology. Meanwhile the princes sought permission to retire from the Diet. The Landgrave of Hesse left without permission on August 6th. A mixed commission of Catholics and Protestants was appointed to see how far an agreement could be attained. Melanchthon, Melanchthon's in his desire for peace, yielded so much that his friends were Weakness. dismayed. Luther wrote: "I hear that you have begun a marvellous work, namely, to reconcile Luther and the Pope; but the Pope will not be reconciled, and Luther begs to be excused." Melanchthon, dreaded war, and the subjection of the Church to the princes. But all hopes of a compromise were destroyed by the unyielding attitude of the Romanists as to the points deemed essential by the Protestants. Melanchthon's Apology was offered to the Diet on September 22nd, 1530, and refused. On the next day he left Augsburg, in company with the Elector of Saxony, the Duke of Luneberg and the Prince of Anhalt. The Diet Edict of broke up, after passing an edict granting the Protestants six Augsburg. months in which to come to an arrangement with the Emperor and the Pope, on condition that they should join the Emperor in crushing the Anabaptists and the opponents of the sacrament, and that they should print nothing, nor draw any into their sect, "since the Confession had been soundly refuted by Holy Scripture." The Protestants, of course, refused to subscribe to such conditions, and everything presaged war.

Protestantism had now fairly taken its stand. Beginning in Germany with one man, Martin Luther, it had become a semi-national movement. The Confession Although Melanchthon was mainly the author of the Confession and the of Augsburg, it was drawn up on lines sketched out by Luther Apology. in his Articles of Marburg, Schwabach, and Torgau; but Melanchthon's scholarly style and moderation made it more conservative and palatable to opponents. In the "Apology," which he revised after leaving

Augsburg, and completed at Wittenberg in April, 1531, Melanchthon produced a finer work than the "Confession," and seven times as long. "It is the most learned of the Lutheran symbols," says Dr. Schaff.

Had not Charles V. felt the real strength of the Reform movement, he would have crushed by force of arms the States which supported it. It is greatly to the credit of the German princes that they, with Luther, showed an attitude of determined resistance to compulsion, which convinced the Emperor that it would be very hard to stamp out Protestantism. The Confession of Augsburg marks the firm establishment of the Lutheran churches, which led on naturally to the peace of Nuremberg and the full recognition of Protestantism at the Diet of Augsburg, in 1555.

AUGSBURG.

CHAPTER XIV.

Luther's and Melanchthon's Last Years; Lutheranism to the Concord of 1557.

Luther's heavy Labours—Smalcald League—Religious Peace of Nuremberg—Wurtemberg gained—Luther's Bible Completed—Pope Paul and the Council—Luther and Vergerius —Conference on Unworthy Communion—Articles of Smalcald, 1537—Luther's Later Years—Amsdorf made Bishop of Naumburg—Consecration by Luther—Catholic Dignitaries Reform—Luther still Hostile to Swiss Reformers—Longs for Death—Pamphlet against the Popedom—Death—His Character and Influence—His Preaching—His Personal Appearance — Melanchthon—His Timidity—Altered Augsburg Confession—Predestination and Freewill—Doctrine of the Eucharist—Smalcald War—Augsburg Interim—Maurice Attacks Charles—Peace of Passau—Augsburg Recess—Melanchthon after Luther's Death—Leipsic Interim—Saxon Confession—Colloquy of Worms, 1557— Melanchthon's Appearance and Character—Controversies—Antinomian—Good Works— Synergism—Osiander—Crypto-Calvinism—Eccentricities and Extremes—Formula and Book of Concord.

AFTER Augsburg we find Luther working indefatigably, to the detriment of his health, translating the Bible, writing his commentaries, **Luther's heavy labours** advising the Elector of Saxony, teaching in the University, and taking Bugenhagen's place as pastor of Wittenberg during the absence of the latter, at Lübeck. Thither he had gone to organise the

Reformed Church in that city. During 1531, he added to his smaller Catechism the section on confession, approving the practice as highly beneficial, and asserting that the confessor, in absolving, conveys the forgiveness of God. Herein Luther went beyond many Protestants, excepting in so far as the minister is authorised to declare that God pardons all those who are truly penitent.

Protestant princes were by no means satisfied that the Emperor would be content with pacific measures, and they thought it best to be forearmed. They met in council at Smalcald, in Hesse, more than once, and considered the lawfulness of resisting the Emperor if he attacked one of their number. Luther had now, to a certain extent, abandoned his previous position of absolute non-resistance. The priests who were consulted were able to make out a case for resisting the Emperor if he infringed the liberties of the States; and Luther declared that in such a case he had nothing to urge against them, but would stand aside. He contented himself with violent attacks on the Emperor's edict—which he refused to attribute to Charles himself—and on the enemies of the Reformers in general.

On the 29th of March, 1531, a league was signed at the town of Smalcald, in Saxony, between the Protestant princes and cities, including Strasburg, Constance, Magdeburg, Bremen and Lübeck, by which Smalcaldic league. they agreed "that as soon as any one of them should be attacked for the gospel's sake, or on account of any matter resulting from adherence to the gospel, all should at once proceed to the rescue of the party thus assailed, and aid him to the utmost of their ability." Some were for introducing uniformity of worship all through the States; but at Frankfort, on the 4th of June, 1531, they resolved to " maintain diversity for fear that uniformity should, sooner or later, lead to a kind of Popery."

Meanwhile Francis I. of France, through his able minister, Du Bellary, was seeking an alliance with the German Protestants against Charles V., and offered to aid them if they attacked the Emperor; but Luther's pacific advice prevented the adoption of active measures. A conciliatory attitude was maintained; and in the summer of 1532, Protestants and Catholics met at Nuremberg, and Charles V. agreed to a compromise by which all differences were left in abeyance until the meeting of a free Christian council, the Lutherans being permitted to preach and teach according to the Religious peace Confession of Augsburg. They, in return, pledged themselves of Nuremberg. to be loyal to the Emperor, to help him against the Turks, and not to protect either the Anabaptists or the Zwinglians. Nothing in Luther's character is more emphatic than his want of tolerance for the Zwinglians; Le

VIEW OF NUREMBERG.

classed Zwingli with the followers of Münzer. Soon after the Nuremberg peace, the Elector John of Saxony died. His piety and firmness of principle had been most valuable to the Protestant cause, especially at the Diet of Augsburg.

Soon after this, in 1533–4, Protestantism gained a success in the restoration of the young Duke Christopher, of the duchy of Wurtemberg, by Philip of Hesse, who defeated the Austrian army at Laufen in 1533. His State became an important addition to the Protestant forces. About the same time the Reformation made decided advances in Baden, Anhalt, Augsburg, Holstein, Pomerania and Mecklenburg. *Wurtemberg gained.*

In 1534 Luther's German Bible was at length completed, including the Apocrypha. Of the New Testament sixteen new editions and fifty reprints had been published up to 1533. *Luther's Bible completed.*

Luther's later years were often embittered by the fact that his doctrines and his vigorous efforts to instil morality and religion into the Germans seemed to produce so little result. He had, perhaps, expected a sudden and great reformation in public morals, but he was obliged to confess himself sadly mistaken and disappointed. We now see that no great movement accomplishes all that has been expected of it by its founders, that hereditary vice often appears to defy all efforts to extinguish it, that the upward progress of mankind, even under the gospel, has been exceedingly slow. But none of us would wish to return to the days of the Fathers, or even to those of Luther and Calvin. Progress is made, though one lifetime may discern little of the broad effects which a study of centuries discloses.

Before the end of 1532 Charles V. had gained Pope Clement's promise to summon a council, but this promise was accompanied by such conditions that the Protestants could not accept it; and in 1534 Clement withdrew his proposal. In October of that year Clement was succeeded by Paul III., and with him the modern period of Roman Catholicism was inaugurated. Paul appointed as Cardinals men of such undoubted religious earnestness and sincerity as Contarini, Pole, and Sadolet, and declared himself in favour of a council which should correct the abuses of the Church, and stem the tide of heresy. He convoked the Council at first for 1536 at Mantua, and appointed a preparatory commission, which drew up a set of thirty propositions for the reformation of the Church. Luther could not, after his earlier experiences, believe in the genuineness of any desire for reform on the part of the Papacy; and when *Pope Paul and the Council.*

P

Paul's nuncio, Cardinal Vergerius, came to Wittenberg to have an interview
with him in November, 1535—the first speech he had had with
a papal legate since 1518—Luther showed himself unbending
and rough in manner, and plainly intimated his opinion of the insincerity
and inadequacy of the Pope's proposals. He went on to say that his party
had no need of a Council, being fully assured about their own doctrine, although other poor souls, who were led astray by the tyranny of the Papacy,
might need one. Yet he promised to attend the proposed Council, though
he should be burned by it. It is a significant fact that ten years afterwards Vergerius himself became a convert to the Reformed doctrines, and
exchanged his bishopric for a humble pastorate in the Grisons.

Luther and Vergerius

In 1536 a conference was held at Wittenberg between Capito and
Bucer and other representatives of south German towns, and Luther and
other Lutherans, in order to come to an agreement, if possible,
on the question whether unworthy and godless communicants
really partook of the Lord's Body. The impossibility of deter-
mining such a question by argument does not seem to have occurred to the
disputants, who took up the matter as if it were a most vital point.
Melanchthon, as usual, was requested to draw up the articles of agreement,
recognising the receiving of Christ's Body by those who "ate unworthily,"
thus accepting the essence of Luther's view. The Swiss Reformers, however, never assented to this.

Conference on unworthy communion.

At the end of 1536 Luther drew up, at the request of the Elector of Saxony,
a Confession to form a basis for the consideration of the proposed Council.
It was in the main like that of Augsburg, but was couched in
far more uncompromising terms. For instance, justification is
declared to be the chief article of faith, "upon which depends all that we
teach and do against the Pope, the devil, and all the world." The mass is
denounced as the greatest and most horrible abomination, purgatory as a
Satanic delusion, the Pope as antichrist, and as caring only for gold, honour
and power. While transubstantiation is expressly rejected, the Lutheran
doctrine of consubstantiation is asserted more strongly than in the Augsburg
Confession. These articles were signed by the Lutheran theologians present
at the Conference of Smalcald in 1537. They were evidently ill-fitted to
form the basis of discussion with a Roman Council. Melanchthon, conciliatory as ever, signed with a qualification, that if the Pope would admit
the gospel, that is to say, its free preaching, the Lutherans might agree, for
the sake of peace, to his retaining his exercise, by human right, of authority

Articles of Smalcald, 1536.

MARTIN LUTHER IN HIS STUDY, TRANSLATING THE BIBLE.

over the bishops. He also added an appendix on the power and primacy of the Pope, refuting the divine right and the temporal power of the Pope, and denying that Christians are bound to believe in them at the risk of their salvation.

We need not here describe the long series of negotiations, invitations, protests, etc., which preceded the actual meeting of the Council of Trent in 1546. Luther wrote more than once to the Swiss in 1538, recognising their piety and expressing friendliness, but expounding carefully his doctrine on the Real Presence of Christ in the Sacrament. During these later years Luther suffered continually from pains and weakness occasioned by stone in the bladder, and was often laid aside.

Among the events of Luther's later years we must chronicle the services of Bugenhagen to the organisation of the Saxon churches, and of the Church in

Luther's later years. Denmark; the declining of the invitation to a Papal Council by the allies of Smalcald; Luther's bitter censure of Archbishop Albert for what he rightly regarded as the judicial murder of Schönitz, his confidential servant; his censure of Agricola's antinomianism, and of Melanchthon's exaltation of man's free will, and acceptance of a doctrine on the Eucharist not far removed from the tenets of Zwingli; the introduction of the Lutheran system into the Duchy of Saxony in 1539, on the accession of Duke Henry; and the acceptation of both Princes of Brandenburg into the Reformers' ranks. The Diet of Ratisbon, in 1541, was marked by concessions made by Contarini, the papal legate, which granted the main features of Luther's doctrine on justification. But the Catholics and Protestants found themselves no nearer to any agreement than before concerning the mass and transubstantiation. The main result of the Diet was the further prolongation of the religious peace of Nuremberg.

In 1541 the town of Halle, long the favourite seat of Archbishop Albert, went over to the Reformers, and Justus Jonas, Luther's friend, was

Amsdorf made Bishop of Naumburg. appointed pastor and director of the Church of that city. The confusion of Church matters in Germany at that time is vividly shown in the appointment of the Protestant Amsdorf as Bishop of Naumburg by the Elector, John Frederick, in opposition to the appointment of another prelate by the cathedral chapter. Luther did not approve of this step of the Elector, but in January, 1542, he consented to

Consecration by Luther. take the chief part in consecrating Amsdorf to the bishopric. He did this in conjunction with three local chief pastors, with prayer and the laying on of hands. The congregation were informed that an honest, upright bishop had been nominated for them by their

THE MARKET PLACE, HALLE.

sovereign and his estates, in concert with the clergy; and they were called upon to signify their approval by an amen, which was loudly given. Thus an ancient custom of election by the congregation, together with the neighbouring bishops, was complied with. It would have been quite possible to continue the orthodox method of consecration by existing bishops in the "Apostolical succession" by the aid of Prussian bishops who had joined the Reformers. But Luther, in this respect, as in others, broke with antiquity, and thus he has incurred the grave reproach of those who strenuously uphold the doctrine of apostolic succession.

In 1543, the prince Archbishop of Cologne, Hermann of Wied, decided to carry out a reformation within his state, and invited Melanchthon and **Catholic digni-** Bucer to aid him; and this aid was cordially given. The **taries reform.** Bishop of Münster also undertook a similar reformation in his dominions. In 1544, at a Diet at Spires, Charles V. again agreed to endeavour to bring about the holding of a General Council in Germany, and also promised to convene another Diet to settle religious disputes, and to bring about general Christian unity and reformation.

Luther never gave up his hostility to Zwingli and his special doctrines. He had seen in the death of Zwingli and the defeat of Keppel a righteous **Luther still** judgment of God, and even found fault with the victorious **hostile to Swiss** Romanists for not extirpating the Zwinglian heresy. In **reformers.** 1543 he once more expressed his resolve to have no fellowship with the Zurich Church. He blamed Bucer and Melanchthon for cultivating relations and compromises with the Swiss reformers. It needs all the charitable allowance we can make for his irritable condition caused by his sufferings from the painful malady of stone, to excuse in any degree the language he used in 1544 in his "Short Confession of the Holy Sacrament." In this treatise Luther testified once more against the "fanatics and enemies of the Sacrament, Carlsbad, Zwingli, Œcolampadius, Schwenkeld, and their disciples," and whom he denounced as "heretics, liars, and murderers of souls, possessed by the devil through and through." Melanchthon was constrained to call this a most atrocious book. Yet, in spite of their divergences, Luther used no harsh expressions in reference to his gentle, compromising friend. Fortunately, he had wholesome work always at hand in the perpetual task of revising his German Bible, but he now longed for death. In 1544 he wrote to the Elector's Consort: "No wonder **Luther longs** if I am sometimes shaky in the head. Old age is creeping on **for death.** me, which in itself is cold and unsightly, and I am ill and weak. The pitcher goes to the well until it breaks. I have lived long enough; God grant me a happy end, that this useless body may join His people beneath the earth, and go to feed the worms. Consider that I have

THE GREAT CHURCH COUNCIL OF TRENT.

Held in the Church of Santa Maria Maggiore from December, 1545, to December, 1563.

seen the best that I shall ever see on earth. For it looks as if evil times were coming. God help His own. Amen."

The Council of Trent was meanwhile summoned for December, 1545, and the German Protestants at the Diet of Worms decided that they could not accept the invitation given them to attend. Luther published

Pamphlet against the Popedom.

a pamphlet "Against the Popedom at Rome, instituted by the Devil," in which he used stronger language than ever, describing the Pope as "the most hellish Father," and concluding thus: "This devilish Popery is the supreme evil on earth, and the one that touches us most closely; it is one in which all the devils combine together. Clearly Luther's time for beneficial action in religious controversy was gone by. Nevertheless, he could still work usefully, as a mediator, in adjusting the differences between the Counts of Mansfeld; and to this piece of service much of his last winter on earth was devoted. He was harassed by pain and weakness, worried by the Catholics and the Zwinglians, discouraged by the immorality still lamentably evident at Wittenberg, in the forms of gluttony, intemperance, rioting, prostitutions, extortion, deceit, and usury. He rejoiced in the thought that the end of things was approaching, a "last day," whose proximate advent has been often foretold since then, but for which the world has still to wait. On the 17th of January, 1546, he is found describ-

Death of Luther.

ing himself as "old, spent, worn, weary, cold, and with but one eye to see with." He died at Eisleben, his birthplace, on the 18th of February, 1546, in his sixty-third year. Among his last words were these: "Take my poor soul into Thy hands. Although I must leave this body, I know that I shall be ever with Thee." He was buried at Wittenberg on the 22nd of February, in the Castle Church, where he had nailed up his theses in 1517.

Every Protestant community mourned Luther as the Prophet of Germany; the Papists exulted at his death. His influence has gone on

Luther's character and influence.

increasing, until within recent years, when the frank acknowledgment of his defects has checked hero-worship with regard to him, and induced a more reasonable estimate of his merits. The period within which he was held to be an unerring guide is past; we live in a time when broader views are requisite than those held by Luther. He considered his Reformed doctrines to be the true and original doctrines of the Church, which the Papacy had perverted. To us the controversy is no longer one between the Pope and Luther, and we have learnt to recognise the possibility of different systems of belief being honestly held, and each being so far true as representing different aspects of the whole truth. He was undoubtedly the strongest opponent, in his time, of the abuses of the Romish system; and his opposition was in great part original,

HOUSE AT EISLEBEN IN WHICH LUTHER DIED, FEBRUARY 18TH, 1545-6.

not suggested to him by others. He was a true leader, and the centre of a movement, not an imitator and follower. Originally intending only to reform abuses, and by nature attached to the Church system, and to the Papal and Imperial governments, he was driven by the opposition he met with to see in the Papacy, first, a corrupted power, used as an engine of obstruction, oppression, and immorality, and then an unlawful, unauthorized, and unscrupulous usurpation. During a long time he hoped to bring about a reform by the election of a new Pope, and by the summoning of a free universal Christian Council; and he would gladly have made use of the imperial power to secure those ends. Like nearly all leaders of great movements, he fell under the domination of ruling ideas, and was inclined to become tyrannical and unreasonable in his demands. He had not the conciliatory temper and the consummate tact of a Paul in becoming "all things to all men;" nor did he possess the magnificent organizing power of a Wesley, or the single-eyed devotion to one object of a Francis of Assisi. In assuming the infallibility of the entire Bible as he knew it, he was, though quite unconscious himself of what he was doing, substituting one human fallibility for another, the fallible human *interpretations* of the Bible for the infallibility of the Church, or the delegated Divine authority of the Pope. The dissensions which immediately arose among the German reformers themselves, to say nothing of the differences that divided them from the Swiss, might have shown them that if honest men could so differ in their interpretations of passages, there was no such infallible, unvarying, and dogmatic teaching to be deduced from Scripture as they declared necessary. The broad outlines being acknowledged, the right course was that towards which we have been approximating during the last century—the acknowledgment of the right to hold, in charity, differences of interpretation, and the necessity of refraining from hurling denunciations of eternal damnation at each other's heads. But it was harder then than now for vigorous natures to refrain from saying, and acting as if they believed, "What *I* think is right." The power of the mediæval Church, driven home by centuries of autocratic interference with, and control over States and individuals, had made it second nature to believe that there can be but one form of Divine truth; that all other representations but the one which displayed that form are erroneous, and must lead to damnation; that it is dangerous to the State and to the public weal to propagate them, and that, accordingly, they must be stamped out by force. But, fortunately for European peace and for the Reformation, Luther held fast to pacific principles and teachings. With strong tendencies to regard his own views as the only right ones, he yet refrained from sanctioning any violent or high-handed enforcement of them, and thus admitted the right of private judgment. He was a sincere moral reformer, and was more grieved at the moral delinquencies of the people, after a generation of reform, than at their deficiencies of belief. He achieved the liberation of nearly half Germany from the Romish Church, and gave the most important directing impulses to the organization of the churches—rightly termed Lutheran, which were set up in its place. But perhaps his greatest gifts to Germany were his translation of the Bible, at once the standard and pioneer of German literature, his hymns, his catechisms, and his commentaries. In several departments of work, as pastor, professor, author, leader, he displayed a master mind. He went wrong, as few strong spirits can help doing, largely through the defects of his qualities. He had strong passions, and was apt to judge others as if they had, or ought to have, passions as strong as his own. He could not be impartial, and could neither understand impartiality in others, nor put up with their partiality when it came into conflict with his own. His scheme of Church organization left much to be desired, but it was partly forced on him by the necessities of his time. Protestants can scarcely regret that he was excommunicated by Rome; for it is difficult to see how all the benefits of reform could have been secured in the Church as it then stood. In the order of the world a new departure had to be made; new ways were to be tried in freedom; the Swiss were certain to have made their own attempt; Henry VIII. must make his. Many things combine to indicate that the process of pouring new wine into old bottles was certain everywhere to result in explosions, and that new wine ought to be stored in new bottles, as the Founder of Christianity with unerring wisdom taught.

A few lines from a Romanist witness, Varillas, give interesting testimony as to Luther's preaching power. Varillas says: "In him nature

Luther's preaching. would appear to have combined the spirit of the Italian with the body of the German; such are his vivacity and his industry, his vigour and his eloquence. . . . He possessed in perfection the highest style of eloquence; he had discovered the strong and the weak sides of the human understanding, and knew the ways by which to lay hold of both. He had the art of sounding the inclinations of his hearers, however various and eccentric they might be. He knew how to arouse or allay their passions; and if the topics of his discourse were too high and incomprehensible to convince them, he could carry all before him by a forcible attack on the imagination through the vehemence of his imagery. Such

LUTHER PREACHING BEFORE EMPEROR CHARLES V.

was Luther in the pulpit; there he tossed his hearers into a tempest, and calmed them down again at his pleasure."

We have not space adequately to deal with Luther's private life, with its many charms and interests. In personal appearance he was well made,

His personal appearance. not much above middle height, emaciated in his earlier years, in later years filling out almost to corpulency. Of an open countenance, with large lips and mouth, broad nose inclining to aquiline, broad forehead with beetling brows, eyes like the lion's or the eagle's, short curling dark hair, his face was impressive and strong in the highest degree. Such was the man, whose words and writings shook the Papacy and nearly all Europe.

Inasmuch as Melanchthon, after Luther's death, was necessarily the chief figure in German Protestantism, it will be well here to note a few

Melanchthon. points in his character and career. Born fourteen years after Luther, in a better social position, brought up under more genial influences, a favourite of the renowned scholar Reuchlin, with everything to aid his linguistic and philosophic studies, his mind was essentially that of the scholar rather than the combatant. He could almost always see more than one side of a question, and thus he was invaluable in many a crisis, from his power of suggesting moderate courses, and the skill with which he could reconcile opposing factions, and show them how much they had in common. Luther appreciated his excellent qualities very cordially. In 1529 he wrote that he preferred Melanchthon's books to his own. "I am born," he declared, "for the work of removing stumps and stones, cutting away thistles and thorns, and clearing the wild forests: but Master Philippus (Melanchthon) comes along softly and gently, sowing and watering with joy, according to the gifts which God has abundantly bestowed upon him." Again and again, when Luther's strong language and intemperate zeal for his own views would have done great injury, Melanchthon was chosen to attend important conferences from which Luther was advised to keep away.

It must be allowed that Melanchthon was constitutionally deficient in courage, and was sometimes inclined to give up too much for the sake of

His timidity. peace. This very quality made him a fitting colleague for Luther, and their co-operation in friendship through so many years is a proof of this. He was always willing to make modifications, if possible, to conciliate the papal party, and sometimes appeared as if he would give up almost the entire body of truth which Luther and he had

Altered Augsburg Confession. laboured to establish. Between 1530 and 1540 he made slight alterations in successive editions of the Augsburg Confession on his own responsibility; but in 1540 he issued an edition so much changed that it has been necessary to distinguish it as the altered or *Variata* edition. The alterations were noted by Eck at the Conference of Worms in 1541, and the Variata edition was often afterwards used with approval in Luther's conferences, churches and schools. After Melanchthon's death the Variata was attacked by several extreme Lutherans as heretical, and a bitter controversy arose, to which we shall have to refer.

One of the principal modifications introduced by Melanchthon in the *Variata* was that he gave up the doctrine of predestination or necessarianism and admitted a subordinate co-operation of the human will, in **Predestination** conversion. Thus he maintained that conversion is not **and Freewill.** mechanical and compulsory, but moral—brought about by the Holy Spirit through the Word of God, with the consent of man, and yet without any merit on his part. This has been called Synergism or Semi-Pelagianism, in allowing man a certain amount of free will after the Fall. This change of view did not in any way lead Melanchthon to give up the doctrine of justification through faith in Christ; but he laid greater stress than in earlier times on man's responsibility for accepting, or rejecting the gospel, and on the necessity of good works as evidences of the possession of saving faith.

With regard to the Lord's Supper, Melanchthon gradually approached the Zwinglian views, and gave up the special points on which Luther so strongly insisted, namely, the literal interpreta- **Doctrine of the** tion of the words of institution, the oral eating of the body of **Eucharist.** Christ, and the ubiquity of the same, a necessary consequence of the power to hold the communion anywhere, as being inconsistent with the nature of a body, and with the ascension of Christ into heaven. Without adopting Zwingli's pure symbolical view of the Eucharist, he taught a spiritual real presence of Christ, and the enjoyment of the benefits of His life through faith. Shortly before he died, he said that a vital union and communion with Christ was the one essential in the Lord's Supper.

As a specimen of the essential differences between the original and the altered Augsburg Confession, we may quote the following article in its two forms (1530): "Concerning the Lord's Supper, they teach that the body and blood of Christ are *truly present*, and *are distributed* to those that eat in the Lord's Supper. And they disapprove of those that teach otherwise." (1540). "Concerning the Lord's Supper, they teach that with bread and wine are truly exhibited (or administered), the body and blood of Christ to those that eat in the Lord's Supper."

Luther, though he disapproved of several of these changes, did not alter in his friendship for Melanchthon ; and shortly before his death said to him, " The matter of the Lord's Supper has been much overdone," that is, too much stress had, he felt, been laid upon it by himself.

Very brief reference must here be made to the Smalcaldic War, which broke out soon after the Council of Trent had met. While endeavouring The Smalcaldic War, 1546-7. to persuade the Landgrave and the Elector of his benevolent intentions towards Protestants, Charles secretly prepared for war ; and the Council of Trent seemed to strengthen his resolve, by its early decision in favour of the authority of tradition, and the principle of accepting the Church's interpretation of the Scripture. He gained over Duke Maurice of the Albertine line of Saxony, and some other Protestant friends, and then proclaimed the ban of the empire against John Frederick the Elector, and the Landgrave of Hesse. War followed between Charles and those who remained true to the Smalcald league. But they were but ill-qualified to cope with the Emperor, and on April 24th, 1547, John Frederick was defeated and taken prisoner at Mühlberg, and his territories were divided between Duke Maurice and Ferdinand, the Emperor's brother. Philip of Hesse soon afterwards surrendered and the two chief Protestant princes were for years imprisoned ; the Protestant territories were overrun, disarmed and heavily taxed ; the cause of Protestantism seemed to be lost

But the very completeness of Charles's triumph carried with it the seeds of his later collapse. He dragged his captive princes with him through Augsburg Interim, 1548. Germany, and this roused indignation and compassion. He presumed himself to promulgate a religious compromise, intended to reconcile both parties, but succeeded in pleasing neither. This compromise was presented to the Diet held at Augsburg in 1548, and was termed the Augsburg Interim, as being a system of doctrine to which all should conform until a free General Council could be held. But at this very time the Pope, alarmed at Charles's success and growing dictatorship, had removed the Council from Trent, where Charles could influence it, to Bologna, and refused to order its return, though petitioned by Charles and the German Diet.

The Augsburg Interim, though drawn up by a Protestant, Agricola, with two Catholics, Pfling, Bishop of Naumberg, and Michael Sidonius, reiterated the chief Roman dogmas of the Pope's supremacy, transubstantiation, the sacrifice of the mass, invocation of the saints, the right of the

LUTHER'S STATUE AT EISLEBEN.

223

Church to interpret Scripture, while only allowing married priests to retain their wives, and permission to give the Eucharist in two kinds. Masses, exorcism, vestments, crosses, images, etc., were retained. The Interim was accepted by the Archbishop of Mayence, as satisfactory, and no member of the Diet had courage to protest. When promulgated, the Protestant divines and laity opposed it strongly, and it was never really carried into effect in northern Germany. The Romanists were equally opposed to it, because of the few concessions it gave to Protestants, and because it encroached on the functions of the Pope in presuming to define articles of religion, and that, too, in concert with an assembly of laymen. From this time the Emperor lost almost all influence with the Pope and his court. The imprisoned Elector, John Frederick, refused to accept the Interim as the price of his freedom; Philip of Hesse, more passionate and less firm, offered to submit unreservedly, but gained nothing by placing himself under the feet of the conqueror. Augsburg, Ulm and other cities were forcibly compelled to submit. Maurice of Saxony excused himself from enforcing the Interim, although he had it proclaimed. But in southern Germany it was vigorously carried out. The old rites were restored, the inhabitants were driven to mass by the soldiery, the Protestant pastors were expelled, and four hundred of them, with their families, wandered away homeless.

Maurice of Saxony, though he had fought for the Emperor, was now dismayed at the increasing injuries done to the Protestants, and felt the
Maurice attacks Charles. accusations of Judas-like conduct brought against him. At last, after concerting measures with some of the Protestant princes, he used the imperial forces which he had led against Magdeburg, to attack Charles in the Tyrol. Assuming the championship of Protestant liberties, and demanding the release of the Landgrave of Hesse, he set out in pursuit of the Emperor himself "to catch the fox in his hole." Charles barely escaped into Carinthia. At the same time Henry II. of France took Metz, and inflicted other injuries on Charles's power. Finally, Charles, through his brother Ferdinand, treated for peace with Maurice and his
Peace of Passau, 1552. confederates at Passau, and after considerable delay, it was agreed that neither the Emperor nor any other prince should offer any injury to those who adhered to the Confession of Augsburg, but that all should be allowed the undisturbed exercise of their religion; that the Protestants should not molest the Catholics; that as soon as the Protestants laid down their arms, the Landgrave should be set at liberty; that

a Diet should be held to settle religious disputes, and prevent them for the future (July, 1552). Thus the overthrow of the arrogant schemes of Charles was brought about by a man who was certainly no Protestant model, and whose action was far more inspired by political and personal motives than by zeal for religion. He was destined himself to fall in battle against Albert of Brandenburg, at the moment of victory; he was cut off in his thirty-second year, after a brief but brilliant career.

In 1555, at the Diet of Augsburg, the principles of the Peace of Passau were formally ratified and promulgated on the part of the Emperor. The Augsburg Recess, as it was called, provided that the civil power in every State should have power to adopt such form of worship or doctrine as it should think fit, and that the Roman hierarchy should claim no jurisdiction in such States as accepted the Confession of Augsburg. But the followers of Zwingli were excluded from the benefits of these provisions, and their enfranchisement in Germany did not take place till a century later, at the peace of Westphalia. Thus Charles V., who had gone forth to crush Protestantism, found himself compelled to tolerate it. This disappointment, together with various other untoward events, contributed to induce him to abdicate the imperial throne.

Augsburg Recess, 1555.

Melanchthon's position during and after the Smalcaldic War was a melancholy one. The studies of Wittenberg were broken up, and Melanchthon himself had to take refuge in Anhalt. He was invited to accept a professorship at the University of Jena, where the Protestant princes tried to collect the dispersed students; but he waited till in the next year he was able once more to resume his lectures at Wittenberg (1547). During the Augsburg Diet of 1547, Melanchthon so unfavourably criticised the proposed form of Interim, that Charles V. again and again demanded that he should be surrendered to him; but he did not obtain his wish. This ought to be some proof to Melanchthon's accusers that he was not so yielding as has been represented, if he could so far rouse Charles's animosity. He certainly was conciliatory as far as he could possibly be with a good conscience; but he was never cowardly, nor did he ever give up the truths he believed essential. Called to Leipsic to deliberate with the Saxon divines upon the religious attitude they should take, he counselled conformity to Rome in things indifferent.

Melanchthon after Luther's death.

He partly drew up what is known as the Leipsic Interim (1548), really a commentary or counter-declaration on the Augsburg Interim. The portions which Melanchthon wrote had to do with fundamental doctrines of justification and good works. But expressions of compliance with the Church Leipsic Interim, 1548. and the Bishops, and with Romish ceremonies, were contained in it, with which Melanchthon was by no means satisfied, though he has been wrongly credited with their authorship. Still he did not repudiate or openly set himself in opposition to them, and his yielding so far as he did, has often been alleged as an evidence of pusillanimity on his part. The fact is, he thought some measure of religious freedom could still be obtained under Charles. He was not a fighting man ; and so long as he was not compelled to abjure what he believed essential, he thought it possible to endure much that he would have preferred to abolish. He had, however, to go through a fire of censure and criticism on the part of his Lutheran comrades throughout Germany. He was accused of seeking to take the people back into Popery. But he replied that he had yielded secondary things, to preserve essentials ; not through fear for himself, but in compassion to the entire nation. He was also accused of having extended too far the definition of indifferent things, and he afterwards considered he had gone too far. It is a question still under controversy, though on broader lines. How much some will sacrifice to keep themselves within the pale of the Romish or the Anglican Churches, with their antiquity or their traditions ! How little some will allow their fellow-men to differ from them in matters of theology or church order in no way affecting their claim to be honest, upright, God-fearing men ! The tendency of modern opinion approximates more and more to Melanchthon's idea of toleration, and of limiting the number of essential articles, than to the exclusiveness of the extreme Reformers, with their many long creeds, which they insist must be believed, as essential to salvation.

The gentle, though firm, reproof of Calvin in 1550, in a letter to Melanchthon, is one of his most creditable productions. But Matthias Flacius, an Illyrian, educated in Italy and at Basle, Tübingen and Wittenberg, where he became Professor of Hebrew in 1544, left Wittenberg rather than submit to the Interim, and retired to Magdeburg, where he was joined by Amsdorf, driven from his Bishopric of Naumburg, and replaced by Pflug. Flacius attacked Melanchthon bitterly, for what he called his want of faith, and his treason to truth ; and termed the Leipsic Interim a "union of Christ and Belial, aiming at the re-instatement of Popery and Antichrist in the temple of God." Although Melanchthon maintained that his beliefs were still those of the Augsburg Confession and of his "Common Places," he lost much of the confidence of the stricter Lutherans.

In 1551 Melanchthon once more undertook the preparation of a formal confession of faith, which should be adapted to the changed circumstances of the times, and intended for the Council of Trent, to which assembly Charles V. had invited Protestant States to send delegates, promising them full protection. Saxon Confession, 1551. This document, at first intended to be a "Repetition and Exposition of the Augsburg Confession," became substantially a new declaration of faith, known as the Saxon Confession ; it freely refuted the theology, worship and government of the Roman Church. It was signed, among the theologians, by Bugenhagen, Major, Eber, and the superinten- dents of Electoral Saxony. Further hopes of any free- dom for the Lutherans at the Council of Trent were soon dispelled, and the "Form of Concord" afterwards super- seded the Saxon Confession. About the same time, the Würtemberg Confession was drawn up by Brentius and other Swabian divines, as representing South German Protestantism.

JOHANN BUGENHAGEN, ONE OF THE SIGNATORIES OF THE SAXON CONFESSION.

Melanchthon did not approve of Duke Maurice's attack upon the Emperor, and reminded him of the legitimacy of Charles V.'s authority, thus enforcing Luther's counsel. When the liberated John Frederick returned home, Melanchthon considered his return more glorious than a bloody victory ; though, but for Maurice's action, John Frederick would, in all probability, never have returned from captivity. Colloquy of Worms, 1557. The Colloquy of Worms, which Melanchthon attended in 1557, with Catholic and Lutheran divines, was interrupted by the death of his wife. The Colloquy effected nothing, owing to the irreconcilable positions taken up by the parties. Melanchthon's divergence from the rigid Lutherans was once more evident, and the Papal party rejoiced at the dissensions among the Reformers. His last years were largely occupied by controversies, of some of which we shall have to speak; and he continued to labour for toleration. His last days were marked by painful incidents and by illnesses, but his piety was conspicuous. His friend Bugenhagen died in 1558. Melanchthon himself died on the 19th of April, 1560, and was buried by the side of his fellow-reformer, Luther.

Thin, short, but well-proportioned, with a longish neck, expressive *Melanchthon's* face, blue eyes, and high forehead, Melanchthon had a gentle and *Appearance and* spiritual expression of face, and his features became extremely *Character.* animated when he spoke. His great industry, early rising, and regular habits enabled him to achieve a wonderful amount of work, considering his weak constitution and frequent sufferings from stone. He aimed at doing everything for the glory of God, and for the benefit of the Church. His learning was wide, and he desired that the Reformation should be attended by the spread of solid knowledge. Of Greek he was especially fond, placing it above Hebrew in importance. He was, doubtless, the greatest theologian of the German Reformation, though, owing to his breadth of mind and tolerance, no writing of his has equalled Calvin's "Institutes" in fame. He gave up too much in the endeavour to secure external unity, and allowed the State too much power in religion, even desiring it to undertake the punishment of heretics. He so far shared the common feeling of his time, that he approved the burning of Servetus. He also held the common superstitions with regard to astrology, ghosts, witchcraft, and compacts with the devil. On a paper, with the perusal of which he comforted himself in his last illness, were written the words: "Thou shalt be free from sin, free from cares, and from the fury of theologians. . . . Thou shalt come into the light; thou shalt see God, and behold the Son of God."

We must now briefly review the controversies which agitated the German reformers during the seventeenth century, and stirred up so much *Controversies:* angry feeling. (1) The Antinomian controversy arose from *Antinomian.* Luther's adoption of St. Paul's saying that the law was dead for those who believed in Christ. Agricola and others, following him, deduced the conclusion that Christians were not bound by the moral law. *Value of good* (2) In the discussion on the value of good works, which Luther *works.* said were not a condition of salvation, Melanchthon laid greater stress on them as necessary fruits of faith; and George Major, a Wittenberg professor, and one of the framers of the Leipsic Interim, taught, in 1552, that good works are necessary to salvation. Amsdorf and Flacius attacked him, and even said that good works are dangerous to salvation. A Synod at Eisenach, in 1556, condemned Major's assertion as not true in view of the Gospel, though abstractly and legally correct; but the latter clause was opposed by Amsdorf and Aurifater as semi-Popish. Melanchthon proposed to drop the words " for salvation," and to say simply that good

ANDREW OSIANDER, THE NUREMBERG REFORMER.

works are necessary, because God commanded them. This was adopted by the Wittenberg professors and the Diet of Protestant Princes at Frankfort in 1558, but rejected by the stricter Lutherans.

(3) The Synergist controversy discussed whether fallen man had any free will left, whether the first impulse in conversion came from the Holy Spirit, or whether man in any way co-operated with God for his salvation.

Amsdorf and others held that man, being totally corrupt, can do nothing but resist God; and salvation affects him by coercing his will, thus making conversion compulsory.

Synergism.

(4) The Osianderic controversy was raised by Andrew Osiander, the Nuremberg reformer, and afterwards Professor at Königsberg, who taught after Luther's death that man was rendered just (justified) by an infusion of the Divine nature of Christ—a mystical idea. He was bitterly attacked, and it was reported that the devil wrote Osiander's books while the reformer was at his meals. After his death, in 1552, his son-in-law, Funck, who led the same party, was executed in 1566, as a heretic and disturber of the peace. Among the opponents of Osiander's view was Striegel, who taught that the principal effect of Christ's death was to change God's attitude towards the whole human race. The Calvinists, on the other hand, taught the doctrines of limited predestination, either before the fall (supralapsarian), or after the fall (infralapsarian).

Osiander.

(5) The Crypto-Calvinistic controversy was really based on Melanchthon's later agreement with Calvin's doctrine of the Lord's Supper. Westpholk, Lutheran minister at Hamburg, attacked Calvin's views, and treated all as heretics who denied the corporeal presence, and real literal eating of Christ's body by believers, and in 1553 upheld the refusal of shelter to John A'Lasco and other Reformed Protestants, refugees from England. Calvin declared that he agreed with Melanchthon, and with the Augsburg Confession, as explained by its author; the holders of this view in Germany were now termed Crypto-Calvinists. The controversy went on throughout Germany with great bitterness. We cannot give the details; but one result was the preparation of the Heidelberg Catechism for the Elector Palatine, and the adoption of the Reformed Confession in the Palatinate in 1563. Peucer, Melanchthon's son-in-law, and naturally a Crypto-Calvinist, was imprisoned for twelve years, and "genuine Lutheranism" triumphed in Saxony, while Calvinists were hated, then and long after, more than Jews or Mohammedans.

Crypto-Calvinism.

The absurdities into which these controversies carried Lutherans may be shown by the following quotation from Schaff's "History of the Creeds": "An eccentric minister in Rostock required the communicants to be shaved to prevent profanation. Licking the blood of Christ from the beard was supposed to be punished with instant death, or by a monstrous growth of the beard. Sarcenirs caused the earth

Eccentricities and Extremes.

on which a drop of Christ's blood fell instantly to be dug up and burned. At Hildesheim it was customary to cut off the beard or the piece of a garment which had been touched by a drop of wine. When Pastor John

JOHN A'LASCO, THE POLISH REFORMER.

Musculus, in Frankfort-on-the-Oder, inadvertently spilled a little wine at the communion, he was summoned before a Synod, and Elector John Joachim of Brandenburg declared that deposition, prison and exile were too mild a punishment for such a crime, and that the offender, who had not spared the blood of Christ, must suffer exemplary punishment, and have two or three fingers cut off."

(6) The Ubiquitarian controversy concerned the omnipresence or at least multipresence of Christ's body, involved in Luther's doctrine of consub-

Ubiquitarian Controversy. stantiation. Luther ascribed also to the human body of Christ the omnipresence of His Divine nature. Melanchthon, in his later years, opposed both these views, and preferred to believe in a personal presence of Christ, of an undefined nature. At a Colloquy at Maulbronn in 1564, the opposing parties discussed the subject, but only confirmed their previous opinions. The Wittenberg and Leipsic professors rejected ubiquity in the Consensus of Dresden, 1571. Many controversies branched out of this one, perhaps because it is one in which evidence is least attainable and discussion most futile.

These protracted and bitter controversies were a source of much weakness, and caused great grief to the more moderate Reformers. Augustus,

Formula of Concord, 1577. who succeeded Maurice as Elector of Saxony—a zealous Lutheran, and one who did not understand the differences between Lutherans and Philippists, and who punished both parties equally, as he happened to be misled by courtiers or partisans—was the political chief who did most to promote unity. The most distinguished theologians who at last secured the adoption of the "Formula of Concord," 1577, were Jacob Andreæ, Professor of Theology at Tübingen, a Lutheran and Ubiquitarian, Martin Chemnitz, Melanchthon's greatest pupil, and Nicholas Selnecker, at first a Philippist, afterwards a Lutheran. Andreæ was a man of indefatigable energy, great learning, and much diplomatic skill, and he made no fewer than a hundred and twenty-six journeys on behalf of unity. Many abortive conferences were held in the principal cities of Germany from 1558 to 1575; but the death of Flacius and some other extremists made union easier to attain. At Maulbronn in 1572, at Lichtenberg in 1576 and at Torgau in 1576, forms of agreement were drawn up, which, after much discussion, formed the basis of the celebrated Formula of Concord, completed by six divines, of whom the above-mentioned were chief, at the Cloister of Bergen, near Magdeburg, in March and May, 1577. It was

Book of Concord, 1580. signed and published in 1580, together with the Apostles', Nicene and Athanasian Creeds, the Augsburg Confession and its Apology, the Articles of Smalcald, and Luther's two Catechisms, the whole forming the Book of Concord. This long book became the creed of the Lutheran churches, to which every clergyman and teacher was required to subscribe. So much enforced belief in time produced revolt either by hypo-critical or thoughtless acceptance, and paved the way for the rationalism of a later time. The Lutheran creed became a new scholasticism, more rational, no doubt, than the mediæval, but quite as incapable of detailed proof by any test precluding differences of opinion.

In the main the "Formula" defers to the authority of Luther, while Melanchthon is never mentioned, and the Zwinglian doctrine concerning the Eucharist is severely condemned. While the Bible is held up as the supreme authority, Luther is treated as its almost infallible exponent. His doctrines of the total depravity of man and his will, of salvation only by God's grace, with no co-operation of the human will, of justification by Christ's imputed righteousness, of consubstantiation and the ubiquity of Christ's body, are stated and adopted; while, on the other hand, his view of absolute predestination is dropped, and the universality of the offer of divine grace is recognised. Man's incompetence to attain salvation is com-pared to that of a column of salt, a statue without mouth and eyes, or a stone. Particular election of the saved and the universality of the call, the inability of fallen man, and his guilt for rejecting what he cannot pos-sibly accept, are also declared, without any attempt to explain the contra-dictions they involve.

This Formula of Concord, from which so much was hoped, produced more controversy than it settled. It was adopted in most of the German Lutheran states, in Sweden and in Hungary; but was rejected in Hesse, Anhalt, Holstein, Nassau, Strasburg, Frankfort, Spires, Worms, Nurem-berg, Magdeburg, Brunen and other cities and states; also in Denmark. The successors of the three electors who chiefly promoted the Concord left the Lutheran Church—the Elector Palatine and the Elector of Brandenberg adopting the Reformed tenets, and the King of Saxony becoming a Roman Catholic. It was converted into a Formula of Discord.

WORMS.

VIEW OF ZURICH.

CHAPTER XV.

Calvin's Supremacy at Geneva—Helvetic Confessions.

Calvin at Berne and Zurich—At Strasburg—Calvin and Melanchthon—Calvin and Sadolet
—Calvin's Marriage—Calvin at Ratisbon—Disorders at Geneva—Calvin invited to
Return—He makes Conditions—His Return—His "Church Ordinances"—Pastors—
Teachers—Elders—Deacons—Causes of Reproof or Prosecution—Calvin's Ascendency—
Censorship of Morals—Forms of Service—Calvin's Labours—Spirituals and Libertines
—Ameaux and his Wife—Gruel Beheaded—Perrin and Favre—Calvin in Danger—
Perrin first Syndic—Monnet—Bolsec—Calvin and Servetus—Servetus Arrested—His
Trial—Reference to other Cantons—His Martyrdom—Calvin's Attitude—Calvin and
Berthelier—Calvin refuses the Libertines Communion—Leading Libertines Beheaded
or Banished—Calvin's Influence Outside Geneva—The College of Geneva—Calvin's
Asceticism and Illnesses—His Death—Calvinism—The "Institutes"—Supra- and Infra-
Lapsarians—Calvin's Church System—Henry Bullinger—Consensus of Zurich—Second
Helvetic Confession—Helvetic Consensus—Cappel, Amyrant, La Place—Literal, verbal
Inspiration—Limit of Offer of Salvation—Adam's Sin imputed to All.

BEFORE he was again restored to Geneva, Calvin was destined to live
through a considerable interval, not without advantage to his knowledge and his cause. Received with something like dismay at Berne,

Calvin and Farel justified themselves before the Council, who wrote to the Genevan Council begging them to moderate their attitude towards these distinguished pastors. Calvin and Farel proceeded to Zurich, where a Synod of Reformers was sitting, and Calvin laid before this assembly the troubles and divisions at Geneva, and demanded freedom in matters concerning the pastorate, the power of discipline and excommunication, and the ordination of ministers by the laying-on of hands, instead of their mere appointment by the magistrates. Their attitude was approved by the Synod, and the Bernese Council, although the Genevese pastors had been opposing regulations they themselves had urged, sent deputies with them to Geneva to secure their reinstatement. But the Genevese proved obdurate, and the pastors were not admitted into the town. *Calvin at Berne and Zurich. Geneva still Obdurate.*

Refusing numerous calls, after a visit to Basle, Calvin went to Strasburg, in September, 1538, by invitation of Bucer and Capito, while Farel was called to be pastor at Neufchatel. The aged Courault died in October, at Orbe. Calvin began to preach to a large congregation of French refugees at Strasburg, then, next to Wittenberg, the most important centre of the Reformation, and especially a centre of conciliation, thanks to Bucer and Capito. Here he was brought into direct contact with Germans of various types, and learnt to appreciate the positions taken up by Luther and Melanchthon. Here also he had opportunity to test experimentally, under no State bonds, the plans of Church order and government which he had thought out, or derived from the New Testament. The congregation of his church were all exiles for conscience' sake, serious and devout, willing to be instructed, and from among them he soon trained men competent to replace him when he should be absent. In 1539 Capito induced him to lecture daily to the students of the Strasburg (evangelical) academy, in the Church of St. Nicholas. He prepared a second edition of his "Institutes," recast his Catechism, wrote on the Lord's Supper, accepting the Zwinglian doctrine, but adding to it a belief in the mysterious or mystical union of Christ with the elements, so that the recipients truly receive the body and blood of Christ. Luther found this a welcome advance on Zwingli. *Calvin at Strasburg.*

Calvin lived on his own little funds, the sale of his library, and small payments from his publishers. At one time he was left without a farthing, but he afterwards received a small salary. He was grieved in January, 1539, by the death of his cousin Olivetan, of whom *Calvin and Melanchthon.*

we have before spoken.   In the spring he went to the Frankfort Conference,

FRANKFORT, THE SCENE OF THE CONFERENCE BETWEEN CALVIN AND MELANCHTHON.

where he had long walks with Melanchthon, who cordially accepted his way of putting things, while Calvin was convinced that the differences between Luther and his own school were not adequate causes of division.

In March, 1539, Cardinal Sadolet, a man of moderate evangelical principles, essayed to gain back the Genevans to the Catholic Church by a letter very skilfully worded. He greatly extolled union with   Calvin and holy mother Church, and endeavoured to show how the Re-   Sadolet. formers had caused seditions and divisions by despising the Church's decrees. But two martyrdoms of Genevese preachers, namely that of Custet, at Annecy, and of Jean Lambert, at Chambery, within a few weeks, were eloquent comments on the Epistle. Calvin, having a copy sent to him, answered it in a letter which is one of his best works, clearly defending his own position and that of the Reformers, and showing the defects of the Church of Rome. He also conciliated many at Geneva by his eloquent defence of them, and by such expressions as: "I cannot direct my attention from the Church of Geneva; I cannot love it less, nor hold it less dear than my own soul." He also wrote to Neufchatel, Lausanne and Geneva, exhorting his old friends to repent, to keep the peace with their pastors, and to call upon God in prayer. His letter to Sadolet caused a revulsion in his favour at Geneva.

Calvin, near twenty-nine years old, married, in August, 1540, a young widow, Idelette van Buren, a refugee from Liège, a woman well fitted to face perils for conscience' sake, though, like himself, of weak   Calvin's health. She was a faithful helper and excellent companion to Marriage, 1540. him, so that he remarks, "Never did I feel the least hindrance from her." She died in 1549, to Calvin's great grief.

Having attended the abortive Conference of Hagenau, in 1540, Calvin was sent as the deputy of Strasburg to the Diet of Ratisbon, in 1541. It was here that Contarini made the most strenuous efforts to   Calvin at present a liberal type of Roman doctrine; but he found it im- Ratisbon, 1541. possible to satisfy the Reformers as to the authority of the Church, and the doctrine of the Mass. Calvin did not approve of the conciliatory methods of Melanchthon and Bucer. "They have drawn up ambiguous and obscure formulæ on transubstantiation," he wrote, "to try if they could not satisfy their opponents without making any real concession to them. But they are too accommodating to the temper of the times." When they came to the question of the Lord's Supper, Calvin declared, "There stood the impassable rock which barred the way to further progress. . . . The act of adoration (of the host) I declared to be altogether insufferable." The

Emperor adjourned the religious debates on the arrival of deputies from Austria and Hungary to demand aid against the Turks, and Calvin gladly departed for Strasburg.

His German stay and travels enlarged Calvin's experience, and he was ready for the next event, his triumphant return to Geneva. The weakness of the successors of the banished pastors, and the conduct of the authorities, caused immorality and disorder to gain ground in Geneva. Many of Calvin's and Farel's partisans stayed away from church and the sacrament. Saunier and several of his colleagues in the academy of Geneva were expelled, with other partisans of Calvin and French refugees. In 1539, however, a more moderate bench of magistrates was elected, and no recovery of Catholicism followed Sadolet's letter. The syndics, who had been active in procuring the banishment of Calvin, became objects of dislike, partly because they had contributed to the surrender of Genevese rights to Berne, partly because of their violence and seditious actions. Two, Chapeaurouge and Lullin, were condemned to death, but escaped from Geneva; Jean Philippe was beheaded, while Richardet, in an attempt to escape by a window on the town walls, fell and soon after died. Friends of the Reformation were elected to vacant places in the Council, and they now formed a majority. Morand and Marcourt, the substituted pastors, resigned in August and September, 1540. The return of Calvin was now sought by both Council and people.

Disorders at Geneva.

Being invited back by special messenger, Calvin was much troubled in his mind, feeling that his position at Geneva might easily become intolerable, and yet desiring so earnestly the good of the Church there that he would sooner have risked his life a hundred times than betray it by desertion. The Strasburg people strongly urged him to remain with them. He himself wrote definitely to Geneva that he was unwilling to return, except as a guide or director, with power to act in such a way as to secure the conformity of the members of the Church with the commandments of God. After taking Farel's advice, he consented to come back after the Diet of Ratisbon. "Were I free to choose," he wrote to Farel, "I would do anything in the world rather than what thou requirest of me. But when I remember that I am not my own master, I offer my heart as a sacrifice to God."

Calvin recalled to Geneva.

He makes Conditions.

Early in September, 1541, he arrived in a quiet manner at Geneva, and on the 13th of September presented himself before the Council, offering to serve Geneva for ever. A committee was appointed to confer with

VIEW OF GENEVA.

him as to the constitution of the Church; and a stipend of 500 florins,

His return. Sept., 1541. with a dole of corn and of wine, was assigned to him. Viret, who had been lent by Lausanne for some months to Geneva, he kept with him; and wished also for the presence and co-operation of Farel.

It was a characteristic of Calvin to do what he did quickly. His first draft of the "Church Ordinances" was presented to the Council

His "Church Ordinances." within a fortnight; but it had to undergo wearisome and detailed discussion, and modification before its final ratification by the people in the end of January, 1542. He begins by defining the duties of four orders of the ministry—pastors, teachers, elders, and deacons.

Pastors. The pastors are charged, in addition to preaching and teaching, with the duty of reproving and correcting in public and private. Calvin's special provision to avoid the evils and inadequacies of popular election was that the existing minister should choose new members of the ministerial order, after examination in doctrine, capacity, faith and manner of life, and should then present them to the State Council. Finally, after their approval, that of the people was to be asked. After such preliminary tests, the consent of the people, however, became very much a matter of form. Imposition of hands, without superstition, was the mode of induction into office recommended; but to avoid arousing prejudice, it was not adopted, though later it was resumed. The ministers and elders were to meet once a week (the assembly being known as the Consistory); if any dispute arose which they could not settle, they were to appeal to the magistrate. Certain sins were declared quite incompatible with the ministerial office; but a list of faults, to be dealt with by admonition and correction, was given, which is sufficient to show that Calvin was not so utterly strait-laced as the Scotch Kirk afterwards became. The Sunday services were to include sermons morning and afternoon, and catechising of children at midday. Three times a week also, sermons were to be preached.

Teachers were divided into two classes—professors of theology, and general teachers of all branches of sound learning. The necessity of

Teachers. having girls' schools was recognised. All teachers were to be approved by the ministers.

The Elders were to exercise some of the most important functions in the Church, especially in watching over the private life of individuals, admon-

Elders. ishing the wayward, and denouncing those who proved refractory. They were to be selected, two from the smaller council, four from the council of sixty, and six from the two hundred, all

men of good conduct and spiritual life; and one was to watch over each
quarter of the town. They might be re-elected or changed
annually. Deacons were to look after the poor, undertake the
administration of alms, and visit the sick.

Deacons.

The Lord's Supper was to be administered four times a year (Calvin,
indeed, desired that it should be given monthly), and the cup was only
to be offered by pastors, elders and deacons.

The most generally interesting portion of the "Ordinances" is the list
of causes for which persons might be reproved or prosecuted. It includes:
dogmatising against the received doctrine, an offence which, if
obstinately persisted in, might be visited by refusal of the communion and accusation before the magistrate; neglect to attend
public services, and contempt of church order. Private vices were to be
privately rebuked, then, if unamended, publicly denounced; such denunciation to be followed by refusal of the communion in cases of obstinacy.
Some public crimes it was necessary not only to denounce, but to punish;
but everything was to be done, not in a spirit of rigour, but with a charitable view, to bring sinners to the Lord. The Genevan Council were careful
to state at the end of the Ordinances that the ministers were to have no
civil jurisdiction, and were only to use the spiritual sword according to the
Word of God; and when any punishment or constraint was necessary, the
whole matter was to be laid before the Council, with whom rested the
decision as to the steps to be taken.

Causes of re-
proof or
prosecution.

Here, then, we have the most complete attempt to carry out the idea
of a godly society after the apostolic standards which the Reformation
had yet produced. It aimed, if not at "making people moral by Act of
Parliament," at least at securing their spiritual welfare and progress by
mutual watchfulness, admonition and correction, with punishment by the
State in the background. According to the light of the time, it was a
noble ideal. The world, under the Romish Church, had remained too immoral; the Romish Church had tolerated too much that was evil. The
Reformers considered that a re-establishment of primitive Christian discipline, with pure simple worship, was the best, nay, the only remedy. They
manfully prepared to do their part; and the innate qualification most of
us feel for judging our neighbours' conduct and pointing out "a more
excellent way," spurred them on to show that Christians in these latter
days could be inspired by primitive zeal, and manifest primitive brotherly
love. This was not a tyranny imposed from without; it was one accepted

R

by the people themselves. Calvin and his Consistory were not set in authority by armed force, but by the people of Geneva, who had found the Roman system, equally with their own free government, inadequate to realize their idea of a free Christian State.

MEETING OF CALVINISTIC DIVINES.

Calvin did not at any time claim the headship of Geneva; he did not even preside at the Consistory, the chair being occupied by one of the syndics. But he undoubtedly took the lead in everything, and as he only advanced what he believed to be based directly upon

Calvin's ascendency.

the Scriptures, and therefore undeniably right, he gained a quasi-dictator-ship which was accepted by all who admitted the authority of the Bible. His sermons, too, plain, unornamented, easily intelligible, deducing every-thing from Scripture, drove his teachings home. He had no rival, for Viret was compelled to return to Lausanne in July, 1542, and Farel was not allowed to leave Neufchatel. Thus his position grew practically auto-cratic, though under the forms of republicanism. And with our experience of autocratic rule, it is surprising that abuses of authority or tyrannical acts were so few as they were. The censorship of private **Censorship of morals.** morals had in Geneva a better chance than anywhere else, and it certainly worked much good; but if this were the fitting place, it could be demonstrated that it generates hypocrisy, dissimulation, a disposition to revolt, a tendency to be satisfied with external conformity, and other evils; and that it is powerless to reform or control the heart. Seeking to create and enthrone an enlightened conscience, it tends to develop an artificial conscience and an external sanction, dethroning the natural conscience, and blocking up the direct avenue of the soul to its Creator.

For some years the new discipline worked without producing any open disturbance, and apparently with success. Immorality was kept within bounds; the church services and sacraments were well attended; children were diligently instructed; no outside attack disturbed the people. Blas-phemy and crime were apparently extinguished; industry developed new resources; men of learning congregated round Calvin. But there was a more trying time to come.

A brief reference to the forms of service, the catechisms, etc., adopted or prohibited by Calvin will suffice to explain their nature. The daily services were marked by prayers, extemporary or chosen by the **Forms of Ser-** minister at will; but on Sunday morning the service opened **vice.** with a sort of general confession of a type like that of the Church of England. No form of absolution followed. Afterwards a Psalm was sung by the whole congregation, the Psalms adopted being Marot's translation, afterwards enlarged by Beza. The children were trained by a singing-master to sing these Psalms to some simple melody; and the people joined in as they learnt the tune. Thus Calvin laid the foundation of congregational singing. Prayer again followed, at the minister's discretion, and then came the sermon, on a well-defined subject, chosen from and illustrated by Scrip-ture. Calvin approved neither of lengthy prayers nor of long sermons, and sometimes admonished Farel on this head. Sermons of the Geneva type were certainly far more edifying than the ridiculous effusions which most of the Romish priests gave forth. A long comprehensive prayer followed the sermon, and then the Apostles' Creed was repeated. Thus the reading of the Bible and the singing of hymns, as so largely developed in modern worship, were absent from Calvin's order.

Calvin's Baptismal service contains a long exhortation, showing the duty and benefits of infant baptism, asserting that "in this Sacrament God attests the remission of our sins." The form concludes with a comment which states that there are many other very ancient ceremonies which are rejected at Geneva, because they are not based on the Word of God. The celebration of the Lord's Supper was similarly simple. It took place after prayer and the recitation of a Confession of Faith, the mode of institution of the Supper, and the assertion that unbelievers must be excluded, including "heretics and all who form sects apart to break the unity of the Church." The exhortation went on to state grounds of hope and comfort and encouragement: the bread and wine were stated to be "signs and evidences" that God accomplishes spiritually in the soul what is signified by the signs, namely, feeding and nourishment. The bread and the cup were distributed by the ministers to the people "with reverence and in order," Psalms being sung meanwhile, and passages of Scripture read. At the close thanks were given. The appended comment defends the mode of administration. "We are well aware what occasion of scandal some have taken from the change made in this matter. Because the Mass has been long in such esteem, that the poor people seemed disposed to think that it was the principal part of Christianity, it has been thought very strange in us to have abolished it. . . . But when they have well considered our practice, they will find that we have restored it to its integrity. . . . Seeing, then, that the Sacrament of our Lord has been corrupted by the many adulterations and horrible abuses which have been introduced, we have been constrained to apply a remedy, and change many things which had been improperly introduced, or at least turned to a bad use. Now, in order to do so, we have found no means better or more proper than to return to the pure institution of Jesus Christ, which we follow simply, as is apparent."

Calvin's labours were incessant, and can only have been performed by a man who toiled continually, giving himself no relaxation. His well-

Calvin's Labours. known lack of humour, of convivial or jovial instincts, supported this idea of perpetual work. But only such zeal could have accomplished what he did; could have planted Calvinism so effectually through the world. In alternate weeks he preached every day;

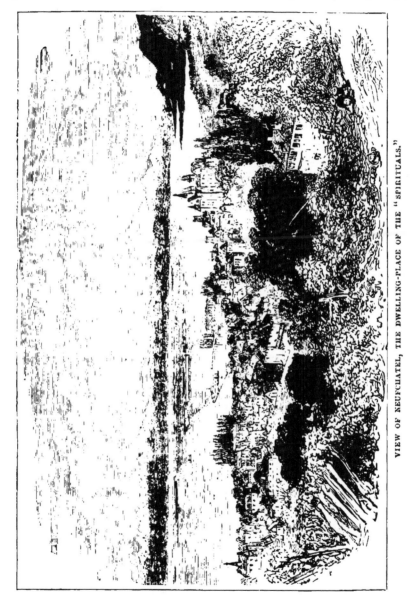

VIEW OF NEUFCHATEL, THE DWELLING-PLACE OF THE "SPIRITUALS."

he gave theological lectures three times a week; he took his share of pastoral duty and visitation of the sick; he directed, though he did not preside at, the weekly meeting of the Consistory. His studies and his writings were carried on at every available moment, from five in the morning. He received visitors and letters from all parts where the Reform movement was progressing, and had to give counsel and information to a large number of correspondents. He found time to write commentaries and sermons on nearly the whole of the Bible, and his commentaries are still among the best expositions of the text. He was a man of principle, and his faults were the faults of his principles. If he had had a more tender, a more emotional human nature, he would have found scope for them in moderating his devotion to his principles; but such was the man, such were his principles, that he was almost as thorough a ruler of his Church as Wesley afterwards became among his Methodists.

For years, with the exception of occasional murmurs, there was little questioning of the new authority which replaced the arbitrary, but often lax, rule of Rome. A refugee from Lyons one day remarked, "How delightful it is to see this lovely liberty in this city!" "Fine liberty!" replied a woman; "we were formerly obliged to go to Mass, now we are obliged to go to sermon!" Calvin was, in fact, a kind of Pope, and dangers arose, as they always have arisen, from such a position. He answered the Sorbonne in a clever ironical fashion; he exhorted Charles V. and the Diet of Spires in 1543; he commented on the Pope's admonition to the Emperor; he attacked Arianism; he translated Melanchthon's "Common Places" into French. His epistle "To the ministers of the Church of Neufchatel, against the fanatical and furious sect of the Libertines, who call themselves Spirituals," in 1544, was a preliminary to a fierce conflict with the Libertines of Geneva, which we now proceed to consider.

The "Spirituals" of Neufchatel were connected with Quintin and others whom Calvin had formerly attacked. Their creed was a sort of Spirituals and Libertines. Pantheism, which, by deifying the inward impulses of every one, gave sanction to much evil. A number of those who, at Geneva, found Calvin's rule too irksome, adopted this doctrine, and were, like them, termed Libertines; but the liberty they claimed was that of leading a life uncontrolled by Calvin's consistorial inquisition. Some began openly to jeer at him; others adopted practices distinctly condemned by the Consistory.

Pierre Ameaux, a maker of playing cards, hated Calvin, who had forbidden the use of cards altogether. His wife, adopting some of the propositions of the "Spirituals," maintained that "the communion of saints" could never be perfect until all things were held in com- *Ameaux and his Wife.* mon among the faithful—goods, houses, and wives. She was imprisoned by the Council, and her husband was declared blamable in the matter. He said that "Calvin was but a new bishop, worse than the former ones; the magistrates who supported him were traitors." He was arrested, and the Council ordered him to make a' public apology. Calvin considered this too lenient a sentence, and demanded either a severer punishment, or that he himself and his colleagues should be put on their trial for teaching false doctrine. The Two Hundred, to whom the matter was referred, found themselves on the horns of a dilemma, and condemned Ameaux to do penance by walking through the streets bareheaded, carrying a lighted candle; and that he should confess his fault on his knees. The Libertines were exasperated, and a few days afterwards made a disturbance during Calvin's sermon. The Council erected a gibbet—a significant hint—which prevented the occurrence of further disorder. But Calvin, self-confident, or rather over-confident in his view of religious authority and State duty, had entered upon a dangerous course, as harmful to liberty, and as tyrannical as the Roman mediæval system itself.

In 1547, Jacques Gruet, formerly a Romish Canon, afterwards a "Spiritual," at that time a Libertine and a profligate, was suspected of the authorship of an abusive treatise directed against Calvin and *Gruet Beheaded.* his colleagues, which was affixed to the pulpit of St. Peter's Cathedral. On inquisition, blasphemous writings and treasonable correspondence against Geneva were discovered in his house. Gruet confessed his guilt, was condemned and beheaded. In the same year the conduct of Amied Perrin, Captain-General of Geneva, his wife, and her *Perrin and Favre.* father, François Favre, who had been previously reprimanded and imprisoned, led to a movement for removing the power of excommunication from the Consistory to the Council, and the latter urged the Consistory to be less hasty in demanding the intervention of the Council to carry out its decisions. Perrin also incurred political censure, but claimed the benefit of his past services; he was, however, deprived of his office as Captain-General. The Libertines were greatly angered at the severe treatment of their prominent members, and the ministers, on December 12th, 1547, after vigorous remonstrances had been addressed to the Favres by Calvin, went to the Council and complained that "a great deal of insolence, debauchery, dissoluteness and hatred was prevalent, to the ruin of the State." On the 10th of the same month, Calvin, alone and unprotected, en-

Calvin in Danger. tered a meeting of the Two Hundred, where threats of violence had been uttered against him. There were loud outcries against him. Swords were drawn. He advanced with a calm, intrepid air, and said, "If you will have blood, shed mine. If you vehemently wish me to be exiled, I will exile myself. If you wish to endeavour once more to save Geneva without the Gospel, you can try." Once again his powerful spirit prevailed, and opposition was quelled. Quarrels were temporarily patched up.

But again, in 1548, the complaint was made that Perrin and others kept away from the communion. Calvin complained of many personal

Perrin first syndic. insults he had received from the Libertines, such as hissing at him in the streets, calling dogs by the name of Calvin in derision, etc. But early in 1549 Perrin became first syndic, having previously merged his captain-generalship. With no disposition to yield, Calvin was skilful enough to have a proclamation made, in which the principal censure for disorder was visited on the pastors, who were enjoined to make it their duty to be more careful and zealous in teaching and admonishing, and in duly reproving vice.

A man named Raoul Monnet, a person of loose morals and life, carried about and exhibited to the young a series of licentious prints and

Monnet. burlesques on the Bible; he was condemned to death in 1549. Even the Libertines had nothing to say in his favour. In 1551 Bolsec, a Carmelite friar, who had renounced Romanism and become a

Bolsec. physician, publicly attacked Calvin's views on predestination as heretical, and as making God the Author of evil. After a two days' discussion before the Council, he was banished for life from Geneva. Calvin, though he did not press for a severer punishment, confessed that he would rather a hundred times be a papist than Bolsec, who survived these events many years, became a Romanist, and published a libellous account of Calvin's manners and morals.

In 1553, at the time when Calvin's conflict with the Libertines culminated in his refusal to admit them to the Lord's Supper, his

Calvin and Servetus. reputation, and the fame of the Swiss Reformation, was tarnished by the martyrdom of Servetus.[1] We have already seen

---

[1] For a full statement of the facts, Dr. R. Willis's able book, "Servetus and Calvin," should be consulted.

that, under the name of Villeneuve, Servetus had sought a conference with Calvin in Paris in 1534. He had since led a wandering life, but had resided for years at Lyons as an editor and corrector of the press, in the service of the celebrated printers, Trechsel. Subsequently he had qualified in medicine and arts at Paris, and had afterwards settled at Vienne, in Dauphiny. In 1546 a correspondence began between Calvin and Servetus, who thought the great Reformer had only as yet gone half-way towards a real reformation, and who offered to teach him his own system, which was to lead to a grander development of truth. Servetus sent Calvin a copy of his "Institutes," freely annotated and criticised; and about the same time Calvin, in a letter to Farel, says: "Servetus wrote to me lately, and, beside his letter, sent me a great volume full of his ravings. . . . He offers to come hither if I approve; but I will not pledge my faith to him; for if he shall come, so far as my authority avails, I shall not suffer him to depart alive." The tone of Servetus to Calvin was even more arrogant and self-sufficient. In 1552 Servetus published privately at Vienne his religious views, under the title "Christianismi Restitutio," which led to his accusation before the Inquisition, and to his imprisonment; but he escaped, and was condemned in absence to be burnt to death over a slow fire. Having evaded the Catholic fire, he felt he must come and combat the equally hostile Reformer at Geneva; and he came, in spite of Calvin's warning.

Essentially, Servetus regarded the orthodox doctrines of the Trinity as involving tritheism, and leading to atheism; he believed in a Trinity of manifestation only. He regarded much of the Reformation as a return to Judaism. His prayer in the conclusion of the main part of his work indicates his sincere spirit and broad belief: "Almighty Father! Father of all mercy, free us miserable men from this darkness of death, for the sake of Thy Son Jesus Christ our Lord. O Jesus Christ our Lord, O Jesus Christ, thou Son of God, who died for us, help us, lest we perish! We, Thy suppliants, pray to Thee as Thou hast taught us, saying, Hallowed be Thy name; Thy Kingdom come; and do Thou, Lord, come! . . . Thou who hast said, 'I come quickly,' wilt surely come, and with Thy coming put an end to Antichrist. So be it. Amen!" *Servetus' teaching.*

After some wanderings, Servetus came to Geneva in the middle of July, 1553, at first lying in concealment. As soon as he was recognised, Calvin summoned him to one of the syndics, and called for his immediate arrest. A young student, Nicholas de la Fontaine, *Servetus arrested.*

Calvin's secretary, at first undertook the office of accuser; but at the trial Calvin came forward as chief accuser, and argued earnestly with Servetus,

MARTYRDOM OF SERVETUS.

His trial. in hope of persuading him to recant. The accusation was mainly founded on the "Christianismi Restitutio." Servetus offered to make good his propositions; but at another time he professed himself ready to recant his errors. He replied to Calvin at first with much anger, calling him a liar, the corrupter of the word of God, a sorcerer, and "Simon Magus." Calvin, sincerely persuaded of the evil contained in Servetus' doctrine, and of its injurious effects if not stayed, used much public and private influence against him, actuated entirely by conscientious motives.

The Council of Geneva asked an opinion on the case from the Councils and ministers of Berne, Basle, Zurich, and Schaffhausen. The trial was greatly prolonged, and was interrupted by differences between Calvin and the Council. The prosecution was taken up by the attorney-general of Geneva, and the grounds of accusation were continually shifted. Servetus was denied aid in his defence, and was kept imprisoned in a loathsome cell. In vain did Servetus protest that he was not a subject of Geneva, that he had committed no offence within its territory, that he was no disturber of the peace, and that, according to the Scriptures and to the early Church, it was not right to make the interpretation of Scripture a subject of criminal accusation. Calvin preached against him, exposing his errors in their most repulsive aspects, and reproaching those persons who had shown sympathy with him. Only irritation resulted from Calvin's intercourse with, or public examination of, Servetus. The responses of the Evangelical Cantons, condemning his heresies, *Reference to other Cantons.* but omitting to declare what was the appropriate punishment, gave an additional impulse towards a capital sentence. On the 26th of October, at a meeting of the Council at which Perrin presided, but from which some of Calvin's opponents were absent, after Perrin had attempted in several ways to save him, Servetus was sentenced to be burnt alive on the next day, and his books were to be destroyed with him. Calvin sought to get the sentence reduced to beheading by the sword; but the majority refused even this mitigation. Servetus, before he suffered, asked Calvin's pardon. Calvin justified his conduct on public grounds, and vituperated his enemy, according to his usual practice. Farel, who accom- *Martyrdom of Servetus, Oct. 27th, 1553.* panied the victim on the way to his execution, tried to induce him to acknowledge Christ as the eternal Son of God; but the prayer of Servetus was: "O God, save my soul! O Jesus, Son of the eternal God, have compassion on me!"

Servetus did not die in vain if his death established the principle that it was irrational and absurd for those who claim religious liberty themselves to persecute men who only make the same claim on their own behalf. Had it not been for Calvin's influence, Servetus might have escaped; but we must remember that even the placid Melanchthon approved of his death. Such deeds were the fault of the age; nor must we be surprised if people who had been by the Roman Church thoroughly persuaded of the righteousness of burning heretics, took a long while to unlearn the lesson, even when the grounds of condemnation were changed. There was on all sides an ardent zeal for truth and a hatred of false doctrine. Men had as yet entirely failed to grasp the idea that truth may be many-sided, and that the knowledge of truth is more easily won by free speech and criticism than by forcible repression. It seemed to the magistrates of the time that the only way of securing public order was to root out all false religious doctrine, which had often been made the basis of political disorder; and they had to learn that burning the heretic makes his error known, leads to examination and often to adoption of his teaching; that the vitality of truth is not best secured by artificial protection; that free and open criticism is the best means of combating and destroying error; and that the final appeal is to human reason, not to brute force. Human reason can control brute force in the long run; brute force can never fetter or destroy the power and right of the human reason to say with Galileo: "Nevertheless, it moves."

While it would be wrong to assert that Calvin was actuated by mere bigotry or by personal motives in his harsh conduct towards Servetus, there **Calvin's attitude.** can be little doubt that he was partly blinded by prejudice, and by the want of reverence and respect Servetus had incautiously displayed towards him. We must condemn many of his acts in this matter, without necessarily calling in question his conscientiousness. It was a profound mistake, which could hardly have been made had Calvin been more human, less intellectual, more tender-hearted. Devoted to logic and disputation, he acted like many logicians, most illogically, in punishing an intellectual adversary, whereas he did not mete the same measure to Papists and Libertines. His memory can never be freed from the stain of Servetus' death.

We now return to the case of the Libertines. While Servetus was slowly being dragged to the stake, Calvin was fighting for the rights of **Calvin and Berthelier.** his own Church against the Libertines and against those who wished to give the civil power complete control over the Church. Philip Berthelier, son of the early martyr of Genevan liberty, had again and again been summoned before the Consistory for his free life and scoffing tongue; and at length, just before the September communion, having been excommunicated, he appealed to the Council against his exclusion. His friends were numerous and influential; and they persuaded the Council to declare that if in his conscience he felt he could communicate, he was free to do so. However much this may be in consonance with present-day notions of liberty, it was not a principle which the Council of Geneva was prepared to extend impartially to all: it was a special case of obliging Berthelier, and of controlling the Consistory and Calvin, whose method of proceeding was by many found too severe; and to refuse such liberty to Servetus, while it was granted to a profligate, was an arbitrary and entirely indefensible act.

Calvin had already done his utmost to warn the Lesser Council. When the case went against him, he betook himself to the Great Council, with all the clergy, and announced with characteristic energy that he would die rather than tolerate the presence of an excommunicated man at the holy table. The pastors declared as one man that they would lay down their offices and leave the churches rather than submit to the decision of the Council. No revocation could be obtained, but the Council privately begged Berthelier not to appear at church at the time of communion.

On Sunday, the 3rd of September, 1553, Calvin preached to a congregation which included a strong body of Libertines, and declared that he would ever guide himself by his Master's rule, which was to him clear and intelligible. If any person who had been interdicted by Calvin refuses the Libertines Communion. the Consistory should intrude himself at the table, he would certainly, as long as he lived, take the course he thought right. Still the Libertines ventured to approach to receive the communion. Calvin, guarding the bread and wine with his hands, said: "You may cut these hands off, and crush these limbs; my blood is yours, shed it. But you shall never force me to give holy things to the profane." The Libertines paused, looked round, saw themselves encircled by reproving faces, and fell back. Calvin had conquered, but in his afternoon sermon he spoke as if he expected banishment.

No thoughtful reader can fail to admire the intrepidity of Calvin in thus upholding, as he believed to be his duty as pastor, the tenets of his form of Protestantism. It would have been well if he had been as careful of the liberty of others as of his own. But his one desire was that what he conscientiously believed to be the truth should triumph and be enforced. He was fatally infected with the idea that truth and moral teaching should be enforced by means of penalties and punishments. He gained strength

CALVIN REFUSING THE COMMUNION TO THE LIBERTINES.

by his victory ; and when Farel, a short time afterwards, denounced the Libertines as atheists, Calvin's influence and his own was such that he was upheld and praised by the Council.

But Berthelier had only retired to renew his attack more vigorously and with better advantage. The rebellion against Calvin's influence was vigorously promoted in 1554, and with profane songs and re- velling, the Reformers were denounced. Berthelier, Perrin and Leading Libertines beheaded or banished. his friends sought to hamper the numerous refugees, to curtail their liberties, and to deprive them of their swords. At last, in May, 1555, an insurrection was attempted, but the state troops soon put it down. Many Libertines escaped, and among them Perrin; others, including a brother of Berthelier, were beheaded; the rest of the Libertines were banished. For years, by their machinations in Berne, Savoy and else- where, they were a cause of offence and injury to Geneva; but they gained no permanent success. If they had gained the upper hand at Geneva in 1555, the Reformation, as there established, would have been rendered nugatory.

It is impossible to give, in detail, an account of Calvin's labours in writing, in correspondence, and advice, or of his influence on outer Pro- testantism. Incidents may be gathered from other chapters on the history of the French, English, Scotch and German Reforma- Calvin's in- fluence outside Geneva. tion. Everywhere his counsel was what might be expected from his conduct at Geneva. He did everything he could to secure the establishment of pure truth, as he understood it. He encouraged those who were about to suffer martyrdom, declaring that they were nobly doing their duty, and were about to earn a heavenly crown. His faith was sub- lime, if his sympathies were by no means fully human. His spirit was strong to the highest degree ; he could endure no paltering with duty or with the faith. He was admired but scarcely loved, except by those who were thoroughly of the same mind with him. Theodore Beza in Geneva, and John Knox in Scotland, having learnt much before they came to him, were established by him in their stern faith, and were prepared to carry on his work after his death. His last years were passed in the exercise of a supremacy scarcely disputed, and John Knox described Geneva as " the most perfect school of Christ that ever existed on earth since the days of the apostles." "In other places," he says, " I confess Christ to be truly preached ; but manners and religion to be so sincerely reformed, I have not yet seen in any other place besides."

One of Calvin's notable services to Geneva was the founding of the Academy and College for higher education. The poverty of the State prevented early fruition of his design. Though land was bought for a building in 1552, it was not till 1558 that the work was taken in hand, supported by a public subscription of 10,000 florins. On the 7th of June, 1559, it was opened, and Theodore Beza was appointed rector, with five professors; two of them to teach theology, and one each to lecture on Hebrew, Greek, and philosophy.

Throughout his life Calvin was in his habits an ascetic. But though always poor, he gave freely to the necessities of others. Pope Pius IV.

Calvin's asceticism and illness. said of him: "What made the strength of that heretic was that money was nothing to him." For several years he was accustomed to take only one meal a day. During his last illness he refused to receive his quarter's salary. He had not earned it, he said; how could he accept it? It is scarcely to be wondered at that, with his labours and habits, he suffered in later years from various painful diseases. Several of his most characteristic treatises were written when he was racked with pain and greatly enfeebled. Early in 1564 his preaching was finally stopped by a violent fit of coughing and a rush of blood into his mouth. He still spared himself no labour, and on Easter Sunday, April 2nd, was carried to church, to receive the communion he had so long administered. Being visited once more, at his earnest request, by the Council, he prayed them to pardon all his faults, and urged on them to keep Geneva faithful to its duty. The pastors he likewise exhorted to perform their office faithfully after his death, and to maintain good order and doctrine. Farel, now eighty years of age, came to see him in May. On May 19th he for the last time sat for a short time at table with the clergy

His death, May 27, 1564. at supper. He lingered till the 27th of May, 1564. His last words were, "The sufferings of this present time are not worthy to be compared with the glory hereafter." His funeral took place on the next day, Sunday, at the cemetery in Plain-palais, where no monument was raised over him according to the Genevese custom of the time.

Calvin founded the system known as Calvinism, which up to the present time has had an even greater vogue than Methodism, its later rival.

Calvin and Calvinism. Renan terms Calvin "the most Christian man of his generation," a distinction he himself would have repelled, and which it is futile to confer upon anyone. His singularly powerful and original intellect has impressed itself upon men so intensely that it must be held to have answered many of the deep feelings, instincts or convictions of humanity. Calvinism seemed to provide a clear scheme of Divine Providence and human redemption and duty. It has been maintained and even intensified by later theologians, but is now giving way to a reaction from its over-severity, and to a broader and more charitable view of human and Divine relationship. But in an age when vice, crime, and lawlessness were rife, the moral self-denying life, the godly conduct, the hospitality to refugees, of the majority of the Genevan citizens, formed a testimony which convincingly justified Calvinism by its fruits. Geneva became a Protestant Rome, with far fewer evils and more holiness. It is doubtful if such a city, as self-denying and religious, now exists. Our modern tolerance tends to become indifference. Doubting what to believe, and hesitating to take the trouble to search for the truth, we do not dare for truth what Calvin and Geneva dared. We ignobly comply with the spirit of our age. Had they done so, Geneva might have failed to create and arouse that new spirit which went forth into nearly all lands and conquered many millions for a faith divested of many superstitious growths and deformities, making no artificial barrier between man and God, if its demands were too rigid, its discipline too stern and unbending, and too regardless of the gentler elements in human nature.

Calvin's " Institutes " is both a literary and a theological masterpiece. The first section deals with theology or the knowledge of God; the second The "In- with Christology or the present redemptive work of Christ; the stitutes." third with soteriology, or the actual salvation of man through the work of the Holy Spirit; the fourth with the Church as an organization, and the sacraments. It is most original in its doctrines of Predestination and the Lord's Supper. Predestination Calvin defined as the eternal decree of God by which part of the human race, without any merit of their own, are elected to holiness and eternal life, part are destined to eternal damnation, in just punishment of their sin. He felt that the latter was a horrible decree, though nevertheless true, and, as God's decree, unimpeachable by man, and compatible with Divine love, justice, and perfection. " Adam fell, God's providence having so ordained it; yet he fell by his own guilt." He believed that God was supreme, to such an extent that sin only took place by His fore-ordination; yet he did not make God the author of sin. Much of his argument was based on the ninth chapter of St. Paul's Epistle to the Romans. One of his great objects was to uproot all human pride in free-will or voluntary efforts, and to strengthen the

S

gratitude and courage of the "elect." It may certainly be said that his doctrine had no tendency to favour licence or careless security. We have sufficiently referred to Calvin's views of the Lord's Supper elsewhere.

The Calvinistic doctrine of predestination was carried on after his death by Beza and others into a "supra-lapsarian" extreme, which made every particular man before the fall, or before creation, the object of election either to salvation or damnation; but this view was never endorsed by the creeds of the churches. The "infra-lapsarian" view has been adopted and incorporated into all Calvinistic confessions. It states that man fell and became condemned by his own voluntary sin, and rejects the belief that God has decreed the existence of sin. This is essentially the view taken in the Swiss, French, Scotch, Dutch, and Westminster Confessions; while the English Thirty-nine Articles, the Heidelberg Catechism, and the other German Reformed confessions expound only the positive side of the doctrine, namely, the fore-election of all who believe, without asserting the fore-damnation of unbelievers. *Supra & infra-lapsarians.*

Calvin's church system involved rigid discipline over the members, government largely by elders, and the maintenance of independence of state interference, though the reception of stipends from the state was not forbidden. In his view all ministers were equal; but he did not object to the retention of episcopacy when it was desired. His recourse to state power in order to punish heretics was a relic of the Middle Ages and of Judaism, which shows how deeply rooted this spirit was in mankind. He attempted to revive a theocracy which should be adequate for all spiritual purposes, and if he failed to accomplish all he desired, he achieved much that was permanent, and his errors teach as much as his successes. *Calvin's Church system.*

After Calvin's death, the first important Reformed creed was the "Second Helvetic Confession," drawn up in 1562 for his own use by Henry Bullinger, the successor of Zwinglius at Zurich, and only second to Calvin as a leader among the Swiss and Reformed Churches. His influence on English Protestantism was considerable, and several exiles were received during the persecution under Queen Mary Tudor in his own house and those of his friends. Bishop Hooper wrote from prison before his martyrdom to Bullinger as "his revered father and guide," and the best friend he had ever found. Many letters addressed to Bullinger from England are published in the "Zurich Letters" (Parker Society). He was friendly with the elder Socinus, as indeed was Calvin, though both en- *Henry Bullinger.*

A SWISS REFORMER PREACHING.

deavoured to restrain their friend's heretical tendency. In 1549, after long
Consensus of Zurich. preliminary correspondence with Calvin, the Consensus of Zurich
(Tigurinus) was agreed to by Bullinger and adopted by both
sections of the Swiss Churches, marking an advance on the Zwinglian doctrine. While the corporeal presence of Christ in the communion is denied,
it asserts that there is a real spiritual presence of Christ's body and blood,
by the power of the Holy Spirit and the faith of the recipient.

Bullinger further elaborated his "Confession" during the pestilence of
1564, when he daily expected death. The Elector Palatine Frederick III.
Second Helvetic confession, 1566. having adopted the Swiss Reformed views and published the
Heidelberg catechism in 1563, was threatened with exclusion
from the Religious Peace in Germany. He consequently requested Bullinger in 1565 to prepare a full exposition of the Reformed
faith, to which Bullinger readily replied by sending a copy of his manuscript. It was so satisfactory that the Elector desired to have it translated
into Latin and German, for the meeting of the Imperial Diet at Augsburg
in 1566. Beza and others helped Bullinger to make it a confession representing the entire Swiss Church, and on its publication it gained great
admiration, and saved the Elector Palatine. It was afterward adopted or
approved by nearly all the Reformed Churches on the Continent. It is a
lengthy theological treatise, but well deserves study. Rejecting priesthood,
priestcraft and exclusive priestly control of the Church, it yet includes
among the duties of the civil power the punishment of blasphemers and
incorrigible heretics; but on other points it is more liberal than Calvin or
Luther. Bullinger died on September 17th, 1575, aged seventy-one.

The last general Swiss confession is known as the Helvetic Consensus of
1675, drawn up to counteract several modifications of teaching introduced
Helvetic Consensus, 1675. by professors in the theological academy of Saumur in France,
namely La Place, Cappel, and Amyrant. Cappel had taught
that the perfect inspiration claimed for the Hebrew Scriptures in every par-
Cappel. ticular could not be upheld, for the system of vowel points was
due to late Jewish grammarians, and that it was in many cases
impossible to be certain that we had the right interpretation. He also
insisted the various readings must be consulted in order to fully understand the text. The new Helvetic Consensus insisted on the literal verbal
Literal verbal inspiration. inspiration of the Scriptures and of the traditional Hebrew texts,
vowels as well as consonants. This extreme doctrine, which is
still held by some persons, led to violent reaction, and has in part stimu-

lated the modern study of the Scriptures by every method of common sense, history, archæology, and literary criticism.

Amyrant had taught that God fore-ordained and desired the universal salvation of man, but made faith in Christ a condition, foreknowing and fore-ordaining that many men would reject it. The Helvetic Con- Limit of offer sensus denied that the call to salvation was ever absolutely of salvation. general, asserting that Christ died only for the elect, and not for all men without discrimination, and also that man was naturally as well as morally unable to believe the gospel without God's grace. Against La Place the Consensus affirmed not only the condemnation of all Adam's posterity as a consequence of his sin (mediate imputation), but also the direct Adam's sin or immediate imputation of his sin to all his descendants, as if imputed to all. they had themselves committed it. It cannot be wondered at that sharp reaction and rebellion against such teaching took place.

HENRY BULLINGER, AUTHOR OF THE SECOND HELVETIC CONFESSION, 1566.

MONKS AND PRIESTS VISITING THE VAUDOIS.

CHAPTER XVI.

The French Reformation from Calvin's Departure to the Revocation of the Edict of Nantes.

Francis I. and Melanchthon—The Sorbonne Alarmed—The Placards—Calvin's Address to Francis I.—The Vaudois Persecuted—Increase of the Reformed Churches—Persecutions under Henry II.—Organization of Reformed Churches—Gallican Confession—Opposing Influences—The Guises—L'Hôpital—Charles V.—Colloquy of Poissy—Beza—Edict of January, 1562—Massacre of Vassy—Battle of Dreux—Pacification of Amboise—Death of Condé—Henry of Navarre—Battle of Moncontour—Death of Jeanne d'Albret—Massacre of St. Bartholomew—Henry III.—The League—Death of the Guises and of Catherine de Medici—Henry III. Murdered—Henry IV.—His "Conversion"—Edict of Nantes—Henry IV. Murdered—Catholicism Restored in Béarn—Huguenots Weakened—Richelieu's Iron Hand—La Rochelle Taken—Louis XIV.—Oppression of Huguenots—The Dragonnades—Revocation of Edict of Nantes—The Emigration.

RETURNING now to the state of affairs in France, Francis I. had supported the Smalcaldic league and the restoration of the Duke of Wurtemberg. It was so much his interest to humble Charles V. that Protestantism might hope for his cordial support and that of his devout sister. He communicated in 1534 through Du Bellay with Melanchthon, Bucer, and Hedis, sounding them as to the extent of the religious changes that would satisfy them, while they did not imperil the unity of the Church. But by arranging the marriage of his second son, the Duke of Orleans, with Catherine de Medici, Francis had already taken a most momentous step with regard to the Reformation. Melanchthon and the two other Reformers were of course ready with their plans of conciliation. Melanchthon, as usual, was prepared to yield much, if errors of doctrine and the Papal office might be reformed. The king ordered a council of clerics, statesmen, and others to sit at the Louvre, and take the proposals into consideration. Francis was so much pleased with the idea of reunion that he himself sketched out a plan based on the offers of the three Reformers. He submitted it to the doctors of the *The Sorbonne* Sorbonne. They were alarmed, and represented to the king *Alarmed.* that the triumph of Lutheranism would involve the downfall of royal power.

King Francis was still hesitating whether he should put himself at the head of the Re- *The Placards.* formation, when, on the 25th of October, 1534, the appearance of certain placards against the Mass startled Paris and France. When a placard which had been posted on the door of his own private apartment was shown to him, the king became violently agitated, and exclaimed: "Let all be seized, and let Lutheranism be totally exterminated."

THEODORE BEZA, COADJUTOR OF CALVIN, BORN 1519; DIED 1605.

All whose Lutheranism was notorious were accordingly arrested. Six were burnt alive in November. Many fled from the country. To expiate the offence done to the Church, a grand procession of the sacrament and of the holy relics was arranged on the 21st of January, 1535. In this procession the king walked on foot as chief penitent, not wearing his crown or robes of state. At the same time he continued his overtures to the German reforming princes, declaring that the martyrs of Paris had suffered for sedition; and he sought to induce Melanchthon to come to the capital. But his sister Margaret now felt she would no longer trust her brother; accordingly she withdrew to her own principality of Béarn, where she gave refuge to many of the persecuted.

THE SORBONNE, PARIS,

A College of Ecclesiastics, whose judgment was often sought from the fourteenth to the seventeenth centuries. The building is now devoted to education.

Towards the end of 1535, Francis, notwithstanding his persecution of

French Protestants, sent Cardinal Du Bellay to Germany to conciliate Melanchthon and the German Protestants; but the attempt to induce Melanchthon to visit Paris was unsuccessful.

Attempts to Conciliate Melanchthon.

WALLS OF THE VAUDOIS, IN VAL LOUISE.

(After a photograph.)

Political struggles which followed and also the increasing infirmities of Francis I., the result of his vicious life, prevented any further accommodation between the Reformers and the French king; and Charles V.

contrived to make peace with him in 1539. In 1540 the Parliament
The Vaudois Persecuted. of Aix, in Provence, ordered the burning of seventeen Vaudois, the expulsion of their families, and destruction of their possessions. The Vaudois were the descendants of immigrants from Piedmont and Dauphiny. They had by their industry converted a bare and robber-haunted country into a flourishing and highly cultivated region. Of late years their pastors, known as *Barbes*, had recognised the Reformers as their natural brethren; and these pastors had printed in Neufchatel the first edition of the Bible in French, translated by Olivetan. The original decree of the Romish Church against them in 1530 was followed by a second in 1540, by which Francis I. offered them pardon on condition that they re-entered the Romish Church in three months.

With unfaltering courage the Vaudois of Provence sent their confession of faith to the Parliament of Aix and to Francis I. The king could find no fault with this document. The bishops of Provence sent three doctors of theology to convert the Vaudois, with the result that all the three emissaries were themselves converted. Ultimately Francis I. was induced to give orders to the Parliament of Aix to put down the Vaudois. The decree was executed with savage barbarity. The people were surprised and massacred, their houses were burnt, their harvests carried off, their wells destroyed. Many Vaudois were burnt alive. The French soldiery committed horrible outrages upon the defenceless mountaineers, many of whom perished miserably in the caves in which they had taken shelter. Two hundred and fifty were executed after a mock trial. The very name of the Vaudois almost entirely disappeared from Provence, and the country they had tilled became a wilderness. The King of France himself was moved by the thought of the sufferings of the Vaudois. In his old age of vice he was, indeed, overborne by Cardinal de Tournon; yet on his death-bed he summoned courage to charge his son and successor, Henry II., to punish the perpetrators of the horrible sufferings inflicted on a harmless community.

Stimulated, perhaps, by the persecution that was meant to destroy it, the Reformed faith advanced in France with great strides during the later
Increase of Reformed Churches. time of Francis I. and the earlier years of Henry II. The Reformed Churches were even reckoned as numbering one-sixth of the population. Families of men belonging to the learned professions in great numbers adhered to the Reformers, together with many of the provincial nobility outside the court circles. Colporteurs

carrying religious books from Geneva, Lausanne, and Neufchatel, spread
the basis of the Reformation far and wide. Many meetings for worship
were held in secret. The arrival of a minister authorised by Calvin or
Farel was hailed with joy. Morals were strictly supervised; luxury was
prohibited; perhaps too ascetic and puritanic an aspect was put on. But
the persecutions and sufferings the Protestants speedily suffered under
Henry II. might well make the Reformers walk in fear, though prudence
might have suggested the necessity of maintaining a cheerful countenance.

Under Henry II. France was dominated by his mistress, **Persecutions under Henry II.** Diana of Poitiers, the High Constable de Montmorency, and the brothers Francis and Charles, the former Duke of Guise and the latter Cardinal of Lorraine. At the coronation fêtes of his queen, Henry caused four Lutherans to be burnt to death; and soon after fierce persecution was extended to all the chief cities of France. The edict

PORTRAIT OF HENRY II. OF FRANCE.

of Chateaubriand, 1551, enacted severer penalties against heretics than ever
and forbade any man to hold office under the crown or to teach
unless he could produce a certificate that declared him to be a **Edict of Chateaubriand, 1551.**
good Catholic. Yet at this time Henry rendered considerable
aid to the Protestant cause in Germany by his expedition into Lorraine and
the annexation of Metz, which promoted the peace of Passau. Persecutions and martyrdoms, however, continued without intermission in France.

In September, 1555, the first Reformed Church in Paris, which met in
the house of M. de la Ferrière, elected as its pastor Jean Maçon de la

Rivière, and also chose elders and deacons, and made arrangements for regular church government. In the same year congregations with pastors were formed at Meaux, Angers, Poitiers, and in subsequent years in La Rochelle, Tours, Orleans, Rouen, and many other towns. In 1558 it was agreed that a national synod should be held in Paris to frame a confession and code of government. This synod met on the 25th of May, 1559, only eleven churches being represented, owing to the great risks run by the delegates. Almost the whole body of French Protestantism looked to Calvin for leadership. Calvin had prepared the first draft of a confession for France, which was modified by his pupil, Antoine de Chandieu, and the Synod of Paris. It is practically a clear summary of Calvin's doctrines, and does not need further description. As to church government, the primary power was in the consistory of each church, consisting of the minister, elders, and deacons, the elders and deacons being in the first place "called" or elected by the congregation, new members having also to obtain the public approval of the congregation. The ministers were nominated (subject to approval by the congregation after three Sundays' hearing) by the district assembly called the Colloquy, consisting of one pastor and one deacon or elder from each congregation. The provincial synod similarly represented all the congregations of a province, and met once a year to decide weightier matters not settled by the Colloquies. Finally, there was the national synod, consisting of two pastors and two elders from each provincial synod, presided over by a minister chosen on each occasion, and with authority to decide on any important question regarding the Reformed faith in France. Here then we see Calvin's complete non-hierarchical system established in France, and if it had had a fair chance, it might have regulated one-half of the kingdom and prevented the French Revolution. The completeness and the practical nature of Calvin's scheme, and his great influence, were shown by the fact that his system was adopted with little alteration, and has been maintained almost in its original form to the present day.

Organisation of Reformed Churches.

Gallican Confession, 1559.

The Parisians were growing inclined to tolerate the Reformers, and the French Parliament contained men who openly defended them, expressing the opinion that it was unjust to burn men for heresy. When the Council of Trent, which was sitting for the purpose of declaring what was, or was not, heresy, had not finished its deliberations, some of those who ventured to speak their sentiments before the king were imprisoned; but at this critical moment Henry II.

Opposing influences in France.

STATUE OF COLIGNY, LEADER OF THE FRENCH PROTESTANTS.
(In the Rue de Rivoli, near the Louvre, Paris.)

received an injury in a tilting match, and died on the 10th of July, 1559. He was succeeded by his eldest son, Francis II., husband of Mary, Queen of Scots. At first his mother, Catherine de Medici, was unable to engross the entire rule in the State, but had to share her power with the Guises and the Constable. At the same time she temporised with the Protestant leaders, chief among whom were Anthony de Bourbon (afterwards King of Navarre, in right of having married Jeanne d'Albret, the courageous daughter of Margaret, Queen of Navarre), his brother, the Prince de Condé, and Gaspard de Coligny, Admiral of France. Coligny, one of the noblest characters in French history, was born in 1517, became a distinguished soldier, and was an early and consistent adherent of the Reformed doctrines. Jeanne d'Albret professed Protestantism in 1560, and in 1563 she abolished the Roman form of church service in Béarn, and set up the Reformed worship. She founded colleges, sent to Geneva for ministers, and had the Bible translated into the dialects spoken in her dominions.

Our space compels us only slightly to refer to the political struggles in which the fate of Protestantism in France was involved. They are part **Persecution by the Guises.** of the general history of France, and we shall confine ourselves to noting how the interests of the Reformers were affected by them. The Guises, early in the reign of Francis II., forbade meetings of the Reformers on pain of death; and although the Inquisition was not formally established in France, the "Chambres Ardentes" which were instituted were quite as efficacious in searching out and prosecuting heretics, and were served by bodies of watchful spies. Images of the Virgin were set up at the street corners, and the demeanour of passers-by was watched in order to discover heretics. A vast system of slaughter and persecution arose; often the property of the condemned was divided among their persecutors. The Reformed Church addressed to the Queen-mother a protest which she interpreted as a threat, and persecution grew fiercer. After the conspiracy of Amboise to seize the king's person—for Anthony de Bourbon had been crushed by the Guises—the Chancellorship of France was **L'Hôpital.** given to Michel de l'Hôpital, a wise and moderate man, who saved France from the Inquisition by passing a bill to give the bishops exclusive jurisdiction for heresy. In December, 1560, Francis II. **Charles IX.** died, and was succeeded by his brother, Charles IX., a boy of ten years. Anthony de Bourbon was won over by the Queen-mother; and to counterbalance their influence and frustrate their plans the Duke of Guise, the Constable de Montmorency, and Marshal St. André leagued themselves together, and induced the Parliament of Paris to vote the "edict of July," which declared that persons who took part in heretical assemblies should be condemned to death; while other heretics should be handed over to the church tribunals. Thus the right of the Huguenots to assemble for worship was taken away. But the Estates-General, convoked at Pontoise, abolished this edict, and called for a reform of the clergy and freedom of worship for the Huguenots.

An attempt was made to reconcile conflicting parties in religion at a colloquy at Poissy, opened by L'Hôpital in a conciliatory speech, acknow-

COLLOQUY OF POISSY.
(From an engraving in the National Library of France.)

ledging the Bible as the authority for doctrine and asserting that "we must not be so averse to the men of the Reformed faith, for **Colloquy of Poissy, 1561.** they are our brethren, regenerated by the same baptism with us and worshipping the same Christ as we do." Theodore Beza appeared as chief spokesman of the Reformers. He is described later in the century as having a grave senator's countenance, comely, affable, and gaining the reverence of those who loved him least. Beza and his fellow- **Theodore Beza.** pastors were separated by a barrier from the priests and bishops. He pleaded eloquently for the Reformed faith, and described and deprecated the persecutions the Reformers had suffered. Once, when he touched on the

spiritual presence of Christ without transubstantiation in the Eucharist, the
Catholics cried out that he had spoken blasphemy, and Cardinal de Tournon
demanded that he should be silenced.   But Catherine, the Queen-mother,
would not respond to this request; and the Cardinal of Lorraine exclaimed,
" Would to God that Beza had been dumb, or we deaf!"   The Cardinal, being
deputed to answer Beza, could only fall back on the infallibility of the
Church as specially promised by Christ, the prestige of Rome, and the usual
arguments for transubstantiation.   Beza was not allowed to reply publicly ;
and the colloquy broke up after much unprofitable wrangling.   But the

MASSACRE OF VASSY.
(From a print in the French National Library.)

fact that it had been held gave a great impulse to the Reformed faith.
Among others, Viret preached with great success throughout Southern
France.   Palissy, the famous potter, has in his " Memoirs " given lively
and interesting pictures of the movement and its spread and influence.
" In those days," he says, " might be seen on Sundays bands of workpeople
walking abroad in the meadows, in the groves, in the fields, singing psalms
and spiritual songs, and reading to and instructing one another.   .   .   .
Not only had the habits and modes of life of the people been reformed, but
their very countenances seemed to be changed and improved."

The " king " of Navarre now joined the Guises, but L'Hôpital and the

Queen-mother called an assembly of notables at St. Germain, in which L'Hôpital pointed out that Church and State need not absolutely coincide ; many might be citizens, he said, who were not even Christians, a view in which he was two centuries at least in advance of his time.

The assembly passed the edict of January, 1562, by which **Edict of January, 1562, at St. Germain.** the Huguenots were allowed to worship outside cities in open places, unarmed ; but they were not to disturb the ancient worship of the Church in any way. This appeared insufficient where the Reformers were in a majority, and in some places destruction of images

ASSASSINATION OF THE SECOND DUKE OF GUISE BY A HUGUENOT, 1563.
(From a print in the French National Library.)

and attacks on churches followed. Early in March the Duke of Guise suddenly attacked a Protestant congregation while at worship at Vassy, on the frontier of Champagne. A frightful massacre followed, **Massacre of Vassy, 1st March, 1562.** which he could not prevent. The slaughter of Vassy was repeated in many towns of France. The first war, 1562–3, was marked by some Huguenot successes, often followed by deplorable destruction of altars, images, and monuments. The Romanists were in the end successful, and wreaked savage cruelty on the Huguenots. Anthony de **Battle of Dreux, Dec., 1562.** Bourbon died at Dreux on December 19th, 1562, the Huguenots were defeated, Condé was captured, Marshal St. André perished, while

T

Coligny drew off the defeated party with excellent skill. Early in 1563 the Duke of Guise was assassinated by a Huguenot. The Pacification of **Pacification of Amboise, 1563.** Amboise, April, 1563, which closed the war, gave the Reformers free exercise of their religion where they were already predominant, restricted the liberty of preaching in the open country, and allowed the nobles to celebrate the Reformed worship in their own castles. The Prince of Condé for the Reformers agreed to this; but Coligny said it had ruined more churches than the enemy could have knocked down in ten years.

HENRY OF NAVARRE, AFTERWARDS KING HENRY IV. OF FRANCE.

A royal progress through France, with meetings of various princes, was **Second war, 1567-8.** followed by rumours of intended massacres of the Huguenots, which were not allayed by the Duke of Alva's proceedings in the Netherlands. Although the Queen-mother remained neutral, Condé and Coligny decided on open war in 1567; but they won no great successes, and the Peace of Longjumeau, 1568, reaffirmed the Pacification of Amboise.

The French court, however, proceeded to get rid of the Huguenot nobles in detail. Huguenots were assassinated all over the kingdom, or perished in miserable prisons. Condé, when about to be seized, escaped to La Rochelle; **Death of Condé.** Chatillon escaped to England; even L'Hôpital was dismissed from the Chancellorship. Catherine and her son seemed to have taken leave of all moderation. Condé was slain at Jarnac, on the **Henry of Navarre.** Charente. At this moment Jeanne d'Albret rallied to the aid of the Huguenots; and her son, Henry of Navarre, being a possible king of France, made her support of the utmost value. Coligny succeeded to full command; but in 1569 the Huguenots were utterly routed on the disastrous field of Moncontour. Yet Coligny still offered a brave resistance, and by the peace of St. Germain, August, 1570, gained excellent terms, giving the Huguenots freedom _{Huguenot defeat at Moncontour, 1569.} of worship, the right of holding offices, of being members of Parliament, and allowing them four strong cities of refuge, in which they might maintain governors and garrisons.

It is often alleged that these towns were intended to lull the Huguenots into a false security. They were so regarded by many at the time; and

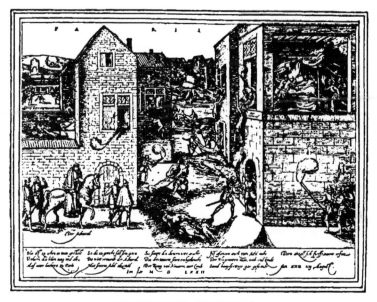

MASSACRE OF ST. BARTHOLOMEW.
(From an engraving of the time.)

the leaders withdrew to La Rochelle with Henry of Navarre and his mother, refusing to come to Court while the Guises were there. Catherine became more and more attached to a high Catholic policy, and determined that Coligny and some other Protestant leaders must be removed. Charles IX., on the contrary, made overtures to the Huguenots, offered his sister's hand to young Henry of Navarre, and met Henry, his mother, and Coligny at Blois. In 1572 all returned to Paris; and now occurred the _{Death of Jeanne d'Albret, 1572.} death of Jeanne d'Albret, Queen of Navarre, it was suspected by poison. The Papists inflamed the populace against the Huguenots, while the Queen-mother plotted against them, and at last recovered her influence over her son. She felt that while Coligny lived her power was unstable, and she planned his death. Meanwhile Henry of Navarre was married to Margaret of Valois. The projected assassination of Coligny failed, and this failure precipitated the massacre of St. Bartholomew. The menaces of the Huguenots frightened the king; Catherine persuaded him that the Huguenots were in arms against him, and had sent to Germany for aid.

Massacre of St. Bartholomew. At last he agreed to a massacre of all the Huguenots in France. The evening of the 24th of August, 1572, St. Bartholomew's Day, was fixed upon, and history records no more treacherous or disastrous slaughter. The two Huguenot princes, Henry of Navarre and the young Prince of Condé, heard Mass to save their lives. Charles IX. was induced publicly to declare that the massacre was accomplished at his command, and he went to view the bodies of the victims. The Romanists exulted, and praised the king to the skies. The greatest guilt in the matter was probably that of the Queen-mother, whose name is indelibly associated with this frightful crime. Dean Kitchin, in his "History of France," says that to some extent the Huguenots excited and provoked opposition, and did themselves harm by mingling political with religious questions.

After St. Bartholomew, a moderate intermediate party, which had been rising, came to the front, and supported the grant of free worship to the Huguenots. In various places they offered stubborn resistance to the royal forces, especially at La Rochelle, and finally by the Edict of Boulogne, July, 1573, they were granted an amnesty, restoration of property and honours, freedom of conscience and of worship in La Rochelle and other cities. The Huguenots dreamt of a federation of independent cities, with a great council in each town, after the Swiss model.

Charles IX. died in 1574, and was succeeded by his brother, Henry III. (Duke of Anjou). He at once announced that no concessions would be made to the Huguenots; they must become Catholics or leave the kingdom. **Henry III.** He put his Catholicism in the forefront, and "was ever either sinning or doing penance for his sins." The Moderates coalesced with the Huguenots for political purposes, and were answered **The League.** by the formation of the "Holy Catholic League" in 1576, under Henry, Duke of Guise, to restore and maintain the sole supremacy of the Catholic Church. Wars and disturbances followed, until in 1584 the death of the Duke of Anjou (formerly Duke of Alençon), heir

HOUSE OF THE ENGLISH AMBASSADOR AT PARIS DURING THE MASSACRE OF ST. BARTHOLOMEW.

to the French crown, made Henry of Navarre the heir and changed his prospects. He was now thirty-one years of age, maturing in character and becoming a great leader. The Leaguers were resolved that he should

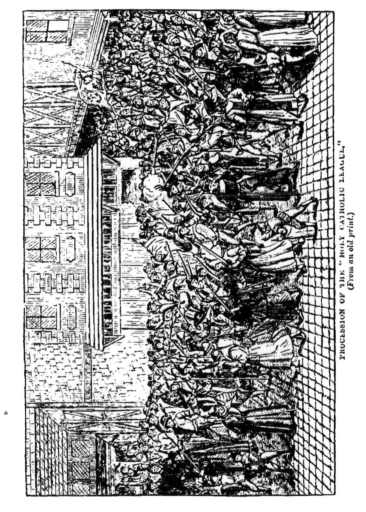

PROCESSION OF THE "HOLY CATHOLIC LEAGUE."
(From an old print.)

not succeed to the throne, and they claimed on behalf of the Church that no heretic should reign. They put forward Henry's decrepit and debauched uncle, Charles, Cardinal de Bourbon, as their candidate for the throne, while the Duke of Guise hoped for the succession himself. The Pope,

Sixtus V., excommunicated Henry of Navarre and his brother the Prince of Condé. The Duke of Guise won great victories over the Huguenots in

Death of the Guises and of Catherine de Medici. 1587, and returned to Paris as practical king. Exasperated by his arrogance, Henry III. caused him to be slain, as well as his brother the Cardinal, just before Christmas, 1588. The Queen-mother died early in January, 1589; and in April, not seeing any safer course, Henry III. came to an agreement with Henry of Navarre, declaring that he would no longer brand the Huguenots as heretics; and the moderate Catholics and the Huguenots became united. They defeated

HENRY, THIRD DUKE OF GUISE, HEAD OF THE "HOLY CATHOLIC LEAGUE."

Henry III. murdered. the League in several quarters; and in the midst of these things Jacques Clement, a Dominican friar and ardent Leaguer, assassinated Henry in August, 1589, and Henry of Navarre became Henry IV.

He had to fight for his crown. The Huguenots were much **Henry IV.** weakened; Henry was greatly tempted to conform to Romanism. He conciliated the Moderates, and showed a firm front against the League.

At last, after varying fortunes, he won the battle of Ivry (1590) against the Duke of Mayenne, who was now leader of the Guise party. But reverses followed, and Henry entered into negotiations with the Papacy, and at

His "conversion," 1593. last agreed to profess his conversion. In July, 1593, he received provisional absolution and heard Mass, a step which made him popular with the majority of his people, while it did not prevent him from granting religious liberty to the Huguenots by the Edict of

Edict of Nantes, 1598. Nantes in 1598. He had many difficulties to encounter before his throne was finally secure; and it was only an act of justice to those who had so long stood by him when the famous edict of

April, 1598, was signed. It gave the Huguenots full right to worship except in some special League cities, the right to hold court offices; and established Protestant chambers in the provincial parliaments. Four colleges were to be founded for their benefit, and their national synod was to meet once in three years. The State undertook to provide stipends for

MURDER OF HENRY IV. OF FRANCE.

the Huguenot ministers; and two hundred towns were put into the hands of the Reformers. But Protestantism had been terribly weakened during the wars and tumults of half a century. So many had perished that the number of Huguenot churches in France had decreased to seven hundred and fifty. However, the peace which followed the Edict of Nantes was most beneficial in consolidating and strengthening the Reformed Church in France.

The assassination of Henry IV. by the fanatic Ravaillac on May 14th, 1610, seriously changed the position. Henry's son, Louis XIII., a boy of nine, became king, with his mother, Mary de Medici, as regent. In 1611 the Huguenots met in a Protestant parliament at Saumur, and demanded the redress of grievances; but the old vigour of the party was lacking. Other meetings were held subsequently at Grenoble, Nîmes, La Rochelle, etc., and in them André Chamier and Dumoulin came to the front. They had to struggle against strong counter-influences in the royal councils, and in 1617 the young king took a strong step in restoring the Catholic worship in Béarn and returning to the Roman Church the ecclesiastical property which had been held by the Reformed Church for fifty years. The soldiery who were sent thither broke open the doors of the churches, burnt the Protestant books, made the citizens kneel when the Host was carried in procession, and drove them to Mass by force.

Henry IV. murdered, 1610.

Catholicism restored in Béarn.

At La Rochelle in 1621 the Huguenots prepared for open resistance to the reaction which seemed imminent. The king attacked and took many of the Huguenot strongholds, and when peace was made in 1623 only two cities were left in their hands: Montauban and La Rochelle. Still they were nominally left in the enjoyment of the Edict of Nantes. They henceforth resolved to live more and more as a people within a people, and to take their own separate line on all questions of religion and politics.

Huguenots weakened.

The iron hand of Richelieu was now beginning to hold the reins of power in France, greatly to the dissatisfaction of the Huguenots, who in 1625 broke out into revolt in several places. Richelieu announced his firm determination to crush them, and resolved that the clergy should pay the whole cost. But it was found impracticable to reduce La Rochelle, and peace was made at Montpellier in 1626. A little later Richelieu resolved to use his whole power against Rochelle, and to take effectual measures to starve the people into submission. At last it capitulated on October 30th, 1628; and after the Church of St. Margaret had been reconsecrated, Richelieu performed Mass there on All Saints' Day. The Huguenot political power was practically extinguished. The exercise of their religion, as a matter of favour, was granted to them; but the spirit and energy of the Huguenots were greatly

Richelieu's iron hand.

La Rochelle taken.

subdued under the stern rule of the great Cardinal. In 1629 he reduced

SIEGE OF LA ROCHELLE.

the Huguenots of Languedoc, under the Duke de Rohan; Montauban
was taken, and its walls demolished. Many so-called conversions to

Catholicism took place, often aided by money. From this time onward the liberties of the Huguenots were such that Richelieu could afford to neglect them in his grand schemes of policy. He made the French monarchy absolute, and practically crushed the Huguenots. When he died in the autumn of 1642, a few months before Louis XIII., he left it a comparatively easy task for Louis XIV. to complete his work by exterminating the French Reformed churches.

Yet during the earlier years of Louis XIV., while excluded from all political influence, the Huguenots distinguished themselves by their in-

Huguenots under Louis XIV.

dustry and their devotion to agriculture, commerce, and manufactures; they transacted much business with foreign lands, and were found to be trustworthy and honourable in their dealings. Many of the Huguenot ministers of this period were men of great excellence, and their literary works testify to their erudition and ability, while the Huguenot academies of Montauban, Saumur, Sedan, and Nîmes were in a flourishing condition. During the supremacy of Cardinal Mazarin the Huguenots enjoyed breathing time. But directly he died in 1661, and Louis XIV. assumed direct sway, he began to attack them. Commissioners were sent through France to examine into all disputes between Catholics and Protestants and the title-deeds of Protestant churches. In most cases the verdict was given against the Protestants, and many churches were in consequence pulled down and schools suppressed. An ordinance was issued banishing " relapsed heretics " for life, namely, those who, having committed some act of partial conformity to Romanism, afterwards were seen to enter a Protestant church. A priest and a magistrate were ordered to visit all sick persons and ask them if they wished to die in the Catholic faith. Children of Protestants were persuaded to abjure their parents' religion, and the parents were compelled to pay for their maintenance in Catholic institutions. Preachers who said anything in disparagement of the Virgin were accused of blasphemy. Many other vexatious restrictions were imposed, but in 1665 the priestly party declared that more zeal was necessary to crush the formidable monster of heresy completely.

Later, when the Jesuits and Madame de Maintenon exercised full influence over Louis, the unfortunate Huguenots were still more rigorously treated. The king was persuaded that every school of opinion contrary to the Roman was an attack on the royal authority. More vigorous measures were resolved upon. In 1681 a regiment of cavalry was sent into Poitou

CARDINAL RICHELIEU.
(*After Philippe de Champagne.*)
283

and quartered on the Protestants, with directions to do pretty much as they liked in the way of oppression and cruelty. A tide of emigration soon set outwards, and all who could do so fled to other lands. In successive years there were revolts in the south against the cruelties practised upon the Huguenots, and they were slaughtered in large numbers. In **The Dragonnades.** April, 1684, an edict was issued that all new converts should be exempt for two years from having troops quartered on them; while those who remained stubborn were specially subjected to this oppression. Many professed conversion to escape continued insults and miseries. At last Louis XIV. thought he had converted so many that the rest might easily be won. The Edict of Nantes destroyed the unity of the kingdom, and sheltered opinions that he held to be both blasphemous and disloyal. The quietness and industry of the two millions who remained Huguenots at heart deceived him. So on October 18th, 1685, he signed the **Revocation of Edict of Nantes, 1685.** revocation of the famous Edict, and forbade all public celebration of the Reformed worship. All pastors

LOUIS XIII. OF FRANCE.

were to leave the kingdom in a fortnight on pain of the galleys for life, and all children were to be brought up as Catholics. There was but one saving clause, which soon proved illusory: "Those Protestants who have not changed their religion shall be allowed to dwell in the cities and places of our realm unmolested till it shall please God to enlighten them, as He has others."

The Revocation was put into force immediately. The great Protestant church of Charenton, capable of containing 14,000 persons, was pulled

FRENCH PROTESTANT FUGITIVES.

(From the painting by Maurice Leloir in the Paris Salon.)

down, and this was followed by the destruction of many other Protestant churches. Troops were sent through the provinces to convert the heretics by force. No one dying a Protestant was allowed Christian burial; only two distinguished Huguenots were allowed to emigrate: Marshal Schomberg, head of the army, and the Marquis de Ruvigny, a great diplomatist; while the aged Admiral Duquesne was permitted to remain at home unmolested. Everywhere persecution was let loose against the Protestants. But so strong was the feeling cherished by many for their religion that they adopted the most astonishing devices and ran the most terrible risks to escape from the country. "They streamed across every frontier; grandfathers and children, tender maidens and strong men, the noble and the artisan, undeterred by the horrors of their lot if caught, struggled onwards in a hundred disguises, with thrilling adventures and escapes; all animated by one spirit,—the determination to join their much-loved pastors, and set up new homes in some less inclement land. They bribed the guards on the frontiers, or they slipped across the open country by night, or they hid themselves in merchandise and were shipped as bales of goods for England; or, finding friendly sailors on the coast, they embarked in little craft, gladly braving the rough autumnal seas, if only they might flee from the curse and bondage of the conversion at home. . . . Here were the thriftiest, the bravest, the most intelligent, the most industrious of Frenchmen, the very flower of the race. . . . In wars, in diplomacy, in literature, in production of wealth, these refugees gave what they took from France to her enemies, for they carried with them that bitter sense

The Emigration.

CARDINAL MAZARIN, CHIEF ADMINISTRATOR OF FRANCE DURING LOUIS XIV.'S MINORITY.

of wrong which made them henceforth foremost among those enemies"
(Kitchin).

Just as the total number of those who escaped or died in the attempt
can never be known, so the loss France sustained cannot be estimated.
Hundreds of manufactories were closed; Lyons, Tours, Nantes, Loss to France.
were almost ruined. It was seen by the stagnation of vast
trades how great a blow the Revocation of the Edict had struck. And
other nations have felt how important to them has been the gain of
the Huguenot refugees. The names of distinction in England Gain to other
are multitudinous; but when we reflect that among the Countries.
better known such diverse names as those of Garrick, Bouverie, Pusey,
Labouchere, Layard, Lefevre, Ligonier, Martineau, Plimsoll, Roubiliac,
Romilly, are of Huguenot origin, with very many more, whose names have
been Anglicised almost beyond tracing, we can faintly realize how much
poorer the English nation would have been without this infusion of honest,
honourable, God-fearing men and women. The reader will find abundant
further information on the subject in Dr. Smiles's "Huguenots in England
and Ireland."

During the following century France was conspicuously barren of
great men; and when they appeared, they were men of destructive minds,
who brought on the great Revolution. France had lost all habit of freedom
with the loss of the Huguenots. She was to be coerced to the point of
explosion, and then enslaved in succession by tyrannies worse than those of
kings. In their turn the Roman Catholic priests and nobles had to flee
from their land, driven, not by Huguenots, but by a maddened and starved
peasantry, led by skilful demagogues.

COMMEMORATIVE MEDALS OF THE MASSACRE OF ST. BARTHOLOMEW.
(From the French National Library.)

HENRY VIII. GIVING THE BIBLE TO THE PEOPLE.
(After an old engraving on the title-page of Cranmer's Bible, 1539.)

CHAPTER XVII.

The English Church and the Reformation to the Death of Henry VIII.

The Lollards—Statute for burning Heretics—Oldcastle and others burnt—Abuses in the Church—Erasmus and Colet—Henry VIII. and the Church—No Doctrinal Reform—Acts against Pluralities and Non-residence—Submission of Clergy, 1532—Appeals to Rome forbidden—Cranmer and Cromwell—Martyrdoms—Bilney and John Frith—Latimer charged with Heresy—Made Bishop of Worcester—Coverdale's Bible—Suppression of Monasteries—The Ten Articles—"Institution of a Christian Man"—Matthew's Bible—Royal Injunctions, 1538—Negotiations with Lutherans—Lambert burnt—Reaction—The Six Articles—Fall of Cromwell—Lutherans burnt—Tyndale's Bible condemned—Cranmer's Reforming Efforts—Bishops' Bible—Henry VIII.'s Primer, 1545—Bonner—The Irish Church—Charities abolished—Death of Henry VIII.—His Influence—No Luther or Calvin in England.

I F not foremost in "protesting against the errors of the Church of Rome," the English Church had long been noted for its resistance to Rome's absolute dominion, and the English crown had often resisted, though it

The Lollards.

had sometimes yielded to, the haughty claims of the Popes. And there seemed some probability after Wyclif's death that these two streams of tendency might be superseded by a more sweeping tide of

283

Lollardism, for its tenets were adopted by many influential men. They rapidly increased in number in the years following Wyclif's death, and even began to ordain ministers, declaring that every priest had the full power to transmit holy orders. In 1394 the Lollards felt strong enough to bring in a bill to the House of Commons, in which it was declared that from the moment the Church of England accepted endowments, faith, hope, and charity began to disappear, and pride and mortal sin to prevail; that the office of priesthood as confessed by the Church was a sham; that the vow of chastity tended to abominable sins; that the pretended miracle of the Sacrament led all but a few into idolatry; that exorcisms and blessings of wine, of the walls of the church, of vestments, etc., were practices of necromancy; that the holding of temporal offices by the clergy was wrong, as were also special prayers for particular dead persons; that pilgrimages, prayers, etc., to the cross and to images were very near to idolatry, and that of all images that of the Trinity was most to be

SIR JOHN OLDCASTLE BURNT.

condemned; that auricular confession and absolution exalted the pride of priests and produced many evils; and that homicide in war or for temporal causes was contrary to the New Testament. But Richard II., returning from Ireland, caused the withdrawal of these proposals by terrible threats.

Early in the reign of Henry IV. the Church was moved to proceed strongly against the Lollards, and induced the king and Parliament to sanction a statute providing that those who were certified to be heretics by the bishops, if they refused to recant or if they relapsed, should be burned in some conspicuous place.

Statute for burning Heretics, 1401.

This statute, passed in 1401, was the first English Act which provided

U

for the burning of offenders against the Church. At once William Saw-try, rector of St. Osith, London, was arraigned for denying that the cross should be adored, and for holding other Lollard doctrines. He recanted, but not so fully as to satisfy his persecutors, for he admitted that bread remained in the Sacrament after consecration. He was burnt at Smithfield on February 20th, 1401. John Purvey, who had been Wyclif's helper, at the same time recanted the principal Lollard doctrines. In subsequent years, Archbishop Arundel issued severe regulations against the teaching of anything by the clergy contrary to Holy Church and against the reading of unapproved treatises of Wyclif and of his translation of the Bible, and enjoined strict inquisition into opinions of students and teachers at Oxford.

We must pass over the story of Sir John Oldcastle, Lord Cobham, a devoted follower of Wyclif and supporter of Lollard itinerant preachers, who Oldcastle and refused to adopt the Roman beliefs on the Mass, image-worship, others burnt. prayers to the dead, etc., and was condemned as a heretic. He escaped, and was concealed in Wales for four years; but at last being taken, he was burnt to death in December, 1418. Many other Lollards, both priests and laymen, were put to death in preceding and subsequent years. No doubt some of them held tenets which seemed to undermine the authority of the State, and many of them went beyond Wyclif in disparaging holy orders. But the Church treated the whole party cruelly, especially in compelling them to assert that no bread or wine existed in the Sacrament after consecration, on pain of death. Many good men lost their lives for refusing to accept this doctrine of mediævalism; many more were frightened into assenting to what they disbelieved.

During the same period abuses were rife in the Church of England: courtiers and royal officers were made bishops and archbishops by pay-Abuses in the ments at Rome; worthless men obtained numerous benefices: Church. and Thomas Gascoigne declared, in the middle of the fifteenth century, that from the year 1403 none was preferred in the Church who knew how to do good to souls, or who could, or would do it. Even a moderate Churchman like Bishop Pecock, who published in 1456 a "Treatise on Faith" to convert the Lollards, giving up some of the extreme pretensions of the Church, was persecuted, compelled to recant, and finally imprisoned for life. Throughout the fifteenth century the Papacy attempted to encroach both on the royal prerogative and on the rights of the English Church; but it was often foiled by Parliament and by bishops. In the latter part of Henry VI.'s reign the Crown became very subservient to Rome, and Lollardy again increased. The appointment by the Pope of Cardinal Kemp in 1452 as Archbishop of Canterbury and legate (obtained by large payments) involved the complete subjection of the kingdom to the

WILLIAM TYNDALE, TRANSLATOR OF THE NEW TESTAMENT INTO ENGLISH, 1525.
(From the monument on the Thames Embankment.)

Pope, and was full of falsity, for Kemp promised full allegiance to Rome, and yet to the king he acknowledged that he held his archbishopric of the king only. He did not live long, but his successors Bourchier and Morton gave over the English Church still more completely to the Pope. Henry VII.

even obtained Bulls from Rome when they could aid his policy; and sellers of pardons were allowed to ply their trade openly. Unfortunately the clergy were very generally immoral and dissolute in their lives; persons absolutely illiterate or ignorant of the English language obtained livings; and the monasteries were often nests of corruption, so that few new ones were founded, and colleges and schools took their place in the regard of pious donors. With notable exceptions, the mendicant friars were to a large extent immoral and liars, and scarcely even pretended to be religious. Chantry priests, ordained solely to say masses for the dead, led more irregular lives than any. Simony was almost universal, and the sacraments had to be paid for. Spiritual penalties were abundantly declared, and then compounded for by money payments. Scarcely anything was done for the religious instruction of the people, except by the Lollard itinerant preachers and their publications.

A beginning of a better state of things arose from the Continent at the end of the fifteenth century. Erasmus, born about 1467, spent the Erasmus and last three years of the century at Oxford with Colet, More, Colet. Grocyn, and Linacre. In 1496 Colet, son of a Lord Mayor of London, had returned from Italy full of the new learning, and though not yet a priest, began to lecture on the Epistle to the Romans, in a style non-scholastic, rejecting much of the usual teaching on verbal inspiration and endeavouring honestly to expound the subject-matter. He urged the following of the perfect but not impossible example of Christ, and that Christians should form a bond closer than that of blood. The intercourse of Erasmus and Colet was so intimate that we probably owe to Colet's urgency the publication in 1505 of the *Enchiridion Militis Christiani* (Handbook for the Christian Soldier), written by Erasmus in 1501, to counteract the belief that religion consists in ceremonies and more than Jewish observances, while neglecting that which belongs to true piety. Many severe blows are dealt in this book against relic-hunting, pilgrimages, and saint-worship. In 1505 Colet obtained the deanery of St. Paul's, and at once commenced to preach real sermons from the pulpit, and by his earnest devotion and plain teaching did much to foster true religion in London. In 1509 Erasmus wrote his *Encomium Moriæ* (Praise of Folly), in which he sharply satirised the evils of the Church and of popular morals. When printed in 1511, it rapidly ran through many editions.

When Henry VIII. came to the throne More, Colet, and Erasmus were in favour with him, and Erasmus received Regius professorships of Divinity and of Greek at Cambridge; but, restless ever, he gave them up in 1513. In 1510, Colet founded St. Paul's School with a large endowment on a singularly liberal plan, requiring that the pupils should be taught good literature, both Latin and Greek—"authors that have with wisdom joined chaste eloquence." In a sermon in 1512 at the opening of a Convocation summoned by Henry VIII. to grant him aid, Colet boldly called for the reformation of the Church, detailing all the evils needing reform. Before long he was accused of heresy, but the Archbishop of Canterbury (Warham) would not entertain the charge. He died in 1519.

Colet founds St. Paul's School, 1510.

OLD ST. PAUL'S CATHEDRAL, LONDON.

The changes in the English Church which took place during the reign of Henry VIII. constitute only one side of the English Reformation. They partially reformed some abuses, but created others almost as injurious; and they tended to recognize a despotic power in the Crown quite as tyrannical as that of the Pope. Reasons of state, selfish private motives, cupidity, as well as national feeling were all operative, while the two main practical results were the liberation of the English Church from the domination of Rome, followed by an equally slavish subjection to the king, and the suppression of the monasteries and the spoliation of their property. Even this latter step had its precedent from Rome, for Wolsey before his fall had procured from the Pope Bulls

Henry VIII. and the Reformation.

for suppressing monasteries in order to endow colleges and found bishoprics.

As to doctrinal reform in the direction of Luther or Zwingli, there
was none in Henry VIII.'s reign. In fact, the king was greatly angered by

No doctrinal reform. Luther's early writings, especially that on the Babylonish
captivity of the Church; and in August, 1521, he published a
treatise on the seven sacraments, in which he inveighed against Luther
so coarsely and confidently that Luther produced an even more violent
reply, while Pope Leo X. granted Henry the title of "Defender of the
Faith." But Cardinal Wolsey was not Henry's abettor in endeavouring to
crush Lutheranism, and both at Oxford and Cambridge he favoured those
who inclined towards the new doctrines. In 1525 the first two editions of
Tyndale's New Testament in English were published at Worms; but their
circulation in England was hindered by the bishops. This led to strenuous
efforts to diffuse them, together with Lutheran books.

The final cause, however, which precipitated active change was the
refusal of the Pope and Wolsey to pronounce Henry VIII.'s marriage with

Acts against pluralities and non-residence, 1529. Catherine null and void. In 1529 Acts were passed, largely by
pressure of the king, against pluralities and non-residence of
clergy, and enacting heavy fines against obtaining licences for
such abuses from Rome. Convocation protested, but suggested numerous
articles of church reform. In 1531 a still more drastic measure was
enforced. Parliament declared the whole of the clergy guilty under the
Statute of Præmunire for having submitted to Wolsey as papal legate; and
they were only "pardoned" on granting a subsidy and admitting the king's
supremacy over the Church, terming him "the singular protector, the only
and supreme lord, and, as far as is permitted by the law of Christ, even the
supreme head of the Church of England."

In 1530 Hugh Latimer, who had been active in influencing Cambridge
University to pronounce for the king's divorce, addressed the king in favour

Submission of Clergy, 1532. of allowing free circulation of versions of the Scriptures. In
1532 the important "Submission of the Clergy" took place, by
which it was acknowledged that the titles and rights of Convocation
depended on the king's will, and that no new canon could be promulgated

Appeals to Rome for-bidden. without the royal sanction. In 1533 the claim of the Pope
to *annates* (first year's income of benefices) was rejected, and a
statute was passed forbidding all appeals to Rome; and while
it was declared that the king and Parliament did not intend to vary

from the Catholic faith, it was left to the king to amend all errors, heresies, and abuses. First-fruits and tenths were now granted to the king. Thus a clerical pope abroad was exchanged for a lay pope at home. The Pope's authority in England was abjured in various ways, and in 1535 his name was erased from all the service-books.

Meanwhile Cranmer had become Archbishop of Canterbury, in 1533,

CARDINAL WOLSEY.

and had pronounced Henry's divorce. Thomas Cromwell, formerly a subordinate of Wolsey, had raised himself to high power by his skilful schemes for securing the royal supremacy. He was guilty of promoting the ruin and beheading of Sir Thomas More and Bishop Fisher in 1535 for declining to assent in words to the royal supremacy and to the Act which declared Henry's divorce valid.

Cranmer and Cromwell.

During Henry's reign persecution and martyrdom of those who held Reforming opinions were by no means uncommon. Thomas Bilney, a Cambridge man who first implanted doubts as to the Romish system in Latimer's mind, and had denounced saint and relic-worship and pilgrimages, was adjudged guilty of heresy in 1527, though he was orthodox on the Mass. Under pressure he recanted and was absolved; but he soon repented, resumed his teaching as before, and was burnt at Norwich as a relapsed heretic in 1531. Several other martyrdoms followed. Among those most active in distributing English New Testaments and other Reformers' books was John Frith, who had been associated with Tyndale on the Continent, and who answered Sir Thomas More's "Supplication of Souls" and Bishop Fisher on purgatory in an able treatise. Frith returned to England, was

Martyrdoms.

Execution of Bilney, 1531.

John Frith Burned, 1533.

PAGE FROM COVERDALE'S BIBLE.

tracked by More, when Chancellor, and thrown into the Tower. He was betrayed into showing a manuscript treatise on the Eucharist, answered More's rejoinder in a very able treatise, and refused to adopt the Catholic views of purgatory and transubstantiation, claiming that they were not necessary articles of faith. He was condemned by the Bishop of London (Stokesley), and burned at Smithfield in 1533. This was martyrdom for an opinion he had never publicly taught, and soon led to the passing of an Act forbidding bishops to proceed *ca-*

officio against heretics. Another man of mark charged with heresy was Hugh Latimer, a popular Cambridge preacher, who after lengthy proceedings against him was in 1532 excommunicated, and **Latimer charged with heresy.** afterwards made a submission which saved him from punishment. In 1533 he was again preaching against purgatory, worship of saints, and pilgrimages. But he gained **Made Bishop of Worcester.** the king's favour, and was active in the proceedings against the Maid of Kent and her adherents, and in 1535 he was made Bishop of Worcester.

About this time the severity of the civil government in dealing with heresy was shown by the burning of fourteen Dutch Anabaptists at Smithfield and elsewhere. In 1535 Henry proclaimed that the Sacrament ought to be taken by the whole con-

ARCHBISHOP CRANMER, BORN JULY 2ND, 1489; BURNT AT OXFORD MARCH 21ST, 1556.

gregation on pain of damnation, and that such clergymen as had taken wives should not exercise any ministry. In the same year **Coverdale's Bible, 1535.** Coverdale's Bible was published by the aid of Cromwell; it was taken under Henry's patronage, and two editions were rapidly sold.

The abolition of the monasteries was now undertaken, and after a visitation of the smaller establishments in 1535 they were suppressed and their lands confiscated by Act of Parliament in 1536. In **Suppression of Monasteries, 1536-40.** 1536-7 other visitations were successful in causing many abbeys and monks voluntarily to resign themselves to the king's will. It is possible that the commissioners, several of whom were men of bad character and utterly subservient to the Court, exaggerated some of the evils they found; and the suppression was not, as in the Lutheran States, the result of genuine change of conviction on the part of the inmates, but an arbitrary act, while in most cases the revenues were confiscated to the Crown. By the end of 1538, owing to suppression and resignation, only a few of the larger abbeys were left; and in 1539 all the acts of the visitors were legalised, and the lands and incomes of the

HUGH LATIMER, BISHOP OF WORCESTER, BORN ABOUT 1490; BURNT AT
OXFORD OCTOBER 16TH, 1555.

abbeys given to the king. Some great abbeys (Reading, Colchester, and Glastonbury) were declared forfeited because their abbots were attainted

of treason on slight grounds. Many of the abbey estates, purposely
undervalued, were granted to courtiers for various services, and thus served
to found many great houses. There is no doubt, however, that the granting of these estates worked for freedom by making many local magnates
independent of the Crown. Six new bishoprics were created; several
abbeys became collegiate churches; and, by the intervention of Sir

PREACHING AT ST. PAUL'S CROSS, LONDON.

Richard Gresham, St. Bartholomew's and St. Thomas's Hospitals were
preserved for the benefit of the poor.

At the meeting of Convocation in 1536 Bishop Latimer preached a
sermon denouncing many abuses,—especially the sale of masses, **The Ten Arti-**
holding services not in the common tongue, and the gross super- **cles, 1536.**
stitions of image-worship and pilgrimages, but Convocation (a body of

church representatives) was induced by the king to assent to his "Ten Articles," which really represent a considerable advance on the Roman position. We do not give them in detail, as they were abrogated in 1539 by the "Six Articles." Immediately after the passing of the Ten Articles the king issued a proclamation enjoining the clergy to preach once every quarter against the Romish usurpation; to teach the Ten Articles, the Creed, the Lord's Prayer, and the Ten Commandments in the vulgar tongue; not to haunt taverns, but to give themselves to the study of Scripture, with other injunctions. The last-quoted is either suggestive of a very evil state of things, or it involves atrocious slander.

After this, at the Convocation of 1537, it was decided to issue a fuller book of instruction in religion; and a committee of bishops and divines drew up "The Institution of a Christian Man." It is a **"Institution of a Christian Man," 1537.** practical, devout book, expounding the Creed excellently, and treating episcopacy as only one grade of the priesthood, not as a distinct order. Saint-worship is omitted, and nothing is said of the intercession of the Virgin. This book was licensed by the king, and widely diffused.

PAGE FROM TYNDALE'S NEW TESTAMENT.

"Matthew's Bible," 1537. In the same year (1537) appeared what is called "Matthew's Bible," from the name assumed by John Rogers, its editor, who compiled it from Tyndale's translation (so far as completed before his martyrdom in the Netherlands in 1536) and from Coverdale's version. Marginal comments and notes were added, of a decidedly reforming tendency. This again was licensed by Henry VIII. through Cromwell's skill.

In 1538 the injunctions issued by Cromwell in the king's name show the high-water mark of the Reformation under Henry VIII. The reading and study of

Royal Injunctions, 1538.

the Bible were enjoined on every Christian man; and the clergy were bidden to preach, at least once every quarter, a sermon "in which they are to declare purely and sincerely the very gospel of Christ, and to exhort their hearers to works of mercy and religion, and not to trust in works devised by man's fantasies, as in wandering and pilgrimages, offering of money, candles, or tapers to images or relics, kissing or licking the same, saying over a number of bedes not understanded, or in such-like superstition." Yet

TITLE-PAGE OF COVERDALE'S BIBLE.

Henry had refused to accept the Confession of Augsburg, though he had certainly engaged in negotiations with the Lutheran divines. Luther had written to him in an apologetic way, and Melanchthon had dedicated to him his "Commentaries on the Epistles,"

Negotiations with Lutherans.

receiving in return a letter of thanks and a large present. A deputation of Lutherans, including Burghart, Vice-Chancellor of Hesse, and Frederick Myconius, minister at Gotha, visited England in 1538. In concert with Cranmer, three bishops and four doctors met them and drew up articles of agreement in religion; and although they were not then adopted, some parts of them were afterwards closely followed in the Thirty-nine Articles. The Germans went on to insist on communion in both kinds, the abolition of private masses, and the marriage of priests. The king would not hear of these points being granted, and drew up an answer in conjunction with Bishop Tunstal; while in November, 1538, a proclamation was issued forbidding married priests to give the Sacrament or to hold benefices, and expelling all who had married.

In the same month John Nicholson, or Lambert, who had adopted Zwinglian opinions on the Eucharist, was condemned, after argument before **Lambert burnt.** the king and bishops, and burnt with barbarous cruelty. The fortunes of the English Reformation henceforward declined during Henry's life; popedom had its usual effect: men must be of his **Reaction.** opinion or perish. The Pope's Bull of Excommunication against Henry, for years held in reserve, was probably published in 1538, but had no effect in England. On the other hand, the mission of Burghart and other Lutherans, with conciliatory proposals from Melanchthon, came to nothing. Royal proclamation enforced a series of rites and ceremonies condemned by the Reformers, such as those of "holy bread, holy water, processions, kneeling and creeping on Good Friday to the cross, and on Easter Day setting up of lights before the Corpus Christi," etc.

The reaction in the king's mind was fully shown when, early in 1539, he was able to enforce on Parliament, against the opposition of Cranmer, Shaxton (Bishop of Salisbury), Lati- **The "Six Articles," 1539.** mer, and other bishops, the celebrated " Act for abolishing of diversity of opinions," known as the " Six Articles." These affirmed (1) transubstantiation in the Eucharist, and that no wine or bread remains after consecration; (2) that communion in both kinds is unnecessary, and that "in the Flesh under the form of bread is the very Blood, and with the Blood under the form of wine is the very Flesh"; (3) that priests may not marry; (4) that vows of chastity are

PAGE FROM TYNDALE'S PENTATEUCH.

binding; (5) that private masses are lawful; (6) and that auricular confession is expedient and necessary. Offenders against the first article were to be burnt; against the others to be imprisoned and to forfeit property; for a second offence death as felons. Absence from Mass and confession was held to be an offence against the articles. By another Act the king's proclamation was declared to have the force of law; by another the king was empowered to create new bishoprics and to appoint bishops by letters patent. The king's injunctions forbade all circulation of heretical books. The Church was completely enslaved.

On the passing of the Six Article Act Shaxton and Latimer resigned their bishoprics, and were committed to custody; Shaxton, however, changed his mind, conformed to the Act, and turned persecutor. To Cranmer the king showed special favour though he

THOMAS CROMWELL, BORN ABOUT 1490; BEHEADED JULY 28TH, 1540.

was known to be married. In 1540 the king's anger rose against Cromwell for persuading him to marry Anne of Cleves; and, in spite of Cranmer, the compliant minister was beheaded. **Fall of Cromwell.**

1 Melanchthon remonstrated with Henry VIII. on the Six Articles in c an indignant strain.

s   The anti-reform party were now in the ascendant. Three Lutherans, Barnes, Gerard, and Jerome, who could not be indicted under the Six

Articles, were condemned to be burnt by special bill of attainder; and,

Lutherans burnt. at the same time, three priests who denied the king's supremacy were hanged. In 1540 and 1541 a number of other victims suffered. In 1543 "an Act for the advancement of true religion"

Tyndale's Bible condemned. was passed, condemning Tyndale's Bible and all books contrary to the Six Articles, and forbidding the reading of the Bible to all but gentlemen and gentlewomen. The Psalter, Primer, Paternoster, Ave, and Creed in English were allowed. While the laity were exempted from death for heresy, and accused persons were permitted to bring witnesses, it was provided that the king might set aside the Act or any part of it. In 1544 an Act further modifying the rigour of the Six

Cranmer's reforming efforts. Articles was passed. For his share in this and other reforming proceedings Cranmer was severely attacked, and only saved by the king's special intervention. Cranmer was gradually preparing for the reform of the services in England. The "Great" or "Bishops'"

Bishops' Bible. Bible appeared in 1539; and in April, 1540, it was published, with a preface by Cranmer, pointing out the great value of the moral teaching of the Scriptures. In May the king issued a proclamation permitting the Bible to be freely read in churches; and in 1543 it was added that the curate of each parish should on festival-days read to the people a chapter from the Old Testament after the Te Deum and one from the New Testament after the Magnificat. The king in 1545 issued

Henry VIII.'s Primer, 1545. a Primer or Book of Prayers to supersede Cromwell's Primer of 1539, into which a good deal of reform had been introduced. This Primer included the first authorised English Litany, intended to be sung in procession; it was freed from many of the old superstitious invocations. A mixed commission of old and new Churchmen revised "The Institution of a Christian Man," and produced "The Necessary Erudition of any Christian Man," in which transubstantiation and the king's supremacy were strongly asserted.

In these years Bonner, who at first was a follower of Cromwell, and had tended towards reform, became a slavish supporter of the king and

Bonner. detecter of heretics. A youth of fifteen and a young man who read and expounded the Bible in St. Paul's were among his victims; but so many were prosecuted that it was found expedient to stop the persecution.

In 1536-7 most of the English Acts affecting the Church and the king's supremacy were adapted to Ireland, and passed by the Dublin

and nobles. In
granted to Henry
one of " Lord."

By an Act of Parliame.
hospitals, and free chapels," &. immen   . of endowmen
private masses for deceased persons and many religious hospitals   Chantr.
were given over to the king; and this was the last important   abolished.
Act of Henry's reign for alienating ecclesiastical revenues. But it was

TOWER OF LONDON: THE TRAITOR'S GATE.

not the last of his capricious persecutions and judicial murders. The Earl
of Surrey was the last to suffer; his father, the Duke of   Death of Henry
Norfolk, escaped by the death of the king himself.   VIII., 1547.

Under Henry VIII. the Church of England was freed from the Papacy
and its tyranny. This was undoubtedly accomplished with the assent of
the mass of the people; but it arose through the personal   Henry VIII.
matter of the king's divorce. It is conceivable that some   and the
   Reformation.
other occasion would certainly have arisen whenever Henry's
strong will was thwarted, as it must have been if the Papacy retained

...e Church. His
...specially his ruth-
...ministers or bishops, when
...me service in promoting or
...g translations o_ ...e and po_..ions of the service into English,
in the publication of the two important treatises "The Institution"
d "The Necessary Erudition of a Christian Man." But he was intolerant
and a persecutor; and, though
the temper of the times is
partly to blame, he is greatly
to be condemned for much of
the bloodshed of his reign.
No doubt he did much which
prepared for the English reformation of doctrine, as by
sweeping away the papal
power he freed the country
from Rome. It is singular
to note how different a course
the Reformation took in England from that which it
pursued on the Continent,
practically because the Continental monarchs were not
prepared to repudiate the
Pope's influence in their
realms, all feeling too in-

CHAINED BIBLE OF THE REFORMATION-TIME.

secure without the Pope's support and that of his bishops; while in
England Henry had no fear whatever of losing his crown by any act
against the Pope.

Another notable point about the Reformation in Henry VIII.'s time
was the lack of great men of the type of Luther, Zwingli, and Calvin.
No Luther or Calvin in England. Had Wyclif left intellectual descendants, this could hardly have
happened. Later, England produced men of more powerful
mettle; but in Henry VIII.'s time opportunism was apparently the refuge of ability. Of course there was always the danger

that Henry would behead or burn any individual, and we know not what greatness was lost to us through this impending peril. Frith, for instance, may have had such possibilities of greatness. The lesson is that tyranny and absolute power often render great intellect of no avail by reason of the mere physical process of the chopping off of heads; further, that the first duty towards progress is to put an end to such kind of absolute power. If it can by no means be prevented, then the conduct of such men as Cranmer, weak and unheroic as it often seemed, is at least intelligible. Continuing to watch for such gains as he could make for truth, Cranmer felt that he was doing more by pursuing this course than by yielding up the contest. He certainly prepared the way for a great work in the next reign.

EDWARD VI. AND HIS COUNCIL.

CHAPTER XVIII.

The English Church under Edward VI. and Mary.

The New Council and Lord Protector—Visitation of Churches—First Book of Homilies
—Royal Injunctions—Destruction of Pictures and Paintings—Gardiner imprisoned—
—Repeal of Six Articles — Reformed Office of Communion — First Prayer-book —
Influence of Continental Reformers — Alterations from Previous Usage — Marriage
of Clergy allowed—Religious Rebellion in the West—Bonner and Somerset deposed—
Destruction of Old Service-books—Scarcity of Preaching—Latimer and Hooper—New
Ordinal — Joan Bocher burnt — Private Religious Assemblies — Hooper Objects to
Vestments—Cranmer on the Sacrament—Revision of the Prayer-book—Articles of
Religion — Ecclesiastical Laws — Somerset executed — Tunstal deprived — Irreligion
prevalent — Founding of Grammar Schools and Hospitals — Religion in Ireland —
Northumberland's Acts — Results of Edward's Reign — Mary's Accession — Bishops
released from Prison—Romanists encouraged—Cranmer and Holgate imprisoned—
Other Bishops deprived—The Mass and Celibacy restored—Gardiner, Lord Chancellor
—Royal Injunctions—Pole, Papal Legate, Grants the Realm Absolution—Laws against
Heretics—Repeal of Anti-Roman Laws—Martyrdoms—Monastic Revival—Royal and
Papal Proceedings—Cranmer's Trial—Latimer and Ridley's Martyrdom—Pole's Plans
—Cranmer's Recantation and Final Declaration—His Greatness—Death of Mary—
Influence of Marian Persecution—Elizabeth's Moderation—Parker Primate—Return of
Reformers from Abroad—Revision of the Prayer-book—Restoration of Reformed
Religion—New Bishops—The Bishops' Bible—The Thirty-nine Articles—The Reforma-
tion Settlement.

THE accession of a young king already impressed in favour of the
Reformers, and plastic under the influence of Cranmer—who now
was able to show clearly his sympathy with them—together with the

election of the king's uncle, the Earl of Hertford (afterwards Duke of Somerset), as Lord Protector, led the way to notable changes in the services and doctrines of the English Church. Bishop Gardiner was omitted from the King's Council appointed by Henry VIII.; and the majority soon freed themselves from Lord Wriothesley and Bishop Tunstal, the only two anti-Reformers included in it. The first act of the Council affecting the Church was to require the bishops to take out new licences from the Crown. Many Reformers whose voices had been hushed in the latter part of Henry's reign came forward boldly and began to destroy images, encouraged by Ridley, Cranmer's chaplain, and soon afterwards Bishop of London. Bishop Gardiner complained of this, and defended the state of things left by Henry, in a series of letters to the Lord Protector.

The New Council and Lord Protector.

The Protector and Council decided to hold a general royal visitation, during which episcopal powers should be suspended, and all preaching forbidden except by a few licensed preachers. A book of Homilies (now the First Book of the Church of England), prepared during Henry's reign, was ordered to be read in churches every Sunday. Its severe tone towards the old system and abuses, and its omission to mention the Eucharist made it very obnoxious to the old Church party. A translation of Erasmus's Paraphrase on the New Testament, containing many hits at the modern state of the Church, was published, dedicated to the king, and set up in every parish church. The visitors went through the kingdom, carrying with them and selling the new books, and issuing a series of Injunctions partly reproducing those of Cromwell and Henry VIII. In various points a further use of English in the services was enjoined; processions were abolished, and the Litany was to be sung kneeling. The Primer of Henry VIII. was declared to be the only permitted manual of private devotion; and his form of bidding-prayer, which permitted prayers for the dead, was retained. Two lights were to be still set up on the high altar before the Sacrament; but all others were forbidden. A few superstitions were still permitted such as the use of holy water, blessing with the holy candle, making wooden crosses on Palm Sunday, etc. But to image-destruction was added an order for the destruction of all pictures and paintings of feigned miracles, etc., in windows or elsewhere, in churches or houses; and thus began a most disastrous destruction of works of art.

Visitation of Churches.

First Book of Homilies.

Royal Injunctions.

Destruction of Pictures and Paintings.

Gardiner protested that he would receive neither the Injunctions nor the Homilies, on the ground that they were contrary to "The Erudition of a Christian Man," and that the Injunctions contradicted the Homilies in many points. He was committed to the Fleet Prison. Bonner also resisted, and was committed, but afterwards conformed, and was released.

Gardiner resists, and is imprisoned.

In November, 1547, Parliament met, and its first Act was one approved by the Convocation of Canterbury, enforcing communion in both kinds, and severely censuring every one who ventured to ridicule the Sacrament, an offence to be punished with fine and imprisonment. Another Act ordered all bishops' appointments to be by letters patent from the king. The Act giving the king's proclamations the force of law was repealed, as were all Acts of the late reign making anything treason or felony which was not so previously. This involved the repealing of the Six Articles and of the restrictions on the publication and reading of English Bibles.

Repeal of Six Articles.

The Lower House of Convocation, sitting at the same time, made a bold attempt to regain ancient privileges in an address to Cranmer, demanding that they should sit in Parliament, that the remodelling of church services should be committed to them, and that a committee to revise the canon law should be appointed. No answer was vouchsafed. Meanwhile there were issued proclamations in which, while some old things were maintained, the use of ashes and palms and candles on Candlemas Day, creeping to the cross on Good Friday, holy bread, and holy water were dropped. All clergy were forbidden to minister elsewhere than in their cures; only certain licensed preachers were allowed to discourse publicly anywhere; and an order in Council commanded the removal from churches, and the destruction, of all images.

Other Reforms.

From the beginning of 1548 a commission, including Cranmer, Bishop Ridley, and other reforming prelates and doctors, sat at Windsor to draw up a reformed office for the Communion. They were greatly indebted to the "Consultation" of Hermann of Wied, Elector-Archbishop of Cologne (mainly by Bucer), based on Luther's form prepared for Nuremberg. The earliest part, the consecration, was left in Latin; but there were added directions and exhortations in English, and a general confession to be said by all the people. The promulgation of this gave rise for a time to much dissension. During 1548 disorders were frequent; and proclamations had to be issued against quarrelling and shouting

Reformed Office of Holy Communion.

in churches, bringing horses and mules through and into the churches, the mobbing of priests, the stealing of church furniture, etc. The Lord Protector tried to appropriate to his own use the estates of Westminster Abbey.

At last, in November, 1548, a new Prayer-book was produced by the Windsor Commission, and became law in January, 1549. Severe penalties were denounced on those who failed to use it or who misused it. Its composition had been considerably **First Prayer-book of Edward VI.**

influenced by the notable Protestant refugees who had now settled in England, such as Martin Bucer, made Divinity professor at Cambridge in 1549, who died in 1551; Peter Martyr, formerly an Augustinian monk, afterwards Divinity professor at Strasburg, appointed Divinity professor at Oxford in 1547 (he quitted England in 1553, and settled at Zurich till his death in 1562); John a Lasco, a Pole, whom Cranmer

PETER MARTYR, ITALIAN PROTESTANT REFORMER, APPOINTED PROFESSOR AT OXFORD, 1547.

made superintendent of foreign religious bodies in England (he also was allowed to leave England on Mary's accession). A long letter was sent by Calvin to the Lord Protector giving his well-known views, and concentrating all under three heads: "Teach **Influence of Continental Reformers.** the truth; extirpate abuses; castigate vices." He feared there were but few lively sermons heard in England. "Let there be a form of doctrine published, received by all, and taught by all. Let all your bishops and parish priests maintain that; and admit none to any office in the Church who will not swear. . . . Let there also be a catechism for the young and ignorant; . . . and as to the order of prayers and rites in the churches, I strongly approve that there be a certain form from which the minister may not depart." There is no doubt that, although the new church service was the work of English divines, it was considerably influenced by Continental Reformers. Cranmer in 1548 published an English catechism, translated from a Lutheran catechism of Justus Jonas, and including somewhat strong teaching of the corporal presence in the Eucharist.

It should be noted that under the Roman jurisdiction there had been a great variety of service-books in use in England. Local saints and local observances complicated the matter, and the "Use" of each diocese was in itself complex and difficult to understand. Thus there was much reason for introducing a simpler and more uniform style of service.

Alterations from Previous Usage. The Sarum Use, the best established and most approved, was taken as a partial basis. The recension of the Roman breviary (about 1535) by Quignon (Cardinal of Santa Croce), which omitted two-thirds of the saints' days, all the offices of the Virgin, and many other superfluities, was also before them. But the Commissioners boldly cut out the services entitled "The Hours," which were mainly a monastic accretion, and retained only the morning and evening services and the Litany. Some of the most conspicuous features in which this first Prayer-book of Edward VI. differed from present Anglican services were that the Exhortation, Confession, and Absolution were not at its beginning; public prayer began with the Lord's Prayer, was followed by the Versicles and the Venite (Ninety-fifth Psalm), and ended with the Third Collect. The Communion Service lacked the Commandments; the name of the Virgin was mentioned; prayer was offered for the dead; water was mixed with the wine; and in delivering the elements to communicants only the first clauses of the words now used were introduced. The sign of the cross was twice made during the consecration and at other services. The consecration was now entirely in English. Many gestures and actions of the priest, significant of stages in Christ's passion, were omitted; the sacrifice on the cross was declared "a full, perfect, and sufficient sacrifice, oblation, and satisfaction for the sins of the whole world. The elements were called 'creatures of bread and wine,' as if to exclude any idea of transformation. The entire service, now termed 'Supper of the Lord and the Holy Communion, commonly called the Mass,' was to be said or sung plainly and distinctly." Forms of exorcism and anointing were retained. In the Burial Service prayer was offered for the deceased. The Athanasian Creed, formerly repeated daily, was to be said only six times a year. There was a great reduction from the former Use of musical versicles, canticles, and responses. The Collects were remodelled, and many of them were beautiful new compositions or translations.

The same Parliament which enforced the new Prayer-book released the clergy from compulsory celibacy—a change already approved by Convocation. Another Act enforced fasting on Fridays and Saturdays **Marriage of** in Lent, and on other fast-days. Much discontent prevailed **Clergy allowed.** in England during 1549, the first year of the new regime, and many districts were in insurrection, partly owing to changes in tillage and to the actions of the new lords of church and monastic **Religious Rebellion in the West.** property. But many complained of the alterations in the services, and the insurrection in the west of England was due to this cause.

Particular injunctions and inquiries were found necessary to prevent the retention of many acts of the popish Mass. Two previously retained were now forbidden, namely, the two lights on the altar and the "sepulchres" to contain the "Host" before Easter. Bonner encouraged those Roman practices, and when ordered to preach at Paul's Cross in favour of the new settlement, discoursed chiefly on transubstantiation. When accused, he made a bold defence, but was deprived of his **Bonner and** bishopric and committed to the Tower. Early in October the **Somerset Deposed.** Duke of Somerset was deposed from the protectorate by his powerful rival, Warwick. His autocratic manner and deeds had made him hated, and few regretted his fall. He was, however, restored to the Council on the marriage of his daughter to Warwick's son.

In December a new Ordinal (or Ordination Service) was ordered to be drawn up by six prelates and six others. By another Act it was made a penal offence to possess any of the old service- **Destruction of Old Service-books.** books, and various officials were deputed to destroy them wherever found, as well as all remaining images of any kind. An enormous amount of vandalism was accomplished under this tyrannical Act.

All this time, when the Reformation in England has been supposed to have been particularly active, preaching was extremely **Scarcity of** rare, except in London, Oxford, and Cambridge. The parish **Preaching.** priests were forbidden by the Council, and but a few licensed preachers travelled through the country, discoursing publicly where they were permitted, but only on Sundays. Meanwhile the young king was constantly preached at, and endured all with satisfaction. After Latimer by his plain-speaking had accomplished much good, the Court grew tired of him, and he left London to preach up and down the country, a bishop without a diocese. Hooper, formerly a monk, for years resident at Zurich, and a follower of Zwingli, Bullinger, and Calvin, succeeded to his place as chief preacher before the king. He denounced the vices of the age as unsparingly as Latimer; but he went farther in denouncing altars and favouring plain communion-tables and the reception of the Eucharist standing or sitting. He opposed oaths and certain vestments prescribed by the new Ordinal. To him has been given the title of the Father of Nonconformity, not indeed as a separatist from the Church, but as one who objected to the interference of the State in religious matters.

Latimer and Hooper.

The new Ordinal was published in March, 1550. It discarded the old Roman minor orders, and left only those of deacon, priest, and bishop. Vestments were much reduced, deacons and priests only wearing a plain alb (a long coat of white linen, with a girdle). The ordination of bishops was most of all shorn of ceremonies. The bishop elect wore a surplice and cope (semicircular vestment worn over the surplice, varying in colour with the season, fastened at the neck, open in front, and reaching nearly to the feet). All had to take the oath to the king's supremacy, bishops also having to take an oath of obedience to their archbishop. The bishop received with the chalice and the bread a Bible. It is admitted even by opponents of this Ordinal that, though much that was venerable and desirable was omitted, everything essential to orders was retained. Heath, however, one of the commission, who had replaced Latimer as Bishop of Worcester, refused to subscribe to the new Ordinal, was unconstitutionally committed to the Fleet, and before Edward's death was deprived. Ridley was promoted from Rochester to London by letters patent, after many of the estates of the bishopric had been granted to royal favourites. Ridley soon showed himself active in supporting the Prayer-book of the Reformation. He broke down the high altar at St. Paul's, and set up a table in its place.

New Ordinal, 1550.

England was still not without its Anabaptists and other Dissenters. Joan Bocher, or Joan of Kent, was an Anabaptist, who in April, 1549, obstinately maintained her belief "that our Saviour was not very man, nor had received flesh of His mother Mary." She

Joan Bocher burnt, 1550.

was excommunicated by Cranmer, given over to the State, and condemned to be burnt. She was kept in prison for a year; bishops and divines tried to convert her, but she continued firm, and the warrant for her execution was signed on April 27th; on May 2nd, 1550, she was burnt alive. Cranmer and Latimer must bear part of the blame for this martyrdom, though not present at the Council which finally condemned her: About the same time it is related that numerous private assemblies were **Private Religious Assemblies.** forming in Essex and Kent, including persons who denied the doctrine of predestination, and that children were born in original sin. Henry Hart, Cole of Faversham, Cole of Maidstone, Vaughan of Heven, and

others, were among the leaders questioned, and in some cases punished.

In 1550 Hooper was offered the bishopric of Gloucester, on the death of Wakefield; but he refused to wear the vestments and to take the oath prescribed by the new Ordinal. **Hooper objects to Vestments.** He scrupled to admit that sacraments confer grace; "They seal, they testify grace, not confer it," he said. Yet letters patent were made out for his appointment.

BISHOP HOOPER, BORN ABOUT 1495; MARTYRED 1555. Who has been called "The Father of Nonconformity."

Ridley, who considered these things indifferent, could not overcome Hooper's scruples. Hooper replied that they lacked the authority of Scripture. Several of the foreign Reformers, settled in England, sided with Hooper, among them John a Lasco. Bucer said the vestments were permissible, but might well be given up; Peter Martyr expostulated with Hooper for making a disturbance about indifferent things. Hooper published a vigorous "Confession of John Hooper's Faith," one noble passage of which was the following :—

"As concerning the ministers of the Church, I believe that the Church is bound to no sort of people, or any ordinary succession of bishops, cardinals, or such-like, but unto the only word of God, although there be diversity of gifts and knowledge among men: some know more, and some less; and if he that knoweth least teach Christ after the Holy Scriptures, he is to be accepted. . . . I am sorry therefore with all my heart to see the Church of Christ degenerated into a civil policy."

Early in 1551 he was committed to Cranmer's custody, and thence to the Fleet Prison, where he at last gave way, and was consecrated bishop in the fashion he had objected to, although he was afterwards permitted to discard his vestments, except when preaching before the king.

We now approach the transition to the more Calvinistic period of Edward's reign. Cranmer had been much influenced by Ridley, and in

Cranmer on the Sacraments. 1550 he published "A Defence of the True and Catholic Doctrine of the Sacrament," arguing in favour of a special gift or grace and a real spiritual presence, but denying transubstantiation, corporal presence, the eating and drinking of Christ by wicked recipients of the Sacrament, and the propitiatory sacrifice of the Mass. Gardiner and Dr. Richard Smith replied with great vigour, the former asserting that Cranmer attacked Catholic doctrine on pretence that it was popish.

Three important labours, in which Cranmer bore the principal part, occupied the last years of Edward's reign, viz., the revision of the Prayer-

Revision of the Prayer-book. book, the drawing up of articles of belief, and also of ecclesiastical laws. Various objections had been made to the first Prayer-book by bishops, as well as by Bucer, Peter Martyr, Calvin, and other Reformers; and it was intended to make the book more perfect, and the fashion of service more earnest. The revision was undertaken by a commission, apparently similar to the former one, without express appointment by Convocation; and Cranmer's hand is very marked in the alterations, as indeed it is in the original book. In January, 1552, Parliament and Convocation met, and the new book was laid before them. In April a second Act of Uniformity legally sanctioned the book, together with a revised Ordinal, still further diminishing the use of vestments, omitting the delivery of a chalice and bread to the priest at ordination and the placing of a Bible on the neck, and the pastoral staff in the hand of a bishop in consecration. It was enacted that presence at any other form of service was to be punishable on the first offence by six months' imprisonment, and on the third by perpetual imprisonment,—another evidence of the intolerance of the age.

In the new Prayer-book, at morning and evening prayer the Sentences, Exhortation, Confession, and Absolution were prefixed to the Lord's Prayer, with which the service had previously begun; and Changes in the prayers were added after the Third Collect. In the Com- New Book. munion Service important changes were made. The reading of the Commandments, with prayers for grace to obey them, was introduced. The name of the Virgin Mary was omitted from special mention. The invocation of the Word and the Holy Ghost, the sign of the cross, and the mixing of water with the wine were omitted. Instead of the long, comprehensive Prayer of Consecration, three prayers were substituted, the first for the Church Militant, the second that of Consecration, the third being the first form of the Prayer after Communion. In delivering the elements to the communicants, one important change was made. For the first clauses as now used, the second—"Take and eat this in remembrance," etc.; "Drink this in remembrance," etc.—were substituted, evidently marking a tendency towards Calvin's, or even Zwinglian, views. In baptism the exorcism, anointing, and triple immersion were omitted; in the service for the visitation of the sick the anointing and directions for private confessions and for reserving portions of the elements from the public communion, and in the Burial Service prayers for the dead, were left out.

The "Articles of Religion," forty-two in number, grew out of a private set of articles drawn up by Cranmer, to be subscribed to by all who would be licensed to preach, or to lecture, in Divinity. In 1551 the Council Articles of instructed Cranmer to frame a book of Articles of Religion Religion. "for the preserving and maintaining of peace and unity of doctrine in this Church." Such articles were drawn up in conformity with the doctrines embodied in a Code of Ecclesiastical Laws, and circulated among certain bishops. They were completed in November, 1552, and published in 1553, as "agreed upon by the bishops and other learned and godly men in the last Convocation at London." Inasmuch as they agree substantially with the thirty-nine subsequently adopted in Elizabeth's reign, we will defer a full analysis. The articles included in the forty-two, but omitted in the thirty-nine, were those on blasphemy against the Holy Ghost, on the obligation to keep the moral commandments, on the resurrection of the dead, on the state of the soul after death, against the Millenarians, and against the doctrine of universal salvation. A clause was included in the third of the forty-two describing the spirit of Christ as leaving His body in the tomb, and descending into hell.

There was a strong protest against the ubiquity of Christ's body, and against the real and bodily presence of Christ's flesh and blood in the Eucharist. The majority of the articles are held in common by a large proportion of Christians, and conspicuous skill is shown in dealing with controversies and in conciliating as many as possible without offence. As to things necessary to be believed, it was denied that the Church had the power to decree anything against or beyond Scripture. The freedom of the will was asserted in an article different from the present. Justification by faith alone was asserted in general terms. Good works were not defined. The clergy were ordered to subscribe to these articles, and they did so very generally during the few remaining months of Edward's reign.

The commission of thirty-two appointed in 1550 "to examine the ecclesiastical laws and gather and compile such laws as might be con-

Ecclesiastical Laws. venient to be practised within the realm in all spiritual courts," which included eight bishops, eight divines, eight civilians, and eight lawyers, was reduced to eight, including Cranmer and Peter Martyr. It produced the valuable *Reformatio Legum Ecclesiasticarum*, not published for twenty years and then rejected by Elizabeth's Parliament. We need not examine it here, since it was never enacted.

Meanwhile events had been occurring which were by no means of unmixed benefit to religion. The Duke of Somerset, having again sought

Somerset executed, 1552. to recover his predominance, was charged with treasonable conspiracy and acquitted, but found guilty of felony and sentenced to death. His execution took place in January, 1552, and thenceforward Warwick (now Duke of Northumberland) was without rival.

Tunstal deprived. Tunstal, Bishop of Durham, was imprisoned on a charge of treason and at last deprived by a lay commission, who allowed him no counsel. Cranmer had refused to take part in this act. Practical religion was not gaining much among the people. The continued spoliation of church property, and especially that of bishops, prepared the people to rebel against the new regime in the next reign. Preachers were few,

Irreligion. and in many cases the parochial services were not performed, livings being often given by nobles to laymen. Disorder was abundant. Ridley succeeded in calling the king's attention to the spolia-

London Hospitals. tion of the charities for the London poor, and by his request the Corporation of London diligently set to work to found Christ's Hospital, to revive St. Thomas's and St. Bartholomew's, and to establish Bridewell. Fortunately, too, the young king had a zeal for education which led him to found many grammar schools throughout the kingdom, particularly in 1552-3, that of Birmingham being the greatest. Of course the funds came largely from confiscated ecclesiastical and corporate property. *The King's Grammar Schools.*

In the first years of Edward the Reformation made no headway in Ireland. The new Office of Communion was scarcely used anywhere. When bishoprics were vacant, the Pope appointed *Religion in Ireland.* his nominees, as did the English king. But in 1550 the new Prayer-book in English was enforced; and the people, who could not understand, and who hated English, left the churches and attended the services of such Romish priests as could enter the kingdom. The Archbishop of Armagh (Dowdal) refused to conform, asserting that he would not be bishop where the Mass was forbidden.

Northumberland in the last year of Edward outdid previous acts of spoliation. St. Paul's and a multitude of parish churches were stripped of valuables; chantry lands, property of bishoprics, and other estates were *Northumberland's Acts.* appropriated. The Duke became haughty of speech to Cranmer; he was hated by the

EDWARD VI.

people; but he thought to secure himself by marrying his son to Lady Jane Grey and inducing the king to appoint her his successor in default of male issue of his cousin Frances, Duchess of Suffolk. Cranmer unwillingly agreed to this scheme. How it failed needs not to be detailed here.

The reign of Edward VI. did not probably hasten very greatly the true progress of the Reformation in England. Of Knox's influence in the latter part of his reign we shall have more to say in the chapter of the *Effect of Edward's Reign.* Scottish Reformation; but the authorities were in favour of the death of notable heretics and of violent enforcement of the new doctrines.

While the people remained staunch in their repudiation of papal supremacy, they were generally attached to the ancient ceremonies and services of the English Church; and as preachers were lacking who could instruct them in religion, the most powerful influences that affected them were the scandalous waste of church property and the general neglect of church duties. The autocracy of Henry had been exchanged for the personal rule of Somerset and Northumberland; and Cranmer, while deserving much credit for his preparation of Bible, Prayer-book, Articles, etc., was unable to establish a condition of true religious liberty and a proper discharge of religious duties. Everything was ready for a reaction on Mary's accession, and without the martyrdoms of her reign it is conceivable that the Reformation might not have gained the hold in England, so soon as it did.

Cranmer by his reluctant consent to the sovereignty of Lady Jane Grey, and Ridley, by preaching in her favour and against Mary at Paul's Cross, added to their previous offences in Mary's eyes. But a violent change seemed at first far distant. The five imprisoned bishops were released and restored to their sees; but Cranmer was allowed to bury the deceased king according to the new Prayer-book. The queen had Mass said before her, and in August, 1553, issued a proclamation forbidding all preaching without her licence, and recommending her own religious belief to all her subjects. Many of the Reformers disobeyed, and were imprisoned; many others fled the kingdom, including the foreign preachers, ordered to leave by proclamation. Northumberland's abject recantation of Protestantism on the scaffold had greatly damaged the cause. Cranmer refused to escape, and strongly asserted his beliefs in a document defending the English Prayer-book. The Council on this committed him to the Tower, whither he was followed by Latimer and by Holgate, Archbishop of York. Ridley was already in prison; and Bonner, once more Bishop of London, wrote to his agents that they might order all things at their pleasure. Bonner, Day, and Tunstal were appointed to inquire into the marriage of bishops, and several who had married resigned or were deprived. The queen sent to the Pope her assurances of fidelity and entreaties for the absolution of the kingdom, though without being able to promise the restoration of church estates.

Mary's Accession, 1553.

Imprisoned bishops released.

The Romanists encouraged.

Cranmer, Latimer, and Holgate imprisoned.

Other bishops deprived.

Mary's first parliament soon settled that there was to be no restitution, and no return to the papal supremacy; but they annulled the divorce

of Mary's mother, repealed the principal ecclesiastical Acts The Mass and
of Edward's reign, including the Acts of Uniformity, restored celibacy of
clergy restored.

MARY TUDOR. QUEEN MARY I. OF ENGLAND.

the Mass, and re-established celibacy of the clergy. Wyatt's rebellion,
however, with its failure, exasperated Mary against the opponents of the

Y

Papacy, and both her foreign and her English advisers counselled severity.

Gardiner Lord Chancellor. Gardiner, who had been made Lord Chancellor, incurred part of the blame of the executions which followed. He had formerly sought to enforce the Six Articles; now he desired to restore the ancient ecclesiastical courts and even to introduce the Inquisition. He also distinguished himself in the cruel treatment of the Princess Elizabeth. A committee of Convocation sitting at Oxford condemned Cranmer, Ridley, and Latimer as heretics; but Parliament was dissolved without having granted power to burn them. Convocation passed a resolution affirming transubstantiation.

In March, 1554, a series of injunctions to the clergy was issued by royal authority, requiring the removal of married priests, the giving up of

Royal injunctions, 1554. the oath of supremacy, the restoration of Latin processions, ceremonies, etc., and many other things current in Henry VIII.'s time. This was but following the example of both Henry and Edward. Mary's great concern now was to re-establish Roman rule. Her cousin

Cardinal Pole comes as papal legate. Cardinal Pole had been appointed legate to England with full powers, but it was not till after Mary's marriage to Philip of Spain that it was deemed safe for Pole to return. He came armed with authority even to consent to the alienation of church lands. A parliament, in the main favourable to the old religion, was elected, and after hearing Pole describe the greatness of the papal see and its claims on England, the Lords spiritual and temporal and the Commons expressed repentance for having done anything against its supremacy, promised to

Grants the nation absolution. repeal such Acts, and sought absolution, which Pole granted. Sermons, masses, and Te Deums in abundance celebrated the joyful occasion. The clergy in Convocation similarly sought and obtained absolution. Meanwhile Peter de Soto, who was for long Charles V.'s confessor, was made Professor of Theology at Oxford; and various other Spanish divines were promoted to high office, and figured in the subsequent martyrdoms of bishops. Gardiner agreed to the Roman headship, which he had formerly opposed. Hooper from his prison maintained his anti-Roman and reforming views in various letters, and joined with other distinguished prisoners in a supplication to the queen and Parliament, claiming the right to public discussion of their alleged heresies.

Parliament in 1554 re-enacted the old Acts against heretics, again

Laws against heretics. making it unorthodox to say or do anything against the Pope and to hold private conventicles. It also repealed in 1555 all

Acts against Rome passed since 1528, at the same time guaranteeing all grants of church lands to the laity.

Some secret assemblies were detected holding the forbidden English service and communion, and many persons were imprisoned. Others followed, who were accused of holding free-will doctrines Repeal of anti-opposed to Calvinism. The Reformers, bishops and others, Roman laws. encouraged one another by letters which passed from prison to prison.

MARTYRDOMS AT SMITHFIELD.
(*From an old print.*)

Early in 1555 the political prisoners in the Tower were set free, and Holgate with them, while Miles Coverdale was permitted to leave the kingdom. But as soon as the new Act against heretics came into force Gardiner, Tunstal, four other bishops, and several of the Council caused Hooper, Rogers, Bradford, and ten others to be called before them, and asked them to join the Catholic Church as now constituted. They denied that they had ever dissented from the Catholic Church, and denied also that the Bishop of Rome had more authority than any other bishop. Hooper denounced the Pope's doctrine as contrary to that of Christ, and the Pope as not worthy to be accounted a member of Christ's Church. On a later occasion a larger commission disputed with the prisoners; and Rogers, despite the terrible prospect, showed great skill in meeting Gardiner, who put forward the extravagant proposition that "when a parliament hath concluded a thing no private person has authority to discuss whether they have done right or wrong." Nearly all were condemned. It is true that pardon on recanting was offered them to the last; but seeing what happened in Cranmer's case, we may doubt if they would have escaped. Rogers suffered first with heroic courage. Bonner degraded Hooper from the priesthood, his episcopacy not being acknowledged, as also others; and they were sent to various places to be burnt, Hooper to Gloucester, Taylor to his parish of Hadleigh, in Suffolk. A second series of martyrdoms, especially taken in hand by Bonner, followed them, including a number of laymen. Bishop Ferrar, of St. David's, was sent down to Caermarthen to be tried by his successor Morgan, and was burnt on March 30th.

Martyrdoms February and March, 1555.

The statue of Thomas à Becket was raised (to be soon maimed by the populace) over Mercers' Chapel, and the shrine of Edward the Confessor once more set up in Westminster Abbey. The Friars Observants were reinstated at Greenwich and Southampton; the Black Friars (Dominicans) were housed at Smithfield; the Bridgetite nunnery of Sion, near Brentford, was repaired. The queen asserted her desire to restore all church lands she held. The bishops did not appear sufficiently active in persecution, so the justices and gentry were bidden to be vigorous in promoting conformity and repressing heresy, and to appoint men to give secret information in each parish. The queen, not needing spur from Philip, personally urged the bishops to greater activity; and Bonner showed himself very obedient. Cardmaker and Bradford were burnt after considerable attempts to convert them. A royal proclamation forbade the importation, buying, selling, or keeping of the books of the Continental Reformers, and also of Tyndale and Cranmer.

Monastic revival.

A Bull of the new Pope, Paul IV., offered plenary indulgence after fasting for three days, confession, and communion. Another Bull purported to revoke the whole recent alienation of church property, but the legate soon found it necessary to obtain its recall as regarded England. A third Bull granted the archbishop's pallium to Heath of York, in terms studiously insolent to the country, the late bishops being called "schismatical," and the late kings "pretended." Fortunately Pole resisted Loyola's offer of Jesuit help.

Royal and papal proceedings.

Passing over numerous martyrdoms in London, Canterbury, Norwich, etc., we come to the notable Oxford trials. It had been decided to treat the previous condemnations of Cranmer, Latimer, and Ridley as void, because they occurred before the "reconciliation" of the kingdom to the Holy See. The Pope was requested to allow Cranmer to be tried; he first summoned Cranmer to Rome, then named a deputy, who appointed another, Brooks of Gloucester, a bishop, to try an archbishop

Cranmer's Trial.

MEETING OF LATIMER AND RIDLEY AT THE PLACE OF MARTYRDOM.

and primate. Cranmer was charged with blasphemy, incontinency (his marriage), and heresy. He refused to acknowledge any representative of the Pope. Martin, a civilian proctor, charged him with disobedience to his oath to the Pope, taken at his consecration, and with an immoderate desire of promotion. He also accused him of having successively maintained three different doctrines about the Sacrament. In answering the interrogatories, Cranmer professed himself as bound to give account to every man of the hope that he had in Christ Jesus, but not as acknowledging the competency of his trier; further, he denied that he was in schism. Pole

The Pope sentences Cranmer. wrote a long epistle in answer to Cranmer's arguments, while the decision of the case was dutifully referred to Rome. On December 4th the Pope pronounced Cranmer excommunicated and condemned as "a notorious heresiarch, a follower of heresiarchs, like Wyclif, of damned memory, and Martin Luther."

Meanwhile Pole issued a commission for the trial of Latimer and

Trial and Martyrdom of Latimer and Ridley, 1555. Ridley, three bishops, including Brooks, sitting on this occasion. They denied the authority of their judges, and only answered under protest. On October 15th they were degraded, and on the 16th they were taken to the ditch in front of Balliol College, and both fastened to one stake. Their last moments were marked by many affecting words; and as the lighted faggot was laid at Ridley's feet, Latimer said to him, "Be of good comfort, Master Ridley, and play the man: we shall this day light such a candle, by God's grace, in England, as I trust shall never be put out." Ridley suffered extremely from the slowness of the fire, his feet being consumed while he still lived.

The Parliament of autumn, 1555, was, with great difficulty, persuaded to pass an Act to allow the queen to give up various church revenues,

Death of Gardiner, 1555. including first-fruits and tenths; but, contrary to her intention, first-fruits were abolished, and tenths and other funds were given to improve small livings. Gardiner died in November; many of the Spaniards were recalled from England; and the queen, Pole, and Bonner conducted the remaining affairs of the reign. Pole was ambitious to hold

Pole's ambitious Plans. a general Anglican synod and to legislate permanently for the Church. The synod was held by royal licence, and important subjects were propounded: a new confession and homilies, a translation of the New Testament, and many other things. He had his own plan for the reconstitution of the English Church, but it need not detain us here.

Martyrdoms continued in several dioceses in the latter part of 1555, in Canterbury and London especially, the most notable in London being

Cranmer's Recantations. that of Archdeacon Philpot. Early in 1556 orders were given by the queen and council to stop the boisterous admiration of crowds at brave martyrdoms, and to apprehend all who encouraged the martyrs. No more pardons were to be offered at the place of execution. Cranmer, while awaiting the Pope's sentence in prison, was shaken in his resolution, and at last signed several forms of submission to the queen, the laws, and the Pope. He was degraded by Bonner and Thirlby (Bishop of Ely); but he appealed to a general council of the Church. He was ordered

THE MARTYRS' MEMORIAL, OXFORD.

to be burnt, in spite of his submissions. A form of absolute recantation was given him, which he signed, we know not under what pressure; but he recovered his mental balance, and when set in His Final Declaration.

St. Mary's Church, Oxford, to declare his changed opinions, just before his death, he renounced all he had lately written contrary to the truth, "for fear of death and to save my life, if it might be." "As my hand offended in writing contrary to my heart, therefore my hand shall first be punished. For if I may come to the fire, it shall be first burned. And as for the Pope, I refuse him, as Christ's enemy and antichrist, with all his false doctrines." At the stake he gloriously fulfilled his promise. Thrusting his right hand into the flame, he exclaimed, "This hand hath offended," and held it there till it was consumed. So, stand-ing perfectly still, without a tremor, he died with extraordinary fortitude. As Canon Dixon well says, "His merits and services were greater than his faults. He had gravity, gentleness and innocency, boundless industry and carefulness, considerable power of fore-cast; and he lived in a high region. He preserved the con-tinuity of the Church of England. He gave to the English Reformation largeness and capacity. He was a greater man than any of his con-temporaries." He has set his mark indelibly on the English Church by his influence on the English Prayer-book. He is more indelibly engraved on the heart of the English nation as the noblest martyr of all the English race.

His Martyrdom, March 21st, 1556.

His Greatness.

We need say little of the remaining proceedings of this reign. A fiercer persecution than ever was set on foot in 1556–7. Even the bodies of dead Reformers, such as Bucer and Fagius, were exhumed and burnt. Pole became Archbishop of Canterbury, but lost favour with the Pope; the queen resented this, and Pole was reinstated as legate. Finally came the disaster of Calais and the deaths of Mary and Pole, on November 17th and 18th, 1558.

Death of Mary and Pole, 1558.

The Marian persecutions settled the English people strongly in favour of the Reformation. Nothing has ever established great causes like the proved willingness of their advocates to die for them, especially when aided by consistent lives. As Huss had suffered, as Luther and Calvin certainly were ready to suffer, so Cranmer, Ridley, Latimer, and Hooper, and their fellows, set a seal to their beliefs which constrained Englishmen to examine the doctrines of national religious liberty and liberation from superstitions, which they supported. The 286 English martyrs in Mary's reign (which included forty-six women) were the invulnerable guarantee of a new and lasting revolt against Rome.

Influence of the Marian Persecutions.

Fortunately for stability, the return of the English Church and

CRANMER COMMITTED TO THE TOWER.

kingdom to reformed principles was accomplished without undue haste. Elizabeth, who succeeded to the throne without opposition, had been well educated, but had conformed, under practical compulsion, to Roman rites during Mary's reign, and appeared resolved to be

Elizabeth's Moderation.

QUEEN ELIZABETH.
(From a painting by Zucchero.)

guided by politic considerations. Sir William Cecil, afterwards Lord Burghley, at once became her chief counsellor, and to him the wisdom of many of her acts is attributable. Eleven of Mary's councillors were retained, and eight of reforming tendencies were added. To Bonner

Elizabeth showed distinct disfavour, and Bishop Oglethorpe, who crowned her, was ordered not to elevate the Host in her presence. Much depended on the new Archbishop. Elizabeth chose Matthew Parker, a grave, learned,

Matthew Parker Primate. and moderate man, Master of Corpus College, Cambridge, under Henry VIII., and Dean of Lincoln, under Edward VI. He lived quietly and obscurely under Edward and Mary, and was selected as the one sensible man to be found, who, as Froude says, "was religious without being a fanatic, and a Christian without being a dogmatist." He was very slow to accept the appointment, but was consecrated in December, 1559.

Without waiting for an archbishop, a commission of divines had been appointed in December, 1558, to revise the second Prayer-book of Edward

Return of Reformers from Abroad. VI. Meanwhile all religious teaching or preaching, except the Gospels, Epistles, and Commandments in the vulgar tongue, and the use of the Litany, Lord's Prayer, and Creed in English, was forbidden. No counsel was taken with Convocation, which was known to be almost unanimous for Romanism. A large number of exiled reforming divines and laymen had now returned from abroad, and brought many strong opinions with them: Bishops Ponet, Barlow, Scory, Coverdale, and Bale; deans, archdeacons, and divines afterwards well known, such as Grindal, Cox, Sandys, Jewel,

MATTHEW PARKER, PROTESTANT ARCHBISHOP OF CANTERBURY
FROM 1559 TO 1575.

Reynolds, Foxe. Many of these had settled at Frankfort, where there had been discussions (detailed in " The Troubles of Frankfort ") between those who wished to use the Edwardian Prayer-book and those who wished to conform to the Calvinist services. Thus they returned to England with germs of division already vigorously developed. Cox, Grindal, and others were on the commission for revision, but the chief influence fell to Edward Guest, afterwards Bishop of Rochester. The result

BISHOP JEWEL, AUTHOR OF THE FAMOUS "APOLOGY FOR THE CHURCH OF ENGLAND."

was a moderate revision of the Prayer-book of 1552, both clauses in administering the elements in the Eucharist being combined, *Revision of* as at present in use. All vestments and ornaments of the *Prayer-book.* Church that were in use by authority of Parliament in the second year of Edward were restored; but this had little practical effect in Elizabeth's reign, only copes and surplices being used.

The first Parliament of Elizabeth (1559) restored the royal supremacy, the title being changed from supreme " head " to " governor "; it also re-enacted the Act of Uniformity sanctioning the Prayer-book, and *Restoration* gave back first-fruits and tenths to the Crown. The Act of *of Reformed* *Religion.* Supremacy repealed all Acts touching religion in Mary's reign, and enforced penalties against those maintaining the papal supremacy. The queen was empowered to create a commission to visit, reform, and amend all heresies, errors, schisms, and abuses, though nothing was to be punished as heresy but according to the word of God (*i.e.*, according to the commission's rendering of the word of God), the four early councils, or national or provincial synods. This was really an inquisitorial power, most detrimental to religious freedom.   Fourteen out of fifteen remaining Marian bishops refused to take the oath of the queen's supremacy, and were deprived; thus a wholesale new consecration of bishops was necessary.   Barlow and Scory were confirmed in Chichester and Hereford; Grindal became Bishop of London, Cox of Ely, Sandys of Worcester, Jewel of Salisbury, Guest of Rochester.   Including the fourteen bishops, however, only 189 clergy were deprived in all England for nonconformity.   But many of those who conformed had no real care for religion, and abuses were rife; many superstitious practices and evil customs remained.   The queen issued injunctions based on those of Edward VI., with some minor alterations.   At the same time she was sanctioning the wholesale alienation of manors belonging to bishoprics, exchanging for them tithe-charges.   Many manors were then granted to courtiers, including Cecil, Leicester, Walsingham, North, Hatton, and Raleigh.

New Bishops.

A temporary set of eleven principal articles of religion, to be read out in church twice a year, was issued in 1561, asserting the main positions of the Reformed English Church.   A scheme was made for revising Cranmer's Bible, bishops doing most of the work; it was not published till 1568, when it was known as the " Bishops' Bible."   In 1561 also the queen commanded the ecclesiastical commissioners to see that Divine service was celebrated with due order and ceremonial, much laxity being allowed by some bishops.

The Bishops' Bible.

In 1563 the Forty-two Articles of Edward VI. were revised, four being omitted, on grace, blasphemy against the Holy Ghost, the moral law (transferred in substance to another), and against the Millenarians.   Four were added, concerning the wicked recipients of the Communion, communion in both kinds, the Holy Ghost, and good works.   Seventeen were altered more or less.   After presentation to Convocation, three relating to anabaptism were struck out.   The Articles were passed by Convocation in February, 1563, and finally enacted by Parliament in 1571.

The Thirty-nine Articles.

The Thirty-nine Articles have been the subject of an astonishing variety of interpretation and latitude of subscription, some representing them as mainly Lutheran, others reading into them much of the theology of the Council of Trent, Calvinists finding in them substantially their own creed, while those possessing a much less positive and dogmatic belief have also been content to subscribe them.   In brief, the Articles are catholic as to the doctrines of the Trinity and the Incarnation,—in this agreeing with all the Protestant confessions of the Reform period, and partly adopting the words of the Augsburg and the Wurtemberg confessions; they are Augustinian on free-will, sin, and grace, again agreeing with most of the Continental Reformers; in regard to Scripture and tradition, justification, faith, and good works, and the number of the sacraments, they reject the same errors of the Roman Church which Luther, Zwingli, and Calvin rejected in common; as to predestination and the Lord's Supper, they are moderately Calvinistic, but Arminians can accept them because nothing is extremely stated; as to baptism, they are more Lutheran than Calvinistic, retaining the Catholic doctrine of baptismal regeneration; they teach a close union of Church and State, and grant the sovereign supremacy in matters ecclesiastical, after the manner called Erastian. Article 36, in reference to the Prayer-book and orders, is specially Anglican and Episcopalian, and has always been objected to by Puritans.

An attempt was made in 1563 to induce Convocation to reduce the number of holy days to Sundays only, to disuse the sign of the cross in baptism, to use the surplice only, and to make it optional to kneel at the Communion. This was only rejected by one vote. *Second Book of Homilies.* A second book of homilies was sanctioned, largely written by Jewel. A catechism of a Calvinistic cast prepared by Nowell, Dean of St. Paul's, was rejected. The short catechism of Edward's *Catechism.* book was enlarged, but the explanations of the sacraments were not added till 1604, and it was finally revised in 1662. In 1562 Bishop Jewel published in Latin his famous "Apology for the Church of England," *Jewel's "Apology."* which was soon translated into English by the wife of Lord Keeper Bacon, and in succession into seven other languages. It was ordered by Convocation to be placed in churches and in the houses of church dignitaries.

Thus we see the Reformation, at first secular and political under Henry VIII., then partially secular, but also largely religious, under Edward VI., after being totally overthrown under Mary, carried out with conspicuous moderation under Elizabeth. It might have been *The Reformation Settlement.* feared that a savage vengeance would have been taken for the burnings of Mary's reign; but, fortunately, though sufficient rigour was observed, no burnings of Romanists took place during the reign of Elizabeth. The Church was settled on a broad, moderate, yet somewhat too inelastic basis. It was not foreseen that honest differences of opinion might be held on many matters decided in the Articles, and perfectly consistent with a genuine Christian faith; and it was not realised that a desire for such variety, or absence of, ceremonial as we now see, would be legitimate. The times were hard; people wished for a steady, strong form of worship and church order, and were only beginning to exercise that right of private judgment which, whatever churches may order, or governments decree, will continue to exist and to win victories as long as man can think.

GREAT SEAL OF MARY.

JOHN KNOX BEFORE MARY QUEEN OF SCOTS.

CHAPTER XIX.

The Scottish Reformation; John Knox.

The Scottish Church — Luther's Books proscribed, 1525 — Patrick Hamilton martyred 1528—Alesius—Seyton and Forrest—Bishops proscribe English Testament—Beaton's Persecutions — George Wishart — John Knox — Ordained a Priest — Influenced by Wishart — Preaches Reformed Doctrines — Carried off to French Galleys — Reaches London, 1549—Preaches at Berwick and Newcastle—Made a Royal Chaplain— Kneeling at the Communion—Refuses a Bishopric—Preaches against Evils at Court —Lands at Dieppe, January, 1554—Visits Switzerland—Called to Frankfort—Disputes at Frankfort—Returns to Geneva—Visits Scotland—Settles at Geneva—His Blast against Women-rulers — Exhortation to England — The Lords of Congregation — Walter Myln martyred — Knox returns to Scotland, 1559—Brief Religious War— Knox Minister of Edinburgh—Death of Queen Regent—French Army withdrawn— Scotch Confession, 1560—First Book of Discipline—Education—Church Revenues— Knox and Queen Mary—The Romanists encouraged—Knox disputes with Kennedy —Mary seeks Knox's Aid—Knox and Mary's Marriage—Attacks on Knox—Knox and Darnley—"History of the Reformation"—Mary's Abdication—Parliament ratifies Reforming Acts—Knox's Last Days—His Death—His Character—Bishops appointed and again abolished—Second Book of Discipline.

WE need not recount the abuses of the Church in mediæval Scotland; they were much the same as in England, excepting in so far as the greater distance from Rome rendered it easier to spread a **The Scottish** superstitious reverence for the Pope. The ignorance of many **Church.** of the clergy was only equalled by their immorality. The Bible in the vulgar tongue was forbidden to be read. The least sign of disbelief in the articles of the Romish faith was severely punished.

But the kingdom could not long be kept in darkness after Luther's vigorous action against indulgences in 1517. His writings and those of his followers began to find their way into Scotland so abundantly that in 1525 the Scottish bishops persuaded the Parliament of Edin-

Luther's books proscribed, 1525.

burgh to pass an Act forbidding the introduction of any of Luther's books or those of his disciples, and ordering that no one should rehearse or discuss Luther's heresies, except in the way of confutation. Probably some of the tendency to the acceptance of Lutheran doctrines was derived from the Lollards who had settled and spread in secrecy in various parts of Scotland, and had again and again been censured for heresy, though preserved from death by the king's clemency.

The new Act was soon to have a victim. Patrick Hamilton, a descendant of the Scottish royal family, born about 1504 and at thirteen made an abbot, was educated at Paris about 1520, and no doubt there imbibed much of the teaching both of Erasmus and of Luther.

Patrick Hamilton martyred, 1528.

He took priest's orders in 1523, but in 1527 was charged by Archbishop Beaton with holding Lutheran heresies. He prudently withdrew to Germany, where he visited Wittenberg and Marburg, and especially profited by Lambert's instructions at the latter place. After six months he returned, courageous enough to speak his mind on the abuses of Rome and the errors of the Church. Early in 1528 he was accused of heresy at St. Andrews, and having maintained certain articles of Lutheran opinion before Beaton, he was adjudged guilty, and died after torture of several hours by slow burning on February 29th, 1528.

This martyrdom had a decided effect in strengthening the hold of Lutheranism in the country. Sir David Lindsay, gentleman-usher to the boy James V. till 1524, in 1528 presented to the king his "Dreme, or

Sir David Lindsay.

Marvellous Vision," a poem in which he graphically described the disorders of the Church; and followed it up by " The Complaint " in 1529. A convert of Hamilton's, Alexander Alesius, a canon of the Augustinian priory of St. Andrews, soon had occasion to suffer for his conversion. His own prior, Hepburn, dragged him with violence

Alesius.

from his seat in the chapter-house, kicked him, and appeared to intend to kill him; he was rescued alive only to be imprisoned, with all the canons who had taken his part. In 1530 he succeeded in escaping to France, thence reaching Wittenberg, and playing a considerable part in the

MARTYRDOM OF PATRICK HAMILTON.

ST. GILES'S, EDINBURGH (WEST END RESTORED), IN WHICH JOHN KNOX PREACHED FOR THE
FIRST TIME IN JUNE, 1559.

Reformation history. Alexander Seyton, a Dominican, confessor to James V., stood forth as a Reforming preacher in 1530 or 1531. He declared there was no true bishop in Scotland, judging by St. Paul's requirements. Beaton influenced the king, and Seyton had to fly to England for his life. Henry Forrest, another follower of Hamilton, was not so fortunate, and, after long imprisonment, was burnt about 1532.

Seyton and Forrest.

The effect of the circulation of copies of Tyndale's New Testament in Scotland became so apparent that in 1532 a proclamation was issued by the Scottish bishops prohibiting the sale, possession, or use of copies of the Scriptures in the English or Scottish tongues. This led Alesius to write a protest to James V. from Wittenberg, and a violent controversy between himself and John Cochlæus took place.

Bishops proscribe English Testament.

z

The Pope granted James the tenth of all benefices in Scotland, above

ST. GILES'S CHURCH, EDINBURGH : INTERIOR.

twenty pounds in value, for three years, in return for which severe measures were again adopted against the Lutherans. In August, 1534, a large number were accused at Holyrood, some of whom fled to England, while others were burnt at Edinburgh. On March 1st, 1539, four martyrs were burnt at one pile on the Castle-hill at Edinburgh. Cardinal Beaton, having succeeded his uncle as Archbishop of St. Andrews, urged on a severe persecution. Yet Sir David Lindsay, who had continued to satirise the Church in "Kitty's Confession," was able, by a representation of his "Satire of the Three Estates" before the king, to induce James V. to urge the bishops to promote reform; but Beaton, who had not been present, was indefatigable in seeking higher office from Rome, and was supported by the king. Severe acts against heresy were passed in 1541; all religious discussion was forbidden, and also all questioning of the Pope's authority. Then came the death of the king in 1542, and the sharp struggle between Beaton and the Earl of Arran for the regency during the minority of the infant princess Mary. Early in 1543 an Act was passed allowing all persons to read the Scriptures in their own, or the English tongue.

Persecutions by Cardinal Beaton.

Death of James V.

Arran Regent.

The next period is marked by the martyrdom of George Wishart and the assassination of Cardinal Beaton. Wishart, a young man of good position and education, was prosecuted in 1538 on the strange charge of teaching Greek, and particularly the Greek Testament, at the Grammar School of Montrose. He withdrew into England, and in 1540 visited Switzerland, where he studied the First Helvetic Confession and translated it into his native tongue. In 1541 he returned to England, and resided at Corpus Christi College, Cambridge, where he engaged in teaching. Coming back to Scotland in 1543 with the envoys who had concluded an alliance with Henry VIII., he found Arran in the power of the Papists, and acting in their interests. Wishart began preaching at Montrose, chiefly on the Ten Commandments, the Apostles' Creed, and the Lord's Prayer. But the fact that Beaton was made Chancellor in 1543 endangered Wishart's position; and the Cardinal in the next year perpetrated cruel martyrdoms at Perth. Wishart was driven from Dundee, and preached in the west of Scotland, sometimes in the open fields. He returned to Dundee when the plague broke out there in 1544, and laboured incessantly for the bodily and spiritual comfort of the sick. Early in January, 1546, he undertook to maintain the Reformed doctrines at a public disputation; but Beaton caused him to be apprehended at Ormiston by the Earl of Bothwell, who promised him safety. Bothwell gave him up to

George Wishart.

Beaton in a short time, and Wishart was thrown into the castle tower at St. Andrews, where he was kept in irons. On February 28th, 1546, he was accused of many heresies, especially as to the seven sacraments, and, with little semblance of fair trial, was condemned and finally burnt on March 1st. Just before his death he said, "For the word's sake and the true evangel which was given to me by the grace of God, I suffer this day not sorrowfully, but with a glad heart and mind. . . . I beseech Christ to forgive them that have this day ignorantly condemned me to death." In less than three months Norman Leslie and others, to avenge Wishart's death and private enmities, seized the castle of St. Andrews, and assassinated Beaton.

We must now take up the story of John Knox, the most commanding figure in the Scottish Reformation. He was born at Haddington in 1505,
John Knox. educated at the local grammar-school and at Glasgow University, where he came in contact with John Mair or Major. This man was Professor of Philosophy and Divinity, and had studied in France and imbibed the sentiments of Gerson and D'Ailly in restriction of the universal authority of the Pope. His teaching that a general council was superior to the Pope, who had no right to temporal supremacy, and his censures on the papal court and the episcopacy no doubt had considerable effect upon Knox. It appears that Knox left Glasgow without proceeding to a degree, and his life for some years afterwards is involved in obscurity. He is said to have been ordained as a secular priest in 1530,
Ordained a Priest. and to have been for more than ten years attached to a religious house near Haddington. Gradually, as Beaton's cruel persecutions brought the Reformed doctrines more into notice, Knox imbibed more of their spirit, and had to seek refuge from the Cardinal by becoming
Influenced by Wishart. tutor in the house of Hugh Douglas, of Longniddrie, in East Lothian. He gained much instruction from George Wishart, whose martyrdom brought him to avow most fully the principles of the Reformers.

Some time after Beaton's murder, which he appears to have held lawful, Knox was received into the castle of St. Andrews (Easter, 1547),
Preaches Reformed Doctrines. where the Reformers held out against the regent; and there he continued to teach religion and expound the Bible until the assembly were impelled to give him that public "call" to the ministry which is such a cherished ideal of Scotchmen. Knox, unable to speak, burst into tears and left the room. His emotion was due to his

vastly enlarged conception of the office of the ministry since his earlier ordination. Soon after he undertook to prove in the parish church of St. Andrews that the Roman Church had departed farther from apostolic purity than the Jewish Church from Moses when it condemned Jesus. His powerful defence of his position created a great stir, and made many con-

JOHN KNOX, PRINCIPAL LEADER OF THE SCOTTISH REFORMATION.

verts; but his preaching was brought to a violent end by the arrival of the French fleet at the end of June, 1547, after which the castle was invested both by sea and land, until it capitulated on the last day of July. Knox had now to suffer in chains the indignities of the French galleys, combined with constant endeavours to force him to conform

Carried off to French Galleys.

to Roman rites. He was carried to Rouen and Nantes, and then back to the east coast of Scotland in the summer of 1548. He was seized with a fever, which he bore with much fortitude; afterwards he wrote a bold confession of faith, which he was able to send to Scotland to his friends. In February, 1549, he was set at liberty, and was able to reach London. Here he was welcomed by Cranmer and the lords of the Council.

Reaches London, 1549.

We have already indicated how far Knox had travelled from Rome; his strong Puritanism and his leaning towards the Swiss Reformers had already been plainly shown at St. Andrews, long before he visited Switzerland. He held that " in the worship of God, and especially in the administration of the sacraments, the rule prescribed in Holy Scripture is to be observed without addition or diminution, and that the Church has no right to devise religious ceremonies and impose significations upon them." He would probably have been delighted to produce such a uniformity and simplicity as Mohammedanism has secured; but he had no notion of the cramping, narrowing effect of such uniform monotony on the mind. This result was scarcely surprising, considering what an example he had before him of varying from the apostolic standards in the case of the Church of Rome.

Knox was soon put upon the list of preachers paid by the king's council, and was appointed to Berwick, on the Scottish border, and having a large garrison of English soldiers. Already well imbued with the influence of a time of conflict, his sermons were of a combative, courageous type, vehement in their denunciation of the errors of Rome. Here he made many converts. Bishop Tunstal of Durham, was ill satisfied with his zeal; and having been accused of asserting that the sacrifice of the Mass was idolatrous, Knox was summoned before him and the council of the north in April, 1550, when he vigorously defended his assertion; and Tunstal did not venture to pronounce any ecclesiastical censure upon him. He was thus left free to continue what he had practised ever since his arrival at Berwick—the administration of the Communion according to its original form, sitting at a table, without kneeling; he also substituted ordinary for wafer bread, thus anticipating the practice afterwards followed in Scotland and elsewhere by Puritans and Presbyterians.

Preaches at Berwick and Newcastle, 1549-53.

In May or June, 1551, Knox was transferred to Newcastle-on-Tyne. During his stay at Berwick he had become betrothed to Marjory, daughter of Richard Bowes, captain of Norham Castle, whose mother had consulted him in deep religious trouble. At Newcastle he continued his outspoken

JOHN KNOX A GALLEY-SLAVE.
343

preaching, with strong anathemas on those who taught any other doctrine.

Made a royal chaplain. He had been appointed one of the king's chaplains and preacher in the north about December, 1551, and was consulted with the other royal chaplains about the articles of religion drawn up by Cranmer. The Duke of Northumberland appears to have heard him preach, and in October, 1552, strongly desired that he should be made a bishop, in order that he should not continue his ministration in the north contrary to the first Prayer-book of Edward VI., and to check the growing immigration of Scots to Newcastle.

A sermon that he preached before the king in 1552 against kneeling at the Sacrament was much complained of, but the majority of the Council were not affected by it. When the articles included in the second Prayer-book of Edward were ready for publication, Knox addressed to the Council a lengthy "confession," strongly stating the arguments against kneeling at **Kneeling in the Communion.** the Sacrament as implying worship. It appears that this protest led to the addition of a "Declaration on Kneeling" to the Communion Service, asserting clearly and plainly that no adoration of the elements was intended or meant by kneeling. It declared that, "as concerning the sacramental bread and wine, they remain still in their natural substances, and therefore may not be adored, for that were idolatry to be abhorred of all faithful Christians; and as concerning the natural body and blood of our Saviour Christ, they are in heaven, and not here; for it is against the truth of Christ's true natural body to be in more places than in one at one time."

In December, 1552, the bishopric of Rochester was definitely offered to Knox, but he steadfastly declined it. The Duke of Northumberland endeavoured to persuade him personally, but found him, to use his **Knox refuses a Bishopric, 1552.** own words, "neither grateful nor pleasable." Certainly Knox would not bow obsequiously to the wily nobleman, full of self-seeking projects, and Knox's conscientious and unbending manner was unlikely to please Northumberland. He again preached at Newcastle on Christmas Day. In a remarkable "Epistle to the Congregation at Berwick," he gave reasons for his conduct, and yet recommended, for the sake of charity and peace, that kneeling should be adopted at the Communion, and stated that he himself would conform to the regulation if compelled. His ministry at this time was seriously troubled by accusations before the Privy Council and other threats of his enemies. Finally, in April, 1553, he left Newcastle and returned to London to preach before the Court. Several of the royal chap-

JOHN KNOX PREACHING. (*After Wilkie*)

lains had spoken plainly of the evil conduct of the king's household and others in high places. Knox with entire sincerity laid bare the evils **Preaches against evils at Court.** arising to the State through evil counsellors, for, as he afterwards affirmed, " under that innocent king pestilent Papists had greatest authority," meaning especially Northumberland, who had rejected Cranmer's reform of the canon law.

In April, 1553, an attempt was made to induce Knox to accept the vicarage of Allhallows, in the city of London. When questioned about his refusal, he confessed that he thought there were

THE TOLBOOTH, EDINBURGH.

many things imperfect in the Church of England, one being that a minister had no authority " to divide and separate the lepers from the whole " (the evil from the good), " which was a chief point of his office." Also he still objected to kneeling at the Lord's Supper, as contrary to Christ's example. A great dispute arose between him and the Council, including Cranmer; they said they were sorry that his mind was contrary to the

JOHN KNOX'S PULPIT.
(In the Museum of the Scottish Antiquarian Society.)

common order; he replied that he was sorry that the common order should be contrary to Christ's institution. During June, *Preaches in Bucks, Kent, and Newcastle.* Knox went on a preaching tour in Bucks, and preached at Amersham on July 16th, nine days after Edward VI.'s death, predicting great woe to the country as the result of Mary's accession. Strangely enough, he continued to preach in Kent till near the end of September under his royal patent; and he probably, under the clause of the new Act restoring the old service - books *Lands at Dieppe, January, 1554.* after December 20th, went on preaching until that date. He was at Newcastle in the middle of December, preaching every day. His safety was endangered, and he was compelled to take refuge in flight beyond sea, landing at Dieppe on January 20th, 1554.

Knox visited Switzerland and its leading Reformed churches, and after a second visit to Dieppe in May repaired to Geneva, where he formed a close personal friendship with Calvin. On a third visit to *Visits Switzerland.* Dieppe in the summer he learnt how many had conformed to Rome again, and wrote a "Faithful Admonition to the Professors of God's Truth in England," in which he painted the persecuting Romanists in the blackest colours. He returned to Geneva, and applied himself vigorously to study, though almost fifty years old. At Hebrew he worked diligently, having had no chance of learning it early in life.

Towards the end of 1554, when the English Protestant exiles had settled in various parts of Europe in large numbers, Knox was called to Frankfort-on-Main by the English congregation there, which had obtained permission to use the French Protestant church, provided their form of worship approached nearly to theirs. The English refugees agreed to omit the Litany, audible responses, the use of the surplice, and various ceremonies. Certain exiles at Zurich and Strasburg were dissatisfied with this departure from the English Prayer-book, and stirred up dissensions at Frankfort. Calvin was appealed to, and his opinion of the English Prayer-book was sought. His reply was that though he found many tolerable fooleries in it,—tolerable at the beginning of a reformation, but to be removed later,—yet he thought it reasonable that the English at Frankfort should themselves draw up an order more conducive to edification. Knox was appointed, with three others, to do this; and mainly under his guidance an order was agreed upon partly taken from the English Prayer-book. This was harmoniously brought into use in February, 1555. But a month later Dr. Cox, lately preceptor to Edward VI., with other strong adherents of the English Prayer-book, arrived at Frankfort, made disturbances, intruded themselves into the pulpit, and caused such dissen-

Called to Frankfort.

The "Troubles of Frankfort."

THE HOUSE OF JOHN KNOX, EDINBURGH.

sions that Knox, having imprudently urged the admission of his new opponents to vote, was by the majority so created discharged from preaching, and he returned to Geneva with a heavy heart. Probably the **Knox returns to Geneva.** "troubles of Frankfort" had an important share in producing the future Puritan struggles in England. Many of Knox's adherents followed him to Geneva, where they formed an English congregation, and adopted the earliest order of worship drawn up by Knox and Whittingham at Frankfort, and afterwards known in England and Scotland as the "Order of Geneva." It was published as "The Forme of the Prayers and Ministrations of the Sacraments, etc., Used in the English Congregation at Geneva, and Approved by the Famous and Godly Learned Man John Calvyn." This was printed during Knox's absence in Scotland.

Knox being much pressed to fan the flame of reform in Scotland, left Geneva in August, 1555, and embarking at Dieppe, reached Scotland near **Visits Scotland, 1555-6.** the Berwick border. He appears now to have formally married Marjory Bowes. He secretly visited the Reformers in Edinburgh, West Lothian, and Ayrshire, preaching and dispensing the Lord's Supper, and addressed a letter to the queen-regent (Mary of Guise) begging her to protect the Reformed preachers. Finding no advantage was to be gained by remaining in Scotland, he accepted the call of the English congregation at Geneva to become their minister, and returned thither with **Settles at Geneva, 1556-9.** his wife and her mother. Here he was now settled from July, 1556, to the spring of 1559, during which period two sons were born to him. He lived in the greatest amity with Calvin and the other Reformed pastors, and commended Geneva to his friends as "the most perfect school of Christ that ever was in the earth since the days of the apostles. In other places," he said, "I confess Christ to be truly preached; but manners and religion so sincerely reformed I have not yet seen in any other place beside."

Still eagerly watching all the religious and political movements in Scotland, Knox held himself ready to return thither at any moment when **His Blast against Women-rulers.** he could be useful. But his indignation was roused by the evils he saw caused by the government of both England and Scotland by women (Mary Tudor and Mary, Queen of Scots), and in 1558 he published "The First Blast of the Trumpet against the Monstrous Regiment of Women," expressing the opinion that "to promote a woman to bear rule, superiority, dominion, or empire above any realm, nation, or city, is repugnant to nature, contumely to God, a thing most contrarious to

His revealed will and ordinance; and, finally, it is the subversion of all
equity and justice." So great censure, however, was caused by the intemperate language of this first "Blast" that Knox refrained from blowing
the two others he had contemplated; and he found that his publication
was the cause of his being forbidden to pass through England when in
March, 1559, he desired to reach Scotland.

Another vigorous address by Knox, "A Brief Exhortation to England
for the Speedy Embracing of Christ's Gospel, heretofore by the Exhortation to
Tyranny of Mary Suppressed and Banished," is dated at Geneva England, 1559.
(1559). It was a fiery exhortation to awake from conformity to Rome and
to reform all abuses in religion. The strength and intolerance of Knox's
views may be shown by the principles he lays down "that none ought to
be freed from the yoke of church discipline, nor permitted to decline from
the religion of God," and that "that prince, king, or emperor who should
go about to destroy God's true religion once established and to erect
idolatry, which God detesteth" (meaning Romish superstition), "be adjudged
to death according to God's commandment." As we have again and again
seen, the early Reformers were almost as tenacious of their views and as
resolute in enforcing them as the papal party; but it must be said, to
Knox's credit, that he never shed the blood of his opponents in religion
when he afterwards had opportunity.

During Knox's absence from Scotland, the lords who had embraced
the Reformed doctrines had become more closely banded together, encouraged by frequent communications from Knox. At Edin- The Lords
burgh on December 3rd, 1557, a "common band" or bond was Congregation,
made by several lords, including the Earl of Argyle, promising   1557.
mutual support and lifelong devotion to the evangel of Christ and to
use every effort to obtain faithful ministers of His sacraments. They
afterwards resolved that the English Prayer-book and lessons should be
read in their parish churches weekly, and private preaching of the gospel
should take place till they might have it publicly. Archbishop Hamilton
endeavoured to arrest Argyle's preacher, John Douglas, but failed; he
next attacked an aged priest, Walter Myln, who maintained
his ground stoutly, and was burnt as a heretic in April, Walter Myln,
                                                         martyred,
1558. This, the last Protestant martyrdom in Scotland,   1558.
stirred the people mightily; and they were so strongly excited against
the Roman priests and superstitions that an era of disastrous image-
breaking and defacement of churches set in. "In Edinburgh was that

great idol St. Gile first drowned in the North Loch and afterwards burnt."

In a succession of petitions the Protestant leaders laid their requests before the queen-regent, asking her to repress abuses in the Church, and to grant them liberty of religious worship under certain limitations. She promised them redress as soon as it should be in her power, and granted them her protection. The bishops would agree only to partial concessions, and the queen-regent showed them that she was really on their side. Nothing was done in favour of the Reformers, and early in 1559 a proclamation was issued forbidding any one to preach or administer the sacraments without the authority of the bishops. John Willock and others disobeyed this order, and the town of Perth openly adopted the Reformed worship. The bishops suggested that offenders should be proceeded against as rebels as well as heretics. This was accordingly done, and Willock and the rest were tried at Stirling on May 10th, 1559.

Meanwhile Knox had arrived at Leith from Dieppe, and reached Edinburgh on May 2nd. Knox at once took in the situation, and joined the body of gentlemen from all districts who were proceeding to Stirling to support their ministers. The queen-regent by vague promises persuaded them not to advance further, and then outlawed the ministers for not appearing on the day of trial. Next day—May 11th—at Perth, Knox preached a sermon against idolatry, which a priest followed by going up to celebrate mass. Stones were thrown, and all the instruments of "idolatry" were demolished very quickly. Outrages in other churches followed. The regent hearing of this, vowed "utterly to destroy the town, man, woman, and child, and to consume the same by fire, and thereafter to salt it, in sign of a perpetual desolation." Thus began a religious war, happily not severe and prolonged. The Reformers assembled too numerously at Perth, and the citizens were left unmolested in the exercise of their religion. In advancing, the Reformers' party found the regent's troops continually in retreat, and finally they entered Edinburgh without a blow being struck. Their army, however, dwindled away, being only levied and provisioned for a few weeks; and the regent was soon able to impose unsatisfactory terms on them. We must note the destruction done to churches and monastic buildings during the Reformers' march, destruction which lovers of architecture and antiquity must ever deplore.

[marginal note] Knox returns to Scotland, 1559.

[marginal note] Brief Religious War.

In Edinburgh the magistrates and many of the leading citizens met

MEDIÆVAL FANATICISM: IMAGE-BREAKING.

at the Tolbooth, on July 7th, and elected Knox to be their minister; and he, nothing loth, at once entered on his duties as pastor of St. Giles. But he had to travel for a time under the protection of the Protestant lords, by which means he spread the Reformed teaching in many parts of the kingdom. Several lords came over to the Reformers, and after considerable negotiations Queen Elizabeth sent aid in the shape of money, troops, and ships, which, together with the bold action of the Scottish Reformers, caused the French to perceive the necessity of making peace. The queen-regent died on June 10th, 1560, and soon afterwards the French commissioners (representing the young Queen Mary and her husband, Francis II.) agreed to withdraw the French troops; and a new basis of government was settled.

Knox chosen Minister of Edinburgh.

Aid from England.

Death of Queen-regent.

Withdrawal of French Army.

The Parliament of Scotland assembled in August, 1560, Knox preaching daily at St. Giles', and promoting a representation to Parliament favourable to a perfect Reformation of religion. A confession of faith was drawn up in four days by Knox and four other ministers, and adopted by the Parliament almost without opposition. It is known as the Scotch Confession of 1560, and is naturally Calvinistic, yet lacking some of the Calvinistic severity. The Church is declared to be uninterruptedly one from the beginning to the end of the world, "one company and multitude of men chosen of God, who rightly worship and embrace Him by their faith in Christ Jesus, Who is the only Head of the same Church." No particular form of worship or Church government is laid down in this confession, which allows freedom in ceremonies. Edward Irving termed it the pillar of the Reformation Church of Scotland, which rallied the people for a whole century afterwards. As a specimen of its style, we may quote from the article on the "Marks of the true Kirk." "The notes, signes, and assured takens whereby the immaculate Spouse of Christ Jesus is knawen fra the horrible harlot, the Kirk malignant, we affirme, are nouther Antiquitie, Title usarpit, lineal Descence, Place appointed, nor multitude of men approving ane error. . . . The notes therefore of the trew Kirk of God we believe, confesse, and avow to be, first the trew preaching of the Worde of God; . . . secondly, the right administration of the Sacraments of Christ Jesus; . . . last, Ecclesiastical discipline uprightly ministred, as Godde's Worde prescribes, whereby vice is repressed, and vertew nurished."

Scotch Confession, 1560.

The same Parliament forbade the celebration of Mass or of baptism according to the Roman rites under severe penalties, and declared that the

Bishop of Rome had no authority or jurisdiction in Scotland. A commission was given to Knox and his four coadjutors to draw up a plan of Church order and government. The result was the "First Book of Discipline." It was largely a development of Calvin's system at Geneva; but in addition to settled ministers, a certain number called superintendents were appointed to exercise semi-episcopal functions over large districts, and the churches, ministers, exhorters and readers therein. Six were appointed, funds being insufficient for more. They were chosen and ordained in the same way as ordinary ministers. The office died out with the first holders, and the country became supplied throughout with regular presbyteries. After 1581, when the "Second Book of Discipline" was authorised, the Church was governed by regular Kirk Sessions (of one congregation), presbyteries (of several neighbouring Churches), provincial synods, and finally the General Assembly, composed of ministers and elders chosen by the presbyteries, and meeting two or three times a year. Thus the French system adopted in 1559 was closely followed. Public worship was conducted according to the "Order of Geneva," with slight variations.

[sidenote: "First Book of Discipline."]

[sidenote: Presbyteries, Synods, General Assembly.]

Knox and his coadjutors were careful to provide for education in their Church scheme, and herein showed themselves in advance of England. They proposed to found a school in every parish, to teach religion, grammar and Latin; a college in every considerable town, and three national universities. But this part of the scheme was not destined to immediate fruition.

[sidenote: Education.]

Notwithstanding the influence of Knox, worldly motives crept in. The "First Book of Discipline" was not generally approved by the nobles; it was perhaps too complete, and had had no adequate evolution on Scottish soil. It demanded a larger proportion of the Church revenues for the Reformed Church than the lords felt inclined to give. At last, after much discussion, the Privy Council, which was now supreme, allowed two-thirds of the Church revenues to be given to the ejected bishops for their lives, to revert afterwards to the nobility,—a more moderate imitation of the English spoliations,—while the remaining one-third should be divided between the Court and the Kirk ministers. "Well!" was Knox's exclamation on hearing of this plan, "if the end of this order be happy, my judgment fails me. I see two parts freely given to the devil, and the third must be divided between God and

[sidenote: Church revenues claimed by nobles.]

the devil." The regulations for Church order were, however, subscribed by the majority of the Council, and generally adopted without Act of Parliament. The year 1560 was further marked by the first meeting of the General Assembly, by the death of Knox's wife, and also by the death of Francis II. of France, husband of Mary Queen of Scots.

Affairs became critical after this event,—which occurred in December, 1560,—and the return to Scotland of his young widow, Queen Mary (August, **Return of Queen Mary.** 1561). She at once gave orders for High Mass to be celebrated at Holyrood Palace on the first Sunday after her arrival. She was skilful enough to win several of the Scotch Lords of Congregation to protect her in the enjoyment of her religion; but when instructions were given for a more elaborate Mass, Knox preached forcibly in St. Giles' against idolatry, saying at the close that " one Mass was more fearful unto him than if ten thousand armed enemies were landed in any part of the **Knox and Queen Mary.** realm, of purpose to suppress the whole religion." Thereupon Mary sent for Knox, and held the first of several conversations with him in which the intrepid Scot spoke the whole of his mind, though with no intentional arrogance or rudeness. Naturally, his assertion that subjects, having the power, might resist princes when they exceeded due bounds, was distasteful to the queen, educated in the absolutism of France. His vindication was so clear and confident that the queen said, " I perceive that my subjects shall obey you, and not me; and will do what they please, and not what I command; and so must I be subject to them, and not they to me." Knox replied that " his travail was that both princes and subjects might obey God." The queen avowed Rome as her Church, which Knox termed " a harlot, polluted with all kinds of spiritual fornication, both in doctrine and manners." The queen offered to provide persons to answer him; but Knox, while willing to meet the most learned Papist in Europe, replied that " the ignorant Papist cannot patiently reason, and the learned and crafty Papist will never come, in your audience, madam, to have the ground of their religion searched out."

After this interview, Knox felt that the queen could not be won to his views, and his attention was given to the dangers of the Protestant lords being caught by the Court so that their zeal should cool. This was the result in many cases, and Knox was not sparing of warnings in his sermons, prayers, and conversation, often couched in strong language. In May, 1562, when the massacre of Vassy had elated the Guises, Mary gave a ball to her foreign retainers, which led Knox to preach against the vices

MARY STUART, QUEEN OF SCOTS.

..eir fondness for foolish pleasures. The queen, hearing ..moned him and gave him a long lecture on having spoken of .everently. Knox answered that she had heard false reports from ..atterers, and repeated his sermon to her. Mary confessed that his words, though sharp enough, had been differently reported to her. All marvelled that Knox was so little influenced by the queen's beauty of manners, and was not afraid. "Why should the pleasing face of a gentlewoman affray me?" he asked. "I have looked in the faces of many angry men, and yet have not been affrayed above measure."

In the autumn of 1562 the Earl of Huntly took up arms, hoping to rescue the queen from the control of the Protestant lords; but they by wise measures put down the rising; while Knox was active in preventing similar attempts in the south by exhorting the Protestant leaders to be on the alert. But the queen continued hopeful within a year " to have the The Romanists Mass and Catholic profession restored through the whole king-encouraged. dom." The Romanist clergy began to preach publicly, and Quintin Kennedy, uncle of the Earl of Cassilis, and Abbot of Crossragnel, offered to dispute with any of the Reformed leaders. He had already put himself forward as a Roman champion; but when Knox offered Knox disputes with Quintin to answer Kennedy's articles at Kirkeswald, the Abbot did not Kennedy. appear, and Knox himself preached. On September 28th, 1562, however, they met at the house of the provost of Maybole. The Abbot's points of contention were even more uninteresting and unprofitable than most scholastic disputes. Both sides claimed the victory.

Early in 1563 Knox was appointed by the General Assembly to examine a case of alleged immorality by a minister, who, submitting himself Knox's severe to discipline and confession, found the discipline so severe that discipline. he retired to England. Knox herein set the example of that bitter severity towards evil-doers which has more than anything else stamped the Scotch character till later years. In May, 1563, the queen Mary seeks tried to gain Knox's support for a relaxation of proceedings Knox's aid. against those who celebrated Mass, but in vain. She then endeavoured, not without success, to gain his interference in a domestic dispute between the Earl and the Countess of Argyle.

Mary's first Parliament (1563) followed, but she was skilful enough to prevent the Acts of the Parliament of 1560 from being ratified, thus leaving it open to the Romanists to say that the Protestants had no law on their side. Mary was corresponding with her uncle, the Cardinal of Lorraine, and with the Pope, as to how she could restore Romanism; and the Earl of Murray was so far persuaded to act in her interest that Knox now quarrelled with him. He also preached very freely against the reported projects for the queen's marriage, predicting dreadful evils if the sovereign married a Papist. Knox was ordered into her presence, and the queen addressed him in a passionate strain, ending, " And yet I cannot be quit of you. I vow to God I shall be once revenged "; on which she burst into a flood of tears. "What have you to do with my marriage? or what are you in this commonwealth?" she asked. Knox fully asserted himself in reply as " bound to obey Him who commanded him to speak plainly, and to flatter no flesh on the face of the earth." His further conversation again produced tears and sobs from the queen. Knox bore himself (harshly and cruelly, as some think) with un-altered countenance, protesting that he took no delight in the distress of any creature, but he had given her no just reason of offence, and only discharged his duty. She ordered him to quit her presence, and insisted on a judgment from the "Lords of Articles" whether his words in the pulpit were not actionable; but no prosecution took place. The two were indeed ill-matched: the one learned, conscientious, upright, severe; the other young, beautiful, wayward, polished, but used to dissembling. Had Knox behaved differently, is there any probability that a better result would have been attained? Those who think there is may yet refrain from condemning him for following conscience.

Knox and Mary's marriage.

In the autumn of 1563 it was thought that Knox had been caught in an actionable default. He had sent letters to Protestant gentlemen to be present at a trial of two Protestants for interrupting the Mass at Holyrood when the queen was absent. The Privy Council adjudged his letter treasonable, but Knox would acknowledge no fault in what he had done. He argued so ably before the extraordinary Council summoned to try his case, that in spite of the queen's evident desire for his conviction, the Council, with the exception of the Court dependents, voted unanimously that he had not committed any breach of the laws. He was afterwards supported in his conduct by a vote of the General Assembly.

Attacks on Knox.

After remaining a widower three years, Knox married, in March, 1564, Margaret Stewart, daughter of Lord Ochiltree. During the autumn of the same year, during which serious attempts were made by the Court party to restrain the liberty of the Reformed preachers, Knox himself was attacked before the General Assembly by Maitland of Lethington, the secretary of the Council, for his mode of praying for the queen's conversion as a doubtful event, and speaking of her as still "under the bondage of Satan." He also censured Knox's limitations of the authority of princes, and his admission of the right of the people to control evil rulers. Knox, as usual, answered vigorously, and no vote of the General Assembly was taken.

Knox's friendship with the Earl of Murray was renewed early in 1565. Neither liked Mary's projected marriage to Darnley. But Knox took no part in the unsuccessful rising of Murray and his friends. After the marriage (in July, 1565), Darnley, who would attend both Roman and Reformed services, appeared in August in St. Giles' church. Knox
Knox and Darnley. preached and quoted during his sermon the words, "I will give children to be their princes, and babes shall rule over them: children are their oppressors, and women rule over them." Some other expressions offended Darnley so bitterly that he refused to taste food till Knox had been punished. Knox was summoned before the Privy Council, but, as usual, had a strong answer ready. He added that as the king, for the queen's pleasure, had gone to Mass, and dishonoured the Lord God, so would He in His justice make her the instrument of his overthrow. Knox was in consequence forbidden to preach while Mary and Darnley remained in Edinburgh. How long this lasted is not certain, but Knox had various occupations in visiting country districts by desire of the General Assembly,
"History of the Reformation." and in writing his remarkable "History of the Reformation" in Scotland. One journey at least he made into England to visit his two sons, who were being educated there. Another of his occupations was to draw up a "Treatise on Fasting," the Assembly having decided
"Treatise on Fasting." to appoint a general fast, in consequence of the critical state of the Reformed Churches, the decrees of the Council of Trent in favour of the extirpation of Protestantism, and the cruelties practised on Protestants by many states and princes. Mary continued her plans for re-establishing Romanism, and gave her adhesion to the "league" formed by the Cardinal of Lorraine; and many other preparations for the restoration of the old religion were made.

We cannot here follow the series of events which overturned all
Mary's Abdication, 1567. previous plans—the murder of Rizzio, followed by that of Darnley, February, 1567; the queen's marriage to Bothwell, May, 1567; her captivity and enforced abdication in favour

of her infant son, James VI. (July, 1567); and the appointment of the Earl of Murray as regent. When the infant king was crowned at Stirling,

PORTRAIT OF JAMES STUART, EARL OF MURRAY.

Knox preached the sermon, but the Bishop of Orkney anointed the little sovereign—a ceremony to which Knox objected— while the superintendents of Angus and Lothian assisted the bishop in placing the crown on the king's head.

James VI.
Crowned.

Knox now advocated that Mary should be tried by the Estates of the Realm, and that if she were found guilty of Darnley's murder and of adultery with Bothwell she would be put to death; and though he afterwards agreed to her detention in confinement, he considered, when a civil war had been occasioned by her escape, that the nation suffered for criminal lenity.

During Murray's regency a Parliament met (December, 1567) which ratified all the Acts of the Parliament of 1560 in favour of the Reformed doctrines, and the tenure of the throne was made dependent on taking **Parliament of 1567 ratifies Reforming Acts.** an oath to maintain the Protestant religion. None but Protestants were to be admitted to public offices. The various ecclesiastical jurisdictions under the General Assembly were defined; but lay patronage of benefices could not be abolished, though the Church asserted its right to refuse unqualified men. Unfortunately the peaceful progress of Reform was interrupted by the assassination of the Regent Murray on the 23rd January, 1570. Again follows a troubled period, in which Edinburgh Castle was held by Queen Mary's friends. Knox, who had barely recovered from a stroke of apoplexy which the strain of events had produced, quarrelled with and openly censured Kirkcaldy of Grange, who held the castle, and found it necessary, in May, 1571, to leave Edinburgh for St. Andrews, where he remained for fifteen months. There he preached constantly. Though very weak, when warmed to his sermon " he was so active and vigorous that he was like to ding that pulpit in blads, and fly out of it."

Knox returned to Edinburgh on August 23rd, 1572, and a small part of St. Giles' was fitted up for him to preach in, owing to his weakness. **Knox's Last Days.** In September, when tidings came of the terrible St. Bartholomew's Day in France, he put forth all his remaining strength in denouncing the vengeance of Heaven against " that cruel murderer and false traitor, the King of France," and all his house. On November 9th he took part in the induction of his successor, James Lawson, and then, leaning on his staff and an attendant's arm, returned to his house for the last time. A pathetic description remains of his last illness, during which he had to answer an attack by Maitland of Lethington directed to the Kirk Session of Edinburgh.

He was still able to defend himself vigorously. In his last address, in his room, to his colleague Lawson and the elders and deacons of St. Giles', he testified that he had had it for his sole object to instruct the

ABDICATION OF MARY QUEEN OF SCOTS.

361

ignorant, to confirm the faithful, to comfort the weak, the fearful and the distressed, by the promises of grace, and to fight against the proud and rebellious, by the Divine threatenings. "I know," he said, "that many have frequently and loudly complained, and do yet complain, of my too great severity; but God knows that my mind was always void of hatred to the persons of those against whom I thundered the severest judgments. I cannot deny but that I felt the greatest abhorrence at the sins in which they indulged, but I still kept this one thing in view, that, if possible, I might gain them to the Lord." Many noblemen and others visited him, and all received counsel and admonition as vigorous

Knox's Death and Funeral, Nov., 1572. and conscientious as ever he had given. He died on November 24th, 1572, in his sixty-seventh year. A vast number of people attended his funeral on November 26th, in the churchyard of St. Giles', the newly appointed Regent, the Earl of Morton, pronouncing the following sentence when the body was laid in the grave: "Here lieth a man, who in his life never feared the face of man; who hath been often threatened with dagge (pistol) and dagger, but yet hath ended his days in peace and honour."

It is natural that Knox should have been represented in contrasting colours by partisans. The Scotch view is substantially that of Richard

Knox's Character. Bannatyne, Knox's favourite servant. Knox was "the light of Scotland, the comfort of the Church within the same, the mirror of godliness, and pattern and example to all true ministers, in purity of life, soundness of doctrine, and boldness in reproving of wickedness." An opposite view is held by those who support the Divine rights of monarchy or episcopacy. Few will deny to Knox the virtues of honesty, devotion to truth, unquenchable earnestness, much courage, and entire obedience to conscience. Ungovernable as his temper appeared to some, it flamed forth only when he believed the occasion fully warranted it. Throughout his many vicissitudes, trials, dangers, and persecutions, he maintained his fearlessness and strength of character. That he was uncompromising and stern, rigid in his demands, and severe in discipline, is undoubted. But he had also considerable tenderness of heart behind his sense of duty; and both wit and humour as well as scorn and censure at command. He was unique among the Reformers. Unlike Luther, Melanchthon, Zwingli and Calvin as originators, he was, rather, an assimilator of what Calvin had well thought out, and a man able to turn a nation largely by his own vehement force of character. For a dozen years

JAMES DOUGLAS, EARL OF MORTON.

in Scotland it was as important to know what Knox said, as what any queen, regent, or noble might say. And his character not only greatly influenced Scotchmen while he lived, but even more intensely after he died. Of small stature, lean and weakly, his whole life was a victory over physical defects. If he had not all the qualities of a great reformer, he had many of them—sufficient to stamp a nation with his impress. That he was often harsh and intolerant was characteristic of his age, and of the deadly fight which had to be waged in order to expel Romanism from its seat of tyrannical authority.

In 1571, not long before Knox's death, the jealousy of the old Scottish nobility of the new Church authority was evidenced by the grant given **Bishops Appointed.** by Parliament to the Earl of Morton of the revenues of the (Roman Catholic) Archbishop of St. Andrews, who had just died, Morton appointing a minister with a small portion of the money. In January, 1572, the Earl of Mar convened at Leith an informal meeting which acted as a General Assembly. It included the "super-intendents" and some other ministers; and under the influence of the nobles it restored the titles of archbishop and bishop, and the old boundaries of dioceses, the bishops to be chosen by a chapter of learned ministers, and not to have any more power or revenue than the superintendents already appointed. These bishops were popularly called "Tulchan Bishops," or Bishops of Straw. The General Assembly of August, 1572, condemned, but was too weak to effectually oppose, these offices. But this particular attempt to restore episcopal form really robbed episcopacy of its claims to respect, and ensured its downfall.

And again Abolished. When Andrew Melville, Knox's true successor, came upon the scene in 1574, progress was made towards a stronger and more definite organization of the Church. In 1581, the "Second Book of Discipline," in which Melville was chiefly concerned, was sanctioned by the General Assembly. The offices of bishop and superintendent were alike abolished, and it was decreed that those already appointed should be known by their own names and not by titles. No superior title in the ministry was admitted beyond **"Second Book of Discipline," 1581.** that of a teaching presbyter or minister. It was strongly asserted that no minister should be intruded on a congregation against its will, and especially that lay-patronage ought to be reformed, for it led to intrusion, and was incompatible with formal election. The "Second Book of Discipline" was not formally ratified by Parliament, but in its main outlines it remains the standard of the Scottish Established Church.

It might have been thought that the mind of Scotland had been sufficiently declared against episcopacy; but we find that numerous attempts, several of them successful, were afterwards made to re-establish it, and to recount them we should have to give an outline of Scottish history to the accession of William III. Sad indeed was the history of the Scotch Church during the seventeenth century; but a brighter period succeeded. At scarcely any time, however, has Scotland been without serious religious dissensions.

MARTYRS AT THE STAKE.

CHAPTER XX.

The Reformation in the Netherlands—Terrible Persecutions.

Rise of Reformation in Low Countries—Effect of Luther's Work—Charles V.'s Proclamation—Early Persecutions—Voes and Esch—John de Backer—The Anabaptists—50,000 Heretics put to death under Charles V.—William Tyndale—Menno Simons—Inquisition: severe Edicts—Charles V. abdicates—William the Silent—Cardinal Granvelle—Growth of Protestantism—Belgic Confession, 1561—Guido de Brès—Granvelle and William—Philip's double dealing—"Les Gueux"—Field Preachings—Extensive Image-breaking—Concessions of Regent—Philip's Duplicity—William withdraws to Nassau—The Duke of Alva Arrives—Egmont and Horn beheaded—Council of Blood—Indiscriminate Slaughter—Incidents of Persecution—Risings against Philip—Sieges of Haarlem and Alkmaar—Alva Recalled—Protestant Divisions—Holland Prohibits Romish Worship—William's Successes—Union of Holland and Zealand—Pacification of Ghent—First Synod of Dort—Union of Seven States—Philip seeks William's life—Is abjured by Holland—William Provisional Governor—Is shot by Gerard—Character of William—Dutch National Reformed Church—James Arminius—The Arminian Controversy—The Remonstrance—Great Synod of Dort—Triumph of Calvinists—Remonstrants Expelled—Unjust Punishment of Grotius and Barneveldt.

W̱E have already mentioned some of the early movements towards the reformation of religion in the Netherlands, the followers of Waldo, the "Brethren of the Common Life," and the pietism of Thomas à Kempis.

It was the Netherlands that gave birth to Erasmus, born at Rotterdam in 1467, and destined to show the dark spots in Romanism in lurid or ridiculous lights, without himself formally joining the ranks of the Reformers. Another Reformer in essence, Doctor

Rise of Reformation in Low Countries.

365

Wessel of Groningen, in spite of tempting offers from the papacy, wrote against the Mass, indulgences, prayers for the dead, and the Pope's supremacy. He maintained that popes might err, and when they did err that they ought to be opposed. In many points he held the same opinions as those subsequently put forward by Luther. He died in 1489, having suffered much persecution, which at last rendered him very cautious and moderate. These

ANTWERP FROM A CROSS ROAD.

two examples suffice to show how necessary is courage, as well as knowledge and right thought, in order to secure any reform. It was Luther's courage and boldness more than his opinions that made him so valuable an instrument in the Reformation.

Luther's bold stand against Indulgences, and against Pope and Emperor, excited much interest in the Netherlands, now directly under the government of the young Emperor Charles V. As early as 1521, Charles found it necessary to issue a proclamation in the Low Countries against Luther, in which he says: "Not to repeat all the said Luther's errors, for that would be endless, it seems to us that the person of the said Martin is not a human creature, but a devil in the figure of a man, and cloaked with the habit of a monk, to

Effect of Luther's work.

Charles V.'s Proclamation.

enable him so much the better and more easily to bring the race of mankind to everlasting death and destruction." Consequently the acceptance of Luther's opinions, or harbouring or reading his books, was condemned. Severe punishments were denounced against the disobedient, and, in fact, notice was effectually given of persecution unto death being in store against the obstinate. In 1522, Cornelius Grapheus, secretary

Grapheus. of the town of Antwerp, was prosecuted for a preface to a book on the Liberty of the Christian Religion, printed long before the proclamation appeared. He was condemned, made to recant his very mild heresies, and then treated for years with a succession of vile punishments and indignities. The Augustinian Convent at Antwerp was suspected, and many of the monks were arrested. The Prior, Henry of Zutphen, escaped from prison, afterwards preached in various cities, and in 1524 was murdered in Holstein by a mob instigated by priests. Two of the monks of Antwerp

Voes and Esch. were burnt on July 1st, 1523, at Brussels, namely, Henry Voes and John Esch, singing the Te Deum until the flames ended their life. Erasmus wrote of the affair: "Two were burnt at Brussels, from which time Luther's doctrine began to be in request in that town." In another place he wrote of putting heretics to death, that it was the work of hangmen, not divines; but he did not separate himself from the Church which acted thus.

About 1524, the pastor of Mels, near Antwerp, preached against the abuses of the Church to great congregations. He was forbidden to continue his meetings outside the church, but a layman named Nicolas,

Persecutions: Nicolas Drowned. who took his place on one occasion when he was absent, was seized, condemned by the magistrates, and drowned in the river in a sack. Many nuns forsook their cloisters; and in some parts of Holland the populace drove the monks out of their monasteries. But the Inquisition set to work vigorously. John de Backer, a priest, who had

John de Backer strangled and burnt, 1525. preached against the Imperial decrees, and had married a wife, was thrown into prison and several times severely questioned. His firmness was equalled by his argumentative power, so that the President of the Court, Joost Lawrence, uttered some detestable sentiments against him. He was first strangled at the stake, and then burnt to ashes at the Hague, in August, 1525. Several other sturdy Lutherans were imprisoned and variously persecuted; and in September a proclamation was issued forbidding all open or secret meetings to preach or interpret the gospel, and all disputes about matters of faith and the Church.

ERASMUS IN HIS STUDY.

While this persecution was being vigorously conducted, the Anabaptist doctrines began to spread in Holland, and three Anabaptists were roasted on a slow fire at the Hague in 1527. Still more severe **The Anabaptists.** edicts were published against Protestants, and many martyrs suffered death for their beliefs, without the formality of trial, but upon the most summary examination; a large portion of their property being given to their accusers. It is but a repetition, with slight variations, of the same dreary, melancholy tale, to record how under the administration of

Mary of Hungary, sister of Charles V., from 1530 onward till 1555, the reading or possession of the Bible was forbidden, all new books were proscribed unless licensed by the court, priests, monks; men and women suspected of heresy were imprisoned, and either made to recant or ruthlessly strangled and burnt.

It has been calculated that even on a moderate estimate no **50,000 heretics** fewer than **put to death.** fifty thousand heretics were put to death in the Low Countries during Charles V.'s later years. There was no power which could adequately resist the

VIEW IN UTRECHT.

imperial forces; the Inquisition, backed by the infamous placards, and by high rewards to informers, had full play. If we recorded a tithe of the narratives of persecution our space would be over-full. We must endeavour to trace more especially the methods and the course of events by which freedom was ultimately obtained. We only **William Tyndale martyred, 1536.** pause to record that William Tyndale, the translator of the Bible into English, was pursued by the vengeance of the Church into the

B B

Netherlands, apprehended at Antwerp, taken to Vilvorde, and there strangled and afterwards burnt as a heretic on October 6th, 1536. The Anabaptist excesses, which in some respects ran as high in Holland as in Germany, caused very many of the executions, for Anabaptism far more than Lutheran Protestantism struck at the Divine right of kings; but Anabaptists were executed as heretics rather than as rebels, that being an easier way of satisfying the rulers' conscience as to the necessity of the death penalty.

A sect of the Anabaptists, called Mennonites, was founded by Menno Simons, who was born at Witmarsum in Friesland in 1492, ordained a **Menno Simons.** priest in 1515 or 1516, and appointed sub-pastor near his native place. By study of the Bible he was led to give up many tenets of the Roman Church, and in 1531, when he was made pastor of Witmarsum, an Anabaptist martyrdom impressed him so much that after further study he was convinced that infant baptism was wrong. He retained his office, however, till 1536, when he resigned and began to preach Anabaptist doctrines in secret. His influence was directed against that loosing of the moral law which various parties among the Anabaptists advocated. Menno was induced to become an elder among them, and he was of the greatest service in restraining outbreaks of wild enthusiasm and fanaticism. He lived in various towns in Holland, often having a price put on his head; but in 1545 he was expelled from the Netherlands, and in 1546 settled at Oldeslohe in Holstein, where he established a printing press, and from which as a centre he visited the Anabaptist congregations. He died in 1559 at Oldeslohe. His character and influence were sufficient to establish the Mennonites as a distinct sect or type of Anabaptists, whose history we cannot follow further here.

In 1550 a foretaste of future severities was given by the issue of a proclamation at Brussels by which justices and officers were "requested **Inquisition:** and desired by the Inquisitors of Faith" to seize and appre- **severe edicts.** hend all persons suspected of heresy. This hint was readily taken by the well-informed people of Antwerp; and, indeed, many of the foreign merchants departed, and trade languished, owing to general fear and uncertainty. The Regent Mary was constrained, on the urgent request of the people of Antwerp and the Council of Brabant, to journey to Augsburg, to persuade her brother, the Emperor, to modify the obnoxious placard, which he did to a slight extent, leaving out all mention of the Inquisitors, but denouncing heresy quite as severely. The sturdy Antwerp magistrates, however, would only publish the edict with an appendix insisting upon their own ancient rights and privileges. But the business of heresy-hunting went forward unremittingly in many of the considerable towns of the Low Countries, and even Antwerp was unable to keep out the Inquisitors.

At last, in 1555, came the abdication of the Emperor Charles V. and the

ABDICATION OF THE EMPEROR CHARLES V.

accession of Philip II. As he entered the hall at Brussels, Charles leaned on the shoulder of William Prince of Orange, a young man of twenty-two, whose family had long enjoyed great influence and possessions in the Netherlands. Still a Catholic, a frank and genial politician, but with a capacity for holding his tongue which served him well on a memorable occasion, he was the

Abdication of Charles V., 1555.

William Prince of Orange.

stadtholder, supreme judge, and military commander for Holland, Zealand, and Utrecht under Philip.

The Bishop of Arras, afterwards better known as Cardinal Granvella, counselled Philip's earliest proceeding against heresy,—the reissue of the Edict of 1550. But it was not at first very generally executed, for several states refused to do so, and Philip's

Bishop of Arras, Cardinal Granvella.

WILLIAM THE SILENT, PRINCE OF ORANGE.
(*From an old print.*)

need of money for war purposes prevented him from pressing a persecution at present. He gained his end, and then, by the brilliant military gifts of Count Egmont, won victories in 1558 from the French at St. Quentin and Gravelines, which strengthened his power and gratified his vanity. But he had most of all set his heart upon

Philip's Victories over France.

the extirpation of heresy. At Cateau-Cambresis, in February, 1559, a treaty was made between Philip and Henry II. of France; the Prince of Orange had been chosen as the preliminary negotiator with France, in which office he had shown great skill. Afterwards, when sent, with the Duke of Alva, to France as (temporary) hostage for the due execution of the treaty, the King of France revealed to him the plot concocted between Philip and himself to put to death all Protestants both in France and in the Netherlands. The Prince of Orange earned his name of " the Silent " on this occasion by giving no indication that this scheme was news to him. It was further laid bare that Spanish regiments were to be left in the Netherlands to secure the execution of this scheme and overpower native resistance.

Treaty of Cateau-Cambresis, 1559.

William "the Silent."

This revelation fixed the life purpose of William, to rid his country of the Spanish tyranny, and he was soon able to rouse his countrymen's feelings against the continued presence of the Spanish troops. He felt that " an inquisition for the Netherlands had been resolved upon, more cruel than that of Spain, since it would need but to look askance at an image to be cast into the flames." He was not yet a Protestant, but his compassion was excited by the thought of so many virtuous men and women being thus devoted to massacre. The death of Henry II., in July, 1559, as we have already seen, deferred the execution of the scheme in France till St. Bartholomew's Day; but there was no relaxation in the cruel persecution commenced in the Netherlands. Margaret, Duchess of Parma, half-sister of Philip, was left as Regent when Philip quitted Holland for Spain in 1559; but the real power was in the hands of the Bishop of Arras. Philip added thirteen to the number of bishops (four) in the Netherlands, intending them to serve as inquisitors of heresy. The Bishop of Arras was made Cardinal Granvella, and when Philip was bidding farewell to the country, he reiterated through him his intention of extirpating all sects and heresies, and charged all governors and other authorities to carry out his commands. The inhabitants of Antwerp refused to receive the bishop sent to them, and were able to maintain their refusal.

The Regent.

Cardinal Granvella real Ruler.

Protestantism grew rapidly under the persecution which ensued. Executions were multiplied, and the Spanish and Roman officials became utterly hateful to the populace. Somewhat sluggish in starting on a new course, the tide of popular feeling, when once it turned, set continuously in the direction of anti-Romanism. In

Persecution and growth of Protestantism.

some places on the French border, as at Tournai and Valenciennes, some of the Reformers met in the public streets to sing Marot's and Beza's French Psalms. At the latter place two preachers were seized, and were long kept prisoners, owing to the unwillingness of the local governor to execute them; but when the Duchess of Parma insisted, and they were about to be burnt, the populace rescued them and set them free.

During these terrible troubles the first Netherlandish Confession of Faith appeared, quietly and unobtrusively. Guido de Brès, born about **The Belgic Con-** 1540 at Mons, became a convert to reformed doctrines in early **fession, 1561.** youth, and took refuge in England with other exiles during Edward VI.'s reign. He afterwards studied at Lausanne, and preached in **Guido de Brès.** south-east Belgium and north-east France. In 1561 he drew up, with the aid of Adrien Saravia, professor at Leyden, and others, what is known as the Belgic Confession of Faith. It contains thirty-seven articles, and follows the Gallican Confession mainly, but with less of controversial matter. It has been termed the best statement of the Calvinistic creed, with the exception of the Westminster Confession. It was presented to Philip II. in 1562, in the vain hope of gaining toleration from him, the petitioners declaring that they were no rebels, but would obey the Government in all lawful things, and that they represented a hundred thousand souls, but that, rather than deny Christ before men, they would "offer their backs to stripes, their tongues to knives, their mouths to gags, and their whole bodies to the fire." The Confession was adopted by a Synod at Antwerp in 1566, and afterwards by other synods, and finally, after some revision, by the celebrated Synod of Dort, in 1619. It is still held by the Reformed Churches of Holland and Belgium, and by the Dutch Reformed Church in the United States. Guido de Brès had but a short life, for he was hanged on May 31st, 1567, for disobedience to the orders of the court at Brussels, and especially for administering the communion to the Reformed congregations.

In 1560 the Spanish troops had at last left the Netherlands on a convenient excuse; but Cardinal Granvella behaved with as much arrogance **Granvella and** as ever, and soon became deeply obnoxious to William of **William of** Orange and Counts Egmont and Horn. In August, 1561, **Orange.** William married, at Leipsic, his second wife, Anne of Saxony, daughter of Maurice, and granddaughter of Philip of Hesse. He gave assurances that she would live in the Netherlands as a Catholic, but it was understood that she could go over the border for Lutheran services. This marriage alienated him still further from Granvella, who continued to urge

PROCESSION OF NOBLES TO MARGARET OF PARMA.

on the inquisitors in their cruel work, while heresy grew apace, and the psalms of Marot were constantly sung at the stake. Granvella became utterly hated by the people, and at last, in March, 1564, King Philip consented to his removal, after receiving urgent remonstrances from William and the other counts, and from several of the States. He was bitterly hated for many years afterwards in the Netherlands, and Philip never brought him back, though he gave him other employments. He died in Madrid in 1586.

William of Orange and Counts Egmont and Horn now returned to the

LAMORAL, COUNT EGMONT.

regent's council table, and after a long and eloquent speech by William against the ill-judged persecution of the Reformers, in which he said that, though a Catholic himself, he could not approve of princes exercising dominion over the souls of men or depriving them of freedom of faith and religion, it was resolved to send Egmont to Madrid to appeal to Philip. The latter cajoled the Count with double-meaning promises, and when he returned, sent letters to the regent, urging a still keener

Philip's double Dealing. persecution of heretics. "The prisons swarmed with victims, the streets were thronged with processions to the stake." The population were maddened by the cruelties inflicted upon men usually of blameless lives. The Decrees of the Council of Trent were published, and subscription to them enforced. Police regulations forbade inns to receive guests, almshouses paupers, graveyards dead bodies, unless upon satisfactory proof of orthodoxy. Only midwives of unimpeachable Romanism were suffered to exercise their profession.   But at last the states and chief

INAUGURATION OF THE LEAGUE OF THE GUEUX.

cities began to protest vigorously, and to interfere with the inquisitors in their labours. Philip conceived the ingenious idea of diminishing popular tumult by putting heretics to death in the prisons at midnight, usually by drowning.

But his increased severity both excited the denunciations of William of Orange, Egmont, and Horn, and also stirred up the people to call on these leaders to save their religious liberties. Early in 1566 a league was formed by some nobles, including Count Brederode, Charles of Mansfeld, and Louis of Nassau, brother of William the Silent, and thousands of others, to resist the Inquisition and defend one another. Several hundreds of the confederates arrived at Brussels, and marched in procession to place their grievances before the Regent, Margaret of Parma. Count Belaymont, a keen Spanish partisan, stigmatised them as beggars (Gueux), a designation they gladly accepted. After temporising, the regent issued a proclamation that heretics, instead of being burned, might merely be beheaded or hanged—but only if they did not stir up riots or tumults. But there was no relaxation in the persecution. Despairing of any improvement in this way, the Protestants resolved to hold their worship in public, in open spaces outside the cities; and they met sometimes to the number of fifteen thousand outside the chief cities, well-known ministers travelling from place to place to preach to them, while men with pikes and guns guarded them. Though forbidden, these field preachings became extremely popular, and the magistrates failed to put them down.

League of "The Beggars."

Field Preachings.

In August, 1566, however, an era of iconoclasm set in, which devastated hundreds of churches, crosses, shrines, and statues in the streets; and the cathedral of Antwerp suffered very great injury. Very many churches in Holland were entirely stripped of their images and Romanist symbols; but no assaults were committed on men and women. The Duchess of Parma was so much alarmed that she promised that the Inquisition should be abolished, and that the Protestants should be free to worship and build churches wherever their worship had already been held. The nobles agreed to dissolve their confederacy, and to prevent Protestants from going armed to services. Much of this was due to the representations of the Prince of Orange. But its effect was only temporary; for as soon as Philip heard of the sacrileges which had been committed he was extremely enraged, and swore to extirpate the heretics of the Netherlands. Among his numerous measures of utter duplicity, he sent messages offering

Extensive Image-break-ing, 1566.

Concessions of the Regent.

Philip's Duplicity.

pardon, and pretending to abolish the Inquisition, at the same time sending secret orders that the Regent's concessions, having been obtained by force, were not to be held binding, and that any one might be put to death in spite of pardon. He sent money to enlist regiments exclusively from Romanists, which at once alarmed William of Orange, Egmont, and Horn.

William, who was now a Lutheran, became more and more obnoxious to the Regent, while Egmont and Horn remained Romanists, and had punished the image-breakings in Flanders and Tournay with much severity. William's suspicions of Philip's intentions grew to certainty, and after recommending him to adopt wise measures for tolerating various forms of religion, he resigned all *William resigns Offices, and retires to Nassau.* his offices, and retired in April, 1567, to his principality of Nassau, first warning Count Egmont of the fate that awaited him if he remained in Flanders. Large numbers of the

ANTWERP CATHEDRAL.

most industrious people in the Netherlands left the country about the same time.

William's departure was the signal for increased persecutions, prevention of all Protestant meetings, and martyrdom of all who had *The Duke of Alva.* attended them, when discovered. Philip now sent his trusty deputy, the Duke of Alva, with about 10,000 picked soldiers, to commence a yet more disastrous period of tyranny and persecution. Counts Egmont and Horn, who had been secretly accused of treachery by the

ARRIVAL OF THE DUKE OF ALVA IN BRUSSELS.

Egmont and Horn beheaded, 1568.

Duchess of Parma, were arrested, and after several months' imprisonment, were beheaded on the 5th of May, 1568.

LAST HONOURS TO COUNTS HORN AND EGMONT.

Alva set up a "Council of Tumults," better known as the "Council of Blood," the majority being Spaniards, with powers above every charter and right of the Netherlanders. This council made it treason **"Council of** to present any petition against the Inquisition or the placards; **Blood."** to permit Protestant worship; to have refrained from opposing the field-preachings; to assert that the king had no right to take away the ancient privileges of the provinces. Practically, as one of the members of this council put it, all the Netherlanders were adjudged guilty of treason. "The heretics broke into the churches, and the orthodox did not hinder it;

TORTURE OF THE RACK.

therefore they ought all to be hanged together." "There was nothing now," says Brandt, "but imprisoning and racking of all sexes, **Indiscriminate** ages, and conditions of people, and oftentimes, too, without any **Slaughter.** previous accusation against them. . . . The gallows, the wheels, stakes and trees in the highways, were loaden with carcases, or limbs of such as had been hanged, beheaded, or roasted. . . ." Philip obtained from the Spanish Inquisition a decision that, with the exception of a select list of names, all the Netherlanders were heretics and abettors of heresy, and guilty of high treason; and with inconceivable malignity he proclaimed, in February, 1568, this sentence, and ordered its immediate execution without respect of persons.

It is impossible to conceive the wickedness of the martyrdoms of this time. Persons were charged by scores in the same paper by inferior councillors, and if their death were recommended, Vargas, the practical factotum of the Council, signed the decree without hesitation or inquiry. If perchance a death sentence was not suggested, the document was sent back for amendment, with reproaches. A man who had persuaded a rioter not to fire upon a magistrate was condemned because this act implied that he had influence over the rebels; a woman who had struck a little image of the Virgin with her slipper was drowned in a hogshead, together with her maidservant, who had been present and had not denounced the crime. "Men were tortured, beheaded, hanged by the neck and the legs, burned before slow fires, pinched to death with red-hot tongs, broken upon the wheel, starved, and flayed alive. Their skins, stripped from the living body, were stretched upon drums, to be beaten in the march of their brethren to the gallows" (Motley). These are but a few items which indicate the varied and multiform ingenuity of these relentless persecutors.

Incidents of Persecution.

William of Orange, his brother Louis of Nassau, Count Hoogstraaten, and other nobles were cited before the Council of Blood, and failing to appear, their estates were confiscated. William's eldest son, aged thirteen, was captured, and sent to Spain as a hostage. Now began—and we cannot but wonder at the long-suffering of the Netherlanders—the series of efforts, sometimes successful, often failing when success seemed just within grasp, by which finally William of Orange was enabled to free the country from the Spanish yoke. These wars we can only briefly refer to here, with fuller notices of the religious consolidation of the country; but the Netherlanders' revolt against Philip's tyranny is one of the most striking chapters of history. In 1569 a synod of Protestants at Emden declared that no church should exercise dominion over another, and that no minister, elder, or deacon should have rule over others of the same degree. This synod adopted the Belgic and Gallican confessions.

Risings against Philip.

In August, 1572, the massacre of St. Bartholomew dismayed the Dutch Protestants, but they resisted the Spaniards heroically for seven months at the siege of Haarlem, which was only taken at the cost of twelve thousand men and an emptied treasury. The Spanish

Siege of Haarlem, 1572-3.

treachery after the surrender, in July, 1573, was diabolical. The horror

MARTYRS LED TO EXECUTION.

of such cruelties strengthened the Protestant cause. Finally, the Spaniards

Siege of Alkmaar. were compelled, after great losses, to raise the siege of Alkmaar by a partial inundation arranged by the Dutch; and now disasters began to crowd thickly upon Alva, who was recalled by Philip, and Alva recalled, 1573. succeeded by the Duke of Medina Cœli. He, however, no sooner saw the wretched state of affairs than he retired also, his successor being Don Luis de Requesens, a man with a reputation for moderation.

Meanwhile the Reformers of Holland had become divided into somewhat hostile camps, and, in addition, the Anabaptists in their various Protestant Divisions. degrees of excess were numerous among them. The Lutherans and the Calvinists held not a few public disputations, sometimes ending in mutual revilings. They were not yet prepared for forbearance and toleration. Another question came before the States of Holland at Leyden in 1573; and against the persuasion of William of Orange, who had now passed from the Lutherans to the Holland prohibits Romish Worship. Calvinists, they resolved to prohibit all public Romish worship. But it appeared to them that the cunning devices and treacheries of the Romanists at that time were so dangerous to the State that its safety was imperilled; and it was on this ground that an infringement of toleration was decided upon. Private Romanist services were, however, winked at; but public worship according to the Genevan model was introduced into the churches of Holland, with toleration for private meetings of other sects. The Southern Netherlands, largely corresponding to what is now Belgium, did not rally to William's standard, and remained largely Catholic.

Further disasters befell the Spaniards; their fleet was destroyed. Louis of Nassau, however, was defeated and slain at Mock, near Cleves, in William's successes. 1575; but William's courage rose with the emergency. At last the resolute resistance of the Dutch, aided by their power of opening their dykes and flooding the land, almost wore out the Spaniards' patience. The governor, Requesens, died after the raising of the siege of Leyden in 1574; his troops, unpaid, mutinied, and sacked Antwerp, murdering thousands of people. William was now practically Union of Holland and Zealand. king of Holland and Zealand, under the style of governor or regent; he sought to unite with him the other Netherland "Pacification of Ghent," 1576. provinces, on the basis of a repudiation of Spanish tyranny. The States, meeting in November, 1576, during the interregnum following the death of Requesens, agreed to the " Pacification of Ghent," by which it was resolved to govern the Confederate States by the States-General, to suspend Philip's edicts concerning the Inquisition and heresy, and to tolerate Protestantism in the Romanist provinces.

In June, 1578, the first National Synod of the Reformed Dutch, German, and Walloon Churches met at Dort, and distinguished itself by sending a truly catholic petition to the new Spanish governor, First Synod of the Archduke Matthias, and his Council of State, requesting Dort, 1578. them to provide for the free exercise of the Reformed religion, and also

GATEWAY AT HAARLEM.

" that both religions might be equally tolerated till God should be pleased to reconcile all the opposite notions that reigned in the land." A measure to this effect, drawn up by William and signed by the Archduke, was presented to, and approved by, the States-General; but the Romanist nobles refused their adhesion, and tumults were aroused, which resulted in the entire alienation of the southern from the northern provinces.

Consequently William had to be content with the more limited number of seven states, formed at Utrecht in 1579, the first germ of the " United Provinces." Don John of Austria, the new Spanish governor, finding that

he must either accept the "Pacification" or return to Spain, adopted the
former course, and dismissed all Spanish and Italian troops.
Don John's duplicity led to his rejection by the States, who installed William of Orange as governor of Brabant. Amsterdam, though
Romanist, joined with the States of Holland early in 1578, giving toleration to Protestants. So many Protestants had formerly been exiled or had
left Amsterdam that on returning they became a majority, and established
the Reformed religion ; the Lutherans and Anabaptists being also allowed
to meet publicly, while the Romanists might worship in private.

Union of Seven States, 1579.

Despairing at last of overcoming William of Orange, Philip in June,
1580, offered, at Cardinal Granvella's suggestion, twenty-five thousand
crowns and a patent of nobility to any one who should deliver
him up, dead or alive. It was upon this revelation of Philip's
unflinching hatred that William published his famous "Apology," addressed to the Confederate States, detailing his own services, but much
more exposing the actions, motives, and crimes of Philip. "I am in the
hand of God," he said ; "He will dispose of me as seems best for His glory
and my salvation." The Confederate States thereupon, on
December 13th, 1580, entirely abjured Philip, whose nominal
authority they had hitherto recognised; and on July 5th, 1581, William
accepted from the States of Holland and Zealand "entire authority as
sovereign and chief of the land" as long as the war should continue.
Later in the month, July 26th, 1581, the representatives of the seven
united provinces assembled at the Hague, renounced Philip, and declared
their independence. William of Orange acted as provisional
governor, while the Duke of Anjou, brother of the French king,
was asked to become permanent governor.

Philip seeks William's life.

Philip abjured by Holland.

William made provisional governor.

On March 18th, 1582, an attempt to shoot William was made by a
Spaniard, and nearly proved successful. William recovered, and in August
accepted the sovereign countship of Holland and Zealand; but
in 1583 he steadfastly refused to accept sovereignty over the
whole united provinces, or the dukedom of Brabant, which was
also offered to him. Attempts continued to be made upon his life, due to the
Spanish ban put upon him; and on July 10th, 1584, Balthazar Gérard, a
Catholic fanatic, having obtained access to the prince at Delft,
under the name of Francis Guion,—pretending to be a Protestant, the son of a martyred Calvinist, and a bearer of the news
of the Duke of Anjou's death,—shot him with a pistol through the heart.

Attempt on William's life. 1582.

He is shot by Gérard, July. 1584.

William died almost immediately, exclaiming, " O my God, have mercy on my soul! O my God, have mercy upon this poor people!"　Gérard's death sentence was one of astonishing barbarity, only explicable by the

MURDER OF WILLIAM OF ORANGE.

feeling of revenge for all the horrors of Philip's rule and of rage at the loss of the beloved William. The reward which Philip had promised to William's murderer was paid to Gérard's parents in the form of three estates in Franche Comté, which properly belonged to William, and which placed them among the landed aristocracy.

William of Orange, surnamed "the Silent," the creator of Dutch independence, thus cut off at the age of fifty-one, was beyond all his contemporaries a liberal prince and statesman. Devoid of personal *Character of William of Orange.* ambition, he was ready to support any ruler who would govern justly; while, tolerant at heart, he was unwilling to compel any to travel his own road in religion. He was a deeply religious and a truly broad-minded man, with faith in God and love for his fellow-creatures; but he was by turns regarded with suspicion by all religious parties. It is eminently satisfactory to find that the Reformation struggle, beginning

VIEW OF LEYDEN.

with men who, in their enthusiasm for their view of truth, denied that there could be any other, had at last produced a statesman who could see that truth had more than one side, that human capacity for discerning truth was limited, and that it was rational to allow every man to hold in peace his own deliberately formed and conscientious opinions. With a constancy undiminished by isolation, defeat, poverty, treachery, and unheard-of difficulties, he strenuously combated tyranny, especially that of the Inquisition; and he is almost singular in this, that he never put himself forward as the one possible saviour of his country, or as a man endued with a special mission from heaven. The Dutch, sluggish to rise, needed all the stimulus of his actions and words to make them realize their proper course. Without him it is conceivable that the united Netherlands would not have come into existence, and that Protestantism would have been driven out of the Low Countries.

Then followed the long period of active warfare during which the Dutch, under Prince Maurice and his successors of the line of Orange, gradually secured their independence, which was finally acknowledged by Spain in 1648. During this period the Calvinistic or Reformed Churches of Holland had gradually *Dutch National Reformed Church.* consolidated themselves into a national Church, which was regarded with very jealous eyes by the German Lutherans, who had rendered Holland no aid when in sore straits.

The Dutch Church was constituted so as to be less independent of the State than the Genevan. Candidates for the ministry, after strict examination by the elders of the Church and after acceptance by the congregation, had to be presented to the magistrates for their *Constitution of that Church.* approval. The minister had to swear allegiance to the civil authorities "in all things not contrary to the will of God." In other respects the order of Church government corresponded closely with that of Geneva. The elders with the pastors formed in each town a court of morals, ready to inform the authorities of any facts important for them to know. But this supremacy of the magistrates grew partly from long-standing customs, and partly from the almost uniform sympathy of the magistracy with the Reformed Churches. It was natural in a country containing a majority of Calvinists that leading Calvinists should be chosen magistrates.

We must conclude our account of the Reformation in Holland by a brief exposition of the Arminian controversy, which was the subject of discussion at the celebrated Synod of Dort, in the years 1618 and 1619. James Arminius, born in Holland in .1560, was educated at Leyden University from 1576 to 1582, and then under Beza at *James Arminius.* Geneva. After a visit to Italy in 1587 he returned home, and in 1588 was chosen minister at Amsterdam. At first a strict Calvinist, his examination of Koornhert's writings against the punishment of heretics, predestination, and the absolute subjection of the human will, convinced him that the will was free, and the offer of grace universal. His changes of view gradually made themselves evident ; and when in 1603 he was called to the chair of Divinity at Leyden, attacks were made upon him, *Arminius Professor at Leyden, 1603-9.* especially by his colleague Francis Gomarus, a strong and irrepressible "supralapsarian." Arminius believed that God's decree as to individual salvation depended on the acts of the persons themselves, that saints might by their own act fail to persevere so as to cause Divine grace to be ineffectual, that every believer might be certain of his salvation, and that it is possible for a regenerate man to live without sin. He hated the idea of a uniform orthodoxy, which he believed to be unattainable. His zeal for truth was extreme; in the search for it he sought to "die with the good God on his side, even if he must needs incur the hatred and ill-will of the whole world." He died in 1609, worn out by controversy: but his doctrines lived, and have been accepted, with more or less alteration, by various Christian bodies; they form indeed an important factor in the theology of the great family of Methodist Churches.

Simon Episcopius, successor of Arminius at Leyden, and James Uytenbogaert, preacher at the Hague, took up the leadership of the Arminians, and were supported by John of Barneveldt and Hugo Grotius, two of the most famous statesmen and scholars of Holland. Uytenbogaert drew up in 1610 a remonstrance, which was signed by forty-six ministers, against the Calvinists. It rejected five Calvinistic propositions: (1) absolute predestination to eternal life or death before the Fall; (2) that God exempted some by His grace after the Fall; (3) that Christ died only for the elect; (4) that the elect are saved by irresistible grace, withheld from the rest; (5) that this irresistible grace, once received, ensures perseverance to the end. The Remonstrance declared that these doctrines are not contained in the Bible, nor in the Heidelberg Catechism, and are dangerous and unedifying. Five positive articles were affirmed: (1) conditional predestination, determined by God's foreknowledge of men's deeds: (2) that Christ died for all men, and no one is lost but by refusing His atonement; (3) saving grace is due alone to God, man being by nature unable to accomplish anything truly good; (4) that God's grace is necessary always, but it may be resisted; (5) that it is not proved from Scripture that grace, once given, can never be lost.

The Arminian controversy.

The Remonstrance, 1610.

The Calvinists issued a counter-remonstrance, and, after ineffectual conferences and other attempts to secure peace, it was decided by the States-General of the United Provinces to summon a National Synod at Dort in 1618, to which each of the foreign Reformed Churches was invited to send three or four divines, who should have a right to vote. A hundred and two divines and laymen, including thirty foreigners, assembled at Dort on November 13th, 1618. The English deputies included Carleton, Bishop of Llandaff, Davenant, Bishop of

Great Synod of Dort,1618-19.

Salisbury, and Joseph Hall, afterwards Bishop of Exeter. James I.'s instructions to the English delegates were to mitigate the heat on both sides, and to advise the theologians not to deliver disputable things from the pulpit. The delegates chosen by the French National Synod were forbidden by the king to leave that country. The whole of the Dutch delegates were orthodox Calvinists, for the three Remonstrants elected by the Utrecht Provincial Synod were excluded in favour of three orthodox men elected by the minority of that province. The Calvinists held the

THE TOWN OF DORT, WHERE THE GREAT SYNOD WAS HELD, 1618-1619.

field, and there was no hope of their yielding. Episcopius and his friends were summoned to the Synod as defendants; but while entering into a full discussion, they declined to promise unconditional submission to the judgment of the Synod. Thereupon the States-General, in defiance of toleration, required that they should submit, but this demand had no Triumph of Calvinists. effect upon them. The Synod unanimously rejected the five articles of the Remonstrants, and adopted five Calvinistic articles in contradiction of them, together with the Heidelberg Catechism and the Belgic Confession. The Remonstrants were condemned as innovators, and sentenced to be deprived of all ecclesiastical and academical functions.

The States-General banished them from the country; but this decree was

Remonstrants Expelled. recalled in 1626, and the Remonstrants, who, to the number of two hundred, had been expelled, returned with freedom to exercise their worship. They established a theological college at Amsterdam, and still exist in considerable numbers as the Remonstrant Church.

Of the two chief lay-leaders of the Arminians, Grotius was condemned, largely through the political jealousy of Prince Maurice, son and successor

Unjust Punishment of Grotius and Barneveldt. of William, to perpetual imprisonment, but escaped by the aid of his wife in 1621. Unfortunately, the illustrious John of Barneveldt was condemned for alleged crimes, of which he was guiltless, and was beheaded at the Hague on May 13th, 1619.

It is worthy of note that the Synod of Dort is the only assembly of the Reformed Churches that enjoyed a sort of general or universal constitution. The Remonstrants found it intolerant; the Lutherans regarded it as strongly hostile to their views. One thing is certain: it commenced an era of dry theological abstraction of formulas and scholasticism, which till Wesley arose threatened to bind religion in fetters antagonistic to healthy growth and development.

MEDAL OF THE LEAGUE OF THE GUEUX.

ARREST OF PURITANS ABOUT TO LEAVE ENGLAND.

CHAPTER XXI.

The English Church and the Puritans.

Intolerance of Reformers—Rise of Puritanism—Attempts to Influence the Church—Parker's "Advertisements"—Many Clergy deprived—Puritans or Precisians—The First Nonconformists—Puritans' Objections to Church—Bill to Enforce Subscription, 1571—Cartwright — The Admonitions — Wandsworth Presbytery — Anabaptists burnt, 1575 — Prophesyings—Puritans put to Death—Robert Browne—Independence of Churches—Brownists—Emigrate to Holland—Browne Conforms—Presbyterianism within the Church—Whitgift's Articles—Court of High Commission—Puritan Parliament overruled—Mar-prelate Libels—John Penry—Nicholas Udal — Severe Measures against Puritans—Sabbath Observance—James I.—The Millenary Petition—Hampton Court Conference—Whitgift's Death—Bancroft's Primacy—New Tests—Growth of Puritanism—Archbishop Abbot Checks Catholics and Arminians—Rise of Laud—Further Restrictions on Puritans—Laud's Administration—Scotch Bishops—New Scotch Liturgy a Failure—Solemn League and Covenant—The *Et Cætera* Oath—Laud's Fall—The Root and Branch Bill—Abolition of High Commission Court—Bishops expelled from House of Lords—Growing Puritanic Feeling—Episcopacy abolished—The Covenant enforced in England—Committees on Religion — Ravages on Churches and Cathedrals—Stern Puritanism in Manners—Growth of the Independents—Triumph of Presbyterianism—Laws against Heresy—The Council of State—Church Property confiscated—The "Engagement" — Barebones' Parliament — Cromwell's Religious Ordinances — The "Triers"—Charles II.'s Letter from Breda—The English Church restored—Savoy House Conference—Act of Uniformity—2,000 Nonconformist Ministers Retire—Conventicle and other Repressive Acts.

WE have seen that the reaction from Roman superstition and complicated ceremonies produced at Geneva and elsewhere a _{Intolerance of} simplified doctrine and a plainer worship. The Reformers, _{Reformers.} however, were as intolerant in spirit as their Romanist opponents: one

303

view of religion was true, all others were false; all others, therefore, were to be put down.

In Geneva, partly by agreement, and partly after contest, with the civil authorities, the Church was free to hold inquisition into the beliefs and morals of the people, and the State supported its action and punished those deemed worthy of punishment; witness the death of Servetus. The Lutherans had been compelled by the political conditions under which they lived to acquiesce in State control to a great extent; but they likewise did not believe that two views of religion should be tolerated. Long struggles were necessary before that idea gradually arose and prevailed.

In England there were complications which induced controversies such as took place nowhere else. There was now a Reformed English Church, with a continuity of benefices and partially of endowments from pre-Lutheran times; and the vast majority of the clergy who officiated under Mary retained their posts under Elizabeth. Yet, partly from independent study, partly from the residence of Continental Protestants in England during Edward VI.'s reign, and of English Protestants on the Continent during Mary's reign, a movement arose having its strength in the ability and pertinacity of its chief advocates—a movement that sought

Rise of · for a hundred years to impress itself upon the English Church,
Puritanism. and that very largely influenced the English nation. We refer to the Puritan movement, which rejected to a great extent the vestments retained by the English Church, and gradually gathered to itself the resistance to doctrines symbolised by ritual and the opposition to government of the Church by the State.

The first important manifestation of Puritanism in Elizabeth's reign was when in 1563 the Lower House of Convocation rejected by only a

Attempts to narrow majority a petition insisting that Sundays should be
influence the the only holy days; that in all parish churches the minister
Church. should read the service distinctly, and turning to the people; that the sign of the cross in baptism should be disused; that kneeling at the Communion should be left to the discretion of the minister; that a surplice should be a sufficient garb for a clergyman at all ministrations;

Parker's and that the use of organs should be prohibited. As a matter of
"Advertise- fact, ritual was often loose and very varied and slovenly, so much
ments." as to anger the queen greatly. In 1566 Archbishop Parker issued a "Book of Advertisements," to secure order in public service, and in the apparel of the clergy. The regulations were expressly de-

scribed as merely temporal, for decency and order, not of necessity binding
the conscience. The use of the cope and surplice was particularly referred
to; but copes were ordered to be worn only in cathedral churches. This
order went far lower than the second Prayer-book of Edward II., and the
use of copes was thenceforward considered illegal in parish **Many Clergy**
churches. Parker attempted to enforce his "Advertisements" **deprived.**
in 1566 on the London clergy, and more than one-third refused obedience,
and were suspended or deprived.

Thus originated the first body of clergy deprived for the sake of vestments. The party about this time began to be termed Puritans, **Puritans or**
as being desirous of returning to the purity of apostolic **Precisians.**

ANCIENT ENGLISH CHURCH.

Christianity. Fuller says the name was first used in 1564. Neal, the
historian of the Puritans, defines a Puritan as "a man of severe morals,
a Calvinist in doctrine, and a Nonconformist to the ceremonies and
discipline of the Church, though not totally separated from it." But at
first the Puritans were merely those who wished to restore ceremonies and
doctrines to apostolic purity. Those who were deprived in 1566 published
a "declaration of the doings of those ministers of God's word and sacraments in the city of London which have refused to wear the upper apparel
and ministering garments of the Pope's Church." They objected to the
church vestments as having been adopted from heathen sources and

having encouraged idolatry and superstition. To enforce them was contrary to human liberty. Upon this the publication of books against the queen's ordinances was forbidden. The University of Cambridge, including several masters of colleges, refused to conform, and it was long before they did so. A number of earnest and able opponents of vestments met and agreed to conform so far as they might, since the word of God and the sacraments were duly administered. These included Foxe, Coverdale, Lever, and some others. But several of them resolved to refrain from

The First Nonconform-ists. public worship, and to assemble in private houses, to worship according to their consciences. They laid aside the English liturgy, and adopted the Genevan service-book. This was the true visible beginning of Protestant Dissent or Nonconformity. The separation was not encouraged by the leading foreign Reformers, such as Bullinger, Beza, and Knox.

Objections had also arisen to other things besides vestments. Neal says that the Puritans objected (1) to the superior rank and power of bishops,

Puritans' Objections to Church. their temporal dignities, and their engaging in secular employments; (2) to the titles of deans, etc., belonging to cathedrals, as unscriptural; (3) to the spiritual jurisdiction claimed by bishops and their chancellors in their courts and to excessive punishments for small offences; (4) to the promiscuous admission of persons to Holy Communion; (5) to many points in the liturgy, such as " With my body I thee worship " in the marriage service, and in that for burial to the phrase "in sure and certain hope of the resurrection to eternal life "; (6) to the ordination of those who could not preach and expound the Scriptures; (7) to the keeping of saints' days and other Church festivals, to fasting in Lent, and buying and selling on Sundays; (8) to the cathedral modes of worship and to organs, to the sign of the cross in baptism, to the exclusion of parents from being godfathers and godmothers; (9) to the confirmation of young children and to its sacramental efficacy; (10) to kneeling at the reception of the Holy Communion and bowing at the name of Jesus; (11) to the use of the ring in marriage; and (12) to the vestments which had been rendered abhorrent to them by Roman superstition and idolatry. Although these views may not have been held in their entirety by the early Puritans, they very soon came to characterize them in general, and may be accepted as a convenient summary of the tenets of the early Puritans.

In 1571 a Bill to enforce subscription to the Articles of Religion was carried, and afterwards the queen put great pressure on the bishops to enforce it. Although by the terms of the Act only those articles were to be enforced on all ministers which concerned the Christian faith and the doctrines of the sacraments, many Puritans were in consequence deprived of their benefices, and some were imprisoned and otherwise punished. The most distinguished man who

Bill to enforce Subscription, 1571.

ARRAIGNMENT OF CARTWRIGHT.

suffered for his Puritan doctrines was Thomas Cartwright, the learned and popular Margaret professor of divinity at Cambridge, who was deprived of his professorship and fellowship by Whitgift, afterwards Archbishop of Canterbury. Retiring to Antwerp, he was the guiding spirit of the "Admonition to Parliament," written by Field and Wilcox, ministers of London, strongly attacking the constitution and ordinances of the Church, and advocating its transformation

Thomas Cartwright.

The "Admonitions."

to the Genevan type.   The authors, who presented it to Parliament, were, by the bishops' influence, committed to Newgate in 1572.   But Cartwright, having returned from the Continent, wrote a "Second Admonition," to which Whitgift replied, while Cartwright soon rejoined.   In 1573 the "Admonitions" and their "Defence" were suppressed by royal proclamation, and Cartwright left England to avoid arrest.   He did not return to England till 1585, but he had continued to exercise much influence as the leader of the Puritans.   Matters had now reached such a pass that open rebellion might have been apprehended.

In 1567 or 1568 an Independent or Congregational Church was founded in London.   Its origin appears to have been as follows :—A group of persons were in the habit of meeting for worship at Plumbers' Hall.   But any services, except those authorized by the Established Church, had been made illegal, and in June, 1567, this private meeting was discovered, and its members imprisoned in the Bridewell.   There they resolved to form a Church, and they elected a pastor, one Richard Fitz, who died of gaol-fever. On their release the survivors appear to have continued to meet at Southwark.   Other persons were no doubt gradually coming to hold similar opinions.   In truth the Independents were a section of the Puritan party, who, we judge, despaired of further reforms within the Church, and who, doubtless, as they would say, by study of the New Testament, and also possibly by reason of persecution, held that each congregation should manage its own affairs; further, that the Church should consist only of people who were truly worthy.   In this point they would differ fundamentally from the Church of England, for that Church embraced all persons who were duly baptized.   A leader appeared to give voice and shape to the principles of the Independents.   This was Robert Browne, who was sprung

Robert Browne.   from a county family in Rutland, educated at Cambridge, and afterwards became a schoolmaster in London, where he preached in Islington on Sundays in the open air.   He afterwards, about 1578, resided with Greenham, rector of Dry Drayton, near Cambridge, where he preached in the adjacent villages.   When he was ordained is uncertain, but he was called to a cure in Cambridge, where he preached with great vehemence and fervour.   He objected to episcopal or presbyterian ordination, and

Independence of Churches.   believed that every Church was rightly independent of every other, and should consist only of truly worthy persons.   He associated with him an old fellow-student, Robert Harrison, and gathered

Brownists.   around him a group of believers in Norwich, who became known as Brownists.   The denomination, afterwards so powerful, grew and became known as the Independents. At Bury St. Edmunds people assembled to the number of a hundred at a time in private houses to hear Browne. Freake, Bishop of Norwich, in 1581 caused him to be arrested, but his kinsman Lord Burghley released him, and afterwards befriended him. Still the Brownists sought for freedom to worship unmolested, and in the autumn of 1581 a large number emigrated in a body to Middleburg, in Holland, where Cartwright and Fenner were already **Emigration to** ministers of the Puritans. The two congregations and their **Holland.** leaders disagreed; Browne and Cartwright wrote books against each other,

which were circulated in England; and in 1583, after a royal proclamation had forbidden their possession or circulation, two ministers, Thacker and Coppin, were hanged for circulating them. Meanwhile Browne quarrelled with Harrison, his Middleburg Church broke up, and he went to Scotland. Returning to England, after some years of preaching and many imprisonments, he was excommunicated by the Bishop of Peterborough in 1586, and thereupon gave up his Dissent, was appointed master of Stamford Gram- **Browne con-** mar School and **forms.**

ARCHBISHOP GRINDAL (1519–1583).

afterwards rector of a church, in the county of Northampton. He died about 1633 in Northampton gaol, to which he had been committed for a blow given to a constable in anger. But long before this, in 1592, Sir Walter Raleigh said he feared there were nearly 20,000 Brownists in England.

In 1572 Puritans were bold enough to form a presbytery according to the Genevan model at Wandsworth, including Field and **The Wands-** Wilcox, and afterwards Travers and other ministers and lay- **worth Presby-** **tery, 1572.** men. Eleven elders were chosen, and thus was formed the first Presbyterian Church in England. Its members kept their proceedings secret, and were not prosecuted. Although many clergymen and laymen were proceeded against for refusing to subscribe to the Articles of Religion

JOHN FOXE, THE AUTHOR OF THE "BOOK OF MARTYRS."

and to the entire rightness of the Prayer-book, their punishment did not go beyond occasional imprisonment, heavy fines, and deprivation of livings; severe punishments indeed, but fortunately lacking the terrible character of the martyrdoms under Henry VIII.

Anabaptists burnt, 1575. and Mary Tudor. But as to burning Anabaptists no such scruples were felt, and for denying that Christ's flesh was of the substance of the Virgin, that Christians might be magistrates or take an oath, and for asserting that baptized infants must be rebaptized when adults, eleven Dutchmen were

in 1575 condemned, nine of whom were banished, and two were burnt at Smithfield, notwithstanding the prayers of the Dutch congregation and of John Foxe, the martyrologist. The queen was inexorable.

During Grindal's primacy (1575–1583) the Puritans suffered comparatively little. They made use of the "prophesyings" or discussions **Prophesyings.** among the clergy, or sometimes in public, to debate many of the points in which they objected to the Church order and doctrine. The queen strongly pressed Grindal to crush these "prophesyings," but he steadfastly refused, and was suspended from his office in 1577. The other bishops were more complacent, however; and they yielded to the queen's desire to put down the "prophesyings." About 1580 the Puritan spirit became more and more roused by the growing scandals and inefficiency in the Church, and satirical pamphlets were published describing the non-preaching clergy as dumb dogs, and severely censuring the pride of the bishops, the proceedings of the Court of High Commission, etc. The queen in 1580 obtained the passing of a severe Act against any defamatory publication against her, or which might encourage insurrection or rebellion. Offenders, on proof by two witnesses, were to suffer death and Under this statute several Puritans were put to death. Another Act punished Papists and Protestant Nonconformists alike for absence from public worship, under penalty of twenty pounds fine per month to the queen.

<small>Some Puritans put to death.</small>

The Puritans who remained within the Church resolved as far as possible to govern themselves on the Genevan model, on which Cartwright and Travers had based their "Book of Discipline." A meeting of about sixty Puritan clergymen was held at Cockfield, in Suffolk, on May 8th, 1582; and after adjourning to Cambridge and then to London, they agreed to form a society of clergy within the Church, to whom candidates for the ministry were to apply. If approved and "called," they were then to apply to the bishop for legal ordination. The associate clergy agreed to use no more ritual than was absolutely necessary, and in cases of difficulty the general body was to be consulted.

<small>Presbyterianism within the Church.</small>

It was even agreed that the churchwardens, etc., might be elected so as to become elders, deacons, etc., on the Genevan model. The formation of provincial synods and a national synod was also contemplated. Thus a bold attempt was started to make the Church of England Presbyterian from within.

Whitgift in 1583 issued stringent Articles to be required of every clergyman, preacher, and schoolmaster, especially demanding full acceptance of the queen's supremacy, the Prayer-book, and the Articles of Religion; and he

<small>Whitgift's Articles.</small>

ARCHBISHOP WHITGIFT, 1533-1604.

followed up this step by founding (or reviving, according to some) the Court of High Commission, with inquisitorial powers, and leave to dispense

D D

with legal forms and outside evidence, the object and result being fre-
Court of High Commission. quently to condemn clergymen on their own answers. Some
hundreds of ministers refused to accept Whitgift's Articles, and
were suspended and deprived. Some subscribed them "as far as they
were agreeable to the word of God." So severe did the English inquisition
grow that some of the Puritans became violently agitated; and "The
Practice of Prelates," issued in 1583 or 1584, described the new Articles
as the work of one man's rigour and as instigated by Satan. Travers was
just now nominated as Master of the Temple, but was rejected by Whitgift
because his " call to the ministry " was derived from a Presbyterian congregation at Antwerp. His objection led to the appointment of Richard
Hooker, author of the " Ecclesiastical Polity."

The Parliament of 1584-5 contained a strong Puritanical element in
the House of Commons, which petitioned the Upper House in favour of
Puritan Parliament overruled. granting most of the special Puritan tenets, and against Whitgift's severe proceedings. But the influence of the queen and of

PURITANS IN THE PILLORY.

Whitgift prevailed,
and nothing came
of the petition, while
Whitgift got the
Convocation of Can-
terbury to pass new
and stringent canons
as to ordination, ex-
communication, and
inquisition of clergy
by the bishop.

In 1586-7 the
Puritans in the
House of Commons
again made vain
attempts to obtain
legislation in their
favour; and after
this failure, 500 of
them subscribed the
"Book of Disci-
pline," and the ques-

tion arose whether it should be practised at once or when civil authority sanctioned it. From this question arose a great controversy, generally signified by the name of the "Mar-prelate Tracts."

The first note in the controversy was given by "A Treatise containing the Æquity of an Humble Supplication in behalf of the Country of Wales," printed at Oxford in 1587, and

"Mar-prelate Tracts."

SITTING OF THE STARCHAMBER COURT.

written by John Penry, a young Welsh "Independent" clergyman. For this very moderate tract Penry was carried before the High Commission, early in 1588, and charged with treason and heresy. The abusive style in which he was examined did not affect Penry, who was able to show his innocence so clearly that after a month's imprisonment he was discharged. But the suppression of his reasonable book and his treatment excited great indignation. The bishops were still infected with the tyrannical and pompous style of Romanist bishops. It was natural that their opponents should attack them wherever they could. But no book might now be legally printed except under the censorship of Whitgift and the Bishop of London, and no printing-presses might be possessed except by certain members of the Stationers' Company in London and by the universities of Oxford and Cambridge. Penry was driven to secret printing. He managed, by the aid of private relations and friends, to hide his press successively at East Moulsey, Fawsley (at Sir R. Knightley's), Coventry, and other places, and thus he evaded the strict search of the Government from

November, 1588, to August, 1589. The pamphlets, however, were not all written by Penry, others taking part, but all using the same name: "Martin Mar-prelate."

There is no question that many passages of the "Mar-prelate" pamphlets are abusive, coarse, and violent, according to modern notions; but we should rather gauge thereby the hatred which the Court of High Commission had excited than condemn the controversialists entirely. Those who replied to them were equally coarse and abusive. We need not describe the contents of these works. The press was at last discovered and seized, and the printers and others were fined heavily. Penry had so skilfully arranged matters that nothing could be proved against him. But Nicholas Udal, a minister of about Penry's age, another of the pamphleteers, was tried at the Southwark Assizes in February, 1591, charged with being the author of "The Demonstration of Discipline." He was

Nicholas Udal sentenced to death. offered a pardon if he would sign a recantation. He refused, and was sentenced to death. James VI. of Scotland, Sir Walter Raleigh, and others interested themselves on his behalf; and it is said that Whitgift consented to his life being spared on condition of banishment. But when it had been arranged that the Turkey traders should take him to Guinea to remain two years, a condition was made that he should never return except by the queen's licence. But the pardon was never signed, and Udal died in prison heart-broken about the end of 1592. Penry, set free, went to Scotland, and continued to write violent pamphlets. In 1593 he returned to London, hoping to gain permission to go back to Wales and

Penry exe-cuted, 1593. preach. He was at once seized, accused, condemned to death, and executed in May, 1593, for "seditious words and rumours" uttered against the queen, the charge being based on papers found in his study. We have but to consider how impossible such an execution would be in these days to gauge the immense difference between the liberty we now enjoy and the repression existing in the days of Elizabeth, sometimes held up to us as far superior to our own.

In 1593 the queen determined on sharper measures against Nonconformists. A law was carried in the Commons to punish obstinate refusal to go to church or persuading to refuse, presence at unlawful assemblies and conventicles, or printing and writing anything against the queen's

Severe measures against Puritans, 1593. ecclesiastical authority, by imprisonment until open submission was made, or after three months' obstinacy by banishment. Returning without leave was to be punished by death. The possibility of passing such an Act is explained by the fact that the nation had

EXECUTION OF BARROW AND GREENWOOD.

not been persuaded by the Puritans, and that Parliament was now extremely subservient to the queen. Many Puritans gladly took refuge in banishment. Numbers went to Holland. Two leaders among the Independents, Henry Barrow and John Greenwood, were in this year condemned for their publications, and were hanged at Tyburn April 6th, 1593.

KING JAMES I. OF ENGLAND AND VI. OF SCOTLAND.
BORN 1566, DIED 1625.

From the time of the emigration of the principal Puritans to Holland, few within the Church ventured to speak much of their Puritanism during the rest of Elizabeth's reign. One line of work in which they were able to proceed was the development of Sabbatarian observance. In 1595 Dr.

Sabbath observance. Nicholas Bound published a book on this subject, claiming that the moral obligations of the Jewish Sabbath were continued to the Christian Lord's day; that on that day all games, sports, feasts, and ordinary employments should be given up. This teaching was partly opposed, because of its detraction from saints' days and holy days; but it gained much vogue, and is reputed to have influenced many. Of course the Puritans, already inclined to a grave and somewhat severe life, acquiesced in it at once. Whitgift suppressed the book as far as he was able, and forbade it to be reprinted; but it was republished with large additions in 1606, after his death, and had great influence in making Sabbatarianism a mark of the Puritans.

When James I. came to the throne, the fact that he was the head of the Scotch Presbyterian Church gave great hopes to the Puritans, since **James I.** he had more than once expressly boasted of the excellence of Presbyterianism. What was called the Millenary Petition, **The Millenary Petition.** signed by nearly 800 clergy, was presented to him, desiring the reform of abuses in the Church, and asking relief from many points of ceremony and discipline, such as we have already summarised.

The universities of Oxford and Cambridge were very angry at some points in the petition, and censured the petitioners most severely; while the bishops, with their extreme subservience, impressed James with their views, and he was induced to declare that the constitution of the Church of England was agreeable to God's word, and very close to that of the primitive Church. He called a meeting in January, 1604, between both parties and himself, and known as the Hampton Court Conference. The Church was represented by nineteen persons, the Puritans only by four, whom the king chose himself—viz., Reynolds, Sparks, Chaderton, and Knewstubbs. Such a conference was necessarily a failure. The king took a prominent part,

Subservient bishops.

Hampton Court Conference.

and dictated his own views. On one occasion, when the king supported the compulsory oath of the High Commission Court, compelling a man to criminate himself, Whitgift expressed his delight thus : " Undoubtedly your Majesty speaks by the special assistance of God's Spirit."

Whitgift died on February 29th, 1604. He is termed a great man by those who hold High Church views ; but others regard him guilty of great cruelties and intolerance. On March 5th, 1604, the

Whitgift's death.

CHAPEL IN THE TOWER OF LONDON.

king showed that he had been converted from his opinions when in Scotland by issuing a proclamation declaring the Prayer-book and the doctrines of the Church of England unexceptionable, and calling on all men to conform to them. Thus began the Stuart intolerance of Puritanism.

One of the king's speeches deserves reproduction here. When Reynolds made suggestions tending towards Presbyterianism, James broke out, saying he found they were aiming at a Scots Presbytery, *James against Presbyteries.* "which agreeth as well with a monarchy as God and the devil; then Jack, and Tom, and Will, and Dick shall meet, and at their pleasure censure both me and my council. . . ." Turning to the bishops, he said, "My lords, I may thank you that these Puritans plead for my supremacy, for if once you are out, and they in place, I know what would become of my supremacy, for 'no bishop, no king.'" The delight of the bishops knew no bounds. Yet the king opened his first session of Parliament by acknowledging the Roman Church to be his mother Church, though defiled with some infirmities and corruptions, and by desiring to unite the "two religions." The Puritans, or Novelists, as he called them, had but a confused form of policy and purity, were impatient of any superiority, and were insufferable in any well-appointed commonwealth.

Bancroft, Bishop of London, who had already shown much intolerance towards the Puritans, was appointed Archbishop of Canterbury in succession to Whitgift, and he soon began to enforce a more stringent test of subscription to the Articles, those who had already *Bancroft's primacy.* signed them being required to assert that they *willingly and ex animo* subscribed to three articles especially: (1) that the king was the supreme head of the State in all causes spiritual, ecclesiastical, and temporal; (2) that the Book of Common Prayer contained nothing *New tests.* contrary to the word of God, and that they would use it, and no other; (3) that the Thirty-nine Articles were all and each agreeable to the word of God. About three hundred of the clergy were ejected for refusing to comply. King James at the same time ordered the universities to impose a new oath which no Presbyterian would take, for it adopted Episcopacy and rejected Presbyterianism as inconsistent with a monarchy.

This treatment had its natural effect in promoting Puritanism. In 1605 the "Apology of the Lincolnshire Ministers" declared more strongly against certain ceremonies than the "Millenary Petition," con- *Growth of Puritanism.* tending that they were unlawful, dangerous, and even sinful. Many resigned their cures, and fled to Holland. It is claimed by some that Bancroft's acts benefited the Church and purified and elevated religious worship, and that in his later years his influence increased the intelligence and vigour of the Church. He died on November 2nd, 1610, and was succeeded by George Abbot, a strong Calvinist and Puritan, Archbishop master of University College, Oxford, and chaplain of the Earl Abbot. of Dunbar, a favourite of the king. Abbot had been made Bishop of Lichfield in 1609, and of London in the following year; and his rapid promotion to the primacy was a serious shock to those who took a broader view than the Puritans of the duties and position of a national Church. He at once sought to repress Catholicism and Arminianism alike—which had been growing—by severe use of the High Commission Court. Unfortunately, he supported, though he did not initiate, proceedings against heretics; and when in 1611 Bartholomew Legate and Edward Checks Catholics and Wightman were charged with Arianism and other heresy, Arminians. Abbot was decided in his determination to punish them, urging that the judges should be selected from those who "make no doubt that His persecutions. the law is clear to burn them." Early in 1614 Legate was burnt at Smithfield, and Wightman at Burton-on-Trent. In another case Abbot approved of torture. If such a leading Puritan could still approve such acts, we may gather how little the true principles of freedom had yet penetrated the ranks of the Reformers. There is no doubt of Abbot's sincerity and conscientiousness, yet he could approve the burning of these men, the last cases of judicial murder for heresy in this country.

One of Abbot's very questionable acts was to persuade King James to demand the ejection from the professorship of theology at Leyden of Conrad Vorstius, an Arminian, whose views were said to be tinctured with Arianism. This request, very urgently made and backed up by James's theological arguments, was granted. To counterbalance this, Abbot treated well a Spanish recusant from Romanism, Antonio, formerly Archbishop of Spalato, and obtained for him the deanery of Windsor. In 1619 Abbot reconciled the Calvinists of Jersey to the Church of England. He was deeply concerned at the issue (in 1618) of the king's declaration to encourage recreations and sports on the Lord's day, and would not allow it to be read in his church at Croydon; but Mr. Trask, a Puritan minister, who wrote a book in defence of strict Sabbatarian views, was set in the pillory at Westminster, and whipped from thence to the Fleet prison, where he was kept a prisoner.

In the latter part of James's reign he made several concessions to Romanism in view of a Spanish match for his son. He also endeavoured to restrain preachers greatly in their choice of subjects. No one but a bishop or dean was to treat of predestination, election, and the doctrine of grace. No preacher was to set limits to the royal prerogative, or to use railing speeches against Puritans or Papists. Under some bishops these regulations were strictly enforced, and produced much murmuring. Fear of a return to Romanism drove Abbot to address a strong remonstrance to the king. The Parliament of 1624 was markedly puritanical; but the king's death in March, 1627, introduced a new regime, resulting in the triumph of Puritanism in the Commonwealth period.

Further restrictions on Puritans.

We have now to note the rise of William Laud, a most vehement anti-Calvinist and supporter of a semi-Romanizing and High Church doctrine. In his exercise for the degree of B.D. he had maintained that Episcopacy was of Divine origin, and that no congregation which was not under the government of a bishop could be considered to form part of the Church. He was elected president of St. John's College, Oxford, in 1611, and gradually acquired great influence at Oxford. He became Bishop of St. David's in 1621, and a few years later Bishop of London.

Rise of Laud.

The early years of Charles I.'s reign were marked by the full establishment of Laud's influence, and by his success in inducing the clergy to preach in favour of the royal supremacy. Parliament in vain endeavoured to repudiate Laud's work and assert Puritanism. The dissolution of Parliament in 1629 produced a violent feeling against Laud and all who supported the king's arbitrary power. During the next eleven years Laud was almost absolute in the Church, while exerting much influence politically. He had a

Laud's principles and administration.

KING CHARLES I. SUCCEEDED TO THE THRONE 1625, BEHEADED 1649.

clear view of the ends he sought, which were not, strictly speaking, Popish, but correspondent in many respects to the modern High Church movement. In spite of Archbishop Abbot, he was as powerful before his own accession to the primacy in 1633 as after. He used the royal prerogative as the sole source of authority in the Church, and by the mouth of the king put forth interpretations of the Articles of Religion, censured bishops for

ARCHBISHOP LAUD. BORN 1573; BEHEADED 1645.

their sermons, and issued instructions, some very reasonable, others relating to points of ceremonial on which there must always be differences of opinion. Several of these points of ceremonial related to simple decency and order, and were not objectionable except in the method of issuing and enforcing them. Non-resident bishops, an evil which had grown great and injurious, were required to live in their dioceses. But Laud neutralised many good features in his administration by his arbitrary, irascible, and haughty behaviour. His belief in the Divine right of kings led him to sacrifice the liberties of both State and Church. We need not here detail the incidents of Laud's primacy, often marked by injustice, unscrupulousness, and misuse of the Courts of Starchamber and of High Commission. Numerous clergymen were silenced or deprived, and others expelled from the universities, while many took refuge in emigration to America. Some of the Puritans, among whom, it is said, were John Hampden and Oliver Cromwell, were prevented from sailing. Gradually the Church of England assumed a condition of almost complete subservience to Laudian principles. The arrangements for the position of the communion-table and the railing before the space occupied by it excited much antagonism, but it was necessary to beware of open opposition, for it ensured heavy penalties. The prohibition of all extemporary prayer during service was another infringement of liberty which greatly vexed the Puritans. External order was preserved, but there were elements of discontent in the air, and they exploded with

JENNY GEDDES HURLS THE STOOL AT THE HEAD OF THE BISHOP.

much violence within a few years. Edward Hyde, afterwards Earl of Clarendon, in 1639 warned Laud that the people were universally discontented, and that every one spoke ill of him as the cause of all that went wrong.

One great cause of Laud's fall was his interference with the Scottish Church, and his attempt to make it equally subservient with the English

and to enforce his views upon it. King James had re-introduced bishops
into the Scottish Church, but they were responsible to the General
Scotch Bishops.
Assembly.   The attempt to introduce the English or a new
liturgy failed.   Laud, however, was strongly of opinion that a liturgy was

SIGNING THE SOLEMN LEAGUE AND COVENANT.

most desirable for Scotland, and the Scotch bishops prepared one in 1634;
it was further altered, and authorized for use in December, 1636. **New Liturgy**
Its actual introduction, in July, 1637, was followed by the **a failure.**
disastrous riot in St. Giles's, Edinburgh,—in which the bishop nearly lost
his life, and when Jenny Geddes, it is said, threw a stool at his head,—

Solemn League and Covenant. and by the drawing up of the Solemn League and Covenant by a Scotch revolutionary committee, pledging the signers to extirpate prelacy in all its forms in Scotland and also in England and Ireland. Then the king vacillated, allowed the calling of a general assembly, sanctioned the Covenant, and gave up the liturgy. The Assembly denounced and abolished prelacy, condemned the liturgy, accepted Calvinism, and condemned Arminianism as antichristian. The campaign of 1639 against the Scotch did but strengthen the feeling of the Covenanters. The short Parliament of 1640 attacked Laud's proceedings as encouragements to Popery and the discountenancing of the Protestant religion. Parliament was dissolved, but Convocation sat on to finish new canons, countenancing all doubtful proceedings of the Archbishop during the preceding ten years and granting all Laud's demands.

A new oath was prescribed, not only approving of the doctrine of the Church, but asserting that the person taking it would never consent to any The Et Cœtera Oath. alteration of the government of the Church "by archbishops, bishops, deans, and archdeacons, *et cœtera*, as it stands now established." This unpopular oath was made ridiculous by the words *et cœtera* carelessly introduced. Almost everywhere it was refused by the clergy. After some rioting had taken place, orders were given by the king not to enforce the oath till after the next Convocation.

His enforcement of absolutist principles and his arbitrary government of the Church led to Laud's impeachment in 1640 by the Long Parlia- Laud's fall. ment, to his prolonged imprisonment, and ultimately to his being beheaded, under an Act of Attainder, in 1645. Without being decidedly puritanical or Presbyterian, all being members of the Church of England, the House of Commons early gave evidence of its dissatisfaction The "Root and Branch Bill." with the existing order of things, and passed the second reading of a Bill, known as "The Root and Branch Bill," abolishing Episcopacy, deans and chapters, and the whole hierarchical system; but on more mature consideration the Bill did not pass, and the majority contented themselves with impeaching two bishops and threatening to impeach others for their proceedings in the late Convocation. The defenders of the liturgy and the order of bishops, thrown on their mettle, produced such able treatises as those of Bishop Hall and Archbishop Usher. Five Puritans whose initials collectively formed the word "Smectymnuus," the best known being Edmund Calamy, wrote an "Answer" and a "Vindication of the Answer." Milton's pen was forcefully used on the same side.

Parliament was at first concerned to promote uniformity in religion in agreement with the wishes of the people expressed by themselves, instead of by absolute will of the king or the Archbishop. They gained signal victories in obtaining the king's consent to the abolition of the Courts of Starchamber and of High Commission. It was made illegal for any bishop or ecclesiastic to use coercion for any ecclesiastical question or to tender the much-disliked oath *ex officio* In 1642 the bishops' votes in Parliament were taken away by a Bill to which the king reluctantly assented. The bishops, meeting privately, signed a protest declaring illegal all the proceedings of Parliament during their absence. They were summarily committed to the Tower.

Abolition of High Commission Court.

Bishops expelled from House of Lords.

The rising puritanic tide was exemplified by resolutions of the House of Commons in September, 1641, that the Lord's day should be kept and sanctified; that dancing and sports before or after service should be restrained; that "all crucifixes, scandalous pictures of any one or more Persons of the Trinity, and all images of the Virgin Mary, shall be taken away and abolished; and that all tapers, candlesticks, and basins, be removed from the communion-table"; and that all bowing at the name of Jesus or towards the east end of the church should be given up. The Lords would only agree to a few of these points, wherefore the Commons published them on their own authority, desiring the people to wait patiently for the intended reformation, and no doubt hoping that many would conform to their orders. In some few cases there were disturbances in consequence; in other places changes were made with little outward notice. In many, of course, the orders of the Commons had no effect.

Growing Puritan feeling.

The "Root and Branch Bill" was now again brought forward, and passed the Lords early in 1643; thus the fall of Episcopacy was decreed, independently of the Royalists, who had now mostly withdrawn from Parliament.

Episcopacy abolished.

In 1643 also the Westminster Assembly of Divines was convened by Parliament to reform the Church of England "on the basis of the word of God, and to bring it into a nearer agreement with the Church of Scotland and the Reformed Churches on the Continent." The Scotch commissioners now required, as the price of their co-operation with the English Parliament against Charles, the adoption of the Solemn League and Covenant. This was agreed to,

The Covenant enforced in England.

and in February, 1644, it was ordered to be taken by every adult. With this weapon, the Root and Branch Bill, and the employment of the test of loyalty to the king, ejections of Episcopalians from their livings became numerous, and finally amounted to some thousands. A succession of com-

Committees on Religion. mittees of the House of Commons, or appointed by it, considered the cases of "scandalous" and "malignant" ministers, and often ejected them on no adequate testimony. So many vacancies were created that they could not be filled. No attempt was made for nearly a year to fill them, and the churches were left a prey to men of various sects.

Finally, the Westminster Assembly was ordered to draw up a scheme for ordination; the plan adopted was for committees of ministers to ordain by imposition of hands. But it is said that many who had received no proper orders gained possession of benefices, under the protection of Parliamen-

Ravages on churches and cathedrals. tarians. In many cathedrals, churches, and colleges, and still more as the Civil War progressed, ruthless destruction was wrought on the statuary, painted windows, pictures, and other ornaments which remained, so determined were the Puritans in their hatred of Popery. On the other hand, it is admitted that in general particulars the manners of the people at this time were growingly marked by an absence

Stern Puritanism in manners. of open vice and wickedness, so that evil-doers were forced to hide. We may mark the temper of the time by the exhortation of the people to repentance issued by Parliament in February, 1643. One of its paragraphs reads thus: "Among the national sins are to be reckoned the contempt of God's ordinances and of holiness itself; gross ignorance and unfruitfulness under the means of grace; multitudes of oaths, blasphemies, profanation of the Sabbath by sports and games; luxury, pride, prodigality in apparel, oppression, fraud, violence, etc.; a connivance, and almost a toleration, of the idolatry of Popery, the massacre of Ireland, and the bloodshed of the martyrs in Queen Mary's time, which, having been a national sin, still calls for a national confession." The strict religious observance of Sunday was ordained in London, and a monthly fast was enjoined.

The Westminster Assembly laboured to evolve an acceptable scheme

Growth of the Independents. of Presbyterianism, the Independent members, however, strongly arguing against it, and proposing toleration for all sects. No means of accommodation between the two parties were found. The utmost toleration the Presbyterians would grant the Independents was to refrain from compelling them to receive the Lord's Supper. Meanwhile the intro-

COVENANTERS WORSHIPPING IN THE OPEN AIR.

duction of Independents, Baptists, and others into churches went on apace. In the Parliamentary army much informal preaching took place by Independents, and Cromwell's Ironsides were composed almost exclusively of them. Their extraordinary success in war no doubt greatly assisted them in gaining supremacy. The question soon arose, Should Presbyterianism have exclusive sway, or should Independents and all other bodies be tolerated? Within this lay the further question, Should presbyteries

THE WESTMINSTER ASSEMBLY OF DIVINES, 1643–49.

have the power of including or excluding members, or should each Independent congregation wield that power? Parliament undertook to settle the whole matter by ordaining that all persons aggrieved by the action of a presbytery might appeal to Parliament; criminal charges being exclusively reserved for the magistrates' decision. The Directory for Public Worship, drawn up by the Westminster Assembly, was ordered to be used instead of the Prayer-book, the latter being forbidden under heavy penalties. The government of the English Church under congregational, classical, provincial, and national assemblies was decreed ; but it was never really carried into effect.

Cromwell in vain tried to reconcile Independents and Presbyterians.

OLIVER CROMWELL, PROTECTOR OF THE COMMONWEALTH, BORN 1599, DIED 1658.

The latter predominated in Parliament, and in 1648 showed their continued **Laws against** intolerance by enacting that all who denied God, or the Trinity, **heresy.** or the Atonement, or the canonical books of Scripture, or the resurrection of the dead and a final judgment were to " suffer the pains of death, as in case of felony, without benefit of clergy." Even if they recanted, they must remain in prison till they gave sureties to answer that they would never again broach such errors. A long catalogue of heresies of the second class was specified, to be punished by imprisonment till sureties were found. All kinds of heresies were thus attacked, but many simple, honest men might be included within their meshes. Meanwhile the army had become more Independent, and was indignant at the negotiations of the Parliament with the king. Pride's "Purge" followed on December 6th, 1648, and the strong Presbyterians were excluded.

The exclusion of most of the Presbyterians from the Commons left it under the sway of the Independents. The Council of State had as its chief members Oliver Cromwell, Sir Harry Vane, and Henry Marten. The two former were sincerely religious, though their enthusiasm or fanaticism led them sometimes to sanction acts strangely at variance with Christian teaching. A declaration of the army, presented to the House of Commons early in 1649, called for a national profession of Christianity, "so it be not compulsive." It, however, excluded Popery and Episcopacy from this toleration; it protested against enforcing religion by penalties and the perpetuation of tithes. *The Council of State.*

The Rump Parliament in 1649 laid hands on the estates of deans and chapters, and ordered them to be sold for the benefit of the State funds. The lands of bishoprics and the first-fruits and tenths of all livings, formerly payable to the Crown, were applied to the payment of ministers, schoolmasters, or university professors; the aim being to pay each £100 a year. Parliament also abolished the obligation to take the Covenant, and substituted for it what was known as "the Engagement," whereby all ministers were to swear that they would be "true and faithful to the Government established, without king and House of Peers." Many Episcopalians agreed to take this test, but the Presbyterians were strongly opposed to it, as involving the giving up of special religious tests and allowing the Church to be too comprehensive. Other Acts of the Commons in 1650 were strongly against Sabbath desecration, profane swearing, atheistic and blasphemous opinions against the honour of God and injurious to human society. The language of the latter Act shows to what lengths the licence of opinion and expression had gone in the recent wars. *Church property confiscated.* *"The Engagement."* *Acts against immorality.*

Cromwell and Vane began to feel that the Rump Parliament needed renewal. Its delay in framing a scheme for calling a new Parliament and its evident wish to continue in permanence led Cromwell at last,

Parliament dissolved. against Vane's wish, to forcibly turn out the whole House of Commons and declare it dissolved, April, 1653. Vane's withdrawal from the Council of State left Cromwell practically supreme. He soon summoned a Convention Parliament of 156 persons to represent the various parts of the kingdom; and while the idea that they should be able,

"Barebones'" Parliament. truth-lovers, God-fearing, and haters of covetousness was good, the mode of their preliminary selection by the Independent Churches and the Council of Officers led to the inclusion of many fanatics. But as this Parliament achieved nothing of importance and soon resigned its functions into Cromwell's hands, we pass on to consider the religious acts of the Protector—as he soon became.

The ordinances issued by Cromwell between December, 1653, and September, 1654, acknowledged the Christian religion, as contained in the

Cromwell's religious ordinances. Scriptures, as "the public profession of these nations." The Protector's inauguration and all public ceremonies were marked by religious services; fast-days were frequently appointed. All sects and parties except Romanists and infidels were allowed full State rights.

Cromwell's great attempt at ecclesiastical control was made through the commission known as the *Triers*, intended to supply vacant benefices in-

Cromwell's "Triers." stead of leaving it to the "presbyteries" constituted throughout the country, or to local influence. They were not exclusively of one party, as they included Presbyterians, Independents, and Baptists. Practically they constituted themselves judges of a man's conversion and spiritual state; and the behaviour of Hugh Peters, one of the leading Triers in these examinations, was both fanatic and insolent. Other commissioners showed both levity and overminuteness in their inquiries. But there were also grave and reasonable men among them. Cromwell's next measure was directed to the ejection of scandalous, negligent, and ignorant

Ejection of Evil Ministers. ministers. The commissioners were all laymen, which fact was most offensive to the ordained clergy. Ministers were to be supported as usual, but in September, 1654, a commission was appointed to unite small parishes and divide large ones. Church rates had previously existed for repairing churches, providing service-books, and bread and wine for the Lord's Supper. Religious liberty was granted to all sects except Romanists and Prelatists. The clergy, however, of the Episcopal Church, were permitted to worship as they would, provided they did not preach on politics.

As regards the Church under Cromwell, Dr. Stoughton ("Church of the Commonwealth ") says : "Accurately speaking, it was not a Church at all. . . . Cromwell's establishment did not include or recognise any internal organisation whatever of an ecclesiastical kind ; it had no Church courts, no Church assemblies, no Church laws, no Church ordinances." The truth seems to be that Cromwell strove

The "Church of the Commonwealth."

THE SAVOY HOUSE CONFERENCE, CALLED TO CONSIDER THE REVISION OF THE LITURGY, 1661.

to inaugurate an era of sound religious liberty. Thus, the thirty-sixth and thirty-seventh articles in the Council of State's Declaration in 1653 provided that "none be compelled to conform to the public religion by penalties or otherwise; but that endeavours be used to win them by sound doctrine, and the example of a good conversation." Further, the great "Independent" statesman Vane declared, "The province of the magistrate is this world and man's body; not his conscience or the concerns of eternity." This view was not favoured by the Presbyterian party. They strove hard to establish their own form of religion.

Nothing was settled about ceremonies or sacraments. One parish might be Presbyterian, another Independent, another Baptist. Probably Cromwell did not intend to settle such matters, preferring to leave them to the individual conscience. At all events, the key-note of his ecclesiastical policy was toleration.

Not many changes were made by the Parliament of 1656. In his opening address, Cromwell again advocated toleration in religion, and said he would not suffer one Christian to trample on, or revile another. He would not consent to take away the tithes until some adequate substitute could be found. An Act passed for Sabbath observance prohibited all trading, travelling, dancing and singing, etc., on Sundays, and a fine of half a crown was to be levied on those who did not attend church or chapel. No further new changes of importance were made in the administration of the Church until the Restoration in 1660.

Charles II. had, in his letter from Breda to the Convention Parliament, declared " a liberty to tender consciences, and that no man shall be disquieted or called in question for differences of opinion in matters of religion which do not disturb the peace of the kingdom." Further, he expressed **Charles II.'s letter from Breda.** himself ready to agree to an Act of Parliament for fully granting that indulgence. The Presbyterians who visited him at the Hague vainly endeavoured to get him to promise not to allow the use of the Prayer-book or the surplice on his return, but their tone was lowered on discovering the disfavour shown to their party in the country generally.

Passing by the events which led to the Restoration, we have to record that when that event took place in 1660, the English Church resumed its **The English Church restored.** position as before 1641. Yet of the non-Episcopalian ministers nine were made chaplains to the King, and had frequent access to him. He requested them to meet at Sion College, and draw up a list of changes which they desired.

Meanwhile the restoration of the former order of things proceeded apace. All surviving incumbents dispossessed during the Commonwealth period were reinstated, to the number of a thousand. The Prayer-book was once more generally used. New bishops were consecrated. The only point in which the Episcopalians could agree with the Puritan demands (largely made excessive through the influence of Richard Baxter) was that there should be a revision of the liturgy. We cannot wonder at their disapproval of the supervision of bishops by a standing council of presbyters, the abolition of oaths and ministerial subscriptions, and the disuse of ceremonies and of the surplice. *Revision of the Prayer-book agreed to.*

Lord Clarendon drew up a royal declaration, read at Worcester House, in answer to Episcopalians and Puritans, and promising toleration to tender consciences, many improvements in Church work, and a review of the liturgy, while in the meantime ministers might use such parts of it as they agreed to. But the Convention Parliament threw out the Bill enacting this declaration.

The Savoy House Conference was called to consider the revision of the liturgy on March 25th, 1661. It included twelve bishops and twelve Presbyterians, with nine assistants on each side. The Archbishop of York (Frewen), Bishops Sheldon (of London), Cosin, *Savoy House Conference, 1661.* King, Sanderson, and Gauden, were among the Episcopalians; while Reynolds, Dr. Wallis, Edmund Calamy, and Richard Baxter, were among the Presbyterians. The latter being requested to bring forward their demands, drew up a long list of desirable alterations, while Baxter, after working assiduously for a fortnight, produced a complete Reformed liturgy, entirely composed of Scriptural phraseology, and offered it as a substitute for the liturgy when desired. Long discussions arose on these matters, and the four months presented as the limit of the Conference expired before anything was decided.

It is to be noted that neither Independents nor Baptists were present at the Savoy Conference. They did not seek comprehension in the Church; and some at all events of their number were opposed, as are their descendants, to the principle of a State Church.

The new Parliament of 1661 was strongly against the Puritans, and it refused to admit as members any who had not received the Lord's Supper. In many ways it showed a temper of irritation against Noncon- *Anti-Puritan Parliament.* formists. The Commons passed in haste a Bill for uniformity in religion, enforcing the old Prayer-book under strong penalties, but the proroguing of Parliament made this of no effect.

In October, 1661, the king issued a commission to the Archbishop of Canterbury (Juxon) to empower the Convocation of Canterbury to review and modify the Book of Common Prayer, the York Convocation *Revision of Prayer-book.* sending deputies to act with them. The bishops and other divines worked with haste, but were much aided by Bishop Cosin's collection of suggestions, gathered during many years. A number of minor alterations were made in this revision, but very few were in a Puritan direction. The present Preface was inserted; the portions of the Bible were now quoted from the authorised version of 1611; the Sentences, Exhortation, Confession, and Absolution were now first printed at the beginning of Evening Prayer; the Absolution was ordered to be pronounced by the "priest" instead of the "minister"; several occasional prayers were added, including those for Parliament, for all sorts and conditions of men, and the General Thanksgiving; the Prayer for the Church Militant was enlarged by the reference to the saints departed; and several rubrics concerning decency and order were inserted in the Communion Service.

Although Parliament was eager to pass the "Act of Uniformity" with the revised Prayer-book annexed, the King and Council kept the book in Act of Uniformity, 1662. hand from December 20th, 1661, to February 25th, 1662, and some further alterations were made. The House of Lords readily adopted the new book, and the Commons refused even to debate it. The "Act of Uniformity" was passed on May 19th, 1662, requiring every beneficed person before St. Bartholomew's Day (August 24th) to read the prayers according to the new revision, and to declare his unfeigned assent and consent to all it contained; and afterwards every newly beneficed person was to do the same. Every cleric, tutor, and schoolmaster was required to declare it not lawful on any pretence whatsoever to take up arms against the king, and also (during the next twenty years) to declare that the Solemn League and Covenant was an unlawful oath and of no obligation. Every beneficed person not in episcopal orders was to be ejected unless he took episcopal orders before St. Bartholomew's Day.

In consequence of this Act, about two thousand ministers were thrust out from their livings. The day is known as "Black Bartholomew's" in Persecution of Nonconformists. English History. A cruel persecution was commenced against Nonconformists, in direct defiance of Charles's Declaration of Breda; soldiers broke up their gatherings, and numbers were imprisoned. Repressive measures followed, and a dark period of suffering ensued for Nonconformists, in sharp contrast to the religious toleration of the Commonwealth period. Dispossessed divines under the Long Parliament had received allowances to prevent them from starving, but the Nonconformists were allowed no such provision. Even as the Act of Uniformity had been preceded by the Corporation Act in 1661, which prevented a Nonconformist from holding office in a municipal body, so in

1663 the Conventicle Act prohibited any Nonconformist from holding a meeting where over five persons were present not belonging to his family;

EJECTION OF NONCONFORMISTS, "BLACK BARTHOLOMEW'S DAY," 1662.

and the Five Mile Act in 1665 prohibited Nonconformist ministers from coming within a radius of five miles of any corporate borough. Five years later the Conventicle Act was enlarged, inducements were given

to informers, and penalties increased ; while later on, in 1673, Noncon-
Other Repres-formists were excluded from all Government offices, naval,
sive Measures. military, and civil, by means of the Test Act. The persecution
stopped short of burning, but inflicted unutterable suffering, nevertheless.
The imprisonments and famine, the fines, pillories, and harassings were
severe enough ; the gaols were thronged with Nonconformists. Yet the
policy of persecution utterly failed.

The effect of these various enactments was that a man was required
to give his entire concurrence to a book full of controversial matter ;
while the Anglican Church was hedged about from all other Reformed
Churches in Europe. To raise the Book of Common Prayer as a standard
or declaration would be one thing, but to do as the Parliament did—viz.,
make it a large and voluminous Test, the refusal of which was fraught
with severe penalties, was quite another. It was this latter which the
Act accomplished.

COINS OF THE COMMONWEALTH PERIOD.

CANTERBURY CATHEDRAL.

CHAPTER XXII.

The English Church since 1662.

Lasting Effects of Act of Uniformity—Efforts of James II. to Restore Popery—Bitter Perse-
cution of Protestant Nonconformists—James Assumes the Dispensing Power—James's
Declaration of Indulgence—Orders Declaration to be read in the Churches—The Clergy
Refuse to read the Declaration—The Bishops' Petition—Imprisonment of the Bishops—
Trial of the Seven Bishops, 1688—James is Deposed—Toleration Act, 1689—Comprehension
Bill—The Non-Jurors—Doctrines of the Non-Jurors—Non-Jurors in Scotland—Queen
Anne's High Churchism—The Sacheverell Riots—Defoe answers Sacheverell—The Schism
Bill—The Moderate Party—Hoadly and White Kennett—The Bangorian Controversy,
1717—Convocation Prorogued for 150 Years—The English Church in the 18th Century—
Bishop Butler's "Analogy"—The Evangelical Party—Views of the Evangelicals—Rise
of Missionary Societies—The Bible Society—The "Oxford Movement"—Keble's Sermon
on "National Apostasy"—Keble's Pupils—Dean Church on the rise of the Oxford
Movement—The "Tracts for the Times"—Their Aim—Tract 85—Tract 90—Mozley's
Letter on Tract 90—Newman joins the Romish Church—The Gorham Judgment—
Æsthetic side of the Oxford Movement—Effects of the Movement—The Broad Church
Party—Its Views—Dr. Arnold on Apostolic Succession—F. D. Maurice's Theological
Essays—"Essays and Reviews"—Dr. Colenso and the Pentateuch—Dean Stanley on
Scientific Enquiry—The Three Parties in the Church—Its Articles and Polity.

VIRTUALLY, the Act of Uniformity of 1662 was the final settlement
by Church and State of English ecclesiastical matters. Various laws have since been passed for the relief of Nonconformists, and various events have happened affecting the Anglican Church,
but the main conclusions arrived at in 1662 have remained unchanged.

Lasting effects
of Act of Uni-
formity.

In the reign of James II., an attempt to restore Popery was successfully repulsed. The great design of the last Stuart king was to bring back the creed of Rome and to reign as a despotic monarch. Shortly

Efforts of James II. to restore Popery. after his accession he publicly attended mass, causing the chapel doors to be thrown open so that the spectacle might be witnessed of the king of England kneeling at the Roman altar. Evelyn testifies in his diary that Romanists " were swarming at court with greater confidence than had been ever seen in England since the Reformation, so that everybody grew jealous as to what this would tend." Father Petre, an active Jesuit, became the king's confidential adviser, and James went so far as to command certain bishops to prohibit preaching against the Church of Rome.

The Protestant Nonconformists—for of course Romanists were now legally Non-Conformists also—were subjected to a bitter persecution, and

Bitter Persecution of Protestant Nonconformists. these, the sturdiest advocates of civil and religious liberty— though possibly not always wise or consistent advocates—seemed, about the year 1685, to be almost completely crushed. The most stirring and romantic stories could doubtless be told of their contrivances to escape capture and punishment, and of their desperate determination and their manœuvres to hold their meetings in secret places.

At length it seemed evident that some of the more audacious among them had resolved on war, when James, with a blind stupidity which appears almost incredible, resolved on a course which alienated from him

James assumes the Dispensing Power. some of his warmest adherents. Briefly, this was to establish a standing army under his immediate control, largely officered by Papists, to claim the right to dispense with the laws, or suspend their execution.

It is the latter with which we are mostly concerned. Romanists were preferred to benefices in the Established Church, and some of her build-

James's Declaration of Indulgence. ings became Roman Catholic chapels, while Papists were appointed to University posts. In February, 1687, the king issued a Declaration of Indulgence in Scotland repealing prohibitions against Papists, and relaxing them against Presbyterians and Quakers; and in April he issued a similar Indulgence for Nonconformists in England.

These grossly illegal acts filled the cup of his governing iniquities to overflowing. Because—first—they were issued without the consent, or even the consultation, of Parliament; and secondly—although nominally in favour of religious liberty, and as such benefiting Protestant Nonconformists to some extent, yet they were really designed to promote the Romanist religion, which might at any time, on the caprice of the king, become again the established religion and the law of the land.

A second Declaration followed on April 27th, 1688. To a large extent it was but a repetition of the first, adding, however, that the king's pur-

JAMES II. OF ENGLAND AND VII. OF SCOTLAND, BORN 1633, DIED 1701.

pose was fixed, and that only those agreeing with him would be engaged in his service. But on the 4th of May out came an order in Council commanding the Declaration to be read in all places of worship on two successive Sundays.

Orders Declaration to be read in the Churches.

This was the signal for open war. A number of clergy of the Anglican Church met together and refused to read the Declaration. To their lasting honour the Nonconformists of London cast in their lot on this matter with their Conforming brethren. Though the **Clergy Refuse to read the Declaration.** Declaration was nominally in their favour, and the Conformists had persecuted them, they refused to accept the gift of "Indulgence" in so grossly illegal a manner, and were suspicious that it might prove a stepping-stone to Romanist bondage.

Thus started, the movement gathered force. A petition was decided **The Bishops' Petition.** upon to the king, pointing out in a somewhat mild manner that the Declaration was illegal. The petition was signed by Archbishop Sancroft and six other prelates, viz., White of Peterboro', Ken of Bath and Wells, Lake of Chichester, Lloyd of St. Asaph, Trelawney of Bristol, and Turner of Ely.

"This is flat rebellion," cried James when he read the petition, and he ordered the bishops to see that the Declaration was read on the following Sunday. The day came, but in only a very few places of worship was the king's order executed. On the next Sunday the same course was again adopted. The despot had drawn the bow too tight, and it had snapped in his hands.

Thereupon the seven bishops were imprisoned in the Tower. The **Imprisonment of the Bishops.** charge was that of uttering a seditious libel. The people were enthusiastically in favour of the prelates, and lined the river banks to cheer them to the echo as they passed along the silent highway to Traitors' Gate.

Greater excitement, if possible, prevailed on the day of trial. The judges were known to be mostly partisans of the king, though one—Powell—had the courage to declare that the dispensing power assumed **Trial of the Seven Bishops, 1688.** by James was outside his rights. But on this occasion the jury system showed conspicuously that it was indeed the palladium of the people's liberties. It sturdily returned the verdict of "Not Guilty," after being locked up all night, and the joyful words were received with shouts of approval from the thronging people. Even soldiers cheered in the king's hearing at Hounslow when they heard the result.

The verdict was given on the 30th of June, 1688. A few months later the king had absconded, and his son-in-law and nephew, William of Orange, **James is Deposed.** and his daughter Mary reigned in his stead. Indeed, it appears that on the very day that the verdict was given, an invitation was presented to William to voyage to England with troops, the invitation

THE SEVEN BISHOPS COMMITTED TO THE TOWER.

9

being signed by influential noblemen and clergymen. James's violations of liberty and law had roused the people to extreme measures.

Under William and Mary, the Anglican Church remained unchanged as the established religion of the country, but the Toleration Act of 1689 released Protestant Dissenters from persecution, yielding them toleration, and repealing the acts passed in Charles II.'s reign against conventicles, etc. Roman Catholics and Anti-Trinitarians were, however, excluded. The toleration was to some extent limited, and did not relax the Test Act, which provided that all civil and military officers under government should take the sacrament according to Church of England forms, and should also take oath against transubstantiation. In fact, the Test and

Toleration Act, 1689.

MEDALS STRUCK IN HONOUR OF THE PETITIONING BISHOPS.

Corporation Acts were not repealed until nearly 150 years later—May 9th, 1828. There is no doubt but that William himself would have gone much further in his liberal policy; and another Bill for uniting and comprehending all Protestants in a national and liberal Church was withdrawn.

Comprehension Bill.

The chief ecclesiastical event, however, of this reign, as affecting the Church of England, was that connected with the "Non-Jurors." They refused to take the oath of allegiance to William III., regarding James as unjustly deposed. By law they were required to take the oath by the 1st of August, 1689, six months being then allowed to lapse before they were deprived. Several bishops and some four hundred clergymen refused to take the oath, and were deprived on February 1st, 1691.

The Non-Jurors.

Archbishop Sancroft was at their head, and with him was Bishop Ken, author of the Morning, Evening, and Midnight hymns. He declined, however, to dissociate himself from the Church, but Sancroft went the length of denouncing all those who took the oath as guilty of schism.

The doctrine animating the Non-Jurors—who were all High Churchmen—appears to have been the principle that the clergy are ecclesiastically *Doctrine of* and religiously independent of the civil power. This doctrine *the Non-Jurors.* is, of course, held by Nonconformists, but seems incompatible with conformity to a State-established Church. Yet Sancroft, it is said, united with others to obtain the license of the fugitive James to consecrate new bishops! This seems extraordinary conduct on the part of one who refused to obey the king in reading the Declaration of Indulgence. It is also said that having taken an oath to King James, the Non-Jurors felt they could not take it to King William and Queen Mary. But we need not discuss their position, nor need we follow their fortunes. The sect—for such it became—had no great following among the English people, at which we are not surprised. In time it approached to something like Romanism, its members quarrelled among themselves, sought union with the Greek Church, and finally it flickered out some years after the rebellion of 1745, in which some of its adherents appear to have taken part. Yet many of their number were men of great learning, and as a body they were of lofty moral life.

In Scotland, all bishops refused to take the oath, and Episcopacy became practically abolished, while over three hundred clergy were deprived. *Non-Jurors in* Indeed, not until 1788, when Charles Edward died, did *Scotland.* Protestant Scotch bishops "comply with and submit" to the Hanoverian government, while in 1792 an Act was passed for their relief.

High Churchism reigned in the days of Queen Anne. She was strongly attached to the Church of England, and in one of her first speeches to Parliament she declared: "My own principles must always *Queen Anne's High* keep me entirely firm to the interests and religion of the *Churchism.* Church of England, and will incline me to countenance those who have the truest zeal to support it." She had been brought up in the principles of that Church, and under her fostering influence High Churchism flourished exceedingly. A cry was raised for the extirpation of the Dissenting Academies which the Nonconformists had founded—for they were excluded from the national universities—and also for the repeal of the Occasional Conformity Bill—which permitted public offices to be

WILLIAM III. AND MARY II.

F F

held by occasional Conformists. Dr. Henry Sacheverell, of St. Saviour's,
The Sacheverell Southwark, who appears to have been a strange compound of
Riots.   bigot and demagogue, preached ferocious sermons against
Dissenters, the Act of Toleration, and even the Revolution Settlement itself.
He held forth at St. Paul's and before the judges at the Derby assizes.

NEW STATUE OF QUEEN ANNE IN ST. PAUL'S CHURCHYARD.

The attack on the Revolution Settlement stirred up the Government, and Sacheverell was impeached, in 1710, of high crime and misdemeanour. Crowds accompanied him to Westminster, crying aloud, "High Church and Sacheverell," and attacking and wrecking Nonconformist chapels. Nevertheless, the House of Lords found him guilty, and he was suspended for three years. At the lapse of that time he preached before the House of Commons and was presented to St. Andrew's, Holborn.

The great writer, Defoe, who was a staunch Nonconformist, answered Sacheverell
Defoe answers by his famous satire, "The Shortest Way with Dissenters,"
Sacheverell. which at first was received with pleasure by the High Church
party. They did not understand it was a satire. But when they discovered the author was a Nonconformist, their indignation knew no

bounds. Defoe was pilloried, and ordered to be imprisoned during the Queen's pleasure. Yet in the disgrace of the pillory, people crowded around and treated him as a hero, and the pillory was even decorated with flowers.

We need not, however, follow out the controversies of that day. They were generally characterized by the greatest ferocity and strength of language. The ecclesiastical affairs of the reign may be said to have

DANIEL DEFOE, AUTHOR OF THE SATIRE, "THE SHORTEST WAY WITH DISSENTERS."

culminated in the Schism Bill. This was introduced into the House of Commons on May 12th, 1714, and provided, briefly, that no The Schism one should teach as tutor, or become a schoolmaster, unless Bill. he conformed to the Established Church and obtained a licence from the Bishop. The Queen encouraged the Bill, and it was passed, but she died the same year, and it became a dead letter. This was the last great attempt to pass a Bill through Parliament to seriously curtail religious liberty.

While, however, the dominant note of the ecclesiasticism of Queen Anne's reign was High Churchism, a more moderate view was held by a minority. Chief among the leaders of this party was Bishop Burnet, of Salisbury, author of a "History of his own Times," a "History of the Reformation," and a work on the Thirty-nine Articles. Archbishop Tenison also was characterized by great liberality of thought and feeling. These two prelates, together with Archbishop Tillotson, and indeed all the bishops of William III., have been regarded as somewhat broad in theology; but apparently that means nothing more for those days than a moderate Calvinism and a tolerance in their general views.

The Moderate Party.

The line of moderation and of liberalism in the Church may be said to have been continued under the Hanoverian dynasty by Hoadly, Bishop of Bangor, and White Kennett, Bishop of Peterborough. Hoadly, indeed, went so far as to assert in a debate in the House of Lords—in which he courageously advocated religious liberty—that if Nonconformists were ever to be won back to the Church, it would be by "gentle means," and White Kennett bravely declared that the promotion of persecution by the clergy had in the reign of the first Charles brought ruin on Church and State.

Hoadly and White Kennett.

These speeches were made on a Bill for giving relief to Dissenters. In truth, King George, who was a Lutheran, was strongly in favour of equal liberty for all schools of thought—Conformists and Nonconformists alike; but the early part of his reign was characterized by an outbreak against Dissenters and against the Government.

A sermon by Hoadly, preached before the King in March, 1717, on the Nature of the Kingdom or Church of Christ, together with a publication by him against the Non-Jurors, led to the famous Bangorian Controversy and to the suspension of Convocation for 150 years, which events were among the most prominent ecclesiastical occurrences of George's reign. Taking as his text, "My kingdom is not of this world," he argued that Christ had not given His powers to ecclesiastical authority. The gist of Hoadly's position appears to be a denial of the Church's authority over the individual conscience. As may be supposed—especially in those days—such a contention provoked bitter antagonism from the adherents of the opposite view, and a lengthy and fierce dispute followed. In one month, July, 1717, no fewer than seventy-four pamphlets appeared on the subject. Indeed, the chief point in the

The Bangorian Controversy, 1717.

controversy became lost in the various side issues raised. Yet public interest was aroused to an extraordinary degree, so that business in the metropolis was interrupted for some days. The importance in ecclesiastical affairs of the issue raised is obvious, for, if Hoadly were correct, the extravagant claims to authority of Church and clergy fell to the ground. Indeed, he appears to have held the same view as the Nonconformists themselves as to the inconsistency of a Christian Church being controlled in ecclesiastical affairs by the civil power, and also the unscripturalness of the Church controlling the conscience of the individual. The Lower House of Convocation addressed the Upper House on the subject, and complained that if these doctrines were accepted, there was an end to all Church authority. But thereupon *Convocation prorogued for 150 years.* Convocation found itself prorogued, and it was not again called together until 1852 for Canterbury, and 1856 for York. Its power has, however, been much restricted.

It is said that religion declined in England until the commencement of Methodism about 1727 by the Wesleys. Originally a "holy club" guild or society in the borders of the Church, it eventually became a separate organization. But of this movement we shall *English Church in the 18th Century.* have to speak in a subsequent chapter. Whether there was really a decline of religion, or simply a decline of High Churchism, or other particular views of Christianity, it appears certain that about this period there was a growth of Latitudinarianism and of Unitarianism in the country. Chillingworth and Hales were prominent exponents of the Latitudinarian party, which occupied a middle position between extreme Puritanism and extreme High Churchism. The Latitudinarian School arose from a desire for a wider constitution for the Church, and Jeremy Taylor had been a famous exponent of this view. The party came to disregard tradition and authority in the region of faith, and in place thereof asserted reason as the better test of truth. A group of tolerant theologians called the Cambridge Platonists, represented the school in the latter part of the century, and were the first Protestants to make the attempt to wed together Christianity and philosophy; the party may be said to be represented to-day by the Broad Church School. Locke's influence and philosophy contributed to the spread of Unitarianism; but into the Trinitarian controversy of the time we do not propose to enter. The condition of the Church until about the close of the century was in some respects scandalous. Bishops and clergy are represented as being grossly

THE REV. WILLIAM ROMAINE, ONE OF THE LEADERS
OF THE EVANGELICAL MOVEMENT.

indifferent to their duty and to religion itself. The holding of pluralities and the practice of non-residence prevailed to an enormous extent. Yet to this period belongs Bishop Butler of

Bishop Butler's "Analogy." Durham, whose work, "Analogy of National and Revealed Religion," has been described by Herbert S. Skeats—a Nonconformist writer—as "the greatest of all the intellectual defences of the Christian religion."

The Church, about this period, appears as deficient in religious emotion. Then arose what has been termed the Evangelical Revival. It seems to have sprung

The Evangelical Party. originally from the Wesleyans, but while they seceded from the Church—or were forced out of it, according to the view different individuals may hold—others remained in the Church. Such were Romaine of London, Fletcher of Madeley, Venn of Huddersfield. The views of the Evangelical or Low Church party were very similar to those held by many Nonconformists in England and Presbyterians in Scotland.

Views of the Evangelicals. They particularly emphasized the view of the entire depravity of unregenerated human nature, and justification of the sinner by faith only; the need of conversion; the gospel offered freely to all; the authority and the plenary inspiration of the Bible. Perhaps, however, the nucleus and the kernel of the whole was their view of the Atonement of Christ, for they regarded salvation as depending on the acceptance of the Atonement alone. The Evangelical party centred at Cambridge, and became the most vigorous section of the Church.

To this period belongs the rise of the various great Missionary Societies. William Carey, a Baptist Minister, was the first to arouse Protestants effectually to the duty of foreign missionary work.

Rise of Missionary Societies. The Church Missionary Society was founded in 1799, the Society for the Propagation of the Gospel—the High Church Society—having been founded in 1701, but chiefly, if not entirely, on behalf of the American Colonies. In 1804 was founded the British and Foreign Bible Society, it being decided that half its committee should be Churchmen and half Nonconformists. The formation of this Society caused a bitter controversy, to which we need not refer further, except to say that the two chief points seem to have been, first: Whether Churchmen and Dissenters should unite for this purpose—a question which it now seems incredible should be raised; and secondly, whether the Bible should be disseminated without the Prayer-Book. Speaking generally, *The Bible* it may be said that, excepting the Evangelical party, the *Society.* Church was against the Society. The effect of the controversy was, however, beneficial, and it gained the adhesion of large numbers of supporters of the Church.

It has been urged that the Evangelical party did nothing for the Church itself in its corporate capacity. The criticism is probably true, for the essence of its creed was to seek the salvation of *The "Oxford* the individual. A party was to rise, however, which, in the *Movement," or Catholic* opinion of High Churchmen, has supplied the omission. *Revival.* This party has become variously known in history as the Oxford Movement, the Catholic Revival, the Tractarian Movement, etc. Its centre was Oxford, which, from the days of Laud, had been, more or less, the home of the High Church party.

The proximate cause—or one cause—of the commencement of the Oxford Movement was the passing of a law in 1833 to suppress ten bishoprics in Ireland. If accomplished in Ireland, why, it was asked, could not a similar course be pursued in England? And to defend the Church arose the Tractarian Movement. On July 14th, *Keble's Sermon on National Apostacy, 1833.* 1833, Keble preached a sermon at Oxford on National Apostacy, and it was this date which John Henry Newman—who became the leader

ORIEL COLLEGE, OXFORD, OF WHICH THE LEADERS OF THE TRACTARIAN MOVEMENT WERE FELLOWS.

of the movement, and who afterwards joined the Roman Catholic Church, and was made a Cardinal—regarded as the commencement of the movement. In this sermon was expressed a belief, held then by many Churchmen, that the rulers of the country, after the Reform Bill of 1832, would tamper with the Church. The suppression of the Irish bishoprics seemed

THE REV. JOHN KEBLE, ONE OF THE FOUNDERS OF THE TRACTARIAN MOVEMENT.

to countenance such belief, and the sermon was practically a call to arms. How could the altered condition of things be met by Churchmen?

The sermon was followed by a meeting at the parsonage of the Rev. H. J. Rose at Hadleigh, in Suffolk, toward the end of the same month. Neither Newman nor Keble were present, but they were, according to Dean Church, "in close correspondence with the others." At

Hadleigh it appears to have been decided "that there was writing to be done." And thus was born the Tractarian Movement that, in the course of fifty years, has wrought such change in the Church of England.

John Keble, who preached this epoch-making sermon, was the son of the Rev. John Keble, a Gloucestershire clergyman of the type of Ken. In 1815 the son became curate at East Leach, still dwelling at Oxford and taking pupils. Among those pupils was Hurrell Froude, and in that little company arose the impulse of the Tractarian Movement. They desired a great revival in the English Church, and they insisted upon the spiritual character of that Church. But they also emphasized the dogma of apostolic succession, and held that the sacraments conferred grace, while they also maintained the prerogatives of the priesthood. In a word, the movement strongly asserted the authority of the Church, together with the insistence of its spiritual character. *Keble's Pupils.*

Newman heard Keble's sermon on National Apostacy, and during his previous career and his travels in the South of Europe with Hurrell Froude his mind had been tending in the same direction as Keble. The sermon, it has been said, gave the signal for action, and a knot of men, of whom Newman became the leader, began to pour forth a series of "tracts for the times," all devoted to the principle of asserting the authority of the Church. Newman penned the first tract, and among other writers were Keble, Dr. Pusey, Hurrell Froude and Isaac Williams. *The Tracts for the Times.*

Dean Church says: "Keble had given the inspiration, Froude had given the impulse; then Newman took up the work, and the impulse henceforward, and the direction, were his." He continues: "Doubtless, many thought and felt like them about the perils which beset the Church and religion. Loyalty to the Church, belief in her divine mission, allegiance to her authority, readiness to do battle for her claims, were anything but extinct in her ministers and laity. The elements were all about of sound and devoted churchmanship. . . . But it was not till Mr. Newman made up his mind to force on the public mind, in a way which could not be evaded, the great article of the Creed—'I believe in one Catholic and Apostolic Church'—that the movement began." *Dean Church on the rise of the Oxford Movement.*

Generally speaking, the line pursued by the tracts was a middle path between Romanism on the one hand and Low and Broad Church doctrines on the other. They immediately caused a keen controversy, for they attacked both Low and Broad, and even the *Their Aim.*

then existing High Church school, while the Tractarians desired to revive the theology of the High Church divines of the Stuart period. They also insisted on the corporate power of the Church.

At length appeared Tract 90. It was the last of the series, and gave rise to a perfect storm of agitation. Probably Tract 85 had been a tough morsel to many. If this tract meant anything, it meant that the authority of the Church is equal to, or greater even than, the authority of the Bible; that is to say, the tract admitted that emphasis is not placed in Scripture on Confession, Baptism, Absolution, etc., but argued that they are to be developed out of the hints and suggestions of Scripture by appealing to tradition. ·

Tract 85.

But it was Tract 90, which appeared in 1841, that marked the culmination of the Tractarian Movement, and with which the series abruptly closed. This tract was written at the request of some of the party, led by W. G. Ward, that Newman should reconcile with the Thirty-Nine Articles of the Church of England the views he had been enunciating. " It is often urged," says Tract 90, " and sometimes felt and granted, that there are in the Articles propositions or terms inconsistent with the Catholic faith. . . . The following Tract is drawn up with the view of showing how groundless the objection is. . . ." The tract examined the articles regarded as anti-Roman or anti-Catholic, and argued that they were not so condemnatory of Rome after all, but were really aimed at the corruptions of Rome.

Tract 90.

We have no space to review the Tract at length, but may quote from a letter of James Mozley as giving a brief contemporary description. The letter is dated 8th March, 1841. " A new Tract," he says, " has come out this week, and is beginning to make a sensation. It is on the Articles, and shows that they bear a highly Catholic meaning; and that many doctrines, of which the Romanist are corruptions, may be held consistently with them. This is no more than what we know as a matter of history, for the Articles were expressly worded to bring in Roman Catholics. But people are astonished and confused at the idea now. . . ."

Mozley's Letter on Tract 90.

So great was the storm which this tract raised that the series came to an end. The tract was condemned by the authorities at Oxford, and two years later Pusey was suspended from preaching for three years because of a sermon on the Eucharist. The same year that saw Pusey's suspension saw also Newman's secession to the Church of Rome. Other Tractarians followed.

Newman joins the Romish Church.

Contrary to many rumours, Pusey did not join in this secession, and it was chiefly due to his efforts, assisted by Keble, that the number of

JOHN HENRY NEWMAN, ONE OF THE FOUNDERS OF THE TRACTARIAN MOVEMENT.

secessionists to the Roman communion was not much greater. He took up a position between Romanism on the one hand, and the view of Zwinglius on the other.

About 1850, however, occurred another secession to Rome. This was occasioned by what is known as the Gorham Judgment. The Bishop of **The Gorham Judgment.** Exeter refused to institute Mr. Gorham to Brampford Speke Vicarage, because he found that he (Mr. Gorham) did not hold that spiritual regeneration is given in the "sacrament of baptism." Appealing to the Court of Arches, the Court decided against Gorham, and declared that baptismal regeneration was the doctrine of the Church of England. Appealing further to the Privy Council, the Court reversed the judgment of the Court of Arches to a certain extent, finding that certain differences of opinion were consistent with subscription to the Articles. After further litigation, Gorham became Vicar of Brampford Speke.

Many of those who took a strong and decided view as to the efficacy of the sacraments thereupon seceded to the Roman Church. Pusey, however, still maintained his attitude, and the Oxford Movement, which became known as Puseyism, and subsequently "Anglo-Catholicism," continued to grow. Pusey—who died in 1882—became virtually its leader after Newman joined the Church of Rome.

It should be noted also that this movement had, and has its æsthetic side, reviving many of the former practices and usages of the Church. But, **Æsthetic side of the Movement.** as we have indicated, Ritualism is far more than merely an æsthetic observance of public worship, though possibly it is that side which has attracted many persons to it.

In its effects, some persons hold that it has greatly stimulated the life of the Church The increase of restorations of ancient churches and the build-**Movement.** ing of new edifices, the reopening of Convocation, the increase of bishoprics, the revivals of the life of Sisterhoods—all these and many other efforts and energies are traced to this movement, some also **Effects of the Movement.** saying that it has absorbed and adapted certain agencies from Nonconformists. How far all this is equally true may be matter of controversy ; but there can be little doubt that it has given great impulse to the life and work of the Church in certain directions. While approximating to Roman Catholic doctrine and ritual, its adherents decline to admit the authority of the Pope—whom they designate the Bishop of Rome.

Concurrently, however, with this movement has flourished another school within the borders of the Church ; perhaps in point of date it was **The Broad Church party.** before it—viz., the Broad Church party. Some would trace its beginnings to Coleridge, but, in fact, it seems the lineal descendant of the "Latitudinarians," to whom we have already referred. Dr.

Arnold, F. D. Maurice, Robertson of Brighton, Charles Kingsley, and Dean Stanley are among some of the illustrious names which adorn this school of thought and faith.

Speaking generally, it rejects many traditional beliefs, though to a

DR. THOMAS ARNOLD, ONE OF THE LEADERS OF THE BROAD CHURCH PARTY.

certain extent it accords with the Low Church or Evangelical party, in that it attaches no particular value to vestments or matters of ritual; further, it minimises the dogmas of apostolical succession and *Its Views.* of the grace of the sacraments, but it interprets dogmas more broadly and liberally, and asserts a broader freedom in accepting creeds.

An early and distinguished leader of this party was Dr. Arnold, Headmaster of Rugby. To him the High Church doctrines were "a great obstruction to the full development of national Christianity." He regarded the dogma of apostolic succession, says Dean Stanley, "as morally powerless and intellectually indefensible; as incompatible with all sound notions of law and government; and as tending above all things to substitute a ceremonial for a spiritual Christianity."

Dr. Arnold on Apostolic Succession.

But perhaps F. D. Maurice, Professor of Theology in King's College, London, did more to shape the thought of the school than even Arnold. His Theological Essays, issued in 1853, were regarded by Broad Churchmen as a statement of their views, and aroused a keen controversy. The discussion turned chiefly on dogmas concerning the Atonement and future punishment. The Council of the College declared against the volume, and Maurice lost his post.

F. D. Maurice's Theological Essays.

The essays dealt with various doctrines, in addition to those mentioned. To touch on them very briefly, we may say that he regarded the Atonement as a gospel of deliverance from sin and the answer of the Scriptures to a sin-stricken conscience; that the "fall of Adam" was but an incident in the education of mankind, showing their weakness away from Christ; that faith was not accepting precise doctrinal statements, but trust in Christ, and in the power of righteousness; that the "Church," the Bible and the Creeds were only valuable as they held up Christ as the object of faith, while, as substitutes for faith, they were positively mischievous. From these few indications of Maurice's position, the wide difference existing between him and the High Church and even Low Church schools of thought will be apparent.

The publication of the famous volume, "Essays and Reviews," in February, 1860, gave rise to another storm. It contained seven papers, which were regarded by some persons as preaching scepticism. The Convocations of Canterbury and York censured its "pernicious doctrines and heretical tendencies, and 9,000 clergy signed a protest against it. It would be impossible in the space at our disposal to deal with this controversy. Perhaps the best comment upon it is that Dr. Temple, who wrote the first article on "The Education of the World," became Bishop of Exeter, and is now Bishop of London.

"Essays and Reviews."

Following hard upon this controversy was that connected with Dr. Colenso, Bishop of Natal, concerning the Pentateuch. "There is not the slightest reason to suppose," wrote Colenso, "that the first writer of the story in the Péntateuch ever professed to be recording infallible truth, or even actual historical truth." We may indicate his position in the accusations against him. Colenso was charged at Cape Town with denying the Atonement, with believing in the justification of those who do not know Christ, with denying the divinity of Christ and the inspiration of Scripture. He was found guilty, and deposed, and after litigation a new bishop was appointed.

Dr. Colenso and the Pentateuch.

The Broad Church school have welcomed a bold and scientific criticism of Scripture; and as long since as 1863, when Dean Stanley preached his farewell sermon at Oxford on "Great Opportunities," he said: "It is for us to choose whether we will make the worst of all scientific enquiry, or whether we will make the best of it; whether we will treat critical researches into the nature, and authority, and language, and history of the Sacred Books as heretical, infidel, unbelieving attacks; or whether we will hail them, even when mistaken, as contributions to the one great aim in which we are all engaged, of a better knowledge of God's Word, a better understanding of God's will."

Dean Stanley on Scientific Enquiry.

This latter attitude is no doubt characteristic of the Broad Church School. It may be said, therefore, that the party welcomes an honest criticism of Scripture, that it deals far more with the human aspect of Christ's life than do others, and preaches a lofty morality to be developed by the individual's own hard efforts, rather than by depending on "grace" mystically conferred.

Thus, then, within the borders of the English Church exist three great parties or schools of thought, and some persons regard this fact as testifying to its great catholicity and comprehensiveness. Its doctrine is determined—as we have seen—by Acts of Parliament concerning the Book of Common Prayer in 1552, afterwards altered in 1559 and 1661, also by the Act regarding the Thirty-Nine Articles in 1571. Its polity is episcopal, and ardent Churchmen would claim that its bishops are the successors of the prelates before the Reformation. Should Disestablishment and Disendowment overtake it, as has frequently been proposed, there are but few indications that its standard of doctrine or ecclesiastical polity would be materially altered.

The Three Parties in the Church.

Its Articles and Polity.

DEFOE IN THE PILLORY.

CHAPTER XXIII.

Protestant Nonconformity in England: Independents, Baptists, Presbyterians, Quakers, Unitarians.

NOT only did the Uniformity Act of 1662 prove a virtual settlement of ecclesiastical matters as regards the English Church, but it also gave a great impetus to Nonconformity.

Thus it forced many earnest men into active separation and different organization from the Anglican Church; it showed how impossible was further reform in their direction within the borders of that Church, and it brought the root differences between those who were ejected and the Church itself into more marked prominence. In short, it caused a chasm to exist between persons of, broadly speaking, two different schools of thought which has never been outwardly closed, even to the present day.

But, as we have already seen, Nonconformity existed in England before 1662. It was indeed a child of the Reformation, even as the present Protestant Church of England is itself the offspring of the same great movement. Yet Baptists and Congregationalists, who agree on so many points, claim their principles to be those of the **Nonconformity before 1662.** Apostles, and their religious practices to be a return to those of Apostolic times. But, passing by these more abstruse or theological aspects of the question, Nonconformity in essence might be traced to the days of Wyclif himself, for he actually went so far as to send out preachers without ordination.

Lollardy continued quietly to exist until it blended with the Reformation of the sixteenth century. Then appeared the Separatism of Queen Elizabeth's reign, the Separatists being, in brief, **Separatism in Elizabeth's reign.** persons who despaired of what they considered further necessary reform within the Church of England itself.

Moreover, a Baptist Church is said to have been in existence in 1417, and indeed several Baptist Churches claim to have originated before Elizabeth came to the throne. It is possible that these were Lollardist. No doubt the history of such early congregations is lost, or **Early Baptist and Independent Churches.** clouded in obscurity, on account of persecution; but, however these things may be, a Congregational (or Independent) Church, according to a State paper, existed in 1567, at Plumbers' Hall, as we have seen in a previous chapter; while the Congregational Church at Horningsham, Wilts, claims to have originated in 1566.

From these early beginnings, and noting in passing the strongly Nonconformist views, in Edward VI.'s reign, of Bishop Hooper, of Gloucester, of whom we have already spoken, we come to the **Marked and historical commencement of Nonconformity.** more marked historical commencement of Nonconformity in the Separatism in Elizabeth's reign.

'In a lecture on the Rise of Independency, delivered in the spring of 1893 by the Rev. J. Guinness Rogers—whom men of all parties would

G G

regard as an authority on Congregationalism—he declared that Elizabeth's reign became the starting-point of a new era—viz., Separatism **Root principles of Separatism, or Dissent.** from the National Church. Some persons had thought of reform within the borders of that Church, but the Separatists struck out a new path. They maintained the right of self-government in ecclesiastical affairs, and further—and this should be especially noted—they declared that a Christian Church should consist only of true believers in Christ.

This root idea of Nonconformity is, it will be seen, fundamentally different from that of a National Established Church. The position may be put in this way: the Separatists appear to have asked, Did Christ found an outward and visible Church, or did He originate one which is purely spiritual, becoming outward and visible by its principles manifesting themselves in the lives of His disciples? And they took the latter view.

If this conception of the Church be attentively considered, and its logical issues thought out, many of the varying views of Conformist and **Different conceptions of the Church.** Nonconformist will, no doubt, be accounted for. It seems impossible, for instance, that those who hold that Christ established simply a spiritual society, and that all "true believers" form the Church, could also hold the dogmas of an outward and visible Church, Apostolic succession, royal supremacy, transubstantiation, or the "grace" and efficacy of sacraments, the "authority" of the Church, and so forth.

Thus it seems clear that from what we have termed the historical **The Independent view of the Church.** commencement of English Protestant Nonconformity in the Separatism of Elizabeth's reign, it has been animated by a distinctly different conception of the Christian Church from that of the Church of England.

It may here be again pointed out that the great Swiss Reformer, Zwingli, asserted powerfully the doctrine of Independency, or Congregationalism, demanding a return to the liberty of primitive Christianity—as witness his speech at the Disputation at Zurich, October, 1523. The early Independents, or Congregationalists, of Elizabeth's reign therefore did not stand alone.

It may be convenient here briefly to summarise the principles held by the Independents, or Congregationalists. Their distinctive doctrine—which, however, is also held by the sister denomination, the Baptists—is that each local Church—*i.e.*, society of true Christians—should choose its own minister and officers and manage its own affairs; they own no ecclesiastical or religious authority except that of Christ as the only Supreme Head of His Church, and regard the Bible only as their standard of faith, considering that the traditions *General Principles of the Congregationalists, or Independents.* of the fathers of the early Church and Councils, etc., have no authority or ruling power whatsoever. Independents hold that there is no authority in Scripture for uniting the various Churches in different places into one corporation, to be ruled by Synod, or Bishop, or Council, and thus they are compelled to stand aloof both from Episcopacy and Presbyterianism. Nevertheless, they have united freely together in county and national unions for mutual help, advice, guidance, and fraternity. Doctrinally they held much the same views as other Puritan parties,—such as those enunciated by the Westminster Assembly, the Independents present at that gathering, however, repudiating the right of that or any other Council to bind any Churches or people. Holding these views of Independency, it is not difficult to see that Cromwell and his followers would strive to prevent the establishment of a Presbyterian State Church in the time of the Commonwealth.

The difference between Baptists and Independents is chiefly, if not entirely, on the question of Baptism, the former believing that the rite should only be administered on profession of faith, and should be performed by immersion, instead of by sprinkling. At first *The Baptists.* sight this might seem trivial, but when the dogma of baptismal regeneration of the Church of England is remembered, the distinctive view of the Baptists appears as of greater importance. The great historic protest of the Baptists has always been against this doctrine of baptismal regeneration.

Congregationalists are quite as much opposed to this dogma as are the Baptists themselves. Indeed, they appear to go farther, and regard the rite simply as a dedicatory service, or it may be a pledge on the part of the parents that they will nurture the child in the Christian faith.

It is probable that those early Separatists included both Baptists and Congregationalists, — both are Congregationalists as to Church Government,—but, in truth, much uncertainty exists as to the various small religious societies which arose about the years 1570–80. *The Religious Societies of 1570–80.* They were denominated Separatist and also Puritan. But the Puritans—as a party in the Church of England—were not Separatists.

The Separatists were Puritans, but the bulk of the Puritans were not Separatists, until, perhaps, 1662, when so many clergymen were ejected

Difference of Separatists and Puritans. from the Church. The Puritans were bent on reforming the Church from within, and many came to be Presbyterians; the Separatists (Congregationalists and Baptists), acting on a fundamentally different conception of the Church, were content to strike out a new path for themselves, and, being opposed conscientiously to Church Establishments, separated from the State Church.

Concerning Presbyterianism, it has been claimed that it was known in the early Church, and existed in Scotland before the appointment of

The Presbyterians. a bishop—Palladius, in 431—and also in certain countries on the Continent. Calvin, however, virtually gave it the form it has, with modifications, since held, and the opinions of the Puritans—

First Presbyterian Church. as distinct from the Separatists—were in essence Presbyterian. In 1572 a Presbyterian Church was founded at Wandsworth, and others followed.

Speaking generally, Presbyterianism occupies a position midway between Episcopalianism and Independency. The congregation chooses its

Their Views. minister and elders, who constitute the "Session," and have the oversight of the Church spiritually, while deacons regulate its affairs financially. The Presbytery of a district is formed of the ministers and certain of the elders, who superintend the congregations in the district, and to it congregations, or sessions, may appeal. Further, there are Synods and Assemblies, consisting of the union of Presbyteries.

At the meeting of the Westminster Assembly in 1643 many of the Puritans were inclined toward Presbyterianism, though some preferred a mild form of Episcopacy, and others were Independents. And while Presbyterians were the stronger at the commencement of the Civil War, the Independents prevailed subsequently.

Here, then, we have the rise of three great historical Nonconformist denominations of England. It is quite possible that they may not have

Obscure Distinctions between early Nonconformists. been clearly defined in those days, and that the words Puritan, Separatist, Presbyterian, etc., may have been sometimes interchangeable and used indiscriminately. Thus in Strype's Annals, in 1583, Anabaptists and Brownists (Congregationalists) are placed together; but the various principles seem to have been in active operation. The English Baptists, however, must not be classed with the Munster Baptists, or credited with their excesses. The Uniformity Act of 1662 brought these three denominations closer together. Previously, to some extent, their history was bound up with that of the National Church, and it has been referred to in former chapters. Cromwell was an Independent, as was also Milton and Owen, the Vice-Chancellor of Oxford, while a group of Independents, fleeing from persecution and living in history by the romantic name of the Pilgrim Fathers, founded New England over the Atlantic.

Hundreds of Nonconformist Churches were founded after the Ejection in 1662. Yet the congregations were harassed and scattered, and their members imprisoned, and pilloried, and fined. Some conformed; others met in secret, with watchers to give information of the approach of the enemy. These are, no doubt, the reasons why so many old Nonconformist churches are to be found in odd, out-of-the-way places and remote corners both in town and country; and some still bear traces of

CONGREGATIONAL MEMORIAL HALL, FARRINGDON ST., LONDON.

arrangements for giving prompt notice of informers, and means for hurriedly conveying away a minister.

The number of ejected ministers has been matter of dispute. Dr. Edmund Calamy, the eminent Nonconformist, gives them as 2,000, and that has been largely accepted. Some Church historians, however, put them at 800. But the exact number does not minimise the importance of the Act itself in English history. In memory of this great event the Congregational Memorial Hall was completed in 1874, in Farringdon Street, on the site of the old Fleet prison, in which several of the early Nonconformists had been confined.

Upon the society known as the Quakers the hand of persecution seemed to fall with, if possible, a worse vengeance. The Quakers, or, to give

George Fox. them their official name, the Society of Friends, began to appear about the year 1648. The founder was George Fox, possibly an indiscreet man, but pious and enthusiastic. The Quakers declaimed against "Steeple Houses," as they called churches; against a paid ministry, which they regarded as unscriptural; against tithes and against Sacraments. They believed in the spirituality of religion, and in the communication of an "inward light" by the Spirit of God dwelling in them, by which light men might discern the truth. They contended that the spirit of man could commune with the Spirit of God, and that outward forms and ceremonies were not needed.

Had they stopped here, it is possible that the persecution against them would not have been so bitter, and that, under Cromwell, at all events,

The Principles of the Quakers. they would not have been attacked. Indeed, he gave orders for their relief; but they, or some of them, were wont to enter "Steeple Houses" at times and assail both preachers and doctrines in public—a proceeding, in days of fierce controversy, not likely to promote their own lenient treatment. Certain of their views appear to have been only some of the Reformation doctrines pressed a little further to their logical issues; but they also held that the civil power had nought to do with marriage, that oaths were sinful, and that it was not permissible to use arms or physical force for the protection of the country.

While some of those early Quakers, or "Friends," were guilty of indiscretions and excesses, and brought down bitter wrath upon them-

They attack others. selves by their public attacks of others, yet their beliefs and practices have no doubt been grossly maligned and caricatured. The name "Quaker" was given to them in derision of the tremblings exhibited by some of the earlier members; but it has now lost any ludicrous or contemptuous meaning. Another version of the

JOHN BUNYAN.

The author of the "Pilgrim's Progress," and the first Nonconformist preacher licensed under the temporary "Indulgence" of 1672.

origin of the term states that it was given them by Mr. Justice Bennet, of

Derby, when George Fox urged him and those with him to quake at the word of the Lord.

When the storm of persecution burst upon Nonconformists after 1662, the Quakers often disdained to meet in secret, and appear almost to have rejoiced in defying the law. They met openly, and soldiers **Bitter Persecution of the Quakers.** rushed upon them to break up their gatherings, and to stun and hack their congregations with clubs and swords. According to Sewell's History, over four thousand Quakers were in gaol in 1662, five hundred being in London. Many died, and numbers were banished.

We turn from these scenes of persecution to glance at three years of leniency. From 1672 to 1675 a Declaration of Indulgence suspended the Conventicle Act; and it is worthy of note that (according to **Bunyan licensed to Preach.** Skeats) John Bunyan, the author of the "Pilgrim's Progress," was the first Dissenting minister licensed to preach. He received the permission after spending twelve years in gaol. The license given by King Charles speaks of Bunyan's Church as Congregational, and a barn or orchard were the places licensed. It seems uncertain whether Bunyan was a Baptist or Independent; the society, however, over which he presided appears unquestionably to have been a " mixed " or union congregation.

Within ten months of the "Declaration of Indulgence" about three thousand five hundred preaching licenses were issued. Another attempt **Declaration of Indulgence.** at Comprehension followed, but failed; while, in 1675, the licenses were withdrawn, and the storm-cloud of persecution burst again—if possible—with even greater fury than before.

An end, however, was approaching to the shameful story, and we gladly pass on to the next great date in English ecclesiastical history—the **Toleration Act, 1689.** year of the Toleration Act, in 1689. We need not recapitulate the events leading to this wise law; but a proclamation of William of Orange had declared in favour of " the covering all men from persecution for their consciences," and Parliament passed the Bill with alacrity.

Looked at from the Nonconformists' point of view, it was a grudging and ungenerous measure, giving as little as possible; regarded from a **Regarded from Different Standpoints.** High Church or Stuart standpoint, it was a large and liberal concession. It was an admission that in principle the Nonconformists had won, and that the policy of bitter persecution must be abandoned. But repression and injustice were still maintained, and the history of Nonconformity from that day, even to this, includes a long series of efforts and of triumphs to regain, and to hold, equal civil and religious rights.

In 1689, also, yet another attempt was made at Comprehension, and failed, and the multiplication of Nonconformist places of worship proceeded apace. Between 1688 and 1690, nearly a thousand were Comprehension licensed; and in the dozen years from 1688 to 1700, two Again. thousand four hundred and eighteen were licensed. Defoe estimated the number of Nonconformists about the year 1700 to be two millions, and declares they were the most numerous and wealthy of all Great Growth of Non- sections in the kingdom. Skeats, however, in his "History of conformity. the Free Churches," hesitates to accept this numerical estimate, though he testifies to "their great activity, and the wide surface of the kingdom over which they had spread their network of Christian organizations."

Shortly after the Toleration Bill became law, the Baptists held an Assembly in London, and a confession of faith was adopted, in which liberty of conscience was asserted. Associations were formed, Baptist and at most of their gatherings three points seem to have been Associations. most prominent—viz., the need of an increase in personal religion, funds for sustentation of churches, and improved education of ministers. The denomination also was being divided into General and Particular Baptists.

The Independents and the Presbyterians were approaching more closely to each other, and there even appears to have been much talk of amalgamation. Baxter, the great Presbyterian, who had Independents suffered much in the recent troubles, and had ever been in the and forefront of controversy, was now an old man, and seems to Presbyterians. have been much gratified at this concord. The proposals for organic union, however, came to nothing, but the two denominations, with the Baptists, learned in the course of a few years to act together, and in Dissenters 1702 a joint deputation representing them waited on Queen Address Queen Anne. Anne at her accession, Dr. Daniel Williams at their head. The queen showed her dislike to Dissent on this occasion by her silence.

In the same year, the body known as the "Ministers of the Three Denominations" was formed, and some years later, in November, 1732, the Association known as the "Dissenting Deputies" came into The being—a permanent body to defend their civil rights and "Dissenting Deputies." superintend their civil affairs. It originated in a meeting to consider an application to repeal the Test and Corporation Acts. This indicates that the Three Denominations, though separate organizations, have largely acted as one. Almost from the first, after the Toleration Act, this was the case with Presbyterians and Independents. The Quakers, however, appear to have stood apart.

One of the first questions which arose was that of Occasional Conformity. It was characteristic of the grossly incomplete nature of the

Occasional Conformity. Toleration Act that no person could take a municipal office who did not "communicate" according to the forms of the Established Church. Some Dissenters did so, and were yet Nonconformists. Thus Sir Thomas Abney, on being elected Lord Mayor in 1701, partook of the "Lord's Supper" in an Episcopal church to qualify himself for the office, and afterwards at a Nonconformist church of which he was a member. Also four years previously Sir Humphrey Edwin, on being elected to the same office, appears to have done the same thing, for he took the regalia to Pinners' Hall, used as an Independent church.

This Occasional Conformity, as it was called, brought out Daniel Defoe as a vigorous and trenchant political writer. He denounced it

"Bo-Peep with God Almighty." entirely, asking how "Communion" could be a civil act in one place, and a religious act in another. Is not this, he said, playing "bo-peep with God Almighty"? The subject was frequently debated during those years, and finally, in 1711, a Bill passed providing that if a person, after admission to a civil or military office, should be seen in a "conventicle" or religious meeting, other than that of the Church of England, he should be heavily fined, and disabled from holding such office in the future. This shows how heavily the tide set in against Nonconformists. To some extent, however, the Act was repealed

Repeal of the Test Acts. in 1718 by the Bill for "strengthening the Protestant interest"; but the matter was not finally settled until the Test and Corporation Acts were repealed in 1828, the controversy concerning them having lasted no fewer than 140 years.

Yet another most important subject arose soon after the Toleration Act—viz., the foundation and growth of the Dissenting academies. These were

The Dissenting Academies. necessary because of the unjust Act excluding the Nonconformists from the national universities, which the Puritans had loved so well. For, whatever were their faults, they were devoted to learning.

Dr. Fairbairn on the Academies. Dr. Fairbairn, the eminent Principal of Mansfield Congregational College, lately established at Oxford (1886), when writing on this subject, says: "Our fathers and founders were sound scholars and great divines, and they were made what they were by their strong faith, working under the conditions supplied by the ancient universities. In a sense, the spirit and ideal of these universities, as they were known to our fathers, survived, though in a sadly broken and reduced form, in those academies that preceded and produced our later colleges. The Act that shut the Puritans out from the homes of the learning they

DR. ISAAC WATTS, HYMN WRITER AND INDEPENDENT MINISTER. BORN 1671; DIED 1748.

loved did not compel them to renounce the learning—only sent them in search of sheltered spots, where, amid the storm of disabilities and penalties, they could still pursue and communicate it."

Here, then, we have the origin of those Dissenting academies, which accomplished so much, and excited the hatred of certain of the Conformists so greatly. This animosity was one of the inspiring **They Spread over the Country.**

motives of the Schism Bill—described in a previous chapter. That Bill would have wrought great harm to the Nonconformist colleges, which had sprung up all over the country, but it became a dead letter through the death of the queen.

A story is told in Wilson's "Dissenting Churches" to the effect that the first public announcement of the death of Queen Anne was made in old Fetter Lane Congregational Church. On the morning of her death, which took place on a Sunday, the pastor, Thomas Bradbury, was walking through Smithfield, when he met Bishop Burnet. "Why so sad?" asked the Bishop. Bradbury explained that he was thinking if he should have the resolution of the martyrs who had perished there, for he assuredly expected a similar persecution (after the passing of the Schism Bill). The Bishop pointed out that the queen was like to die that day, and he offered to send a messenger to Fetter Lane Chapel, who should enter the gallery and drop a handkerchief if she died. The queen did die that morning, and the messenger arrived and dropped the handkerchief while Bradbury was preaching. In a prayer following the sermon, he gave thanks for the nation's delivery, and sought the blessing of God on King George and the House of Hanover. Bradbury, we are told, often referred to this fact in after life.

Death of Queen Anne first announced in Fetter Lane Chapel.

The first seminary for the poor, we may note, had been established as far back as 1687 in connection with a Nonconformist Church at Southwark; while as for the work of the "Academies," among the men trained in them may be mentioned Archbishop Secker, Joseph Butler, Bishop Maddox, Dr. Watts, Daniel Neal, Philip Doddridge, Edmund Calamy (the third of that name), and Nathaniel Lardner. In time these academies blossomed into the Dissenting colleges, and Nonconformists won a great victory when, in 1826, London University was established. According to Dr. Fairbairn, it became the great ambition of the better Nonconformist colleges to win London degrees; "their efficiency was tested and determined by the number of men they passed, and the honours they obtained. They became, in a sense, University Colleges." We may add that it was not until 1871 that the University Religious Tests were abolished—more than 180 years after the passing of the Toleration Act. Another eleven years elapsed before—in 1882—fellowships and heads of colleges at Oxford and Cambridge were freed from such restrictions.

Distinguished Men trained in the Academies.

Abolition of University Tests.

Yet another great struggle in which Nonconformists were engaged was for the Abolition of Church Rates. They were a tax on parishioners for the support of the Church, and have been traced to a law of Canute. Considerable difficulty was often experienced in recovering the payments, the only method of doing so before George III.'s reign being by process in an ecclesiastical court. In that reign, however, an Act was passed (53 George III., cap. 127), giving jurisdiction to the justices of the peace at the instance of the churchwardens, and parish contention soon blazed forth. Parish after parish refused to make the rate, and in 1834 the first of a number of Church Rate Abolition Bills was introduced into the House of Commons. The agitation continued until 1868, when an Act abolishing compulsory Church rates was passed, except in cases where a local Act existed for their payment. Voluntary rates were afterwards made in some parishes, and possibly paid by parishioners who did not scrutinize their papers closely, or feared to offend. The attitude of Nonconformists to this matter may perhaps be best expressed by Mr. Bright's speech in the House of Commons in 1862, on Sir John Trelawney's Bill. They repudiated altogether a tax which recognised the supremacy of a Church to which they objected, and from which, it may be added, the ecclesiastical forefathers of many had been ejected.

The Church Rates Controversy.

The Attitude of Nonconformists.

Many other grievances of Nonconformists were slowly relieved. Thus before 1836, the births in their families were not registered. Ministers in some cases kept voluntary registers, and the means of proving dates of births legally was by these, or by entries in family Bibles. The same year also saw marriages permitted in Nonconformist places of worship; but an Act enabling Nonconformist ministers to conduct services at Nonconformist funerals in parish churchyards was not passed until 1880. In all these and various other efforts the Nonconformist cause received the most material assistance from the organization which came to be known familiarly as The Liberation Society, which was founded in May, 1844, by the late Mr. Edward Miall and other eminent Nonconformists.

Removal of other Nonconformist Disabilities.

The Liberation Society.

Turning now from the more controversial aspects of Nonconformist history, we notice very important landmarks to arise in the formation of the Baptist Missionary Society in 1792, and the London Missionary Society—which soon became practically the Congregationalist Society—in 1795. William Carey was a Baptist

Missionary Societies.

minister and also a shoemaker, who, by reading Cook's Voyages, had become much impressed with the degraded condition of the heathen. It became a fixed idea with him that men should be sent to preach to them the Christian religion. At length he preached a powerful sermon, which

Baptist
Missionary
Society. caused the Society to be formed, and its first collection amounted to £13 2*s.* 6*d.* The Society was formed in the back parlour of Mrs. Beeby Wallis's house at Kettering, and in less than nine months Carey was on his way to India, where he became a most remarkable Bible translator.

The London Missionary Society was founded on unsectarian lines, and Evangelical Churchmen took part in its formation. They, however,

London
Missionary
Society. soon dropped off when the Church Missionary Society was founded in 1799. David Bogue, a prominent Congregationalist minister, was on the preliminary committee, and preached to an enormous congregation at Tottenham Court Road Chapel in the week during which the Society was founded. "We are called together," he said, "to the funeral of bigotry"—an enthusiastic statement which, judged in the light of succeeding events, was premature, to say the least.

Many distinguished men, such as Marshman and Ward, Duff and Morrison, Livingstone and Moffat, have gone out in connection with these Societies.

The Religious Census of 1851 appears as another prominent feature in Ecclesiastical history. For the first time, something like complete

Religious
Census, 1851. information was gained as to the position of the Church of England and various Nonconformist bodies. Mr. Horace Mann, of the Registrar-General's office, accompanied the returns with some luminous "explanatory remarks." Briefly the Census showed that there were 14,077 buildings belonging to the Church of England, with 5,317,915 sittings, and 20,399 of other denominations, with 4,894,648 sittings. These other denominations numbered thirty-four, of which nine were foreign.

There were five varieties of Baptists and three of Presbyterians,

Immense
Growth of
Nonconformity. while there were seven varieties of Methodists, to which we shall refer in another chapter. We need not enter into any of the controversies which this Census aroused, except to point out the immense growth of Nonconformity which it proves and illustrates.

In the meantime, in 1832, the Congregationalists had formed themselves into a Union for mutual help and guidance, the first annual meeting of the new organization being held in 1833. At that gathering a Declaration of Faith was adopted, it being expressly stated that the Declaration was not intended as a test or creed, and the independence of each Church was affirmed. Similarly the Baptists have also formed themselves into a Union. In short, the Congregationalists, with their fellows the Baptists, seem to have set themselves to solve the problem of guaranteeing the independence and the right of private judgment to each individual and to each Church, with the voluntary union of all for the common good.

Formation of the Congregational Union, 1832.

The Baptist Union.

HOUSE AT KETTERING WHERE THE BAPTIST MISSIONARY SOCIETY WAS FORMED, 1792.

Speaking generally of the two denominations, their history appears to show signs of almost constant growth, and their line of continuity is clear and plain.

Not so, however, with the English Presbyterians. Their organization seems to have declined some years after the Toleration Act. Some became Unitarians, others joined the Independents; and, according to Mr. Justice Kekewich, in his judgment in what was called the Tooting Case, concerning a Nonconformist Church known as

"Suspension" of the Presbyterian Church.

Defoe Church, Tooting, "Until about 1836, well into the nineteenth century, the Presbyterians had no active life as a body; there appears to have been no return of their chapels, and no other evidence of their identity. . . . They dropped out as a body."

If this were so, however, they have endeavoured to make up for their deficiency within the last fifty or sixty years of the century. There were

Revival of Pres-byterianism in England. Presbyterian Churches in England connected with the Scotch Church; and Churches came to be formed connected with both the Scotch Church and with the United Presbyterian Churches. At the formation of the Scotch Free Church in 1843 most of the English

The Presby-terian Church of England. Presbyterian Churches sympathised, and in 1876 the two synods in England joined and assumed the name of the Presbyterian Church of England. A cardinal point in the policy of this Church is the Sustentation Fund, by which each minister receives a stipend. The entrance to the ministry, however, is more safeguarded than is the case with some other Nonconformist denominations.

Historically the earlier Presbyterians may be said to have generally become Unitarians. This change occurred in the course of a few years

Unitarianism. after the fateful date, 1662. It is not intended to imply that Unitarianism or Socinianism was unknown in England previously; thus there were Unitarian or Arian martyrdoms during the days of Edward VI. to James I., and in James's reign Socinianism exerted much influence in England from the continent. But the historical continuity between English Unitarians and the Socinians appears very doubtful—if, indeed, any exists. Generally speaking, Unitarians hold the doctrine of the Divine Unity as opposed to the doctrine of the Divine Trinity, and reject the

Views of Unitarians. account of the supernatural birth of Christ. They also regard the teaching and the example of Christ as the more essential parts of His mission. The philosophy of Locke was favourable to Unitarianism, and Sir Isaac Newton was, it is said, a Unitarian, though, like Locke, he did not formally avow himself such. The distinguished chemist and Dissenting minister, Dr. Priestley, who discovered oxygen gas, did not, however, scruple to declare himself, and the riot against him at Birmingham, where his house was burned and his manuscripts, books, and philosophical

Riot at Dr. Priestley's House. instruments were destroyed, affords a shameful instance of bigotry and intolerance. Dr. Priestley had been educated at one of the "despised" Dissenting Academies in Northamptonshire founded by Dr. Doddridge, and though brought up a Calvinist, came, as he himself said, "to embrace what is called the heterodox side of every question." In one of his first works he declined to accept the orthodox doctrines of the atonement and of the Trinity. The rejection of these remain cardinal features in the views of all sections of Unitarians to this day.

It was not until 1813 that they were legally placed on equal footing with other Nonconformists. Like the Congregationalists and Baptists, their form of Church government is congregational, and like them they have a union—the British and Foreign Unitarian Association. *Given legal Equality with other Nonconformists.*

Signs are not wanting that in this last decade of the nineteenth century the "orthodox" Nonconformist bodies are drawing nearer together for mutual assistance and support. They insist on the essential unity of the Christian Church from a spiritual standpoint, and they seem increasingly disposed to manifest this unity in more organized co-operation, still holding their distinctive doctrines. In witness of this may be mentioned the various Nonconformist Councils and Free Church Congresses which have lately been formed. *Signs of Union among Nonconformists.*

An attentive observer might also distinguish among these denominations two classes answering to the Low and Broad Church parties within the Church of England, or—to change the metaphor—to Conservative and Liberal schools of thought. As to their numbers, it is said by some that the Nonconformists form half of the community, while in Wales they largely preponderate; and that they have become a mighty political and religious force no impartial writer can deny.

WESTMINSTER ABBEY.

EPWORTH RECTORY, THE BIRTHPLACE OF JOHN WESLEY.

CHAPTER XXIV.

The Methodist Family of Churches.

TO a certain extent the history of the remarkable movement known as Methodism was largely bound up with the history of one man.

Originates within the Established Church. Originating within the borders of the Established Church, it grew and spread, until soon after the death of its founder, it broke right away from the Establishment, and became formally, what it was before practically, a new religious denomination.

The step of separation was inevitable. John Wesley, who was the founder, and who was at one time a most rigid High Churchman, came gradually to hold views distinctly Nonconformist in character, Separation inevitable. though doubtless he would not have acknowledged them as such. But in 1784 he actually took the step of ordaining a bishop and presbyters for America, and he wrote to Charles Wesley, his brother, that "the uninterrupted succession (apostolical succession) I know to John Wesley's Views. be a fable, which no man ever did or can prove." Nearly forty years earlier, he held that "originally" each local church was independent

THE HOLY CLUB.

of other churches, that presbyters and bishops were one order, while he built meeting houses without permission of the parish clergymen, and earlier still he baptized by immersion, though at that time also he was such a "High" Churchman, that he refused the Communion to persons,—and declined also to bury those—who had not been baptized in the Episcopal Church. In short, this remarkable man moved through the ecclesiastical semicircle from pronounced High Churchism to something like distinct Dissent, though to the last he repudiated the idea of separation from the Church.

Strong believers in heredity might find confirmation of their views in

these changes. For although John Wesley's parents had both conformed
to the Established Church, yet both his grandfathers had been
His Parents. ejected ministers under the Uniformity Act of 1662.   His
mother's father, indeed, was none other than Dr. Samuel Annesley, who has
been spoken of as "The Nonconformists' St. Paul." She was a very intelli-
Both Non- gent and high-principled woman, and Susannah, the "mother
conformists. of the Wesleys," has become with some persons a well-nigh
perfect model of feminine virtues. She is reported to have been learned
and an excellent teacher, also a pattern housekeeper and a wise disci-
plinarian.

The ecclesiastical changes in the Wesley family might teach charity
to disputants on both sides of the Nonconformist controversy. No doubt
both of John Wesley's parents were conscientious Conformists, even
as their fathers were conscientious Nonconformists.

John Wesley's father was Rector of Epworth, in Lincolnshire, and
the future founder of Methodism was born at the Rectory in 1703.
Wesley saved When quite young, he was saved as by a miracle from a
from a Fire. fire, and he was brought to regard himself as set apart for
some remarkable work. In 1714 he went to the Charterhouse School, and
in 1720 to Christ Church, Oxford, whither his brother Charles also went.

Then in course of a few years it came to be rumoured among the
colleges that some of the students were wont to meet in religious
assemblies. The gathering was called the Holy Club, and
The Holy Club. the beginning seems to have been with Charles Wesley and
a few young men when John was away for a short time. In November,
1729, John and Charles Wesley, Mr. Morgan of Christ Church and
Mr. Kirkham of Merton, commenced to spend some evenings together,
chiefly reading the Greek Testament. Others joined, and so the Holy
Club went on. Some persons called them Bible Moths and some
The name Methodists, because of their methodical habits or exercises.
Methodists. "Here is a new sect of Methodists," a young man of Christ
Church is said to have exclaimed, when struck by their regularity of
life and study, and the name has remained.

They appear to have followed rigidly the discipline of the Established
Church, and they missed no opportunity of attending sermons and prayers.
They devoted an hour night and morning to private prayer, fasted on
Fridays and Wednesdays, and partook of the communion every week.
They also visited the prisoners and the sick.

Before this,—in 1725,—John Wesley had been ordained, and he had also been elected a Fellow of Lincoln College. Two books previously had

JOHN WESLEY, THE FOUNDER OF METHODISM. BORN 1703; DIED 1791.
(From a portrait by Romney.)

exercised great influence over him, Thomas a Kempis's "Imitation of Christ" and Jeremy Taylor's "Holy Living."

Another member of the Holy Club was George Whitefield, who also became intimately connected with the rise of Methodism. Born at the

George Whitefield's early days. Bell Inn, Gloucester, in the closing days of 1714, he gained some schooling at St. Mary de Crypt, and then served his mother as a drawer of beer in her public house. Before this, his mother had contracted a second marriage—for his own father died when he was two years of age—and this second marriage proved unhappy. In the trouble that followed, his brother was wont to read aloud to him Ken's Manual for Winchester Scholars, which appears to have greatly influenced the boy.

In the moments of leisure from beer-drawing and various duties at the public house, young Whitefield wrote sermons and studied Thomas à

He writes Sermons. Kempis. Yet he said of himself, that "If I trace myself from my cradle to my manhood, I can see nothing in me but a fitness to be damned."

Happening to know some friends of a young man who was a servitor of Pembroke College, they were applied to, and George returned to school

Goes to Pembroke College. and studied diligently. Presently his friends' recommendation succeeded, and at eighteen years of age Whitefield went to Oxford.

Before going thither, he had heard, according to Southey, of the young men "who 'lived by rule and method,' and were therefore called

Joins the Holy Club. Methodists," but he hesitated to join them, for "it seems that the sense of his inferior condition kept him back." Charles Wesley, however, saw him often walking alone, and had heard somewhat of his character; so we soon find him introduced to the Holy Club.

John Wesley, who was now an earnest tutor, came under the influence of William Law about 1732, a man whose writings Southey regards as

Wesley and William Law. having completed what Jeremy Taylor and Thomas à Kempis' "Imitation of Christ" had begun. Law was the author of the "Serious Call to a Holy Life" and of "Christian Perfection," and in one of his interviews with Wesley he is reported to have said,— "Religion is the most plain, simple thing in the world. It is only, we love Him because He first loved us." To William Law Wesley applied also, when he was considering whether he should sail as a missionary to Georgia, then a new colony. Law approved of the plan. On October 14th, 1735 (Wesley's father having died the same year), John and Charles Wesley, together with Benjamin Ingham (one of the Holy Club), and Charles Delamotte departed from Gravesend for Savannah. In the same ship voyaged twenty-six Moravians, with whom John **Meets** Wesley became friendly, and from the Moravian Church **Moravians.** much of the Methodist organization came afterwards to be derived.

This ancient body was formed about 1467 under the name "Unitas Fratrum," out of the wreckage of the Bohemian Church. Thus it existed

INTERIOR OF FETTER-LANE (MORAVIAN) CHAPEL.

many years before the sixteenth century Reformation. After a chequered history a branch settled at Herrnhut in 1722. Among Protestant Missions to the heathen, the Moravians were the oldest, being **Sketch of the** established in 1732. The London Association for helping these **Moravian** missions was founded in 1817 by members of other Evangelical **Church.** Churches, and they have greatly assisted the Moravians in their efforts. So great is the foreign missionary work of this Church, that it is estimated about one in sixty of its adults enter that work, compared with one in five thousand of the other Protestant Churches.

It was with some members of this body that Wesley met on his voyage to America. They were sailing to join some of their fellows from Herrnhut, who had gone forth the previous year with the approval of the English Church.

By the Moravians Wesley was much influenced, not only on the voyage, but afterwards when he met some of their number in London. **Spargenberg's pointed Question.** Spargenberg gave him a new idea, or a new view of Christianity, when sailing to Georgia. In reply to some question, Spargenberg asked him, "Does the Spirit of God bear witness with your spirit that you are a child of God?" Wesley says in his journal that he was surprised, and did not know what to answer. In further conversation, Spargenberg pressed the question, "Did Wesley himself know that Christ had saved him?" "I do," replied Wesley finally, but he adds in his journal, "I fear they were vain words."

A few years afterwards, when his intolerance had caused misunderstanding in Georgia and he had returned to London, he met Peter Böhler, **Meets Peter Böhler.** a Moravian missionary, and had much conversation with him. Then on the 24th of May, 1738, he went to a meeting in Aldersgate Street, where some one read Luther's preface to the Romans. Wesley writes in his *Journal*: "About a quarter before nine, while he was describing the change which God works in the heart through faith in Christ, I felt my heart strangely warmed. I felt I did trust in Christ, Christ alone, for salvation, and an assurance was given me that He had taken away *my* sins, even *mine*, and saved *me* from the law of sin and death. I began to pray with all my might for those who had in a more especial manner despitefully used me and persecuted me. I then testified openly to all there what I now first felt."

In the meantime Whitefield had commenced evangelistic labours. He **George Whitefield Ordained, 1736.** had been ordained in 1736, and immediately afterwards he preached at Bristol, where his sermon is said to have "driven fifteen persons mad." Probably it wrought them to a great pitch of anxiety concerning their souls' salvation. He soon became sought for in all quarters, and people travelled miles to hear him. He was wont to preach nine times weekly, and people in London rose before dawn in order to be present at his sermons.

The condition of the people at that time is said to have been very degraded; yet Whitefield was soon able to attract immense crowds. The clergy, however, began to bar him from their pulpits and accuse him of visiting Nonconformists, and of disregarding the parochial system. It is said that at length the Chancellor of the diocese of Bristol threatened to excommunicate him if he preached without the Bishop's license.

Whitefield's Preaching.

This was given; but Whitefield determined to embark on field preaching, and

Whitefield takes to Field preaching.

he commenced with the colliers of Kingswood. "Finding," says he, "that the pulpits are denied me, and the poor colliers are ready to perish for lack of knowledge, I went to them, and preached on a mount to upwards of two hundred. Blessed be God that the ice is broken, and I have now taken the field."

The results

GEORGE WHITEFIELD. BORN 1714; DIED IN AMERICA 1770.

were marvellous. We soon hear of his preaching to ten thousand colliers, and of his seeing the tears pouring down their coal-grimed cheeks. Hundreds, he stated, were brought under conviction. So Whitefield proceeded, preaching wherever he could obtain room. In Bristol he had audiences of ten and twenty thousand people.

Travels with Howel Harris in Wales.

Then we find him travelling and preaching in Wales with Howel Harris, who founded Methodism in the Principality.

But before this, Whitefield had written to Wesley, urging him to preach at Kingswood. Wesley was now on intimate terms with the Moravians, attending " love-feasts " and highly emotional religious gatherings, in

Wesley's Preaching. which he was wrought up to a high pitch of rhapsody. Extra-ordinary physical effects also began to attend his preaching. People suffered extreme agony, and shrieked in pain ; then the suffering would give place to joy, and they believed themselves to possess a heaven of happiness. Sometimes persons would be seized with fits. Not unnaturally these manifestations aroused opposition and dislike. To Wesley's brother Samuel, who appears to have long been an opponent of his excesses—or what he regarded as such—John wrote : " You deny that God does now work these effects ; at least, that He works them in such a manner. I affirm

Replies to his brother Samuel. both, because I have heard these facts with my ears, and seen them with my eyes. I have seen (as far as it can be seen) many persons changed in a moment from the spirit of horror, fear, and despair, to the spirit of hope, joy, and peace, and from sinful desires, till then reigning over them, to a pure desire of doing the will of God."

No doubt there will always exist conflicting views concerning such manifestations. Some persons will see in them the results of fierce excite-

Extraordinary Manifestations. ment ; the physical fear of hell passing to the pleasures of heaven ; the love for the marvellous, or for mysticism, which seems a more or less marked trait of character in many persons or the results of superstition on ignorant minds. Others might urge that the excitement, however produced, did prove a powerful stimulant to turn persons into a different course of conduct ; while others, again, would simply behold in them the direct working of God.

When Wesley received Whitefield's invitation, he opened his Bible to consult God's will concerning the journey—whether he should go or not. The verse he found was unfavourable. Again and again he did the same thing, with similar results. At length lots were drawn at a meeting in

Wesley preaches in the Fields. Fetter Lane, and the lot fell that he should go. He went, and he actually preached in the fields. " I could scarce reconcile myself at first," he says in his journal, " to this strange way of preaching in the fields, of which he (Whitefield) set me an example on Sunday, having been all my lifetime (till very lately) so tenacious of every point relating to decency and order, that I should have thought the saving of souls almost a sin if it had not been done in a church."

Soon he found the churches closed against him, and he was forbidden to preach to prisoners; he therefore spoke more and more in the open air. A

THE FOUNDRY—THE FIRST METHODIST "MEETING-HOUSE," 1739.

difference now begins to appear between Whitefield and Wesley. With all his great gifts, the one was not an organizer; but Wesley began to gather his converts into "Societies," which were divided **First Methodist Chapel opened, 1739.** into class-meetings and bands. Wesley's idea appears to have been that the converts should meet together, and encourage and assist one another in their religious life. In 1739 the first Methodist chapel was opened at Moorfields, Finsbury, London. It was an old Government factory **The Foundry.** known as the Foundry, where cannon had been cast, but was now disused and ruinous. The Wesleyans bought the lease for £115, repaired the building, and there crowds attended to hear John Wesley himself. A bell was rung at five in the morning and nine in the evening to summon the "Society" to prayer, and several social or philanthropic efforts were set on foot : one was a Dispensary, another was a Loan Society, and a third was a Widows' and Orphans' Home. In the same year a Methodist "meeting-house" was raised at Kingswood.

On May 2nd, 1739, Whitefield preached to ten thousand people on Kennington Common, and to double the number on the 5th. On the evening of Sunday, May 6th, he believed "there were no less **Whitefield on Kennington Common, 1739.** than fifty thousand people," while it is said the throng increased to sixty thousand. Persons fainted in the great crush, and one man dropped dead. The controversy concerning Methodism rose high, and in this year no fewer than forty-nine publications were issued regarding it.

The two evangelists were now fairly launched on their career. In **Charles Wesley.** the meantime Charles Wesley had also been preaching in Essex, and, being threatened with penalties, we find him replying by preaching to ten thousand people in Moorfields.

The headquarters of the movement came to be established at The Foundry, Moorfields, where it continued for nearly forty years. This building was in Windmill Street (then called Windmill Hill), at the north-west of Finsbury Square. With London as a base, the evangelists toured the country, working as far north as Newcastle, and as far west as the Land's End. Though the Methodist Societies were forming, and though **Gradual separation from the Established Church.** excluded from the pulpits of the Established Church, neither of the three leaders, John or Charles Wesley or Whitefield, seem yet to have formally separated from that Church. The Communion or the rite of baptism were not administered at their meetings ; the process of separation was gradual.

Wesley's movements about the country appear to have been extraordinarily rapid, especially when the sorry condition of the roads in those days is remembered. But he seems to have carefully mapped out his course beforehand, and as far as possible adhered to it. He was wont to journey on horseback, and thousands would gather together to await his arrival. Riots constantly occurred, and in some cases it is said the clergy incited the mob against the Methodists. At the commencement of his regular preaching journeys, on returning from Newcastle, Wesley came to Epworth. The curate refused to allow him to preach in the church, but in the afternoon a large congregation assembled, a report having spread that he would preach there. At six o'clock, however, he did

WESLEY PREACHING ON HIS FATHER'S TOMB.

preach in the churchyard, standing on his father's grave. "I stood," he says, "near the east end of the church, upon my father's tombstone, and cried, 'The kingdom of heaven is not meat and drink, but righteousness, and peace, and joy in the Holy Ghost.'" For seven evenings in succession did he preach on that spot,

Preaches on his Father's tombstone.

and he says, " Lamentations and great groanings were heard, God bowing their hearts so."

A few months after he had taken the Foundry he severed himself from the Moravian Society. Controversy had arisen, and Zinzendorf, the Moravian leader, announced that the Moravians were not con-

Separated from the Moravians.

nected with the Wesleys. John Wesley had also a difference with Whitefield. Briefly, it concerned the question of predestination, Wesley being Arminian in his views, and Whitefield Calvinistic. Two of Wesley's prominent doctrines were instant conversion and

Difference with Whitefield.

Christian perfection; but though the two evangelists were alienated for a time, they afterwards became reconciled, but their paths were separate. Whitefield was in America at some period of the

Calvinistic Methodists.

dispute, and Calvinistic Methodists in England decidedly tended towards separation during his absence. Whitefield, however, did not himself form a new organization, and his followers either joined the Connexion which the Countess of Huntingdon came to establish, or united with other bodies, or in Wales helped to form a denomination led by Howel Harris, known as the Welsh Calvinistic Methodists. Controversy between Wesleyans and Calvinists broke out afterwards in 1770, and lasted about six years, when Augustus Toplady showed himself, though a devoted pastor, a most abusive controversialist.

Whitefield returned to England in 1741, and was well received by the Wesleys. He embarked on a course of preaching, going to Scotland, and in 1742 discoursing at Moorfields Fair. At this place he was

Whitefield at Moorfields Fair.

pelted with dead cats and rotten eggs, but he held on his way. For three years he journeyed hither and thither on his evangelistic course, and then again voyaged to America. Wesley was also as busily engaged in a similar manner. At many places he met with rioting and violent opposition. At Wednesbury and Walsall his life was in danger. He had preached at the former place without molestation, but in the evening the house in which he was staying was mobbed, and the rioters

Riot at Wednesbury.

cried, " Bring out the minister! We will have the minister!" Wesley's serenity and self-possession never left him, and he asked the mob what they desired with him. He went to the magistrates with them, and his fine voice and masterly self-command told on the people. " What evil have I done? Which of you have I wronged?" he asked. At length the ringleader turned to help him, and finally he was brought back unhurt, save for bruises.

Such riots were most disgraceful, and indicate the lax state of the law then prevailing in certain places. It is said that at Wednesbury the clergyman had incited the people to turbulence. Where the magistrates did their duty, riots were soon stopped, and in course of time the prosecution of a few disturbers had a wholesome effect.

In his journeys, Wesley, as a rule, sought out industrial and populous neighbourhoods, where he might find numbers of colliers, weavers, miners,

RIOT AT WEDNESBURY.

fishermen, and day labourers. He would ride sixty or seventy miles a day, and cover in his journeyings never less than 4,500 miles a Wesley's year, sometimes preaching several times on the same day. His Journeys. open-air preaching places were often such as lent great effect to his words. Gwenap, in Cornwall, a natural amphitheatre, was one of his Some of his favourite spots. He says: "I stood on the wall in the calm, Preaching Places. still evening, with the setting sun behind me, and almost an innumerable multitude before, behind, and on either hand. Many likewise

sate on the little hills, at some distance from the bulk of the congregation.
But they could all hear distinctly while I read, 'The disciple is not above
his Master.'" When seventy years of age he preached there to possibly a
larger audience than had ever gathered to hear him—some thirty-two
thousand.

As a church or a separate denomination, Methodism was a growth,
rather than a fabric deliberately planned and quickly reared. One of

JOHN WESLEY PREACHING AT GWENAP PIT.

the first questions Wesley had to face was the ministration to the
Methodism a various societies which were so quickly arising. He was
Growth. assisted by some clergymen, but circuit preachers were also
appointed. The first of these was Thomas Maxfield. He had been left in
Thomas charge in London as an "expounder" or leader, and from this
Maxfield. work to preaching was easy. Soon Wesley was informed that
Maxfield had turned preacher. Inclined at first to prohibit this "irregu-

larity," Wesley returned to London, but was met by his mother, who said, "Take care what you do with respect to that young man, for he is as surely called of God to preach as you are." Wesley heard him preach, and was satisfied. The next lay-preacher of note was John Nelson, a Yorkshire mason, who had heard Wesley discourse at Moorfields; he was a man of most determined courage, and lived a life of hard service in the cause he had espoused. He appears to have gained as much power over the people as Whitefield himself. Among others were Christopher Hopper and Thomas Lee and John Jane. Some of those early

John Nelson.

JOHN JANE PREACHING IN THE STOCKS.

lay-preachers suffered almost as much as the Wesleys themselves. The circuits were large, and most of the preachers, because of their poverty, had to journey on foot. Nelson's house was demolished, squibs tossed in his face, and a rector at Grimsby hired a drummer to drown his preaching by noise. But after beating his drum for near an hour, Nelson's preaching so affected him that he wept. John Jane, when put in the stocks, preached to the people who came near; he died from exhaustion and fever brought on by fatigue, and all his belongings were not sufficient to pay for his funeral.

Other Lay Preachers.

I I

No salary was paid to those early preachers, but at length it was arranged that each circuit should give its minister three pounds per quarter. Then on one occasion Wesley desired one of the preachers named Mather to accompany him to Ireland on an evangelistic tour. "How shall my wife be supported?" asked Mather, and the question raised a difficulty, which came to be answered by an allowance for married preachers, and a school was also built for their sons. Almost from the very first the contribution of small sums weekly had been encouraged to defray expenses, persons calling for the penny or what not every week, and sometimes discovering also irregularities of life among the members.

Class Leaders. Thus the societies were divided into classes, each with its "leader," who had to visit every one in his class weekly. The system appears to have originated for the object of paying the cost of the meeting-house at Bristol.

So we have Methodism, building chapels, raising funds, and paying preachers. Then in the summer of 1744 Wesley called a "Conference" of some of his helpers. Six were clergymen. Among the objects of the gathering was the classification of societies into circuits, and the settlement of questions of discipline and government. The question also arose: Were the "Wesleyans" or "Methodists" Dissenters? And the reply was No. Although they united in religious societies, yet they "dared not" separate from the Church. Yet that very Conference undoubtedly formed an era in the history of Methodism. As time went on, the tendency to separation from the Established Church increased. The lay-preachers naturally desired to be placed on a level with other ministers, and the societies desired to have the Communion administered by the preachers. Finally, Wesley ordained ministers himself in 1784 for America. Southey regards this as taking "the only step which was wanting to form the Methodists into a distinct body of separatists from the Church," though, in fact, Methodists did not formally separate until about four years after Wesley's death. But in America Methodism was organized as an Episcopal Church.

The first Conference, 1744.

Wesley ordains Ministers.

Charles Wesley strongly disapproved of the ordination by his brother. He was more of a priest at heart than John, and probably also much more of a Churchman. His preaching was unequal, sometimes being very powerful, and then again spiritless. But the great service he rendered to the movement was that of writing hymns. In this respect he shot higher than any of his coadjutors, and has taken high rank as a

Charles Wesley's Hymns.

hymnologist of the Christian Church. It is said that he wrote no fewer than 6,500 hymns. When forty-one years of age, he married Miss Gwynne, and settled down to domestic life. John Wesley's marriage, which took place in 1751, was very unhappy, and ended in separation. His wife, the widow of a Mr. Vazeille, proved a terrible termagant, and for twenty years vexed his life. At length she took some of his journals and papers, and departed. He simply wrote in his journal in Latin : " I did not forsake her, I did not dismiss her, I will not recall her." Nor does it appear that he travelled a mile the less after his marriage, nor after the separation. He died in his **Wesley's death.** 88th year, in 1791, his brother having pre-deceased him in 1788.

The hand of the great controller being withdrawn, the Methodists revolted against their subserviency to the Church —for such they regarded it. No fewer than 278 ministers were connected with the Methodist Socie-

CHARLES WESLEY'S TOMB IN MARYLEBONE CHURCHYARD.

ties at Wesley's death, and it was claimed, in short, that they should exercise functions as other ministers, and that with the laity they should share the power of the " Legal Hundred " or Conference which governed the body. Up to 1784, the Conference consisted of those preachers whom Wesley decided to call together, but then a legal constitution was given it. The first demand—after Wesley's death—was practically granted, and the

Wesleyan Church formally seceded from the Church of England in 1795.
But the admission of the laity to Conference was not granted,

Methodist New Connexion, 1797. and a secession took place, led by the Rev. Alexander Kilham—curiously enough—of Epworth, and in 1797 the Methodist New Connexion was formed which gradually increased to a denomination of much importance. The principle for which the New Connexion contended was to some extent granted in the Wesleyan body, in 1877, when Con-

Lay Representatives Introduced. ference came to be partly an assembly of ministers taking counsel together in pastoral matters, and partly a meeting of ministers and laymen to discuss the general affairs of the denomination. In the *New Connexion* one layman is admitted to Conference for every minister, and the laymen share in all the business, whether "spiritual" or "secular."

The next secession formed the Primitive Methodist body. The proximate causes were the question of the permission for women to preach,

The Primitive Methodists. the propriety of religious camp-meetings, and the admission of laymen to Conference in the proportion of two laymen to one minister. The secession took place in 1810, and the same year saw the formation of the Independent Methodists, who rejected a paid

The Independent Methodists and other bodies. ministry. Five years later the Bible Christians, or Bryanites, followed, chiefly in Cornwall, led by William Bryan, a local preacher, and recognising more fully the value of the laity. The "Fly Sheet" Controversy, about 1844-8, advocating reforms in the constitution, resulted in the expulsion of the supposed writers and their friends, who formed the Wesleyan Reform Association in 1849. A few years previously the Wesleyan Association had been formed by reason of

United Free Methodists. the removal of a few influential pastors, and being of the same principles as the "Reform" Association, the two joined in 1857 to form the United Free Methodists. Their distinctive points are the independence of Churches, and free representation in the Annual Conference.

The organization of the followers of Whitefield was largely undertaken by the Countess of Huntingdon, who had made the great preacher her chap-

Countess of Huntingdon's Connexion. lain in 1748. She also established Trevecca College in South Wales,—removed to Cheshunt in Hertfordshire in 1792,—and founded numerous places of worship. The immediate cause which compelled her to leave the Church of England was a legal decision providing that she should certify these buildings under the Toleration Act. "Now I am to be cast out of the Church," she said, "only for speaking and living

for Christ." At the same time she appears to have held distinctly Nonconformist doctrines.

Whitefield, who married in November, 1741, and was undoubtedly the
most eloquent preacher of that day, is reported to have preached 18,000
sermons in the thirty-four years of his career. He visited Whitefield's
America several times, also Scotland, where, at Cambuslang, his Career.
preaching caused remarkable scenes, and died in 1770, twenty-one years

TREVECCA COLLEGE, SOUTH WALES.

before John Wesley. Whitefield founded the Calvinistic Methodists, and
his followers are also known as the Countess of Huntingdon's Connexion,
which is now practically identified with the Independents.

To Whitefield the great original impulse of the Methodist movement
must be traced. It was he who first embarked on the aggres-
sive effort, and it was he who led on Wesley to do so. His Worldwide
spread of
voice was extraordinary, being very clear and musical, and Methodism.

with it he could reach forty thousand persons in the open air. But John Wesley was really the founder, the leader, and the organizer of Methodism. "His genius for government," says Macaulay, "was not inferior to that of Richelieu." Together with his coadjutors he established a denomination which, with its offshoots, has spread all over the world and counts its adherents by millions

JOHN WESLEY'S TOMB, CITY ROAD CHAPEL, LONDON.

THE DISRUPTION IN THE CHURCH OF SCOTLAND—FREE CHURCH MINISTERS
LEAVING THE ASSEMBLY, MAY 18TH, 1843.

CHAPTER XXV.

𝔐𝔬𝔡𝔢𝔯𝔫 𝔓𝔯𝔬𝔱𝔢𝔰𝔱𝔞𝔫𝔱𝔦𝔰𝔪 𝔦𝔫 𝔖𝔠𝔬𝔱𝔩𝔞𝔫𝔡 𝔞𝔫𝔡 𝔍𝔯𝔢𝔩𝔞𝔫𝔡.

Episcopacy in Scotland—Murder of Archbishop Sharp—The Covenanters—Persecution
of the Scottish Nonconformists—Graham of Claverhouse—Presbyterianism settled in
1690—The General Assembly—Act of Establishment at the Union—Right of Presentation to Benefices—the United Presbyterian Church—The "Disruption," 1843—The
Veto Act—The Auchterarder Case—The Lethendy and Marnock Cases—The Rights
of the Civil Courts asserted—Preparing for the "Disruption"—Dr. Chalmers's Sustentation Fund—The Scene in the Assembly—The Protesters go forth—Founding the
Free Church of Scotland—Its Speedy Growth—The Three Scottish Presbyterian
Churches—Episcopacy in Scotland—The English Prayer-Book Adopted—Constitution
of the Scottish Episcopal Church—The Irish Episcopal Church—Catholic and Apostolic Church—Irving's Views—The Evangelical Union or Morisonians—The "Reunion
of Christendom"—Conclusion.

THOUGH the Second Book of Discipline, adopted in 1578, has remained
in its chief features the standard of the Scottish Church, yet the
Stuart kings strove hard to establish Episcopacy; and on Episcopacy in
occasion almost succeeded. In the reign of Charles II. it was Scotland.
established legally, and James Sharp, who had been a Presbyterian, and

457

had probably been engaged in confidential co-operation with English bishops for the re-establishment of prelacy, was consecrated Archbishop of St. Andrew's. This treachery, as they regarded it, was never forgiven by the upholders of the Covenant. Moreover, his political influence was usually used in favour of severe measures; he became detested by the people, and at length, on May 3rd, 1679, a dozen Covenanters murdered him as he was driving to St. Andrew's with his daughter.

Murder of Archbishop Sharp.

After his death the tyranny exercised against the unhappy Covenanters increased in severity. The Covenanters were those persons who were determined to uphold the Covenant for the preservation of the Reformed Church, and for the "extirpation of popery and prelacy." Expelled from the churches, they met in the open air, and, like the English Nonconformists, persisted in worshipping in what they regarded as the most righteous manner. Especially was this the case in the western Lowlands. Here they were so oppressed that they took up arms and frequently rose in insurrection. Persecuted and tortured, imprisoned and hanged, their story presents as black a page of oppression as any in British annals.

The Covenanters.

Persecution of the Scottish Nonconformists.

In this terrible strife Graham of Claverhouse, Viscount Dundee, has earned an unenviable notoriety. He pursued the Covenanters with relentless activity. They routed him at Drumclog in 1679, but he was a cavalry captain with the army which defeated them at Bothwell Brig a few weeks later; and though apparently guiltless of the infamous Wigtown martyrdoms, where two women were fastened to posts till they were drowned by the rising tide, yet he cannot be absolved of the crime of slaying the martyr, John Brown. After the Revolution of 1688, he took the field for the exiled James, but was shot at the fight of Killiecrankie, in 1689. His name comes down to us, both cursed and adorned by titles which show how strongly he evoked feelings in differing parties. With some he is "Bloody Claver'se"—a monster of iniquity and cruelty; with others the "Bonnie Dundee" of the well-known ballad.

Graham of Claverhouse.

In the end the principles of the Covenanters largely prevailed. A settlement took place in 1690, when Presbyterianism was re-established. The Scottish Estates had met in 1689, and the bishops then decided against abandoning the fallen James. But William and Mary were recognised as the king and queen, and prelacy

Presbyterianism Settled in 1690.

was abolished. When, in the next year, the re-establishment of Presbyterianism took place, the Westminster Confession was ratified **The General Assembly.** and raised as the standard of national belief. The General Assembly was also held, and with few exceptions has met annually ever since.

MURDER OF ARCHBISHOP SHARP ON MAGUS MUIR.

Its constitution was the same as previous to its dissolution by Cromwell. It consisted of ministers and elders from the presbyteries, with elders from universities and from burghs, while **Act of Establishment at the Union.** its connection with the State was recognised by a Commissioner nominated by the Crown to preside over its meetings, together with a minister as Moderator chosen by its members. When, in 1707, England and Scotland were united, a law was passed securing Presbyterianism in Scotland and confirming the ratification of the Confession of Faith.

These enactments no doubt produced a feeling of settlement in the country, but in 1712 an Act was passed which sowed the seeds of future trouble. It restored the right to patrons of presentation to **Right of Presentation to Benefices.** benefices, which the establishment of Presbyterianism in 1690 had taken away. Causing much discontent, many efforts were made to repeal it, but its provisions largely remained a dead letter, until at length the Assembly commenced to act on it; then discontent largely increased. In 1733 the non-contents seceded under Ebenezer Erskine, and formed the Associate Presbyterians popularly called Seceders. In 1761, yet another secession occurred, connected with the patronage law, and was known as the Relief Presbyterians. In the meantime the original Seceders had become divided, concerning the taking of the Burgher's oath to two Synods—the Burgher and the Anti-Burgher; but in 1820 they **The United Presbyterian Church.** were united, and in 1847 they were again united with the "Relief" Synod, and the amalgamated body is known as the United Presbyterian Church. From about the year 1820, the Seceders also took up a hostile position to State-Established Churches.

Yet another secession, however, connected with the patronage law, had taken place from the Established Church. This break was very large, **"The Disruption," 1843.** taking off half the members. It has become known as "The Disruption," and resulted in the founding of "The Free Church of Scotland." Probably it is the most important event in Scottish ecclesiastical history since the re-establishment of Presbyterianism in 1690.

For some time two parties had divided the Church, viz., the "Moderates," who were in favour of the patronage law, and the "Evangelicals," who were opposed to it. The Moderates were for long in the ascendancy, but during the earlier years of the nineteenth century their power began to de- **The Veto Act.** cline. The influence of Dr. Chalmers and of Andrew Thomson was in favour of the Evangelicals, and in 1834 the Veto Act was passed by the Assembly, declaring that no minister should be appointed to a congregation contrary to its will. This Act of Assembly was not considered **The Auchterarder Case.** legal by some persons, and an occasion soon arose when its legality was tested. The patron of Auchterarder "presented" a minister whose "call" had only been signed by three persons, and of

SLAUGHTER OF COVENANTERS AFTER THE BATTLE OF BOTHWELL BRIDGE.

these one did not belong to the parish; while 287 parishioners petitioned against the appointment. Thereupon the Presbytery declined to endorse the presentation, and subsequent appeals to the Synod and to the Assembly, resulted in favour of the Presbytery and of the majority of the parishioners. The case was carried to the civil courts, and finally to the House of Lords, when the decision was in favour of the patron and his presentee.

A similar case occurred at Lethendy, where, however, the nominee of the congregation was settled by the Presbytery in face of a Court of Session's interdict in favour of the patron and his presentee.

The Lethendy and Marnock Cases. For this, the eight ministers of the Presbytery were largely mulcted in costs, and the rejected minister obtained heavy damages against them. These sums of money were paid by the Church. Further, at Marnock, the Presbytery seems to have been in favour of the patron's presentee, though only one parishioner signed the call; but in consequence of the Commission of the Assembly and of the Veto Act they declined at first to institute the presentee, but afterwards endeavoured to do so. The Commission suspended the ministers of the Presbytery, who proceeded to the civil courts, and these decided in their favour.

The rights of the Civil Courts asserted. Other cases occurred, but in all of them the decisions were against the views of the Evangelicals and the Veto Act. The supremacy of the civil courts and the right of the patrons were asserted. Finally, the Evangelicals appealed to Parliament; but this application also proved a failure.

Thereupon the Evangelicals prepared for secession. Holding the views they did, it was the right course for them to pursue. To them, doubtless, it

Preparing for the Disruption. appeared as though their Church was but the servant of patrons who might be atheists or grossly immoral persons, and, further, that it was ecclesiastically, as well as civilly, under the domination of the civil courts. Previously they appear to have thought that the Church could legally refuse to ordain a man not approved by the majority of the congregation; but these legal decisions convinced them otherwise.

Toward the close of 1842, therefore, they met together to consider their future course. The situation was sufficiently disturbing. They would have to leave manse and church, and go they scarce knew whither.

Dr. Chalmers's Sustentation Scheme. Then Dr. Chalmers sketched his plan of a Sustentation Fund in which all should share, and 423 ministers there and then passed the resolution to secede from the State Church.

Next year, on the 18th of May, the great step was taken. It was a memorable day in the ecclesiastical history of Scotland; it was the day when the Annual Assembly was to meet as usual, the day when **The Scene in the Assembly.** the Free Church ministers parted from the Establishment.

DR. THOMAS CHALMERS, FIRST MODERATOR OF THE SCOTCH FREE CHURCH.

The Assembly was held in St. Andrew's, Edinburgh. Her Majesty's Commissioner was in his place to preside, having gone thither in great state; the church was crowded; then Dr. Welsh, the Moderator, read a protest.

"When the last of these solemn sentences had left the Moderator's lips," says Dr. Buchanan, "he laid the protest upon the table of the house, and, turning round towards the Commissioner, who rose in evident and deep emotion, Dr. Welsh bowed respectfully to the representative of the Queen, and, in so doing, bade the Church of Scotland's farewell to the State. That brief, but solemn and significant action done, he lifted his hat from the table, and went forth from the degraded Establishment.   As he moved

THE FIRST ASSEMBLY OF THE FREE CHURCH OF SCOTLAND.
Signing the Act of Separation.

with calm dignity from the chair, Dr. Chalmers, Dr. Gordon, Dr. Patrick McFarlan, Dr. Thomas Brown, Dr. McDonald, the fathers of the Church, men who were its strength and glory, one after another rose and followed **The Protesters** him.   It was a moment of intense and overpowering interest **go forth.**   .   .   .   .   How many were to follow?   .   .   .   The chief law officer of the Crown, who stood beside the Commissioner, looked down from

A FREE CHURCH MINISTER LEAVING THE MANSE.
(From the Picture in the Scottish National Gallery.)

his elevated position, with an anxiety which no effort could disguise, to mark how far his previous representations to men in power, and the facts now before him, might be found to agree. Dr. Candlish, Dr. Cunningham, Mr. Campbell, of Monzie, Mr. Dunlop, and others, familiar names in the struggle which had now reached its close, were seen moving on after those who had gone before. . . . But the quiet country ministers occupying these crowded benches behind,—it is not possible that they can design to cast themselves and their families into the midst of poverty and want . . . . Bench after bench poured its occupants into the stream which kept constantly flowing towards the door of the church. There was no hurry, no rush, no confusion. . . . One entire side of the Assembly, and the whole of the cross-benches, were left untenanted."

About 450 ministers left the Assembly, and, forming into column, marched to their place of meeting, crowds of persons accompanying them. **Founding the Free Church.** The hall to which they went was an old tannery at Canonmills, and there Dr. Chalmers was asked to become Moderator, and the ministers resigned their charges. Thus ended the "Ten Years' Conflict," as it was called, the first movement in the fight having been made in 1834. But it was, in fact, a fight which had been proceeding for very much longer, ever since 1733, when the first secession took place.

The Free Church of 1843 speedily shot up into vigorous existence. The enthusiasm, self-sacrifice, and conscientiousness of the seceding **Its Speedy Growth.** ministers commanded almost universal sympathy and respect. "I am proud of my country," exclaimed Lord Jeffrey, the critic and judge, and many others felt the same. Nearly £3,000 was collected in one meeting-place on the Sunday following, and so strenuous were the exertions, so energetic the action, that before very long almost every parish saw its Free Church and manse rise within its midst. Similar organizations have also appeared in England, Ireland, and the Colonies.

In 1874 the choice of a minister in the Scottish Established Church was given to the congregation, and the right of patronage abolished. **The Three Scottish Presbyterian Churches.** Thus there are three Presbyterian Churches in Scotland, the Established Church, the Free Church, and the United Presbyterian. Union between the two latter has been proposed, and should the Disestablishment of the State Church be accomplished, it is not unlikely that the three may be united into one Free Church.

While the Scots have thus strongly manifested their decided preference for Presbyterianism, the Episcopal Church has continued its existence as a "Free" or Voluntary Communion among them. Its bishops were all Jacobites at the Revolution of 1688, but many of the clergy did **Episcopacy in Scotland.** not object to take the oath of allegiance to William and Mary. Though no doubt hampered by the courts of the Scottish Established Church (Presbyterian), the Episcopalians gained protection by a Toleration Act in 1712. They were, no doubt, prejudiced by their sympathies with the Stuart insurrections, but in 1792 were released from penal laws. In 1863 the Prayer-Book of the English Church was adopted, **The English Prayer-Book adopted.** though permission was given to use the Scottish Communion office, and some years previously—in 1804— the Thirty-Nine Articles of the Anglican Church had been adopted by the bishops and clergy. Before this, forms approximating to the English Prayer-Book had been in use, while certain Churches used a Communion office framed on Charles the First's Scottish Liturgy.

The Scottish Episcopal Church thus presents the

ST. PATRICK'S CATHEDRAL, DUBLIN.
Erected in 1190 on the site of an older Church.

spectacle of a free and self-governing body, electing its own bishops, who elect their "Primus." The Episcopal College, consisting of the bishops, forms the supreme judicial "court," while the **Constitution of the Scottish Episcopal Church.** General Synod forms the supreme legislative body. Further, there is a Church Council, consisting of the bishops, clergy, and lay representatives. There are seven dioceses, and the choice of the

K K

bishops rests with the diocesan clergy and representatives of lay communicants.

In like manner the Irish Episcopal Church, or Church of Ireland, has been, since 1871, a free and self-governing body. Previous to that year it **The Irish Episcopal Church.** was the Established Church of Ireland—a branch of the Anglican Church—and James I. had given to it all the Irish ecclesiastical endowments. But when disestablished and disendowed by the act of 1869, its adherents numbered only an eighth of the population. It is governed by a Synod, consisting of the bishops, eleven in number, with two archbishops, and also representatives of clergy and

ST. DOLOUGH'S CROSS AND CHURCH, MALAHIDE, IRELAND.
The Church is said to have been erected by the Danes.

laity. The bulk of the people still remain Roman Catholics, but Presbyterianism, which was introduced about 1613, prevails in the north-east. Congregationalism and the Baptist denomination are also represented in Ireland as in Scotland.

Two important secessions from Presbyterianism have taken place. The one is known as Irvingism, or the Catholic and Apostolic Church, and **Catholic and Apostolic Church.** the other as Morisonianism, or the Evangelical Union. Edward Irving, who was born at Annan, Dumfriesshire, in 1792, was appointed in 1819 as assistant to Dr. Chalmers, and three years later came to the Caledonian Church, Hatton Garden, London, and subsequently to a new church in Regent Square. He became extraordinarily successful as a preacher, and attracted immense congregations. One of his prominent ideas was "that bodily disease was the direct infliction of Satan, and that therefore faith and prayer, and these only, should be employed as the means of deliverance." He also announced, about 1825, that the second personal coming of Christ was close at hand. In 1829–30 he lectured on "Spiritual gifts," *Irving's Views.* and maintained that miracles were intended to occur throughout the present dispensation. Some extraordinary phenomena were alleged to have then occurred in the West of Scotland, and subsequently in his own church, among these manifestations being miraculous healing, speaking in unknown tongues, and prophesying. Irving was deposed by the Scottish Church in 1831 for heresy, and he died in 1834. In the next year his followers organized the "Catholic and Apostolic Church." A Liturgy is used based on those of the Anglican, Roman, and Greek Churches; also vestments, lights, and incense. Its ministry comprises "angels" or bishops, also elders, prophets, evangelists, pastors,

STATUE OF EDWARD IRVING.

and deacons. Further, it believes that the mysticism and the miracles of the apostolic age are essential to the Church, and it holds itself in constant expectation for the second coming of Christ.

Very different in many important particulars was the secession, or separation, which resulted in the Evangelical Union. In 1843 the Rev.

The Evangelical Union, or Morisonians. James Morison, of Kilmarnock, with three other ministers and their congregations, separated from the Secession Presbyterian Church, of which we have already spoken, because of certain doctrines. They were joined by some Seceders from the Congregational Union of Scotland, and some fifty-six years later had nearly a hundred churches, with a Theological Hall. The distinctive views in which this movement originated may be described as a rebound from the Calvinistic doctrines of predestination and unconditional election and reprobation as represented in the Westminster Confession. Furthermore, so far as the Secessionists from the Presbyterian Church are concerned, their system has become largely Independent, and their formal amalgamation with the Congregational Union of Scotland has been frequently considered, and now appears likely to be accomplished.

Signs of reunion also among other bodies are not wanting as the nineteenth century wanes to its close. It is as though the Children of the

The Reunion of Christendom. Reformation, tired of divergencies and separations, were at last looking more on their points of agreement than of disagreement and while admitting, more or less fully, the right of private judgment, were recognising that such right, among certain schools of thought, is quite compatible with voluntary union on a broad and sound basis.

Looking back on the chequered history of the Reformation, with its tumults and its controversies, its cruel persecutions and its hard-won triumphs, such separations appear to have been, no doubt, inevitable. The right of private judgment was slowly being vindicated; a battle for true liberty was slowly being fought. We see that a perfect outward uniformity is impossible; interference by the State with the consciences of men is productive of terrible evil, and cannot be permitted; absolute identity of faith and practice cannot be enforced, but voluntary action may take its place. These surely are among some of the great legacies of that mighty movement of the sixteenth century, which marks off modern from mediæval Europe, and is known as the Reformation and the rise of Protestantism.

THE END.

INDEX.